In COSELL,

⚜ W9-COW-742

"... THE BAMBINO OF BOMBAST goes the paper route. The result is a continuously readable recitation of Howard's Most Memorable Moments and Stupendously Stellar Stalwarts. ... The man's undeniable virtues shine through here: his candor, his outrage with hypocrisy, his unabashed infatuation with great gamesmen past and present. ...

"A SPORTS FAN'S MOTHER LODE."
—*New Times*

"A FINE BOOK—tough, informative, entertaining and honest." —Gay Talese

"A FASCINATING look at sports from the microphone level and a revealing portrait of a complex, sensitive man."
—*Business Week*

"COSELL could become as popular on the bookstand as Howard is on the air."
—*South Bend Tribune*

The extraordinary autobiography of America's best-known, most listened-to, most argued-about sports commentator, COSELL is a full selection of the Sports Illustrated and Playboy book clubs, and a featured alternate of The Literary Guild.

COSELL
was originally published by Playboy Press.

COSELL

by HOWARD COSELL

with the editorial assistance of
Mickey Herskowitz

PUBLISHED BY POCKET BOOKS NEW YORK

COSELL

Playboy Press edition published 1973

POCKET BOOK edition published August, 1974

L

This POCKET BOOK edition is printed from brand-new plates made from completely reset, clear, easy-to-read type. POCKET BOOK editions are published by POCKET BOOKS, a division of Simon & Schuster, Inc., 630 Fifth Avenue, New York, N.Y. 10020. Trademarks registered in the United States and other countries.

Standard Book Number: 671-78671-7.
Library of Congress Catalog Card Number: 73-84918.
This POCKET BOOK edition is published by arrangement with Playboy Press.
Printed in the U.S.A.

For Emmy, Jill, Hilary, Peter, Justin and Jared,
the ones who are truly what my life has been all about,
and without whom there would be no life at all.

Table of Contents

A 16-page photographic insert appears
between pages 206 and 207.

Preface

This book is being published one year from the time when I spent the most trying and most dramatic moments of my life in a village housing thousands of athletes from all over the world. When a man writes a book about himself he struggles to remember his entire life. For me there was no struggle in remembering above all what happened on September 5, 1972 in the Olympic Village in Munich, West Germany. This is why my book begins with that scene. This is why I have not begun it the usual way—where I was born and how I grew up.

But perhaps this is not totally true, because, in a strange way, where I was born and how I grew up—a Jewish boy in Brooklyn—became inextricably interwoven with my emotions on that day in the Village. How could it have been otherwise? After all, I was in Germany and while Hitler was gone he was part of my youthful life and once again Jews had been killed.

Chapter I

THE 20TH OLYMPIAD

---

*"My God . . . can't they at least
stop the Games?"*

PART 1:

A Problem in the Village

I never dreamed it would turn out to be the worst time of my life—a time when all kinds of doubts would be renewed about the meaning of the Olympic Games. The 20th Olympiad. The Germans referred to it as a *Jungenfestspiel,* a festival of the young. The opening day ceremonies were magnificent. The pageantry, the colors of all the world were there.

The Germans had organized it brilliantly. The Olympic needle rose above the stadium. The torch was lighted. And the Games—Willy Brandt called them "the joyous games" —opened with a flourish of mountain horns and the release of thousands of doves, the music of massed bands playing modern, spirited tunes instead of anthems. Little German schoolchildren scattered rose petals in the path of the parading athletes.

And then another note was introduced. Bavarian bullwhips cracked and exploded and echoed in the clear, sunlit August air, under the curved acrylic dome. The sound was unnervingly like gunfire.

I can't explain what I felt. But standing on the infield

1

of the stadium, surrounded by 80,000 people, with hundreds of millions watching on TV, the sound of the whips unsettled me. I watched the West Germans march into the stadium, and the East Germans, both with a perfection of rhythm, in sharp contrast to the relaxed entry of all the other nations, including the Soviets. I got a sense of World War II and the days that preceded it—it was almost like seeing Warsaw and Prague again. I couldn't shake it. Right then my whole background surfaced in me. I felt intensely Jewish. Suddenly, I knew, I remembered, that Dachau was only 22 miles away.

As I left the Olympic Stadium with my wife, Emmy, a Canadian broadcaster stopped me and asked to tape an interview. He wanted my impressions of the opening day ceremonies. Sometimes, instinct compels you to say certain things. I told the man I was very troubled and that I was leaving the ceremonies with a sense of unease. I thought: This thing may have outgrown itself—and its usefulness to the civilization. My God. Six hundred million dollars in two weeks. Such feudal pomp and circumstance. So much, much money. I spoke of the confusion I felt, the vague sense of discomfort about these Games. The whips: It was as though they were symbolic, an echo of things past and, somehow, a precursor of things to come.

I carried that feeling with me as we followed the crowd out of the Olympic Stadium.

As the days passed it seemed that I was enmeshed in every controversy the Games produced—and they were epidemic. But I never expected to be a reluctant observer of what became the biggest, cruelest news story of the year.

Harry Curtis knocked at my door at the München Sheraton Hotel at seven o'clock, the morning of September 5. Harry was my radio engineer, assigned to me during the Olympics to tape my network shows for broadcast back to the States. He walked in, unstrapped the tape recorder from his shoulder and said, almost casually, "Did you hear the news?"

"No, what?"

"Arab commandos got into the Village, took over the Israeli building, shot some of them dead and are holding the rest hostage."

I stared at him. "Harry, knock it off. Harry, don't kid about a thing like that."

"I'm not kidding. It's absolutely true."

"Harry, you swear to me on your life. On your wife's life—"

"Howard, it happened. It's absolutely true."

My head whirled. "Good God," I said. "I've had an uneasy feeling ever since I got to Germany. It's almost as if I were back in the age of Hitler. I can't sort out my thoughts. I can't describe this damned feeling."

I knew that wasn't a rational thing to say. It was a purely emotional reaction fed by the moment. I picked up the telephone and asked the operator for the room of Pete Axthelm, sports editor of *Newsweek*. I had left him only a few hours before, at three in the morning, in the hotel bar. He was the first person who came to mind. I had to talk to someone; I had a compulsion to repeat this ghastly development.

"Pete, did you hear the news?"

Sleepily he said, "What are you talking about? What the hell is the idea of calling me at this hour?"

I described what Harry Curtis had just told me. There was a pause. When he spoke, Axthelm's voice was coated with disgust.

"You know, maybe some of those guys in the States are right. Maybe you've just gone too far. What kind of terrible joke is this? What kind of Cosellism is that, at this hour of the morning?"

"Pete," I said, "I didn't believe it either. Emmy's standing next to me. It happened. You'd better get dressed and get your ass over to the Village."

He said, "You *are* serious."

"Yes."

"Oh, my God. I'll see you in the lobby in a few minutes." He hung up.

I called Roone Arledge, the president of ABC Sports and the moving force behind our Olympic coverage.

"Roone, you heard—"

"Yes. Get right over to the Village. Jennings is already there for news. Get over to the Village and hold the fort there. We'll get a camera crew to you in the Village."

"Okay." I looked at Emmy. What the hell do you say at a time like that?

All over Munich, people were waking up that morning to the horror of this news. So grotesque, so remote from the spirit of the Games, as though it had happened on some other planet.

In the press dormitories at the Olympic complex, German orderlies moved efficiently through the halls. They knocked on the doors of ABC technical personnel and awakened them:

"There's a problem in the Olympic Village. You're needed at the ABC bungalow."

A problem? A film breakdown maybe? A fight? A dispute over judging? Nothing of the sort. Our whole Olympic broadcast contingent was about to rejoin the real world.

I quickly taped my radio show, covering the previous day's events. I touched briefly on the developing tragedy but I was still without details. I told Emmy to come to the ABC building later with our chauffeur. In the lobby I encountered Tony Triolo, a *Sports Illustrated* photographer working for us during the Olympics, Jim Murray of the *Los Angeles Times,* Shirley Povich of the *Washington Post* and Rick Giacalone, director of photography for ABC. We piled into Rick's car and raced to the company bungalow just outside the entrance to the Village.

We were met there by Marv Bader of ABC Operations. Quickly he told us that there was only one entrance we could get through, far around the other side of the Village. Bader also said we had one film crew already inside and that it was for the use of Peter Jennings, the young film producer John Wilcox and me. We would each have to share it depending on the flow of events. Wilcox and Jennings had slipped in shortly after the news broke around 5:00 A.M., before the increased security, which was now fantastic, had been established.

We drove around to the entrance to which Bader had directed us. No way to get in. Especially, no reporters. So I divested myself of all identification—the ABC jacket, everything. The others did the same. I was now in a shirt, tieless, wearing Puma tennis shoes. We found another entrance. Tony, a burly, earthy-looking fellow, convinced the guards that we were all Puma shoe salesmen and workers in the Village. In we went. We didn't even look back, for fear they were going to stop us. We headed straight for the scene behind the Israeli quarters. Building 31—which in its way was about to become the same sort of tragic landmark as the Texas School Book Depository Building in Dallas, Texas.

It was now 8:30 A.M., Munich time. As we walked I was struck by the fact that the Village looked no different. Athletes strolled past us in both directions, smiling, carefree, obviously unaware of the tragedy that was taking place. And there were the buildings: sterile, gray apartment houses, so constructed that they could be converted to later use as rental or cooperative apartments. In fact, apart from the colorful flags and bunting so much in evidence, one could picture in one's mind a lower-case co-op city such as exists in the Bronx, New York.

I found Wilcox and Jennings and the crew, not at Building 31 but in an area immediately behind the Italian and the Burmese buildings. Both overlooked Building 31, which was under the control of the Arab terrorists and roped off by a massive West German police guard. Jennings was assiduously getting all the data then available, by walkie-talkie, from the Associated Press and the United Press International. The facts as known were these: Shots had broken the quiet of the Village at approximately 4:30 A.M., only a few minutes after ABC had completed its feed of the previous night's coverage back to the States. The Arabs, in disguise—at least one as a woman —had climbed a wall, slipped past the flimsy security at the main gate and forced their way into the Israeli building. The unarmed Israeli athletes awakened to that dreadful sound of other years—the pounding on the door in the middle of the night. Two were murdered as they resisted. Nine were taken hostage. Some escaped.

Murray and Povich went their own way now. Other writers, names familiar to the American people, were already on hand: Will Grimsley, Milton Richman, more to come. They had rushed over from the press building at the first alarm of the incredible drama now unfolding.

And now the vigil began. Word came on the walkie-talkie that Emmy was at the ABC offices. She would wait there from 9:30 in the morning to 11:00 that night, with me constantly trying to get word to her. None of us knew what was going on. Bill Toomey, the decathlon champion of 1968, now working as an ABC commentator, slipped into an athlete's uniform and literally jogged past the guards and into the Village.

We watched all day. We fed reports. Jennings sneaked into the Italian building—how he got past the police I'll never know—and situated himself on an upper floor, from which he had a perfect view of the Israeli building and the events taking place in front of it. Thus, he was positioned to render the vivid and accurate reports that all America heard throughout the day: Reports of German authorities entering the building, conferring with the leader of the terrorists; of the Arabs peering through the windows and from behind doors barely ajar; and, once, a German policewoman being used as a distraction while the police moved into new positions—for what, no one really knew.

The West German police began clearing out the Italian building, threatening Jenning's observation post. Ingeniously, he hid in a lavatory and emerged after they had gone.

In the early afternoon John Wilcox disguised himself in an Olympic sweat suit and darted into the Burmese building carrying a walkie-talkie. He wound up in a room no more than 10 or 15 feet away from the very Arab guarding the hostages. He could look directly into his eyes.

On the balcony of the building, one could now see furtive figures in stocking masks.

Meanwhile, I was based about 20 yards from an underpass that separated the Italian and Burmese buildings and led to the Israeli quarters. All day long, hour after hour, that underpass was a beehive of activity. And I reported on developments there. Never less than a dozen cars were parked in the underpass. Always, as new ones drove up, plainclothesmen would come out. Somehow they all looked tough, athletic, right for the job.

At one point ambulances arrived. They took out some stretchers. The plainclothesmen, even while in their street clothes, could be seen putting submachine guns over their shoulders, partly hidden under the backs of their jackets.

During all of this bustle—call it frenzy—I learned that a close friend of one of the slain Israelis was at the other side of the underpass, just outside the roped-off area in front of Building 31. I ran around and found him and induced him to come back with me for an interview. It was a moving few minutes, as the Israeli told us about his friend, Moshe Weinberg, the wrestling coach; about the way Moshe had lived, his aims and dreams, and the baby daughter born a week or so before whom he would never see.

(About a week later this same Israeli sought me out at the Sheraton Hotel. He now realized, he said, that the West Germans would have paid him up to a thousand dollars for such an interview. He felt that I should compensate him instead. I was shocked. Horrified. I told him I thought he had spoken out of love for a friend and that payment was unthinkable. I walked away. I never saw him again.)

At two o'clock I learned that athletic events were still going on. Even as two Israeli athletes lay dead, even as time was running out on the lives of nine others, as the anguish and torment mounted with each hour, crowds cheered at soccer and field hockey and volleyball matches. It all seemed a bad dream. At the Boxhalle, heavyweight Duane Bobick, the U.S. hope for a gold medal, was meeting Teofilo Stevenson of Cuba. The day before it had seemed important. There was no way I would cover it now.

I thought it was obscene for the Games to continue while the Olympic Village was being turned into a death-trap. It was insane, the tired old men of the IOC debating whether or not to postpone, or even interrupt, their precious pageant, even as blood still bathed the steps of Building 31. They would, finally, suspend the competition around four o'clock.

As the vigil continued, more cars pulled into the underpass. German police garbed in athletes' uniforms poured out of them, their submachine guns and pistols plainly visible, and vanished into the buildings adjacent to the Israeli quarters. Snipers, equipped with rifles and telescopic lenses, climbed to the nearest rooftops. One sensed they would attempt to rush the Arabs. A shoot-out would be inevitable. From his vantage point John Wilcox monitored the police activity. A lone Arab guard nervously patrolled the balcony. Wilcox said starkly: "They can shoot the Arab guard dead, *at will*. He is an open target."

Yet no one moved. The Germans were playing for time. No one wanted to risk a misstep that might panic these men and lead to the slaughter of the helpless Israeli hostages. Suddenly I got word that people in America— parents—were worried about the safety of our athletes. I ran about 500 yards, grabbed two American athletes, got them back to where we were and quickly did a film piece in which they assured everyone back home that there was no danger—at least as far as they were concerned.

Now dusk came—and with it the eeriest scene I have ever witnessed. I did my last film piece on the back slope of a hill. I had them turn the cameras on a spot 300 yards away where hundreds and hundreds of athletes had congregated, held back by police guards and ropes. The number grew as the day wore on. Athletes of every country, male and female, watching and waiting. It was like the Roman arena of ancient days. They waited for a shoot-out that would not come until hours later—and then not in the Village but at an airport miles away.

The only people allowed close to the rear of the Israeli building were my crew and a man named Willi Sheffler, a ski instructor who had emigrated from Germany in Hitler's time to the United States. He worked all day in the Village with us, operating the walkie-talkie, staying in touch with our studio people. We were joined by Cooper Rollow, the sports editor of the *Chicago Tribune*. I convinced the German police he was part of our group. We were sprawled, belly down, all of us, on the back slope of the hill. The police insisted that we hug the ground; no one could predict when the shooting might start. Less than 30 feet away from us lay two German snipers, guns ready. But, mostly, the police tried to drive us away. We resisted. Pete Axthelm wrote later: "Cosell stood them off with typical Cosell put-downs."

Most eyes were now riveted on the snipers moving across the rooftops. A climax of some kind seemed at hand. We were going to film it. I was going to describe it. In a weird way, totally disconnected from reality, I felt I was back doing the opening scene in a military movie spoof by Woody Allen, called *Bananas*. It was unreal. The eerie atmosphere, the athletes, tense and transfixed, waiting irresistibly for the final scene.

It was like watching a fire. You simply could not take your eyes off Building 31. What was happening in there? How many were dead? What a nightmare this must be for the hostages, bound and gagged and defenseless, knowing that at any instant their lives might end.

And who were these men who had traveled thousands of miles to bring murder to the Olympics? By what incredible circumstances had they intruded on this innocent place and spoiled our fun and games?

You wished you could turn off your mind. But the thoughts kept coming until there did not seem to be room for them in your brain. The games seemed remote, distant. Yet 500 yards from where we stood I could see athletes casually moving around the recreation area, playing chess and shuffleboard and ping-pong. I cursed them for their indifference and callousness. "I don't give a damn what country they're from," I thought, "how can they?"

With each new rumor your heart raced. Yes, they had decided to charge the building. More deaths. But at least an attempt to free them, to end the agonizing suspense. No, they would not risk it.

Now, a deal. The Germans had agreed to fly the Arabs and their captives to another country. Is that how the vigil would end, with no ending at all, just a postponement of whatever fate the Israelis faced?

Hour after hour after hour it had gone on, the excruciating doubt and uncertainty. The young Israelis—a team that came to Munich with less hope perhaps than any other nation of winning an Olympic medal. Any medal. And yet they came to compete and to share—and received the largest ovation of any team from the multitudes that witnessed the opening ceremony. The Germans were saying, in a special way, that the Israelis were welcome; the cheers and applause were telling them that the crowd knew what they and their country had suffered and endured for so many years.

Now this. If you had a drop of sensitivity you hurt for them. You alternated between rage and frustration and pure helplessness. At one point a young U.S. soccer player, dressed in his sweat suit, pleaded with me: "Mr. Cosell, isn't there anything we can do? Is there any way we can help? My God, at least can't they stop the Games?"

We paced aimlessly on small patches of grass, tortured by thoughts. What must the Israelis be thinking? Of their homes, their families? Were they wondering, all this time, what the world was doing about them?

Well, you're not human if your life doesn't spring before your eyes. I'm a man born of Jewish parents who grew up in Brooklyn. My father was old-worldish. I myself had received no formal religious training. I married a Protestant girl. My older daughter married a Catholic boy. So I'm a hybrid character. But I did grow up in Brooklyn, of Jewish parents, in the age of the Depression and the threat of Hitler. Again, I had never felt so intensely Jewish as when I watched this scene: two Israelis already dead; more to die here in Germany, where Hitler inflicted his scars; the Arabs, incredibly, this tiny coterie of desperadoes, holding forth. I found myself wanting to scream at the German authorities: "YOU DIRTY BAS-TARDS! Where was your security? Did you purposely allow this to happen? You know what the international situation is. Why were there no guards around the Israeli building?"

I wasn't being rational or really fair: No one wanted things to be right more than the West Germans. There may have been a laxness of security. That's debatable. But one thing is certain: The West Germans were driven by a desire to erase the awful memories of World War II; what happened was the last thing on earth they wanted. Another point ought to be made. There is a limit to security and a limit to control. Even with infinitely more security the same tragic events might have occurred. Who's to say?

The day turned to night and the shoot-out hadn't come. We were all exhausted. But then there was a sudden scurrying. Cars moved out. The police emerged from the buildings and scattered in all directions. Some were changing back out of the sweat suits and into their uniforms. We could no longer film because of the lighting factor, but we were still unable—emotionally and by training—to leave the scene. Near us was a plaza over which flew the flags of all the nations in the Olympics. Now the police began to rope it off.

I approached the head police official and asked, "What goes on here?"

"A deal," he said. "A deal has been made. The helicopters will be here. In moments they come."

I reported it on the air. But the helicopters didn't land, not for 15 minutes, not for 30. The helicopters came more than an hour later but not there, not at the plaza. They landed in a field behind the Village. The rest is part of the history of our times.

Our vigil on the back slope of the hill, overlooking Building 31, was done. I finally got instructions from ABC that I could leave the Village. I went straight to the studio. There, Roone Arledge told me I was needed to do a voice layover on the Bobick-Stevenson fight. I didn't want to do it. I told Roone so. I was exhausted and had no taste for it, in the wake of all that had happened. Roone said, "If you don't want to do it, I understand. The only thing I'll say is that the *New York Times* tomorrow will not only report the tragedy. You'll still see a write-up of the fight."

He had a valid point. I gave in. And I did it.

By now it was after one o'clock on the morning of September 6. In the studio Jim McKay was joined by Jennings and Lou Cioffi, our bureau chief in Bonn. It had been some day for McKay. God, it had been endless for him. Before I left, Jim had broken the news that all of the Israelis were dead. They had died in the flames and gunfire on the runway at Furstenfelder Airport, as German soldiers attempted, in vain, to pick off the Arab terrorists. The shoot-out had indeed come. Bound and blindfolded, the Israelis never had a chance. A confusion of news bulletins—it was at first reported they had survived—only heightened the final horror.

I went back to the hotel and found Emmy upstairs, in bed but awake. I told her they were gone, all of them. And she started to cry. We went to sleep, or tried to. But I never got to sleep that night. The phones started to ring.

To my amazement, at least a dozen overseas calls reached me from the United States. One was from a lady in New Orleans who told me they were going to start a foundation in Louisiana for David Berger, formerly of Cleveland, who had gone to school down there. A weight lifter, young Berger had moved to Israel only two months before in the express hope of representing that country in the Olympics. He had not yet even had time to learn Hebrew. Another call came from California, an older man with a Jewish accent. "Only you will tell us the truth," he said. "What is happening there?" The phone rang all night.

Weeks later, in a piece on the Olympics in the *New York Times Sunday Magazine,* Erich Segal made a point of it. "For all the criticism Cosell gets," he wrote, "people believe in him. All during the Olympics, he's the one who got the steady flow of calls from America. 'Tell us what's really happening,' they would ask him."

My mind was filled with so many thoughts. All of the inevitable questions. I told Emmy that I just wanted to get home. I didn't want to stay in Germany. I didn't ever want to go back.

Later that morning we went to the Olympic Stadium for the memorial services that were being held in honor of the slain Israelis. I almost couldn't get Emmy in. Admission was being granted only to those who came with tickets for the athletic events that were to have been held that day. I was outraged. One would have thought that we were going to just another entertainment.

But that outrage was nothing compared to the disgust and indignation that overwhelmed us as we listened to Avery Brundage, the president of the International Olympic Committee, speak. No thought or suggestion of suspending the games. Instead, unbelievably, an apparent attempt to equate the murder of the Israelis with the issue that had preceded the Games—whether or not Southern Rhodesia should be admitted. "The Games of the Twentieth Olympiad," Brundage declared grimly, "have been subjected to two savage attacks. *We lost the Rhodesian battle to naked political blackmail. . . .*"

Regurgitating the Rhodesia question at such a time was offensive to all, but particularly to the young black Africans sitting in mourning in front of him. Some got up and left the ceremony.

Brundage went on: "I am sure that the public will agree that we cannot allow a handful of terrorists to destroy the nucleus of goodwill and cooperation. . . . The Games must go on."

He then declared a day of mourning. Incredibly, he made it retroactive to 4:00 P.M. the day of the tragedy. Why? So the games could resume more quickly? The effect could not have been more stunning. It was as though he were unaware, or unconcerned, that until a few hours before the charade of the memorial service, much of the world still believed the hostages had escaped.

Emmy and I got out of there. We felt unclean. Undignified. We were not alone. Leaving the stadium I said bitterly to Emmy, "There was a time for Avery Brundage, that of William of Orange." I later used that sentence on the air, and it became a kind of catchphrase, quoted everywhere.

There is no way I can describe Avery Brundage. I have known him since 1956. At that time, when I was really just a beginner in broadcasting, I did a series of one-hour network radio shows called "The Olympic Games: Sports or Politics?" I did them with Avery Brundage. He is, in some ways, one of the most remarkable men I've ever known. By his precepts he is a completely principled man. And that's all right, assuming his precepts are right. He is an extraordinary man physically. In his eighties, he stands straight, walks tall. The pace is crisp, the speech is clear, and so is the hearing. There is an almost unending vigor about him. You always know where he stands, and he'll fight anyone for what he believes in. He has many admirable qualities. The only trouble with Avery Brundage is that he believes in all the wrong things. He loves having power. He loves it! He believes in pomp and circumstance. He believes in superficial things. He has a curious unconcern about what is going on in the world in terms of people, and the legitimate hopes and aims and aspirations of people. I don't suppose he ever showed it more than the day after the tragedy, at the ceremonies.

As we left we bumped into a contingent of U.S. basketball players. Their heads were bowed. I talked to them and they expressed their own feelings about what they had just heard and seen. As we walked away from them, one said, "Some Olympics." (Later his team would lose a basketball game to Russia that it had, in fact, won.)

For me, the Olympics died with the Israelis. But not my job.

PART 2:

Case of the Empty Blocks

---

*"He can go on being a coach.
What can I go on being?"*

In an almost parklike setting, Olympic athletes strolled down a winding path, past a reflecting pool in which some of them waded and out a gate not more than 20 yards from the headquarters of the ABC staff. Between the two points was an area that served as the bus depot for the Olympic complex. From there the buses departed every few minutes for a specific destination in the vast, rolling fairground that Munich had created as a monument to German taste and efficiency.

The gate to the Olympic Village stayed busy. Buses and people came and went. We had a window to the athletes in the doorway of the ABC building, officially known as "Barnathan's Bungalow." It had been named in honor of Jules Barnathan, the network's vice-president in charge of operations. Inside worked Julie's staff, who were among the unsung heroes of the endless television coverage America watched. The bungalow featured a flea-bitten cafeteria that served the worst food you ever tasted.

There was constant traffic of ABC personnel through the bungalow. Some would come in to grab a sandwich and risk ptomaine poisoning. Or to pick up their mail. Or just to relax for a moment in the reception room, where a color television set carried the Olympics around the clock.

On September 1, 1972, I left the Boxhalle shortly after 4:00 P.M. when the afternoon Olympic boxing competition had terminated. I headed for Barnathan's Bungalow and got there at approximately 4:20. There was a lot of excitement going on, judging by the way members of the ABC crew were gathered around, talking among themselves and gesturing. They were either right outside the reception room or in it, watching the television screen.

Jim Murray, the syndicated columnist of the *Los Angeles Times,* was standing outside. Jim, a tall, attractive man with black hair, glasses and an everpresent Irish twinkle in his eyes, was of a different mood at the moment. He was watching the others, and he was clearly distracted.

"What's going on?" I asked.

"Something—something wild has just happened," he said.

He and some of the others began to fill me in. (Jim would be with me for the next two to two and a half hours, and that night would file the only eyewitness news report on the flow of events during that time. He did a superb column, which appeared in many of the papers in the United States the next day.)

As it was described to me, I had just missed Eddie Hart, Rey Robinson and Robert Taylor, America's sprinters in the 100-meter dash, and their coach, Stan Wright. In an almost ghoulish scene, they had been casually lounging in the doorway of the reception room at Barnathan's Bungalow, watching the television screen. Unbelievably, they saw the runners lining up for the quarter-final heats of the 100 meters—*in which they were entered*.

I stood there, getting this slightly garbled account of a moment that had overtones of tragicomedy. The runners had at first thought they were viewing a replay of the heats they won earlier that day. They thought so, that is, until they heard Jim McKay announce that our boys—Hart and Robinson—were not in the starting blocks.

Suddenly an ABC executive, George Milne, screamed out that Robert Taylor could still reach the track in time for his heat. Stan Wright was clearly shattered, frozen, his head in his hands, mumbling over and over, "Oh no. Oh no . . ."

Our people literally pushed them into an ABC car. A young man named Bill Norris, a part-time worker, climbed behind the wheel. They drove frantically to the stadium where Taylor, with no warm-up, unpeeled his sweat suit, hurried directly to his lane and finished second to Valery Borzov, of Russia, by a yard. That was to be the finish in the finals, as America lost the 100-meter title for the first time since 1960.

Immediately after Taylor's heat, the distraught Stan Wright went to the Olympic officials. He appealed for Hart and Robinson to be given another chance to qualify. In his panic, Wright at first claimed that they had been caught in a traffic jam. His appeal was denied.

At ten minutes to five a bus pulled up to the depot outside the door of Barnathan's Bungalow. Stan Wright and Eddie Hart got off. Some youngsters asked poor Eddie for his autograph. He just shook his head and said, in a quiet and gentlemanly way, "Not now, kids, it's the wrong time." He turned toward the entrance to the Village.

Stan Wright kept his head down. Tears were in his eyes. I felt for him. We all did. "Stan," I said, "it's a terrible, terrible thing and a terrible time to ask you, but you're going to have to say something on television to the American people. Who's to blame? What happened?"

"Howard, I'm to blame. But I can't talk to you now. I've got to see Bill Bowerman." As the head coach of the U.S. team, Bowerman was Wright's boss.

"I understand," I said. "But when can I see you?"

"At five thirty in front of our building, Number Fourteen."

The next bus pulled up and unloaded a group including Wayne Collett, John Smith, Chuck Smith and Rey Robinson, who was beside himself. The bitterness and disappointment spouted forth from his lips like water gushing from a fire hydrant into a New York City street during the summer as he excoriated Stan Wright. Jim Murray described it in his column the next day as "the language of the deepest ghetto."

"If you want to come in and tell it like it is," I said, "I'll put you on the air."

"I sure do," he said.

Robinson did the interview. He modified his language to exclude the profanities but he made it painfully clear that he held Wright responsible. So did others. "He has just one job," said John Smith, the 400-meter runner, "to get those guys to the track at the right time. That's what he's paid for."

Wright's obvious grief left Robinson, in the heat of his own hurtful moment, unmoved. "The man is a coach. He can say he's sorry. But what about three years? What about torn ligaments, pulled muscles, a broken leg? He can go on being a coach. What can I go on being?"

There it was. Years of work and pain and sacrifice. It had all come to nothing for Eddie Hart and Reynaud Robinson. In the meanest kind of irony, in a sport ruled by the clock, they had not gotten to the track on time. The Olympics had left without them.

After the interview with Robinson some of our ABC people got Rey through on the phone to his family in Florida so that he could explain to them what had happened. Once again he made no effort to disguise the bitterness that engulfed him.

In the meantime I went to see Roone Arledge. "I don't think we can, or should, play this interview," I said, "unless we have Stan Wright on to answer it."

Roone agreed. "Let me try to get him," I said.

I struck out for Building 14 in the Olympic Village. With me were Jim Murray and Terry O'Neil, a brilliant young Notre Dame graduate who had been hired by ABC as our Olympics researcher. We reached the quarters of the U.S. team at 5:25 P.M.—five minutes before the time Stan Wright had set to see us. There was an American reporter already waiting outside the building, Larry Merchant of the *New York Post*. He wanted to see Wright but said he couldn't get in. I suggested he wait with us for the meeting Wright had promised us at 5:30. The appointed time came and went. So did 6:00 o'clock. Still no sign of Stan Wright. I yelled up to his room on the third floor and, once, I thought I spotted him at the corner of a window looking out. I might have been mistaken.

By then I could wait no longer. I was to represent the ABC announcing team at a banquet that night at a Munich restaurant, to be attended by the film producers with whom ABC does business. Before I left I told Terry O'Neil: "Stay on top of this. The minute anything happens, here's my number. Get me."

At a quarter to ten I got a call from Terry. "He finally surfaced. There is going to be a press conference at ten fifteen."

I said my good-nights, left Emmy at the party and shot over to the Village to meet Terry.

He filled me in: "It's incredible what happened. It has been a cloak-and-dagger game for all these hours. Somebody in the building called the West German police to keep the press out. Some reporters were roughed up. Larry Merchant tried to get in. He had his credentials taken away."

"You've got to be kidding."

"No. They've tried to clamp it shut."

I learned later that at the time Murray, Terry O'Neil and I had bumped into Merchant in front of Building 14, he and three colleagues had already had their ruckus with three of the West German police. Larry, Paul Zimmerman, also of the *Post,* Ed Ingels of WCBS radio and Dave Marash of WCBS television had gone immediately from the stadium to Building 14 when our sprinters failed to appear on time. According to Zimmerman, Vince Matthews, the 400-meter gold-medal winner, asked them up to his room, and they had gone up perhaps five stairs when they were sent hurtling backwards by the police. Merchant did have his accreditation taken from him, but stayed in the Village and was still holding the fort when we arrived at 5:25 P.M. As Terry spoke I thought of one of the more enduring lines ever written about me: "He makes the world of fun and games sound like the Nuremberg Trials." The writer? Larry Merchant. Now he was finding out that sometimes it *can* be the Nuremberg Trials.

The press conference finally took place, with many prominent U.S. writers not even aware of it. Perhaps the U.S. officials had seen to it that there would be as little communication as possible.

I fired the first question, and then the writers took off. It was not a gentle interrogation. Clifford Buck, the president of the U.S. Olympic Committee, began by babbling away: "We don't know anything about the schedules. We don't know what happened. . . ."

Frank Dolson, of the *Philadelphia Inquirer,* screamed at him, "How dare you tell us that when the *Paris Tribune* had the correct schedule."

The questions piled on: "What! You say the German authorities were responsible? Which ones? When? Who are they? What are their jobs?"

Another writer asked if the U.S. officials didn't check the schedule every day. Stan Wright assured him that they did. He held up a schedule. Paul Zimmerman looked at it. "My God," he said, "that's an eighteen-month-old schedule."

The press conference was a disaster. They had no answers, except to somehow attempt to attach the blame to the German authorities. When it ended I went up to Wright. "Stan," I said, "I've got to be honest with you. Rey Robinson [who was at the press conference with Eddie Hart] did an interview with me earlier and he blamed you. I'm not going to play it unless you have equal time. Do you want to come on and explain to the American people?"

"It's up to Bill. Let me talk to him."

Bowerman left it to Wright. He agreed to come on, by now a spiritless man, resigned to the fact that what had happened would not go away. "I guess," he said, as we walked to the studio, "I'm going to have to live with this forever." His desolation was genuine.

"I'm afraid so, Stan," I said. "But I think the only

thing to do is to go on and talk about it. I think you'll find that somehow, two or three years from now, it will have receded. You'll have bad memories. But it will have receded."

I knew Stan Wright only distantly from the 1968 Olympics in Mexico City. As the coach of the sprinters, he had been swept into the whole protest kick of Tommie Smith and John Carlos and the uncertainty surrounding Lee Evans. Stan Wright seemed destined for problems. But I was sympathetic to him. Only a few days earlier in the Village he had asked me to pose for pictures with him. I had been delighted to do so.

Now as we reached the studio I sought out Roone Arledge. I briefed him on the press conference and the toughness of the questioning. Roone wondered if we should play the footage of the press grilling Wright and the others. I was against it. There was a time problem involved in developing the film. More to the point, I felt Wright was entitled to answer Rey Robinson and the charges raised at the press conference directly.

Arledge then handed me an Associated Press dispatch. It said unequivocally that the Americans had blamed the German authorities. "Is this what was said?" he asked.

Quickly I read the story. "It's a little more complicated than that. But yeah, they tried to duck it." Roone told me to do my thing. To pin down the answers to the confusing, fragmented story that now included outdated schedules and mysterious German officials and phantom traffic jams.

I had never seen a studio more tense as we prepared to do the interview. Stan sat to my left. He was visibly drained. I felt uncomfortable for him—for us both. He is a heavy man, round-faced, gentle-spoken. Some of the younger black athletes describe him as being an "Old World" black man. They do not relate to him. But track has been his life.

In my earset I heard the command from the control room: "Cue Howard." We were on. And here, exactly as the words were spoken on the air, is the transcript of the now famous Stan Wright interview:

COSELL: This is Stan Wright, the coach of the United States Olympic sprint relay team, the key figure in the terrible mishap that occurred today when two very great sprinters, Eddie Hart and Reynaud Robinson, failed to appear on time for their respective heats in the one-hundred-meter dash. Now earlier, Stan, as you know, Rey Robinson said you were the culprit, you were the man to blame for their failure to show. Is this or is this not true?

WRIGHT: Well, that's a pretty harsh word, Howard—culprit. I would simply answer that in that I am responsible for the sprinters, they have faith in me and they had faith in me. There was a misunderstanding of time schedules. I assumed one time schedule and there was another time schedule I had not seen—did not see, and we left the village together to come over, and the only thing I can do is to be a man and take full responsibility as sprint coach for them not being there. It's my responsibility, I'm deeply grieved about it, and will forever, I guess, be sorry on their behalf.

COSELL: Are the athletes in any sense to blame? After all, they're not children.

WRIGHT: No, no, no, no, no, the athletes are not to blame. The athletes are not children, they're men, they're young men, but they put their faith in their coaches. And when I—when we agreed that we were leaving the Village on a certain time to be over, to run on a certain time, then they go along with me one hundred percent. I was going on a basis that the only thing they had on the time schedule there was that the eight hundred meters went at three o'clock, fifteen hundred, and I was going on a basis of after that everything came down the line, and on the sheet as it came down the line the one-hundred-meter second round was after the ten-thousand-meter trials and, not knowing this, they changed it and put the one hundred meters before—

COSELL: But as a matter of accepted routine, with all that's at stake, all the years, really, of work and preparation and so on, don't you check on a given day with the appropriate Olympic authorities—

WRIGHT: Yes, I did.

COSELL: —as to the schedule? What happened?

WRIGHT: I checked as to our heats and I checked the stadium before I left, checked the assembly area, asked them about the schedule I had. They said that's the way it was going to run—be run—and I left on the assumption that that was correct.

COSELL: I feel deeply sorry for you, but we all have to answer to the American public. Why in the world was America the only country to have the wrong information?

WRIGHT: *Well, I can't answer that because those a little higher up on the echelon, as far as I'm concerned—*

COSELL: What do you mean by that?

WRIGHT: *Well . . . I think you know what I mean.*

COSELL: No, I don't. I'd like you to tell me.

WRIGHT: *Well, I'm not in a position to tell you because I really don't know myself,* but I don't feel I have to answer to America; I feel I have to answer to these two youngsters, and this is why I feel so deeply about it. I'm concerned about them. They were the ones that did not make the heat, they were the ones that are suffering the grief of, as you say, long preparation. Great sprinters, outstanding sprinters, representing their country, and they didn't get a chance because there was a misunderstanding on my part on the schedule.

COSELL: I think everybody feels the same way about that, but this other matter you've just implied upon: some other people. Are you trying to tell me that there are people above you who are responsible for this?

WRIGHT: No, I didn't say other people. *I said there might be something in the higher echelon that I'm not—don't quite understand and why the information didn't get to me, that's what I'm telling you.* I'm not blaming anybody else.

COSELL: Do you feel that the breakdown in communications might be attributable to higher authority, not to you?

WRIGHT: No, I'm not saying that either. *I'll say this, that there was, perhaps, a breakdown in communications* and I didn't get the information. And I'm not passing the buck 'cause as far as I'm concerned the buck stops with me. I'm the sprint coach and I have to take the responsibility.

COSELL: Final question. Do you believe that your young men can still have confidence in you as the coach in view of what happened?

WRIGHT: Well, I think so. They have expressed confidence in me later on after the emotions settled down. I understand that Rey said it was my fault, and I don't blame him for saying that. I think they realize that I'm a human being just like all of us are and we make mistakes, and it's just unfortunate that this incredible thing happened. I still can't believe it happened.

The interview ended on that note. Stan Wright stepped out of the hot studio lights and into the hall. Back in Arledge's office, Roone and one of his executive staff, Jim Spence, debated whether to ask for another take. Spence, particularly, felt that although Wright had appeared to accept the blame, he alluded vaguely several times to a "higher echelon"—Americans? Germans?—who were somehow involved and responsible. "I think you've got to follow up on that," Spence said. "And don't forget, the AP story out of the press conference clearly says they tried to blame the Germans. But above all, the schedule. What schedule did he really use? What one did he talk about at the press conference? And dammit, we're still the only country in the world that didn't get the right information."

In that, we knew Spence was correct. Certainly the front pages all over the world the next day would headline the same refrain: ONLY AMERICANS FAIL TO KNOW STARTING TIME.

I asked Stan to return to the studio. "Oh, no," he said,

understandably. "I've done all I'm going to do. I'm just not going to do any more." With that he left.

We still had to have a full package—reportorial balance and, indeed, fairness. We put Eddie Hart on the air. Hart took a softer view than the visceral honesty of Reynaud Robinson. "Yes, Stan Wright was to blame," he said, "but so were a lot of other people. You can't blame any one man."

So we now had the strong statement of Robinson indicting Wright, the more tolerant statement by Hart, and Wright himself. What we didn't have was Wright clarifying his vague references to the "higher echelon." What we also didn't have was a statement Wright had made at the press conference, in which he also involved a member of the German organizing committee. Nor did we have enough on the schedule Stan had used. Jim Spence insisted that I round out the package with a commentary to cover these points.

So I faced the cameras again, and began:

COSELL: So that's the headline story in the Twentieth Olympiad, Munich, West Germany, today from the three principals: Rey Robinson, Eddie Hart and, finally, Coach Stan Wright. Not a happy story. Frankly, it's a rotten mess and a terrible human tragedy. When two decent young men and two very great athletes spend so many years of their lives for the one fulfillment, the one challenge, and don't even have the opportunity to accept that challenge, it has to be the most frustrating and heartbreaking thing possible to those two young people. Now, what about the coach, who has just openly admitted his mistake, who has made a terrible mistake quite clearly, *but who has been a very decent man all his life and a very fine track coach?* At a press conference just a few moments ago, he alluded to an Olympic authority that he spoke to this morning when he presented what was an old schedule—though he did not say it was a year-and-a-half old in my interview with him, as he did at the press conference, it was obviously an old schedule—

and the Olympic authority to whom he presented it
was later identified in the press conference by Stan as
a member of the German organizing Olympic Committee. He also said that at the stadium later today
he had spoken to some Olympic authorities in blue and
white uniforms who confirmed that old schedule. But
without attacking or unnecessarily pillorying Stan
Wright, the plain fact is for you people in America that
only the United States of America had the wrong information. It is clear that the *Paris Tribune* as published today in Munich had the right time information
for those one-hundred-meter heats. It's clear that every
responsible reporter in Munich, West Germany, had the
right time information. The American Broadcasting
Company had the right time information. So, no matter
how they try to pass the buck, no matter how they
try to whitewash, *our people* are to blame. And the
ones who suffer are the ones who are supposed to
flourish: the two decent young men who've had such
dedication and such purpose, and now such terrible,
terrible despair and disappointment. That's what happened here in Munich, West Germany, today, even as
others exulted in the Mark Spitz victory.

You may judge for yourself the firmness and tenor of
the questions and comment applied to Stan Wright. I
described him as a fine, decent man. In that, and other
ways, I felt I gave him the benefit of the doubt.

Not everyone agreed. The next morning I was aware
again of being in the center of a terribly sensitive situation. Yet we had covered every angle of the story, had
gotten the people on the air, were bringing journalism to
the telecasting of the Games.

At breakfast I ran into Julie Barnathan. He was, to
put it mildly, agitated. "My God," he said, "I just spoke
to New York. After your interview with Wright played,
and the commentary, they had four hundred negative
calls."

I started to laugh. "Julie, you're kidding me."

"Like hell," he said. "The switchboard went crazy."

"What are you so frightened about, Julie? I don't give a damn. We hit the issues. And for all the years the writers and the critics have been saying, 'Television never hits the issues.'"

"Well, I know, but a lot of negative calls—"

"Julie," I said, striding off, "you worry about it. I'm not going to. The ones I'm sorry for are the two kids. I gave Wright every opportunity to say what he said at the press conference and he didn't do it."

In my mail slot at the desk were perhaps a dozen telegrams lambasting me. Some accused me of being antiblack. At such moments you pause and wonder what your life is all about; what you have been doing all along. All right. You're a professional. You've been through it before. It won't be the last time. And you tune it out. Or try.

In a day or two the newspaper clippings began to pour in from home. In Milwaukee I was awarded the title of "Mr. Obnoxious." Cosell brutalized the poor black coach. In Chicago, a columnist wrote that "the time has come, once and for all, for ABC to get rid of Cosell. The American people can't go on with . . ."

Never mind that my questions were identical to those asked by the press earlier; questions that begged to be met. Suddenly Cosell's treatment of Stan Wright had become a more emotional issue than the misfortune and denial of the two young athletes. Both had invested their lives in an opportunity that now, for no accountable reason, had simply evaporated.

Too often, one suspects, anger waits not for bad tidings but for the messenger.

I read with particular interest the issue of *Sports Illustrated* of September 24, 1972. It carried on page 13 a "Scorecard" item that said, in part: "Cosell relentlessly badgered the obviously suffering Wright. . . . the gratuitous 'commentary' that followed the interview was cruel and unnecessary. Cosell seems to think himself a crusading district attorney. . . ." The item was captioned: "The Hanging Judge."

On page 21 of that same issue, *Sports Illustrated*'s own

coverage of the Olympics began with these words: "It could have been worse. Stan Wright could have been coaching Mark Spitz or managing the American wrestlers. . . ." This item was written by Pat Putnam who was in Munich and who was at the Stan Wright press conference. The other item was written by a writer in the United States.

I suggest that these three points are emphasized by this whole episode.

First, there will always be people who don't want to hear anything bad that happens in sports and who especially don't want to learn that Americans can make mistakes like anyone else.

Second, the television medium can often provide sympathy for a person who is facing adverse circumstances. Stan Wright is an appealing-looking man with a round, clean-cut face and sensitive eyes, and on the occasion of the interview his dismay and inner torment were etched on his visage.

Third, hard news is often alien to sports coverage but it became an integral part of our Olympic coverage. This in itself was a shock to many. I suspect that had Walter Cronkite, Mike Wallace or Harry Reasoner conducted the same interview I did with Stan Wright, it would have attracted hardly a murmur. It was journalism of the sort they deal with every day, but not of the sort dealt with in sports every day.

I felt sorry for Stan Wright. I did then and I do now. I'm not now and never was at war with this man. But I believe that the U.S. track officials—including Stan Wright—were given credit for an honesty and a candor that their actions did not justify. An admission of guilt can't reduce the damage done to the innocent.

Some weeks later I received in the mail a newspaper clipping from Don Canham, the athletic director of the University of Michigan. It reported certain punitive action taken that day by an investigating council of the NCAA, and it included this statement:

"California State was disciplined for using three ineligible athletes in the 1971 NCAA College division track and field championships and for erroneously certifying 13 athletes as eligible under the 1.6 grad point eligibility rule." Then, in a hand-written note on the side, Canham said, "The coach of Cal State is Stan Wright. Thirteen is a new record."

Curiously, while the press was unsparing in its criticism of me, the coaches and athletic directors who are Wright's colleagues remained eloquently silent.

So now we recapitulate: First, U.S. officials groped for explanations, and could make none stick. Then they divided the blame among them—Buck, Bowerman and Wright. And then they attempted to share it with the German organizers.

Out of this colossal bungle came the certain knowledge that of the 132 nations that competed in the Games, only one nation missed the starting time of an event because of an error by the coaching and administrative leadership. That nation was the United States of America. It still seems beyond comprehension that the proper schedule could have eluded the keenest minds of the United States Olympic Committee.

But the Stan Wright incident did not end with the 20th Olympiad. A letter dated November 8, 1972, addressed to the "American Broadcasting Companies, Inc.," the "American Broadcasting Company," "ABC Sports Inc.," and "Mr. Howard Cosell" arrived in New York. It was from Stan Wright's attorney who advised us that he had been retained in connection with a planned suit for defamation of Stan's character during the course of my interview. The letter ended with this paragraph:

"However, Professor Wright has agreed to have us first discuss this matter with you away from the glare and limelight of the public interest, which such a lawsuit would surely engender. Should you wish to do so, please contact our office within the next ten days."

The ABC attorneys did. Subsequently we played the video tape of the interview and my commentary that followed for Stan and his attorney. We also provided them with transcripts of both.

Finally, on May 23, 1973, almost nine months after

the interview, Stan called a press conference in New York City. He announced that he would not sue either ABC or me because he could not afford the cost of the suit and possible appeals. He characterized my interview as misleading and derogatory. But in his statement to the press he said this:

"While I didn't try during the interview to place the blame on anyone else, the truth of the matter is that I never received from the American officials or from the German officials, or from anyone, any notice of the change in the schedule, and that before leaving the stadium that morning, I showed my schedule for the afternoon events to the proper German official, who said it was correct."

Which was exactly what I was trying to adduce from him in the interview, because it was the gist of what he said, or tried to say, at the press conference in the presence of Bill Bowerman and Clifford Buck.

On May 23, when Stan held his press conference in New York, I was in Room 1318 of the new Senate Office Building in Washington, D.C., testifying before the Senate Commerce Committee. Subject: four proposed pieces of legislation designed to allow for some form of government responsibility with regard to the U.S. Olympic structure so that the multiple American mishaps of the 20th Olympiad—like the case of the empty starting blocks—might never be repeated.

Stan's timing was bad again.

PART 3:

Every Day a Crisis

*"The land of the Free? No.
I can't believe those words."*

By the end of the 20th Olympiad the "case of the empty starting blocks" had become commonplace. Never a day passed without an issue, a mistake or some kind of turbulence. They seemed to be as much a part of the daily schedule as lunch. And, of course, it was my assignment to cover these stories.

Bob Seagren, the world record holder in the pole vault, was the first case. On his arrival in Munich, Bob knew that the International Amateur Athletic Federation had initiated proceedings that could lead to his pole being taken from him. The pole was a fiber glass model, lighter and more flexible than most but clearly within the rules.

But here politics crept in. It was manufactured for Bob in the States. Some vaulters—meaning those who did not have similar poles—felt that he was taking advantage of capitalist technology. Rules or no rules, the IAAF apparently intended to penalize Seagren.

It sounds curious to say it, but there is a special attachment between a vaulter and his pole. Everywhere he goes, it goes. Heifetz had his violin. Jack Nicklaus had his putter. And Seagren had his "catapole," which in the Olympic trials had lifted him to previously unattained heights—18 feet, 5¾ inches.

No sooner did Bob reach Munich than he learned that

the IAAF had ruled in his favor. He would have his pole.
The minute this news broke I shot over to the U.S. building to get Bob for an interview. I couldn't even get
through the door. "No one but the athletes admitted."
That's what I was told by one of the press representatives
for the track-and-field contingent. I insisted I had to talk
with Seagren. He advised me that they had held a press
conference that morning at which Seagren had appeared.
Now we haggled like fishwives. I told him that ABC had
been advised by no one, including himself, of any such
press conference. He said that such conferences were an
everyday routine. I said there was nothing routine about
Seagren being allowed to keep his pole. And around and
around we went.

Finally he went into the building, and out came Bill
Bowerman, the head coach of track and field. This was
my first meeting with Bowerman. He seemed a decent
fellow, looked a little like Bud Grant, the Vikings' coach,
and even had the same kind of personality—dull. Bowerman explained to me that I would have to live by the
rules that had been established. I told him I had no
desire to break them, but the Seagren story was a major
one and I needed to see Bob. He doubted that Seagren
would talk to me, but he agreed to ask. He went back
into the building. While I waited other athletes emerged,
some of them friends from the Mexico City Olympics.
They all told me Seagren was not inside. I began to
wonder about this silly charade. All I wanted to do was
talk with Seagren. I had known him for many years, had
become friendly with him in Mexico, and I knew that
he wouldn't be party to this strange attempt to keep him
secreted away. Actually, what was going on right then
should have alerted me to the cloak-and-dagger procedure that took place the day Hart and Robinson did
not get to the starting blocks.

Bowerman finally came back out, said "Follow me"
and led me through a maze of doors to a room that
seemed to be an annex to the main building. Lo and
behold, there was Bob Seagren, warm and friendly as
ever and delighted to do the interview. He gathered up

his pole, and off we went to the entrance to the Olympic Village where I had a film crew waiting.

On camera Bob explained why the pole was so important to him, how it did conform to the rules. He bluntly called the attempt to outlaw it an effort by some in the IAAF to try to engineer a victory in the pole vault for the East German, Wolfgang Nordwig.

Off camera Bob and I talked about the trouble I had encountered in getting to him. "Same old crap," he said. "They never change. They do everything to get in your way, nothing to help you." He was referring to the coaches and the U.S. Olympic officials. But, overall, Bob was feeling good. He had his pole—or so he thought.

On the very eve of the competition, there was a sudden reversal, and vaulters like Seagren, Steve Smith of the United States and Kjell Isaksson of Sweden had their poles confiscated while they were out of their rooms. Seagren alone lost eight in the raid. The day of the competition I went to the Olympic Stadium with Bill Toomey in order to interview Seagren. I was down at trackside with Toomey when Seagren arrived. Before I could talk to him we were intercepted by a man named Adrian Paulen, of the Netherlands, the very official responsible for disallowing Seagren's pole. He started to tell us that banning the pole was the only fair thing to do. I merely said, "That's arguable," and I motioned Seagren over to us. At first Paulen said we couldn't do the interview. But when I insisted that Bob should make that decision he finally acceded. Bob wanted to do the interview—and then some.

He was almost violent in his expression about the IAAF and his absolute disgust with the 20th Olympiad. He was going to have to vault, he said, with a pole he had never seen before. He had registered objection to this and was told he might be disqualified from the competition for unsportsmanlike behavior. He said, "Frankly, for me this is no Olympics at all. I just want to get out of here." Wolfgang Nordwig won the pole vault. No surprise.

When Bob finally finished vaulting for the day, in his

despair he flung the pole that he had been forced to use in the direction of Adrian Paulen. Seagren left the Olympic Village the next morning.

So that was the beginning.

My permanent assignment, quite apart from coverage of all of the controversies, was at the Boxhalle, a beautiful arena seating 6200 people. Over there they called it *Der Boxhalle mitt der Gloves*. I was there every afternoon and night for six hours. I saw so many fights I got cauliflower eyes. To our surprise the American fighters started off well, and as they piled up early victories there was a growing excitement about them. This was important to our telecasts because boxing took place every day but one during the Olympics. Since we had 61 hours of air time to fill, the boxing competition became a vital element of nearly every telecast.

As the fates would have it, the Boxhalle produced the first vigorously disputed decision of the Olympics—of many to come. It involved an American fighter, a light middleweight by the name of Reggie Jones, a New Jersey youngster who had only turned to boxing a couple of years before the Olympiad. He was pitted in the very first round against a skilled veteran Russian opponent by the name of Valery Tregubov.

I had seen Tregubov first in Russian-American competitions in the past. Jones figured to have two chances: slim and none.

Now the fight was on. Tregubov, with all his experience, was having unexpected trouble with Jones. The American was clearly the aggressor. By the third round he was beating the Russian all over the ring and quite clearly seemed the winner.

At my elbow Andy Williams, the singer, was going berserk. Andy was in Munich for a few days, and I had bumped into him in the lobby of our hotel. He mentioned that he would like to see the fights, and I had arranged for him to sit in the booth with me. Now he was beside himself. The American was apparently beating the Soviet fighter, and patriotism was gushing out all over. Williams was screaming for Jones. The fight ended, and based upon my experience in Mexico City in 1968 I cautioned the viewers that Olympic decisions can be tricky. I advised them not to count what they had just seen as a victory for Jones—not just yet. But I made it clear that I thought Jones deserved the decision.

They gave the decision to Tregubov—and 6200 people erupted. They weren't all Americans in that arena either; they were East and West Germans, French, British, from all over the world; only a handful were from the United States. They began throwing debris into the ring and screaming in half a dozen languages. "Fraud, fraud, fraud." *"Schande, schande, schande"* (shame).

Andy Williams led the way. He was not singing "Moon River," not this time. He was screaming, "Fix, fix, fix!" Over the uproar I continued to talk into the microphone, labeling the decision "a disgrace."

(In the *New York Times* the next morning it was called "the biggest steal since Brink's.")

Even as I poured it on, Williams was urging me to "tell it like it is, Howie." No one would have believed this was the little fellow with the satiny voice who comes on in a lower-case Perry Como way on American television. Andy, in fact, seemed hoarse from screaming as he left the arena with this parting advice to me: "If I were you, I'd come with me and whack out on this damned thing. It's phony."

Instead of whacking out on it, I went to the press room in the Boxhalle and grabbed Reggie Jones and Bobby Lewis, the American boxing coach. I took them back to the ABC Studios with me and interviewed them both. Jones broke down, understandably. I wonder if people can realize what it means to a black youngster from the ghetto to dream of escape, to find the opportunity to fulfill that dream in the Olympic Games via a gold medal and then a professional career and the money to make that escape—and then to have that dream destroyed by the injustice of a bad decision. It was simply too much for Reggie Jones. He cried. He said he might never fight again.

Jones did, in fact, fight again. Not once but three times.

He lost twice. But he has not approached the fighter he was that day. Something went out of him with that decision.

But the fight had one constructive aftermath. Six boxing judges were fired within 24 hours, and 18 others were reprimanded. Even so, it was not the end of bad decisions in the boxing arena. They were numerous, and they reflected one of the scandals of the 20th Olympiad, the scoring in the judgment sports—boxing, diving and gymnastics. Ken Sitzberger, ABC's analyst on diving, Gordon Maddux, our expert in gymnastics, and I repeatedly called attention to this. Inevitably, judges from the Soviet Union and its satellite countries would dominate the scoring. As we clearly pointed out, again and again, this didn't only reflect adversely upon American competitors but could just as easily operate against athletes from other countries. In boxing, for instance, a decision in favor of a West German middleweight over Britain's Alan Minter was even more outrageous than the one against Jones. And I said so. There was nothing cheerleaderish about our statements.

But there were times during the boxing when you could see a man utterly captivate a crowd. So it was with Jesse Valdez, a colorful kid from Houston, Texas. An Army sergeant, a veteran boxer at 26, a classic stylist with more amateur bouts by far than any of our other fighters, Valdez took the Boxhalle by storm in his very first appearance. He was sensational. He just danced around his opponent, Komlan Kalipe of Togo, jabbed and pecked away and earned the first perfect score the judges had given in these Olympics. The crowd stood and gave him an ovation that lasted for several minutes. Jesse had tears in his eyes. It was, he later told me, the greatest thing that had ever happened to him. Ironically, with me in the booth as Valdez soaked up the cheers of the fans was one Bob Seagren.

The most talked-about American fighter, however, was clearly the heavyweight Duane Bobick. He had been the recipient of a well orchestrated buildup in the United States, culminating in the Olympic Trials at West Point.

Working at ringside with me during the trials was Muhammad Ali, who went into all kinds of excesses about Bobick's ability, proclaiming him "The Great White Hope." Even then, his keen instinct for business must have suggested to Ali that here might be an important future payday.

Bobick is one of the most likable young men I've ever met. He always has a twinkle in his eye and a half smile across his lips. His brown hair is wavy, and he appeals strongly to the young ladies. He is not very big for a heavyweight, certainly not built like Foreman, Ali or even Frazier, who, though not tall, has enormous biceps and shoulders. But Bobick does have a good short, crunching right, and with his buildup everyone looked forward to a gold medal. Including Bobick. I bumped into him in the Village one day when the Games had just gotten under way. He cheerily waved and said, "Hi, Mr. Television. I'm glad you're here to see me do it."

A funny thing happened to Duane Bobick on his way to the gold medal. Curiously, he was placed in the same half of the draw with the two toughest other heavyweights, Teofilo Stevenson of Cuba, and Juri Nesterov of Russia. Then he went almost a week until he fought for the first time—against Nesterov, an imposing fighter. Though Bobick floored him twice and won the bout, he came out of it a used-up contender. Just two days later he had to fight Teofilo Stevenson.

This is not by way of an excuse for Bobick, but it was too much to ask of him: to fight Nesterov so fiercely, and next to engage a great young fighter on the very day of the Israeli tragedy. While I wasn't at ringside for the match—there were other priorities that day—I subsequently talked at length to Bobick about it. He had beaten Stevenson once before, in Cuba, but Duane freely admitted that the lad from the sugarcane fields had improved enormously since that time. And he conceded that much had been taken out of him by Nesterov and that his mind was clouded by events taking place in the Israeli building.

It is questionable, however, if he could ever have

beaten Stevenson under any circumstances. The Cuban looks to be a remarkable young fighter, handsome and swift in the manner of the young Ali, proportioned much like the young Ali. Also, Stevenson has a knockout punch. There probably isn't a boxing manager in the United States who wouldn't give up his entire stable to land Teofilo Stevenson. There was a day when I spoke to Stevenson about this, describing how much money he could make as a professional fighter in the United States. He half looked around, as if Cuban military might be at hand. You can rest assured that Stevenson will not be defecting. He will probably be found in Montreal in 1976, winning another gold medal.

So, in a perverse way, even Duane Bobick was caught up in the twisting flow of the 20th Olympiad. And one after another our boxers began to lose, except for an appealing young character named Sugar Ray Seales. But while this was happening I was swept up by the same currents that pulled us all along. With one exception. I had to be there. I had to cover these flash interruptions that jarred the normalcy of every day.

Now Wayne Collett and Vince Matthews did their thing. Momentarily I thought I was back in Mexico City with Tommie Smith and John Carlos. "Get them on the air." Those were the orders. With the aid of Terry O'Neil I got them on the air. And I got the story. It wasn't easy. Before we did the interview, both men openly told me they were afraid they would be treated unfairly. They had seen the shock and indignation their actions caused at the stadium. Why should they expect better from American television?

I told them, simply, that they would get fair treatment and they should judge for themselves after the interview was done.

That afternoon Matthews had broken the tape in the 400-meter run, with Collett finishing second. On the victory stand there was no immediate hint of yet another tempest. In a sporting gesture Matthews reached out a hand and pulled Collett onto the top with him. Then, as the national antem played on, as the crowd grew more disbelieving, they stood at inattention, slouched, chatted, surveyed the scene with casual indifference. The crowd booed its displeasure. Matthews twirled the gold medal that dangled from his neck. It appeared to be blatant disrespect. But why? And was it planned?

As I spoke with the two of them I became absolutely convinced that they had not acted in planned concert, that what each did sprang from instincts deep within him. This was no return of the Smith-Carlos number. Said Matthews: "I did what came naturally to me at the time. If I had wanted to demonstrate, I would have found a better way."

The truth was, Matthews had been nursing a wound. Lee Evans had failed to qualify for the 400 meters in the Olympic Trials. Bill Bowerman had given the impression—at least to Matthews—that he preferred Evans and hoped to find a way to get Lee into the event, instead of Vince. He was deeply hurt and resentful. I don't happen to agree with the method of Olympic Trials. I regard it as unthinkable that the best competitive runner I ever saw, Lee Evans, failed to qualify because on one given day he was running with a hamstring pull that nobody knew about. But that's the way it was, and under the rules Matthews had made it. He deserved not to be made to feel as though he were a freeloader.

So he felt rejected and bitter. It was seething within him. By God, when he won that gold medal he just busted out all over.

I found Collett, on the surface, a more cultured, literate man than Matthews. Boiling within him was the feeling he expressed so clearly in that interview. He spoke of racial injustice and his inability to relate to the "Star Spangled Banner." "The land of the free? No. I can't believe in those words. That's why I did it." It was not premeditated. I'm convinced of that. It was a natural reaction, each man for different reasons. Matthews because of what he felt were the insults of the coaching staff toward him. Collett because deep inside him he nurses what Tommie Smith and John Carlos and Lee Evans nurse, what many black athletes in the whole sporting firmament, and what many black people in all of America, nurse—the undying bitter resentment at being born black in a white man's country; being a second-class citizen.

Both young men knew there would be consequences. But even those who wanted to see them punished were surprised by the manner in which it was handled. It came from the International Olympic Committee, not from the United States and not with due process. Both were barred from ever competing again in the Olympics. Question: Where was the U.S. Olympic Committee?

Both seemed relieved after the interview was over. Both felt they had been treated fairly. Collett joined my wife and me for cocktails later at our hotel. We talked about his future and whether or not his actions would hurt his job opportunities. He felt that they probably would, but he was going back to college and then on to graduate school. It was his overall feeling that things would work out for him. Certainly he was not despondent. I see Vince Matthews from time to time. He lives in Brooklyn. He has become part of the new professional track tour. And he is writing a book. He is a hard young man to penetrate. When he talks with you he always has a trained smile, and you get the feeling that somewhere within him is a persecution complex. I wonder how things will go for Vince Matthews.

Oddly, after those two interviews we got mail from the States accusing me of being too soft on "the black bastards." We had come full circle in the confused American sociology. Remember Stan Wright?

Next came the Jim Ryun misstep. This was to have been another great Olympic confrontation between Jim Ryun, the kid from the Kansas prairie, and Kip Keino, a product of the highlands of Kenya, in the 1500-meter run. Unaccountably the two were in the same heat. The first four finishers qualified. Obviously, America's most famous miler could fail only one way—by falling down.

The race began. Ryun, as usual, lay far back in the pack. Then, suddenly, shockingly, Ryun became entangled with a runner from Ghana as he started to make his move. He fell hard, lay stunned for a moment, then bravely got up and finished hopelessly out of contention. In my opinion he ran a stupid race. But you had to feel for him. He was devastated. His rematch with Keino, who defeated him in the thin air of Mexico in 1968, now seemed gone forever.

Out of nowhere I received a telephone call that night at my hotel. It was Jim Ryun. He planned to appeal. Would I help him draft the language? Could I come over?

No. But I offered to dictate a statement for him over the phone. "Read what you've written," I suggested. I dictated an addition to it, wished him luck and said I would see him in the morning. Privately, I gave his appeal little, if any, chance.

Then came the latest orders: "Live with Jim Ryun."

And so I did. I was with him the next day as he waited—and waited—for news of his appeal. It was growing close to the time of the race itself. Ryun was in his sweat suit, warming up on the practice track. He kept looking for one of the assistant coaches, hopeful that good news was coming. I was there when one of the coaches finally came. I watched them talk and then saw tears well up in Ryun's eyes as he jogged down the track. One of the hardest walks I ever took in my life was up the length of that track to where Ryun had stopped.

Quietly, I said to him, "Jim, I'm sorry, so terribly sorry. Do you want to talk?" Yes, he did. He went on the air and said that he had run his last Olympic metric mile. That he would have to pick up his life, that he would have to take care of his wife and children. He said he simply couldn't understand why his appeal had been treated in the manner it had, why the delay was so long.

I still see Jim Ryun, and I shall always respect him. He did what no man had ever done before, and what man has yet to do since: He ran a mile in 3 minutes, 51.1 seconds. But somehow misfortune seems permanently to have come upon him as a runner. He is a maze of psychological complexities. He analyzes and reanalyzes himself to the point of self-destruction. He has turned professional now, along with his international rival, Kip Keino. In his first official pro appearance he was defeated easily by Keino. In his second appearance he was injured.

I interviewed both Jim and Kip the morning after that first professional match-up in Los Angeles. I bluntly told Jim that there would be no more psychological interviews, that he had became the Floyd Patterson of track and field. Just as bluntly, Jim agreed, and admitted that he had done himself great harm by his introspection the previous year.

The odyssey of Jim Ryun goes on.

Bizarre misfortune continued to haunt the U.S. team. No one suffered a more cruel reversal than Rick DeMont, the 15-year-old California swimmer, an asthmatic, who won the 400-meter freestyle. Six weeks before the Olympics began, Rick had been in Washington, D.C., filling out the necessary forms, disclosing that he suffered from chronic asthma. He filed them with the medical authorities on the U.S. team whose duty it was, under the existing drug procedures, to report Rick's condition to the IOC. Had they done so, the IOC would have advised them that the medication taken by Rick includes the stimulant ephedrine, which was not approved. Another would have been suggested. It was that simple. But American doctors inexcusably failed to report it.

So the youngster won the gold medal, the emotional crest of his young years, and had it taken away from him. He was also subsequently barred from the 1500 meters, his specialty, minutes before he was to compete. I interviewed his coach, Peter Daland, and the chief medical officer of the U.S. contingent. I was very impressed with Daland. He is a no-nonsense guy who was determined to see that the American people knew that Rick DeMont was the victim of yet another bureaucratic U.S. bungle. During the interview, because of Daland's outspoken forcefulness, the doctor—after hemming and hawing—admitted the mistake. Still another controversy. It seemed I couldn't turn around without being engulfed by them.

During all of this I had made a friendship I valued with Erich Segal, serving as our analyst on distance running. He fascinated me and my wife. This emotional, sensitive man who had written a record best seller, *Love Story,* who had been through his own turmoil at Yale and suffered his own abuse, who had a passionate interest in distance running, became deeply absorbed in the boxing scene. I took him to *Der Boxhalle mitt der Gloves* and he positively fell in love with it. He must have gone at least five times. I reminded him about the likes of Hemingway and Mailer and Schulberg. I said, "Don't feel embarrassed by it. All the great writers love boxing."

I responded to the emotion and excitement that always seemed to be close to the surface of Erich Segal. I was in the control room the day Erich was reporting Frank Shorter's superb victory in the marathon. The finish of the race was confused by the appearance of an intruder in track togs who loped into the stadium, even as the crowd braced itself to welcome the winner of this grueling event. The TV cameras had followed Shorter virtually to the lip of the stadium, but now this. The fans blissfully cheered on, most of them totally unaware that the character who now bounded around the track with arms upraised was a phony.

There was a stricken quality to Erich Segal's voice as he said: "That's not Frank. . . . THAT'S NOT FRANK. He's an impostor. HE'S AN IMPOSTOR. Get him off the track. Here comes Frank now. He doesn't know what's happening. My God, look at the anguish on his face. IT'S ALL RIGHT, FRANK. IT'S ALL RIGHT. YOU'VE WON, FRANK."

It developed later that the impostor was a German college student, let out a few blocks from the stadium, who was not there to disrupt the race but to protest—in this fuzzy way—the continuation of the Games in the wake of the Village murders—at least that was one version. The way the AP reported it, the young man was protesting the Vietnam War. It was one of the odder—and lighter—moments of the 20th Olympiad. This time, a harmless aberration. Even Shorter was amused. Erich's concern had been for nothing. Frank confided that he preceded him onto the track, and took his victory lap in unspoiled elation. "I'm sorry," he said, grinning, "if it was spoiled for other people."

I must admit, I felt a twinge of pleasure at seeing somebody else involved in a mixup for a change.

The reason I was in the control room at that time— the final Sunday of the Olympiad—was because of another chain of chaotic events that had occurred at the basketball venue the previous night.

A scoreboard had become the focal point of all Olympic notice: It read: Russia 51, United States 50. The game had ended in mass confusion, disorder and controversy. Adding to the emotion of the moment was the fact that this was *the* American game, invented by us, dominated by us. No U.S. basketball team had *ever* lost in Olympic competition.

What happened, briefly, was this: The U.S. team had struggled all night, fallen behind by ten points late in the game, and finally rallied to take the lead—with the clock stopped at three seconds—on two free throws by Doug Collins of Illinois State. The Russian coach attempted to call a time-out as Collins jockeyed the ball for his second shot. The Russian coach and some of his reserves were edging onto the court, still trying to call time, as their team put the ball in play for a final, desperate shot. It missed. The buzzer sounded. The Americans leaped up and down and pounded each other in pure jubilation.

But, ominously, there was a crowd gathering at the scorer's table. The official at the scene, Dr. William Jones, a Munich resident, had decided that the Russians were entitled to their time-out. He ordered the three seconds put back on the clock.

I must pause to explain that Dr. Jones is president of the Federation of International Basketball Associations (FIBA). There are 21 Olympic sports, each with its own governing body, constitution and police force. Dr. Jones reminded me of Adrian Paulen—remember?—the IAAF authority in the Seagren case. One can go crazy with these petty, pompous organizations.

At courtside there was still one more moment of clean comedy. Only one second was restored to the clock. Another false start. More turmoil at the scorer's table. Three *more* seconds and one more try.

This time, even as the Americans were attempting to find out what happened, even as they were preparing a defense on the court, the Russians heaved a length-of-the-court pass to their leading scorer, Alexander Belov, under the basket. He shoved aside Jim Forbes and Kevin Joyce and dropped it in. The buzzer went off. Again.

Now the Russians were in a state of self-congratulatory hysteria. It was beyond imagination. Two endings. Two outcomes. You could have run a split screen of the two celebrations and they would have been nearly identical. Only the names and nationalities had been changed.

For the life of me, I will never understand why no member of the U.S. Olympic Committee was there at least to voice some official protest on the spot. But none was there, and we saw the unbelievable spectacle of David Wolper, the famed film producer, and David Gerber, the television packager for whom I appeared on "Nanny and the Professor," at the scorer's table fighting for the interests of the United States.

That tableau, by itself, stands as an index to the United States Olympic program.

Later that Saturday night my phone was ringing again, unceasingly. One voice said, "I'm Homer Johnson, of Fargo, North Dakota. You're the only one we can call because you tell it like it is. Now you go down and tell those damned basketball judges that America won that game. Do you understand? You do it right now!"

Yes, sir. Right away, sir.

Another call, this time from Ohio. "I'm sure you'll remember me, Mr. Cosell. I was captain of the Furman basketball team in 1956." Oh, yes, of course. "You've got to change that goddam thing. America won't stand for that crap with the Russians. They didn't win the game."

Yes, sir. You can count on it.

All night the phone rang. I hadn't even *covered* the

basketball. Frank Gifford and Bill Russell had. At 7:30 the next morning, Sunday, Gifford knocked on my door.

"You know what happened last night?"

I nodded.

"Let me brief you." And Giff began bringing out meticulous notes on the game and the controversial ending.

I rubbed my eyes. "I'm sorry about all this, Frank, but I've been up all night answering the damned phone."

"Well," he said, "the meetings are today, the protest and review and everything, and I'd appreciate it if you'd come with me."

"Okay. I'll be glad to, Frank."

We went down and had breakfast. We left Emmy at the hotel and drove to the basketball venue. On the way, Giff laughed and said, "Damn, I felt like you last night, in the middle of that mess. Now I know what you go through."

When we got to the venue, we found people already collecting there—reporters, members of the U.S. team, Olympic officials. The Federation of International Basketball Associations was going to make a determination on the outcome of the game.

We waited and waited and waited. One hour. Two hours. Three hours. During the wait I talked with Kevin Joyce, Doug Collins, Tom McMillen and others on our team. "We never should have gone out on that floor again," Tom said. "Not after we beat them." Privately I agreed.

Finally Dr. Jones and two of his colleagues, together with an interpreter, called the press to order, and the interpreter started reading. In three languages—German, French and English.

At this very moment an ABC man brought me a message. Get over to the Olympic Stadium immediately. Dave Wottle was about to run in the 1500-meter finals, and I was to interview him after the race.

I got there. Wottle lost. I did the interview. And then, in another of the unending mishaps of these unending games, George Woods of the United States finished sec-

ond in the shot put and on the home screen it appeared
that he might have lost the gold medal because his best
put hit a distance marker. And so I interviewed Woods,
who made it clear that the marker had not cost him
the victory. But Woods was an extraordinary interview.
He detailed his disgust with the games, excoriated America's track-and-field coaches, said he was through with
the Olympics and called for a restructuring of amateur
athletics in the United States.

Now I got word that I was wanted back in the studios.
It was now late afternoon on that final Sunday. All that
was left were the marathon that afternoon and the boxing
finals that night. Back I went to the studios, and that's
how I happened to be in the control room when Erich
Segal made an impostor immortal.

By this time I was literally wiped out. This had been
going on, remember, for two weeks. But so was everyone else. I couldn't wait for the night to come and go.
One more job to do—the boxing finals—then home at
last.

It was 5:00 P.M. The boxing finals began at 7:00.
Frank Gifford arrived back at the studios with some of
the kids from the U.S. basketball team and the game's
official scorekeeper. "What happened, Giff?" I asked.
"They turned our protest down," he answered. "Just
what you'd expect. But this scorekeeper is a gutsy little
guy who's willing to tell the truth, that we won the game."

Gifford had done one hell of a job in staying on top
of the story from beginning to end. He had been up
all night, had gone to the studios in the small hours of
the morning with Dr. Jones and other members of FIBA
to review the video tapes of the final minutes of the
game, and had then come back to talk with me at the
hotel. So he was utterly exhausted. And it showed when
he went into the studio to try to collect his thoughts.
He was to do a final piece on the entire basketball fiasco,
including a rerun of the tapes showing the end of the
game and an interview with the scorekeeper. To give
Frank support—we all needed some at this point—Dennis
Lewin, one of our producers, sent me into the studio.

Frank and I then did a seven-and-a-half-minute piece, which wound up with me asking the scorekeeper one final, direct question: "Under the rules and regulations governing Olympic basketball, who won that game?"

He replied: "The United States of America."

As Frank said, a gutsy little guy.

I closed it out and had ten minutes in which to get to the Boxhalle—plenty of time, I thought.

Except that now it pouring rain, and this time there *was* a terrific traffic jam, the kind Stan Wright wished there had been. I got there just in time. We were going live to the States. It was the windup of the major competition of the Olympics, and we were to carry a good part of the action. Our emphasis, of course, was on a marvelous, colorful kid, Sugar Ray Seales, fighting out of Tacoma, Washington, in the light-welterweight division. He was the one remaining American in the competition—our last chance for a gold medal in boxing.

Sugar Ray is a southpaw, with a punishing left that follows a good right lead. He stunned the crowd by using that left to floor his tough and clever opponent, Angel Anghelov of Bulgaria. As good as the show was that Sugar Ray put on, his mother may have put on a better one. She was a wildly enthusiastic spectator at ringside, garishly garbed, singing and shouting and making almost as much noise as the entire crowd in the Boxhalle. I talked to her between rounds of the fight, and she was just great. Then, after Sugar Ray won the decision—and the gold medal—I spoke with him and his mother. He's such a winning kid, I knew the calls would inevitably come—Dick Cavett, Johnny Carson, the talk-show circuit. Sugar Ray was on his way.

I knew it for sure when Sugar Ray told me in the interview that he was going to turn pro, would one day be fighting for the title in Madison Square Garden. Then he looked at me and said, "If you're lucky, Howard, you'll get to call the fight." That's my kind of guy.

As I was leaving the arena that night, Harry Forbes, manager of our boxing team, and Bobby Lewis, the coach, stopped me and handed me a four-foot-long, rolled-up Olympic boxing poster. They unrolled it to reveal inscriptions on the face of the poster from every member of the U.S. boxing team. It made me feel proud, because I had fallen in love with those kids, and I had developed a genuine admiration for Bobby Lewis. Unlike the track-and-field leadership, Lewis had done a superb job of welding his team. Those kids had a sense of togetherness. They comported themselves with a spirit and purpose that made you glow. For instance, little Timmy Dement, the lad who had beaten Bobby Lee Hunter whose prison background had made him a pre-Olympic celebrity, took his own defeat with a strength and a dignity far beyond his 17 years. Bobby Lewis, in a nutshell, took 11 kids and made them feel like they were the 11 best fighters in the world.

And so it was over. Emmy and I left the Boxhalle for the last time. The rains were still pouring down. We drove slowly back to the München Sheraton. ABC Sports was having a big farewell party. We made only a token appearance. And in a strange way I felt I was back at the beginning. Bob Seagren suddenly appeared with his wife. They had driven to Spain, then had come back for the final day. We had a final drink with Jim and Geri Murray, then went up to bed.

We were awake at six the next morning to catch an early plane for Frankfurt and a connecting flight to New York. Frank Gifford was with us. Our last glimpse of Munich was of armed German soldiers, submachine guns shouldered, patrolling the airport.

The flight seemed endless, because my thoughts were concentrated on the cobweb of chaos that had been the 20th Olympiad. All of the questions and all of the doubts had now come into focus. Had the Olympic Games outlived their usefulness? Had they, indeed, merely become a political forum every four years for those who would make them so—Arab desperadoes, black athletes, black African nations, Communist-block countries, whomever? Should the Olympics have been allowed to continue after the slaughter of the Israelis? In the priority of the needs and even demands of civilization, is it any longer right to expend hundreds of millions of dollars on two weeks of "fun and games"?

What about the U.S. Olympic Committee and its terrible mistakes? What about the International Olympic Committee, with its arrogance and pomp and medieval philosophy? You had to think about these things because of what you had just seen and lived through. I knew one thing—that when I got back to the States I was going to dedicate myself to the task of educating the American people about the U.S. Olympic Committee—its inadequacies, its failures, the needless penalties and indignities thrust upon America's young athletes. And here perhaps a point should be made. In another time, a less traumatic time, what happened to Bob Seagren, Jim Ryun, Rick DeMont, Eddie Hart and Rey Robinson and the U.S. basketball team would have been characterized in the sporting lexicon as tragic. But not now. Not here. Not at Munich in 1972.

As we landed at Kennedy, even the Customs officials looked good to us. Emmy and I left Giff at the airport. "See you tomorrow, Giff," I said. "It's seven days to the start of 'Monday Night Football.' "

Gifford groaned.

Chapter II

THE 19TH OLYMPIAD: GAIETY AND BLACK GLOVES

"These Americans, very excitable."

Unlike the 1972 games in Munich, the 1968 Olympic Games in Mexico City are one of my life's more pleasant memories. I remember my initial doubts as to whether or not I'd even be asked to go. The games were to be held in October, and by midsummer some of the other ABC sports announcers had already been spoken to, but not a word had been said to me. Then one day in the lobby of the ABC building I bumped into Roone Arledge and I said, "Aren't I going to be assigned to the Olympics?"

And he said, "Why, Howard, all the announcers going have already gotten their Olympic blazers." Then, as he saw the consternation register in my face, he laughed and said, "Of course you're going," and that was that.

Shortly thereafter the company had a pre-Olympics luncheon at Mama Leone's restaurant in New York City, where all the announcers were to be introduced to press people from all over the country, many of whom would be covering the Olympics. As the luncheon was concluding, Keith Morris of *Sports Illustrated* raised his hand and said, "Let's hear from your boxing expert on our chances in Mexico City."

Roone looked at me, and I gulped as I got up to answer. I didn't know a damned thing about our team at that time, but I suddenly remembered a big kid named

George Foreman whom I had once seen spar with Sonny Liston. So I said that I thought we had a potential gold-medal winner in a 19-year-old heavyweight named George Foreman. After the luncheon several veteran writers surrounded me and asked me about Foreman, and I told them that he had impressed me with his size and punching ability when I had watched him spar with Liston. As subsequent events proved, in the full sweep of my ignorance I had hit it lucky.

We had a big pre-Olympics production meeting presided over by Chuck Howard. All the announcers and the key operational people were there, and I was floored by the degree of organized preparation already accomplished. It was clear that I was to do the boxing competition, perhaps some other events as assigned on a day-to-day basis, virtually all of the interviews and, further, because of the threat of incidents involving our black athletes, I was to stay on top of developments in this area.

At that time there was a threat that the blacks might boycott the games. Professor Harry Edwards of San Jose State was leading a movement in this direction, a major press conference had been held in New York with Martin Luther King in attendance, and it had been made evident that a boycott might take place, or, if not a boycott, then some kind of protest might manifest itself at the Games.

Roone Arledge was as aware of this as I was. He was also aware of the long-standing criticism of sports broadcasting that the announcers were shills, and that in their desire not to offend anybody they could never hit an issue head on. Once and for all, especially in what would be the biggest sports coverage in the history of television, Arledge wanted to put that notion to rest. "Do your thing," he told me. "I don't want any newsman beating us on any story. We're on the scene, we've got the instancy of our medium, and I don't want to get beat."

In this sense Arledge has been consistent in his entire relationship with me. He has never sought to put manacles on me in any coverage or commentary or interview I have ever done. This is an amazing thing in sports broad-

casting and not a easy position for Arledge to adopt.
When you're dealing with the National Football League,
the NCAA, the NBA, the U.S. Olympic Committee and
all the rest, you're not supposed to say anything that will
get them upset. You know that if you do there are two
other networks waiting in the wings to grab the rights to
the events in the future, and the people with whom you're
dealing will have no compunction about moving to another network. Indeed, this is one of the basic reasons
why there is so little journalism in sports broadcasting.
Not only that; getting involved in an issue that produces
mixed reactions among the viewers makes the sponsors
unhappy. On average, the sponsors live to this day with
the childlike theorem that you can and should make everybody happy. Which is the kind of thinking that led
Newton Minow to his "vast wasteland" speech.

But Arledge has some guts, and when Emmy and I
went to Mexico City I was psychologically buoyed by the
knowledge that I would be supported if there was a black-
protest situation that would require direct, head-on reporting. I was also happy about something else. Though
I had never been to Mexico City before, I had been told
about the beauty of its great boulevard, Del Reforma,
and some of the great hotels, and Chuck Howard told
us that we'd be staying in a brand-new hotel, just off
Del Reforma and right across the street from the great
Maria Isabella Hotel where press headquarters were.
All ABC Sports personnel were to be quartered in this
new place, called the Del Angel, and we looked forward
to our stay enthusiastically. Until we got there.

It is possible that, despite all that occurred there in
the athletic sense, my outstanding memory of Mexico
City is the Del Angel. When Emmy and I got there we
found a lobby as small as the New York Knicks dressing
room, which is smaller than the living room of my apartment in New York. The hotel had two elevators, which
never worked at the same time. As we came into the
lobby to register we found Tom Maloney, our gymnastics
expert, at the desk. He had arrived several days earlier,
and it seemed he had sent four shirts to the laundry on

a 24-hour-service basis. Now he was pleading for his shirts in combination pidgin English–pidgin Spanish. The man behind the desk didn't understand, or, if he did, he wasn't about to let Tom know. Maloney, in desperation, began to to scream. "I need those shirts, you understand? I've got to have them." Suddenly the man nodded, issued an order in Spanish to a Mexican youngsters nearby. He went through a door, came back in a minute with four laundered sports shirts and with a triumphant smile the deskman gave them to Maloney. "These are not my shirts, goddammit. I had dress shirts, not sport shirts."

"Better keep them, Tom," I said. "There may never be any others."

"You might be right," he answered, as he took them.

Things never got better at the Del Angel. A few days later, Tony Triolo, the *Sports Illustrated* photographer who was working for us during the Olympiad, delivered some shirts to the desk. "No starch," he carefully told the clerk, pointing to the collars and cuffs. "No starch, you understand?" The clerk nodded cheerfully. Three days later Tony was screaming to everybody who'd listen, "The sons of bitches, I told them no starch, so they removed the collars and cuffs from my shirts. Took them right off. Ruined them. Get me out of this damned place."

Then there was the saga of Parry and Arden O'Brien. Parry was our expert on field events. A massive man, he had been an Olympic gold-medal winner and world record holder in the shot put. But he is a man of surprisingly gentle nature, belying the strength of his body. Good thing, too, because if you got Parry mad, you'd be taking your life in your hands. His wife Arden was a lovely girl, very attractive, tall and slim. One day Parry was on assignment in the late afternoon at the Olympic Stadium. Arden was back at the hotel and she got on an elevator with two Mexican workmen. The elevator door closed, went down a couple of feet and stopped. Arden rang the elevator alarm, word went throughout the hotel that she was trapped on the elevator, but nobody could do anything about it.

The hotel manager's view of the situation was simple

and to the point. It was past working hours and to call in an elevator engineer would mean overtime. No, she would have to wait until the next morning for the elevator to be fixed. Emmy and some of the other girls were beside themselves, and the ABC men who were in the hotel were outraged but could do nothing about it. The hotel manager was adamant. Parry got back to the hotel about an hour later. Apprised of the scene, he went wild. He went up to the floor where his room was, went over to the elevator, called to Arden, who said she was all right, and then, applying those gargantuan hands and shoulders to the task, his feet firmly planted on the floor, he simply broke those elevator doors open, lifted Arden out, hugged her, and off they went to their room. That elevator was out of order for the rest of our stay.

Then there was the day Jim McKay was taking a shower. Or thought he was. He was all soaped up, ready to go. But the water wasn't. Not a drop. It had just suddenly stopped. This happened at some time every day during our sojourn. Jim is a small fellow, but he has a fiery spirit. He got out of the shower, half wiped himself off, put on a robe, stormed down to the lobby, told the clerk what had happened, and shouted, "If it ever happens again, I will keel you, you understand? I will keel you."

The clerk nodded, and as Jim went back upstairs the clerk shrugged. "These Americans," he said, "very excitable."

We still sit and talk and laugh about those days, all of us at ABC Sports. I would go to our Control Tower every morning, the place from which Chris Schenkel would originate as anchor man, and I'd go into the announcer's booth to tape my daily radio shows. It became a big thing, because the whole technical crew knew that on every show I'd give an anecdote about the Del Angel. It would invariably break everyone up and we'd begin the day in a good mood.

At one point during the Games, Chris Schenkel came to me and said, "Hey, I've been talking with the guys, and we all agree you should talk to Arledge to let us get out of here." Arledge, by the way, with the rest of the company brass, was staying at the El Presidente, one of the fine hotels in the city, and thus was blissfully unaware of what we were all enduring—or at least he pretended to be. I told Chris that I thought the idea was good, but that he or McKay should be the one to talk to Roone. The idea died there. Except for this: Two of our directors, Chet Forte and Andy Sidaris, on their own moved out and got rooms at the plush new Camino Real. For a couple of hours, that is. Then Arledge heard of it and ordered them right back. It was company policy that we all suffer together. So back they came, shamefacedly, their treachery exposed.

The last straw was when, after we had all been there for about ten days, Bud Palmer, one of our announcers, went to the desk clerk and asked for the key to his room. The clerk looked at him pleasantly enough and asked Bud his name. Bud could not believe it, because in all the time he had been there he had made it a practice to leave his key with the clerk whenever he left the hotel. So Bud exploded at the clerk, "My name is Bud Palmer."

The clerk looked back at Bud and informed him, "We have no Bud Palmer registered here."

Bud leaned over the counter—all six feet, five inches of him—and he said, "I am Bud Palmer, and you have been giving me my goddam key for two weeks. There's the box with my key in it." Palmer got his key.

One curious thing happened just as the games were about to get under way. Emmy and I got to the Del Angel one afternoon and, of all things, there was a message for me. Jim Bouton, who was to become more famous for his gossip book *Ball Four* than he ever was for his pitching, was holding a press conference at the Maria Isabella at cocktail time that very evening. The subject of the conference was to be the Republic of South Africa.

Emmy and I had already made plans for the evening, but I deferred them because I wanted to see Jimmy and I wanted to help him if I could. We had always been fond of Jimmy and his wife from the time he first joined the Yankees. I thought he was a kid with spunk and spark and I thought he had good instincts. The Boutons adopted a Korean orphan, and Jim always seemed concerned with the underprivileged and with causes that I myself was interested in. On the social side, in the very beginning, the Boutons were naïve kids, and I will always remember their positive delight when, one year at spring training, Emmy and I took them to dinner at the Diplomat Hotel in Hollywood where Steve Lawrence and Eydie Gorme were performing.

I knew the gist of what the press conference would be about, and it couldn't have been more ill-timed. Some time before the Olympics started, there was a growing controversy over whether the Republic of South Africa should be barred from the Games because of its policy of apartheid. The American Committee on Africa opposed the admission of South Africa and called a press conference to make its position known. At that conference were two members of the Yankees, a remarkable man named Reuben Amaro and Jim Bouton. There was Jim, I thought, standing up again when others would not. Subsequently—and, of course, not because of this one committee and its position—South Africa was barred from the 19th Olympiad.

That was the background to Jimmy's press conference, and as I crossed the street to the Maria Isabella I thought to myself, "What's Jimmy after now? The issue is over, at least for 1968."

Jimmy got a very small turnout, and I felt sorry for him. One fine reporter who was there was Murray Olderman of NEA, and he had the same attitude I did. "What's up now?" Well, Bouton wanted the International Olympic Committee to take action, right then and there, to bar South Africa from the Games forever, unless apartheid were renounced. A noble aim, but one impossible of accomplishment, and with the games getting under way and with the great feeling that existed in Mexico, he stubbed his toe badly. Then, when he had to face questions from the few who were there—specifics about the International Olympic Committee; what support, if any,

he had thus far been able to muster; and many other
relevant things—it was clear that Jimmy was in over his
head. After the conference I shook hands with him and
left, depressed. I think he was, too. But not enough to
have diluted his spirit forevermore. Not if you've read
Ball Four.

In the meantime the games had begun. During the first
two days I was there I spent most of my time at the
Olympic Village. I had never been in one before and I
was utterly taken by the scene. Somehow, seeing all those
young people, from all the different countries, of different
colors and creeds, living in such gay harmony gave Emmy
and me an uplifted feeling. It was like watching Utopia in
action, like someone was saying, "Look, here is the proof.
People throughout the world can live together in peace
and harmony. No matter the background, there can be
understanding." That feeling in me never wavered. I had
it all over again in the Village in Munich, despite all the
sorrows of the 20th Olympiad. In fact, it was the feeling
I got in the Village that began to justify the Mexico
City Olympics to me.

Mexico is a poverty-stricken country, and Mexico City
itself is filled with hunger, dirt and decay. Apart from
the Del Reforma, some of the great hotels and restaurants,
it is hard to escape the poverty, and so it was hard for
me, intellectually, to justify a nation's expenditure of multimillions of dollars for two weeks of international fun
and games. It still is. But I must say that those millions
were an investment in national pride and self-respect.
Unless you were there, you could never understand the
pride of the Mexican people in the knowledge that for
two weeks their nation was the capital of the world.
The lowliest peasants walked the streets shouting in
unison to all who would listen, "May-hi-co, ho, ho, ho,"
and they would clap their hands as they sang it out,
their faces wreathed in smiles. No, you couldn't take
this away from them. And when one of their swimmers
won a gold medal, and one of their distance walkers won
a medal, the celebrations were heard as far away as
Cuernavaca and Acapulco. There was exultation every-

where. Mexico was no longer a little country, somewhere on the American continent. It was the host country of the world. and it was as if the peasants, living in their little cottages without adequate facilities, were saying, "Look at us. Look at our land. We can do it, the same as you." And they did it. I wish Munich could have had the joy of Mexico. The Mexico City Olympics were an Olympics with a heart. In Munich they had a computer.

On my first visit to the Village I went straight to the American building to meet with our boxing coach, Pappy Gault. and the members of our boxing team. Gault is a shrewd man, knows his business and knew, despite reports to the contrary. that we had a good team. "We can win as many as five gold medals," he told me, "and George Foreman definitely will win one." I realized he wasn't kidding me. and I knew his background in boxing, which was extensive. so I felt encouraged about the possible excitement in the boxing telecasts. I met most of the team that morning but not Foreman. He was out, somewhere in the Village. So I went downstairs, waited in front of the building with Emmy, spoke with some old friends, like Bob Seagren and Lee Evans, and then suddenly I saw George Foreman. I ran up and introduced myself to him. and he was, in truth, excited to meet me because he had seen me do so many fights on television. Just to meet Foreman is to be impressed with him. Then and now. At 19 he was huge, open-faced, with a warm smile, an engaging manner. Above all, you sensed that this kid was clean. wholesome. No drug problem. Not stupid. On the contrary. thoughtful, with a sense of purpose about life. Even then he told me he would win the gold medal, then become heavyweight champion of the world. Not boastfully. Just factually. He recited some limericks, in the fashion of Ali, then went off to spar. I told Emmy, who had listened to the conversation, "It's just instinct, but that's a terrific kid, and probably a terrific fighter." Nothing has happened since to change my mind.

But many things happened in Mexico City. My first assignment, and I couldn't believe it, was a women's volleyball game involving the U.S. team. Everybody kidded me about it, but I really enjoyed the idea. I had seen the Japanese women's volleyball team in action and I knew what a great game it could be, swift and exciting. So off I went to the volleyball venue, watched the U.S. team get trounced, and then interviewed their very colorful coach, a fellow named Cohen. The interview was played back to the States that night, and posthaste I got a telegram from Curt Gowdy ribbing me for being occupied with "big time" sports. That, by the way, was my last adventure with women's volleyball.

I went on to other, more normal pursuits. Much of the time I was at the Mexico City Arena doing fights. You never knew whether or not what you were doing would go on the air, unless you were going live to the States. That was up to Roone Arledge. I learned something about Arledge in Mexico City. He is without peer as a producer. He rolled his sleeves up, sat in the control room in our Central Control Tower and, with a flood of monitors covering all the different venues in front of him, would switch from one set to another with an amazing sense of timing and judgment. It seemed we always had the right thing on at the right time, and he was the man responsible for it. When we put together taped shows for later transmission, it was Arledge who would decide what to put in the show and what the running order would be. I think Mexico City was the best I've ever seen Arledge.

At the Mexico City Arena our young fighters were doing very well, and I was having a ball. I discovered that amateur bouts are, on the average, much more exciting than professional bouts—nothing but action, and over in three rounds or sooner. I also discovered that the Mexico City Arena could be a dangerous place to be. When Mexicans fought, or whenever a decision was rendered that the Mexican fans did not like, they would heave pesos toward the ring, and if you got hit by one of them your face could get slit open. This didn't happen to me, but it did to some others. One other thing, I learned something about Olympic judging, as a number of decisions were given that made no sense at all. Generally those decisions were in instances where the board of five judges was dominated by the Soviet Union and its satellite countries—a precursor of the boxing controversies in Munich.

As the first week went by, and our fighters were winning, it began to appear that Pappy Gault's prediction of five gold medals had a chance. But things were happening at the Olympic Stadium in track and field, so I had to divide my time between the two venues. My job was to interview the American gold-medal winners, but the trouble was that I had no interview position. I was down at trackside, right next to one of our cameras, but I had no right to be there. When we paid millions of dollars for the rights to televise the Olympics, this did not include interview rights. In the complex hierarchy of administrative bodies that dominate the Games, the Federation of International Athletic Associations controls that situation and they would allow no interviews. Mexican guards were all over the place to ensure that there would be no violations.

Nonetheless, we wanted the interviews and we felt that the American public was entitled to hear from its young people who were winners. So I had to try to get them anyway. By hook or crook I succeeded in getting Al Oerter, Jimmy Hines, Lee Evans, Bill Toomey, Wyomia Tyus and some others. But it wasn't easy. When Jimmy Hines won the 100-meter dash, I broke through the Mexican guards and actually chased him around the track after he had breasted the tape. That's when I almost got thrown out of the stadium. They should have thrown me out anyway for making a farce of the scene. Imagine, at age 48, the ludicrous nature of my pursuit of Jimmy Hines. Imagine it even if I were 21.

At any rate, we managed. The only key interview we missed was with Jim Ryun after he lost in the 1500 meters to Kip Keino of Kenya. These were the Olympics of high altitude, and it was apparent that some athletes were being hurt by it. A great Australian distance runner collapsed. So did some of the swimmers. Some felt Ryun lost to Keino because of it. In any event, Arledge wanted me to get into it, and so I collaborated with Murray Rose, the great Australian swimmer who was working with us, and we did a series of pieces on the high altitude.

But always in the background was the threat of a black protest. It finally came to pass. Tommie Smith set a new record in winning the 200 meters, and John Carlos finished third. Then, on the victory stand came the bowed heads, the shoeless feet and the black-power salute. It should not have been unexpected by the members of the U.S. Olympic Committee, but the way they behaved one would have thought that the black protest had not been a simmering possibility during the past four months. No matter. This was a front-page story throughout the world, the very story that Arledge and I had discussed before we ever went to Mexico, and we couldn't let the papers beat us on it. All we had on the air that night was what happened on the victory stand. After the incident Smith and Carlos vanished. They couldn't be located in the Olympic Village; indeed, they had been ordered out of it. My assignment: Find Tommie Smith, interview him.

Smith was nowhere to be found.

I was up all that night trying every connection I had in Mexico City—sportswriters who were close to Tommie, Olympic officials, friends of Tommie's. No luck. But one of the great people of the world, a member of our broadcast team, Hayes Jones, who was a gold-medal winner in Tokyo in 1964, discovered—I'll never know how—that Tommie and his wife had checked in at the Diplomat Hotel. Hayes called me in the small hours of the morning and by eight that morning I was at the Diplomat. At first I couldn't get through to Tommie's room; they were taking no calls. Then I finally did, and Tommie's wife told me that Tommie would talk to no one. I had never met her or Tommie, but she knew of me. I finally induced her to let me come up to the room.

Once in the room, I felt defeated. Both of them were fixed in their position. Tommie would not grant an interview. I argued and argued, but both said Tommie had never been treated fairly by either the press or broadcast. "You'd think I committed murder," he said.

"All I did was what I've been doing all along, call the attention of the world to the way the blacks are treated in America. There's nothing new about this."

"I admit you have talked about a protest before," I told him, "but it's new when you do it at a world forum. I think you're wrong. I think you should state what you did and why you did it. Then at least some people might understand."

To my astonishment, Smith's wife, who was a school-teacher, did an abrupt turnabout. She suddenly told Tommie she thought I was right, he began to waver, and the next thing I knew we were on our way to our studio at the Central Control Tower. When I got there you could sense the excitement. Arledge came out of the control room, Jim Spence would be talking to me from the control room during the interview, everybody gathered around, and it was as if the Games had come to a halt.

The interview was simple and direct. What did you mean, symbolically, by the bowed head, the shoeless feet, the outstretched fist? He explained: the fist to show the strength and unity of the black people everywhere, black power; the shoeless feet to show the anguish of the black people through all the years; the bowed head because the words of the anthem were not being applied to blacks.

"Are you proud to be an American?" I asked him.

"I am proud to be a black American," he answered.

The interview over, Smith and his wife were pleased that he had done it. "I got fair treatment," he said. I did not see Tommie again during the Olympics. I have seen him any number of times since, when he was with the Cincinnati Bengals trying to make it in professional football as a wide receiver, and most recently at Oberlin College, where he is the assistant director of athletics. I respect him. He and his wife have broken up, and I feel badly about that. She was in New York recently and called me, asking if I could help her get a job as a model. I tried and failed.

The Tommie Smith interview was picked up by papers all over the world. The following night I was in the lobby of the El Presidente Hotel, just inside the door. A car went by, came to a sudden stop, then backed up in front of the door. Out of the car jumped a tall, familiar figure. At first I didn't realize who it was. Then suddenly I knew. It was John Carlos. He came through the door, shook my hand and said, "We're grateful for your fair treatment." And with that he was back in the car and gone.

This was not the end of the black-power incident. There was still the question of Lee Evans, a close friend of Smith and Carlos and another of the so-called black militants. He was the favorite to win the 400-meter run, and the big question was: Would he demonstrate as Smith and Carlos had done? Reporters, broadcasters, everyone would try to get to him before the race, in the Village, to determine his intentions. But he steered clear of everyone, and the tension mounted. As he went into the starting blocks I was at trackside with my earpiece and I heard Jim McKay describe the scene. He related vividly what Evans had gone through that morning and he said, "What will he do on the victory stand if he wins? Howard Cosell is at trackside to find out."

The race was one of the magnificent events in my memory. There has never, in my opinion, been a more competitive runner than Lee Evans. He does not run with style. The arms flail, the legs pump. But nobody has ever run with a bigger heart. Lee Evans won that race and set a new world record. I was the first one to him after the race. The Mexican guards tried to prevent the interview, but Lee wouldn't let them. His first words to me after the race were "Who won?" I said, "You did, you jerk. A new record." He smiled and struggled for breath.

Then the interview. Congratulations first, then the tactics of the race, the fact that he didn't know he had won. And then: What would he do on the victory stand? Evans said he didn't know. He didn't really know. When the time came he was shoeless, but he stood at attention for the anthem and waved to the crowd when it was over. No bowed head, no black-power salute. Immediately thereafter the president of the U.S. Olympic Committee met with a group of us, writers and broadcasters, and smilingly said, "He was fine, just fine. No problem, no problem at all." End of black-power incidents in Mexico City.

Except for one thing. The late Joe Sheehan of the *New York Times* broke a story to the effect that the black athletes—Tommie Smith, John Carlos, possibly even Lee Evans—might have to give back the medals they had won. Purportedly, the U.S. Olympic Committee had evidence that the athletes, in violation of the Olympic rules and regulations, had received compensation, directly or indirectly, from a shoe company—in this case, Puma. The story was leaked to Sheehan by Eppy Barnes, executive director of the U.S. Olympic Committee.

The story gained instant momentum. An eight-column headline in the *New York Times,* October 24, 1968, bannered the news: "OLYMPIC INVESTIGATION OF ILLEGAL PAYMENTS TO ATHLETES EXPECTED TO WIDEN." Shirley Povich of the *Washington Post* did a front-page treatment in the *Los Angeles Times*. But a funny thing happened to the U.S. Olympic Committee. It usually does. News of what the committee was planning to do swept the Olympic Village like wildfire, and the athletes reacted immediately. Harold Connolly, the hammer thrower, said, "What's this all about? There isn't an athlete here who's an amateur, and everybody knows it." Bill Toomey joined in. One American athlete after another rallied to the cause of the blacks. Then the athletes of other countries expressed their indignation at what they construed as an attempt to penalize the blacks because of the black-power demonstration. Dan Ferris of the AAU, the ancient patriarch of track and field, bluntly said, "There is no such thing as an amateur."

Suddenly the U.S. Olympic Committee put out a statement: "There have been rumors spiraling around that Olympic athletes have received money which jeopardizes their amateur standing. At this time we have nothing to substantiate the rumors with respect to athletes subject to our jurisdiction. If anyone has any concrete evidence to offer about the United States athletes in this connection, we shall be pleased to follow up the information."

And the signature under the statement? Eppy Barnes, the very man who leaked the original story to Joe Sheehan.

I remember standing in the lobby of the Maria Isabella with the late Arthur Daley and Neil Amdur of the *New York Times* when that bomb was dropped. Sheehan had been writing for a couple of days about the "investigation" of the black athletes, and now Sheehan's scoop had been exploded by Barnes's turnabout. So Art Daley wrote a column the gist of which was, "There is no such thing as an amateur athlete."

And that, finally, was the end of the "black athlete problem."

But not the end of Mexico City for me. America had a youngster named Wade Bell in the 800-meter run who was the favorite to win the gold medal. In his first trial heat Wade failed even to qualify. I was shocked. The word seeped out that Wade was sick, that the Mexican food and water had disagreed with him (this happened to a number of athletes from all over the world), and that this was why he had failed. I wasn't satisfied with the story, so I went to the American building in the Village early in the morning the day after Bell had lost. I went up to the floor where Bell was quartered, found nobody there except a pleasant-faced, not so young man (29 going on 30), whom I recognized as Bill Toomey, the United State's key entrant in the decathlon.

Though I had never met Toomey, I knew his background and respected him very much. He had grown up in New Canaan, Connecticut, a town right next to Pound Ridge, New York, where we have our home. I introduced myself to him and I told him I wanted to check out the story of why Wade had failed to qualify. He said, "You know, you're the only guy who's done that. Wade's in the hospital. Let's try to see him."

We went over to the hospital in the Village, were not

allowed to see Bell, though it was later confirmed that he had, indeed, been ill. But I liked Toomey immediately, and he liked me. During the next ten days we were together often, and Emmy and I met the girl he later married, a lovely British lass named Mary Rand, who had been a British Olympian. They have two children now, and Bill and I see one another from time to time. I consider him one of my dearest friends.

I also consider Toomey's victory in the decathlon representative of the best of what I take out of sports. The decathlon consists of ten events, spread over 48 hours. It is quite probably the most grueling competition in all of sports. But Toomey was ready for it. His whole life had been one of athletic struggle. When he was but five years old, playing with another child, a piece of ceramic broke in his right hand, severing the nerves from the wrist to the hand. To this day the hand is shriveled, and he has a hard time buttoning the button-down collars on his shirts. But he dreamed of becoming an athlete. Actually he became a schoolteacher, but as he grew up he tried first one event and then another. Track and field was his love. The Olympics was his dream. But he didn't seem to have the talent. Suddenly his name began to appear in little clips in the papers. He was competing in the decathlon in meets all over the world. He had made that shriveled hand work, work well enough to heave the discus, put the shot, carry the pole for the vault, throw the javelin. He paid his own way to Tokyo in 1964 and was inspired by the victory of Hayes Jones. Now he would really make it to the Olympics.

But before he would, this is what he went through: infectious hepatitis that had him lying near death in a West German hospital; a shattered kneecap, which would have ended the career of most athletes; then mononucleosis. It appeared the hardships would never end. But here he was in Mexico City, and the chance for the fulfillment of a dream was at hand. I watched him go through event after event, and now there was only one left—the 1500-meter run. His main competition was expected to be Kurt Bendelin of West Germany, at 23 a younger, stronger man. It did not seem possible that Toomey could win the 1500, and he had to win it to win the gold medal. I sneaked into the athletes' rest room in the stadium and saw Toomey lying there, just before he was called out for the event. He was prostrate with exhaustion. I gave him no chance. It was dusk when they ran the race. The winds had come up, rain had begun to fall. The race began, and seemed to go on endlessly. Then the final lap, and as they approached the stretch, one lone figure began to pull away. Almost incredibly it was the schoolteacher, 29 going on 30, step by step making a runaway of it. I could hardly contain myself. I couldn't believe that at my age I could be so touched by an athletic victory. At 48 there I was cheering like a damned kid. Bill Toomey did it, and as I stood there I realized why I had become emotional. It wasn't the victory. It was Bill Toomey—his whole life, what he had gone through to achieve what he had just done. This is the essence of what is great in sports, a complete manifestation of the sheer magnificence of the human spirit. What a man can do if he but wills it. Bill Toomey made it happen.

For me Toomey's victory was the climax of track and field. But there was still the boxing. Some of our men were beginning to lose, but we still had good representation left. Then the axe began to fall. Our middleweight, Al Jones of Detroit, won, I thought, convincingly over Britain's Christopher Finnegan. But Finnegan got the decision as the pesos flew through the air. (Finnegan, incidentally, went on to win a gold medal, turned pro in Britain and fought a good but losing fight against light-heavyweight champion Bob Foster in London in 1972.)

We came down to the finals with three opportunities for gold medals. One of our lads, a youngster named Al Robinson, was beating the stuffings out of a Mexican lad named Roldan. Suddenly the fight was stopped, and my instant reaction was "Good call by the referee. Roldan is being protected from serious injury." But I never said it, and to my astonishment I discovered the referee had disqualified Robinson for butting. We replayed the round several times, and I advised the viewers to judge for themselves. The sarcasm in my voice was clear, and I remember Laurence Laurent, the distinguished TV critic of the *Washington Post,* writing, "Cosell drily admonished the viewers to judge for themselves, but left no doubt as to where he stood." As for young Robinson, he was heartsick. He couldn't believe what had happened. But in a strange way he wound up with a great deal of national attention and sympathy, and later received a nationally publicized award as the "Sportsman of the 19th Olympiad." A hard way to get it.

A youngster from Kent State University, Ronnie Harris, won a gold medal in his division. He won it on points, fighting in the curious way that most Olympic judges seem to like best. Stay away from the other man, dart in and out with light jabs and pile up the points. If you get tabbed only occasionally, don't worry if the other fellow registers punishment greater than you have scored. Power doesn't matter, damage doesn't matter, even knockdowns don't matter. Just the number of punches that connect. Ronnie did all the right things.

The final major event of the Olympiad was the heavyweight bout for the gold medal. George Foreman of the United States against Iones Chepulis of the Soviet Union. Foreman, 19 years of age, with only 19 amateur bouts under his belt prior to the Games. Chepulis, a veteran, in his late twenties, with more than a hundred fights behind him, a man who could have fought professionally in the States with real effectiveness. Foreman was overpowering. Not skillful as a boxer, but overpowering. Chepulis could not escape his punches, and the wonder of it was that the Soviet fighter would not go down. The referee stopped the bout in the second round, and another new heavyweight champion of the world was on his way. In the excitement immediately after the bout, Pappy Gault put a little American flag in George's hand, which he carried about the ring. Foreman had brought the flag to the bout with him because, as George later put it, he wanted everyone to know where he was from.

But he also made it clear that he wasn't indulging in a preplanned display of patriotism and that he wasn't answering Tommie Smith and John Carlos. "I just do my own thing," Foreman told me, "and make sure of one thing. I'm no Uncle Tom."

Pappy Gault had led me to believe that Foreman would announce at a press conference a day or so after the fight that he would turn pro, with Gault as his manager. So in my postfight interview with Foreman I pressed him on the issue. George refused to commit himself. Shortly after, I understood why. He was going to turn pro, all right, but under Dick Saddler, a crafty boxing man who had been Sonny Liston's manager. And Saddler did very well for George in a boxing sense. There is a question about how well he did for George in a financial sense, which may be why Foreman became his own manager in the summer of '73.

It was a great finishing event to an exciting two weeks that I would always remember. The only drawback was that Emmy had gone home after the first week to be with the kids. She knew I was taking the first plane home on Sunday morning, so she ordered up a limousine for me at Kennedy International Airport. I had ordered up one on my own. Young Don Ohlmeyer, producer-director, ABC sports, flew back with me, and when I found two limousines waiting I put Don in one. He got into the limousine with an air of executive importance that would have made one think he was Leonard Goldenson, board chairman of ABC. As I watched him drive off I thought of how it had begun, with Tom Maloney begging for his four shirts. It ended with a foul-up on limousines. But in between, I felt, there was some of the best damned television in the history of the medium, to be topped only by the telecasts from Munich. I was more sure of it than ever when I got home to Pound Ridge and Emmy and I watched Jim McKay give a touching, brilliant performance on the closing ceremonies in Mexico City.

The next morning when I got to the office I found a copy of the Warren, Ohio, *Tribune* on my desk. The paper was open to a full page advertisement edged in black, which had been paid for by a local furniture dealer. The headlines of the ad read: "SHAME ON HOWARD COSELL—SHAME ON ABC." The thrust of the ad was that I had shamed America, my company and myself and had deliberately introduced controversy to the Olympics by interviewing Tommie Smith and by questioning Lee Evans as to his intentions when he took the victory stand. It was even implied that I might benefit the American democracy by voluntarily departing it.

Also on my desk was a letter from Yale University congratulating me on my work at the 19th Olympiad and inviting me, as a consequence of it, to establish residence as a Hoyt Fellow for a week at the university. For me this still stands as one of the great honors I have received in my life.

That's when I felt good about my role in the telecasts. Middle America was still secure, unchanged, and I had helped bring some journalism to the world of sports broadcast.

May-hi-co! Ho! Ho! Ho!

Chapter III

ONE WEEK IS ENOUGH

"See you on the hill at Iwo Jima."

I now had two Olympiads behind me, unique experiences in my broadcast career. More typical was a week that began on October 22, 1972. I flew to Chicago with Joe McGinniss, the writer, who was to do a piece on me for the *New York Times Sunday Magazine*. Joe wanted to spend a week with me, see how I worked, live with my schedule. He's sorry now that he did, because he wound up with a severe respiratory infection, spent time in the University of Pennsylvania Hospital and never did get well in time to write the piece. But he learned a lot.

Joe and I got to O'Hare Airport at 8:00 P.M. after having watched the Jets beat Baltimore on a freak touchdown pass that afternoon. We went straight to the Continental Plaza Hotel, where there was a message from Chet Forte to meet him, Frank Gifford, Sid Luckman and Irv Kupcinet at a local restaurant. We shot right over. But there was also another message. This one was from Brent Musberger, a Chicago broadcaster who had been a sports columnist and whom I respect very much. He is really trying, on the Chicago scene, to bring some journalism to sports broadcasting. Brent was doing the "Abe Gibron Show" that night (a weekly show done by the Chicago Bears' coach) and he wanted me to guest. So I went with McGinniss to the restaurant, spent 15 minutes with the quartet named above and then left them to do the show. McGinniss was tired, stayed behind with the Giffer and the rest, and I didn't get back to the hotel until after midnight. This was his introduction to the killing nature of my schedule.

At six the next morning I was up and on my way to ABC Radio, Chicago, to do my morning network radio show and to prerecord my two afternoon radio shows. I do three a day, six days a week, come hell or high water. From there I went to the Executive House, where the Bears stay the weekends of home games, and I talked with Dick Butkus and some of the other Bears about the Vikings game that night. Then back to ABC Radio and another show with Butkus.

I think Butkus is a special kind of guy. More than any man in professional football, Dick—with that reckless monster of a body—symbolizes the violence of the game. But inside that awesome frame there is a great deal of warmth and humor and fun and a surprising literary capability.

Larry Linderman, of PLAYBOY magazine, did a PLAYBOY interview with me and in his preface he quoted Butkus as calling me "horseshit." Butkus wrote the following open letter in the next issue of PLAYBOY:

Dear Howard:

Listen, pal, I heard you were mad at me. I heard that you heard that I said you were "horseshit."

This is not true, Howard. I have nothing but the deepest respect for you, for your command of the language, your knowledge of the game, your flair for repartee with Dandy Don and Frank, your dedication to truth, your penchant for calling 'em as you see 'em and really laying it on the line, letting the chips fall where they may. Howard, ole buddy (as Dandy Don would say), you and I are the victims of a misquote. You're in the business, Howard. You know how they splice those tapes. What happened is this:

Some radio guy asked me what I thought of Howard Cosell as a football announcer. "He's a horse," I said. Where I come from—the South Chi-

cago mills—we don't usually talk that way, but I went to school with a lot of farmers and picked up their expressions. When they call a man a horse, they mean he's tops. Then the guy asked me if I thought you were a tough interviewer. I said, "Boy, he's tougher than rat shit." That's another farm-boy localism I picked up at college. Then I talked an hour or so about your good qualities—there wasn't time to say everything—and the next thing I know, some moron with a splicing machine cuts the tape apart, and what's left is me saying Howard Cosell is "horseshit."

I hope that clears up the misunderstanding, old pal. No reason we should ruin our friendship because some smart media guy is trying to split up two of America's idols. Good luck, say hello to Frank and Dandy for me, and keep a clear throat when you do your game against the Minnesota Vikings: Monday night, October 23.

Your very good friend,

Dick Butkus
Chicago, Illinois

See what I mean about Butkus?

After that I went back to the hotel, and by this time McGinniss was up. We had breakfast, and then I took him to our production meeting, which is habitually held at 11:00 A.M. the morning of the game. From there we went to the Sherman House where I was to be the principal speaker at a meeting of the Chicago Touchdown Club. We found a packed house, the largest attendance in the history of the club, standing room only. When I finally spoke—and this was after a number of speakers from the two Chicago baseball clubs—I covered a range of subjects including "Monday Night Football," the 20th Olympiad, some throwaway lines about baseball, and then some straight talk about sports journalism, both in print and in broadcast. Result: standing ovation. I had agreed to make the speech at the request of the sports editor of *Chicago Today,* Rick Talley, and Rick was present, of course, along with a substantial number of Chicago sportswriters.

As we left the luncheon, McGinniss, who is a reserved man, not given to compliments, told me that he thought it was a great speech, forthright and sincere and the kind of thing that should be done in sports more often. I laughed, said I did it all the time and told him that he wouldn't believe the way the speech might be written up in the Chicago papers the next day. He asked me what I meant, and I told him the speech might be totally misrepresented. Joe, who had been a sportswriter in Philadelphia before he went on to more important arenas, was dubious about my position. Writers, unlike broadcasters, are a fraternity and they are resistant to any adverse comments about the clan.

The speech over, we went back to the hotel, rested for a half hour and then went on to Soldier Field where I had to do the half-time highlights. This was when Joe realized that the toughest part of "Monday Night Football" was this part of the broadcast. But he couldn't help observing that the schedule I was living under was backbreaking. "One week," he said, "will be more than enough." He was prophetic.

The highlights done, we shot back to the hotel so that I could shower and change into my ABC blazer. (To some in ABC sports, the wearing of the blazer is more important than the quality of the telecast.) Then we went to ABC TV Chicago, on State Street, downtown, where Herb Granath, ABC's vice-president of TV Sports Sales, was running a cocktail party for "Monday Night Football" sponsors. This is a routine nearly every Monday night, just before Dandy, Faultless and I go to the stadium. It is a chore, especially after the kind of day I go through—because I speak every Monday afternoon during the football season, just as I did in Chicago that day —but it is a legitimate chore. When a sponsor spends $72,000 a minute on "Monday Night Football"—the going price in 1972—he is entitled to have the performers appear at a party for a few minutes the day of the game. By the time of our arrival at the party, McGinniss, who is a tall, thinnish man, was dragging his tail. Usually reserved, Joe was now speaking out, wondering how and why I went through this kind of weekend 13 times in a row each fall. But the best was yet to come.

As we arrived at the party, Herb Granath was waiting for us at the door. He had a copy of the bulldog edition of the *Chicago Tribune* for the next morning, and the headline of the first sports page heralded the "BIG BAG OF WIND," or words to that effect, that had blown into Chicago. The story under the headline was about my speech that afternoon and it bore little if any resemblance to what I had actually said or, equally important, to the way I had said it. It was written by a writer I had never met, and it seemed clear to me, as I read all the old garbage about my conceit and pompousness, together with some attempted smart-ass digressions, that this was just another case of a writer trying to get some attention at the expense of the "controversial" Cosell. So I laughed, gave the piece to McGinniss, who read it and then said, "By God, you were right. It's hard to believe what they do to you." We stayed at the party 20 or 30 minutes, then with the Giffer and Danderoo in separate cars, we went to Soldier Field finally to do the game.

On arrival at the stadium we proceeded up to the press level and the first person we met was Cooper Rollow, sports editor of the *Chicago Tribune*. I like and respect Cooper Rollow. He is a fine man and a fine reporter. I spent some of the most harrowing moments of my professional life with Cooper, on the back slope of that hill in the Olympic Village on September 5, 1972, the day of the Israeli tragedy. I know something about his personal reaction to crisis and, having read his column the next day on our experience together, I know something about his concern for accuracy and his talent for completeness in telling a story.

Cooper greeted us. He knew McGinniss slightly, but mainly by Joe's reputation as the author of *The Selling of the President—1968*. He said, "Hey, I hear you were fantastic at the Touchdown Club luncheon today. You know, I had a man there to cover it, and it will get a big spread in the paper tomorrow."

Whereupon McGinniss said, "It already has. We just read it. It's a far cry from what Howard said and how he said it."

Rollow was taken aback. "What do you mean?"

McGinniss explained. Just then we were joined by Rick Talley, who began to tell Cooper how well the luncheon had gone. Cooper became even more disturbed. Joe and I left for the broadcast booth, and now, at long last, Joe would actually get to watch how we do what the public hears and sees. We had a good game; the Bears upset the Vikings, we had another controversial call by the officials that turned the game, the Giffer had Mike Eischeid punting for both teams, and we went back to the hotel, tired but satisfied. (Later I kidded Frank about Eischeid, but he topped me. "Why shouldn't he kick for both of them?" Frank said. "The guy's a hell of a kicker.") A nightcap, and then bed.

McGinniss woke me up the next morning at 6:30. He was beat and he decided to go back to New York with Herb Granath. I had to go to Washington to make a speech that night, and we agreed to meet on Wednesday in New York. But there was something else. Joe had the Tuesday-morning *Chicago Tribune.*

"Look," he said, "the story of the luncheon is out of the paper."

"You're kidding," I answered. "They must have just moved it to a later page to headline the Bears' upset last night."

"Nope, it's out altogether."

"What do you make of it?"

"I think Cooper Rollow killed it."

"I told you he's an honest guy."

Then Joe McGinniss' "typical week in the life of Howard Cosell" turned into a week of tragic loss for the country and myself personally. In the taxi to Midway, racing for my connection to Washington, I heard on the radio that Jackie Robinson was dead. I don't think I've ever been more affected by a death, not even in my own family. I knew it was coming, of course. I also knew that it was a blessing. But I also knew that part of my life and the lives of literally millions of people went with Jackie Robinson. I thought of Emmy as I rode in the taxi, and of Jill and Hilary, of how they had grown up taking for granted the presence of black players in major-league baseball. To them anything else would have been unthinkable. And then I thought about Rachel, and David, and Sharon, and Jackie, Jr., and about the whole injustice of life, about all that the Robinsons had gone through. I got to Midway, and Washington was the last place in the world I wanted to go. I wanted to go home, discover what the funeral arrangements were to be, see if I could help and then be with Emmy, because I have always believed that Emmy and I have a relationship much like the one Jackie had with Rachel.

When I got to the airport I immediately called Emmy. She had heard the news, of course, and asked if I was coming straight home. I couldn't do that—I had to meet my speaking commitment—but I hold her I'd make the last plane to New York, that I'd see to it that they let me speak early that night.

When I got to Washington, Andy Ockershausen met me at the airport. He runs our Washington broadcast operation and he had asked me to make the appearance that night. He was aware of my relationship with Jackie and was sensitive to the situation on my arrival. He quickly agreed that I could get home that night, but had set up a luncheon with Moe Siegel, the Washington columnist, at the popular eating place, Duke Zeibert's. I said, "Okay, let's go, but first I want to call ABC Sports." I called Roone Arledge in New York, couldn't reach him, spoke to his aide, Jim Spence, and Jim told me that Roone wanted me to do an instant half-hour special on Jackie. I explained that I would not be back till late that night but that I'd get started on it the next morning. I learned later in the day that the funeral would be on Friday.

Duke Zeibert's was packed. It almost always is. Edward Bennett Williams, the brilliant trial attorney and president of the Washington Redskins, was there, and we talked for a few moments, first about Jackie and then about the game the preceding night—a game that now seemed a million light-years away. But Williams is a man of parts and high humor and he kidded about the Giffer having Eischeid kick for both teams. So I shot the Giff's line right back at him. "Why not? The guy's a hell of a kicker." And Williams broke up.

This leavened the mood, temporarily, but then Moe Siegel and I began to talk about Jackie, and we recalled the day in Washington when the all-star game was to be played—baseball's centennial year. It was a day marred by an altercation between Bob Feller and Jackie Robinson. Feller, never known for his intellect, had made a statement, with Robinson present, that at the very least implied that baseball was the heart of the democracy and that outspoken blacks who talked about prejudice in baseball were at variance with the facts and were harmful to "the game." Robinson exploded, answered back with all his pride and anger, and suddenly the room was like 1947 all over again. After Jackie spoke, the writers swarmed all over him, for it was remembered that more than 20 years earlier Robinson and Feller had had major differences. When finally the reporters were done with Jackie, we got into Moe Siegel's car and drove to the White House, where the president was having a cocktail party for all of us in the all-star entourage. So Moe and I reviewed that day, and we agreed it was typical Jackie Robinson.

After lunch Andy drove me to ABC News, Washington, where I did two radio shows, about Jackie, naturally, and then to the hotel where I was to speak. I had about an hour to pull myself together, went down to the cocktail party before dinner and found, to my surprise, that an old friend, John Wilbur, guard, of the Redskins, was there. His coach, George Allen, had excused him from a team meeting so that he could hear me speak, and he hoped I would talk about Jackie Robinson.

I did. And I broke up. For the first time in my life, after talking for about 45 minutes. When I got to the point where I said, "There is only one word to describe Jackie Robinson and that is 'unconquerable,'" I started to cry, and could go no further. The audience was wonderful. They, or at least many of them, had started to cry, too. There were blacks there, and Jews, and Catholics and Protestants. But the important thing was, if they could identify with Robinson, so could millions of others, and maybe the damned racism that infects this nation could yet be diluted, if not beaten. I remember the dinner chairman saying, "You have seen another side of Howard Cosell."

Another side, hell. They were seeing the real Cosell, and what the hell, I wondered, did they think I had been talking about through all the years—who would pinch-hit for the Mets?

Ockershausen drove me to the airport. I just made the plane.

Emmy was still awake. We both wanted to talk. Martin Stone, one of Jackie's closest friends and his personal advisor, had called to tell us of the funeral arrangements. And we talked about all the years, and about the special I had to begin work on. And so to bed.

There could be no meeting with McGinniss the next day or the rest of the week. Chuck Howard, Arledge's head of production, assigned Don Ohlmeyer to produce the Robinson special. It was a felicitous choice. Ohlmeyer, still in his twenties, is a Notre Dame graduate, and I am proud to say that I had something to do with his getting his job in the company. I have watched him grow to where I now consider him as good a producer as there is in the sports-television business. He is bright, he is sensitive and, above all, he has a feel for story line that is not given to many. He is one of the few men in the business who understand that, in a documentary, action footage has its limitations, and that one must shoot according to the dictates of the story. In my opinion Don has much growth before him, not necessarily in sports—although he can always do that—but in motion pictures.

Ohlmeyer knows the way I work. He had produced my memorial show on Vince Lombardi and, together with another young man, Mike McCallum, had done a superb job. So quickly we met and lined up the show. I traced Jackie's life story for Don, naming the key people. Arledge had cleared prime time for the show the very night that Jackie was to be buried. There was precious little time. We must get Bob Blackman, head football coach at Illinois, I told Don, explaining that Blackman had seen Robinson's extraordinary exploits when Jackie was at Pasadena Junior College. Then we must get Bobby Bragan, who in 1947 asked Mr. Rickey to trade him rather than play with a black man. Bragan later became a close friend of Jackie's and wound up managing a team with more black players than any other in baseball. Buzzie Bavasi is another, I said. And Leo Durocher. And more. Then we started hitting the phones. Bragan in Fort Worth. Bavasi in San Diego. Blackman in Champaign-Urbana. Durocher in Palm Springs (we reached him too late). I explained what we wanted, Ohlmeyer got local crews to do the shooting, and in 24 hours we had the material we needed from all over the country. The rest would come at the funeral. With one exception. On Thursday night I went to the home of Dr. and Mrs. Logan, in the West Nineties in Manhattan. They were the closest friends of Jackie and Rachel. Final funeral arrangements were to be made there. Among those present were the Reverend Wyatt T. Walker, Bayard Rustin, key black leaders in the country. I was there with a film crew and interviewed the doctor and his wife.

He told of how Jackie would have had both legs amputated within a year if he had lived. He suffered from the most malignant form of diabetes and could already barely walk. Mrs. Logan told of the travail when the Robinsons moved to the whiteness of North Stamford, Connecticut. The show would be a moving tribute.

Ohlmeyer met me at the Riverside Church the next morning with his film crew. We had decided to end the

show, apart from commentary, with my last interview
with Jackie, done in a limousine after we had left the
Gil Hodges funeral together. But now the task was to
talk to all those at the funeral who had been part of
Jackie's life. We began with Martin Stone. Then it was
catch as catch can: Bill Veeck and Hank Greenberg, who
had brought in Larry Doby at Clevelend, but only after
Jackie had paved the way; Bill Russell, a great man
whose eyes teared as he said, "He never gave up his manhood"; Pee Wee Reese; Ralph Branca; and many, many
more.

Finally, after the services, young David Robinson left
his mother and sister, put his arm around my shoulder
and sobbed, "He left us his courage, faith and belief.
We will have it always."

Don and I drove downtown together. We were emotionally enervated, but the job was just beginning. The
film just shot had to be developed, then transferred to
tape. Editing had to begin according to story line. There
was the task of selecting film from memory so that precious time could be saved.

The show got on but only by a miracle, and by the
poise of Don Ohlmeyer. We never did have time to in-
tegrate the show and put it on tape as a complete package. We only got half done and then, with Roone Arledge
lending support in the control room, Ohlmeyer would
roll the interview inserts while I would ad-lib comments
before and after each piece from the announce booth in
the studio. At the very close, Don said, "We're about
thirty seconds short, Howard. Ad-lib." Which I did.

I'm as proud of that show as I am of anything I have
ever done in my broadcast life—that, and my show on
Vince Lombardi when he passed away. That was Friday
night. Emmy and I left for Dallas eight o'clock the next
morning. Detroit was at Dallas the following Monday
night.

Life has a way of going on. Emmy and I flew to Dallas
with Wally and Ginny Schwartz. Wally was now the new
president of ABC Television, reporting to Elton Rule,
president of the American Broadcasting Companies, and

for ten years we had had a very close relationship as his
growth in the company developed on the radio side. He
first joined ABC in 1963 as vice-president and general
manager of our flagship radio station, WABC, and then
was moved in as president of the ABC Radio Networks,
when we began a whole new four-network structure that
revolutionized the network-radio business in this country.
Wally took the network business, which was dying, and
made it work in the new structure, to the point where
ABC Radio could probably show a $4-million profit in
1973. Then Elton Rule, in a company reorganization,
decided to move Wally to television. Now Wally, getting
his feet wet in the new job—and as a sports fan who had
grown up in Detroit—wanted to see firsthand how "Monday Night Football" was done.

We landed at Dallas in the forenoon, were met by a
former ABC newscaster and old friend named Murphy
Martin and his wife Joyce. We went straight to the Marriott Motor Hotel, registered, then left the girls and
went to the Cotton Bowl to watch SMU lose to Texas
Tech. The next night, Sunday night, Herb Granath had
his weekly cocktail party for the sponsors, and the
affair was going swimmingly, with Humble Howard,
Dandy Don and Faultless Frank holding court. Mickey
Mantle had come to the party, and we were talking about
the fact that he wanted to manage the Texas Rangers,
but it appeared that Yankee coach Dick Howser would
get the job. I remember Mickey saying, "Hell, Short
[the owner] says he wants a guy who learned from Houk.
I'm the guy who played for Houk. Nobody knows more
about Houk's methods than I do." Mantle didn't get the
job, but neither did Dick Howser. It went to a fellow
named Whitey Herzog.

Emmy and I were having a good time, and we were
talking with Cowboy President Tex Schramm and his wife
Millie, old friends who used to live in Greenwich when
Tex was with CBS Sports. Things couldn't have been
more pleasant when Eddie Anderson of the Lions burst
upon the scene. Eddie had been a long-term assistant of
sorts to Bill Ford, the owner of the Lions, and he couldn't

wait to get at me. He interrupted our conversation with the Schramms and said, "There'll be a letter on Arledge's desk tomorrow morning from Bill Ford, demanding that you be taken off 'Monday Night Football' because of what you said about Joe Schmidt." Schmidt was then the coach of the Lions.

I said, "What are you talking about?"

He said, "Your crack in Joe Falls's column."

Joe Falls is a columnist in the *Detroit Free Press*. We had been in Detroit two weeks earlier for the Green Bay-Detroit game, and on the day of the game I got a call from Joe asking if he could talk with me for his column. I explained that I had to go to Tiger Stadium to do the half-time highlights, so he said he'd be at the hotel when I got back, that he'd only need 15 minutes or a half hour. I said fine.

When I got back Joe was in the lobby, came up to our suite, and what he wanted was to fire names at me for capsule characterizations, just as Burt Reynolds had once done with me on the Carson show. This kind of thing is fun, so when he said "Bowie Kuhn," I said, "A decent man determinedly presiding over the death of baseball." When he said "Joe Schmidt," I said, "A once great player who, as a coach, couldn't inspire a frog."

That's what Eddie Anderson was talking about, and the kind of nonsense he was now trying to give me illustrates vividly how seriously some operators in sports can take themselves. So when he talked about a letter to Arledge I said, "Eddie, let's not wait for tomorrow, let's go to Arledge's boss right now, Walter Schwartz." Poor Anderson. He was really shocked. So he did his piece on Wally, and Wally told him he had grown up in Detroit and Schmidt was a great player. Then Wally said he wished that Schmidt could coach like he played. I then offered to bet Anderson $50 that Schmidt would not be coaching the following year. He refused the offer. Schmidt resigned at the end of the season.

The next morning I was breakfasting with Emmy and Ginny Schwartz, and Anderson was at the next table.

As he passed by us he made a crack about the game that night, and I told him to stop with the talk and make sure that his team was up that night, lest Dallas cream them. The next thing I knew, Wayne Walker, the veteran linebacker and an old friend, was down from the team meeting and said, "You bad-mouthing us? Eddie Anderson says you say we're gonna get killed." I set Walker straight, then later bumped into Wayne and Joe Schmidt. Joe confronted me on the Joe Falls item. I told him he needed a sense of humor and I said, "Look what I said about Kuhn and Rozelle."

Whereupon Joe said, "Are you apologizing?"

I said, "Hell no. Concentrate on the game tonight."

At our production meeting after that, Giff said he was going into a meeting with Schmidt to talk about the Lions. I told Giff to tell him not to take himself so seriously, and that I really liked him as a person. The next thing I knew, somebody in Detroit was writing that I sent Giff up to apologize for me. Perish the thought. By the way, I do like Joe Schmidt.

After our production meeting I had to go to the Dallas Market Hall to speak at a luncheon in my honor. Incredibly, 3652 people paid to come—the biggest luncheon in Dallas history. Bobby Bragan and Solly Hemus, old baseball friends, came from Fort Worth and Houston respectively, and we had a great reunion. Then the half-time highlights, then the game. Detroit gave us a good show, even though they lost 28–24.

We flew back the next morning, I went straight to the office, and there was the following letter from Cooper Rollow:

Dear Howard:

In case you didn't see it, enclosed is the final version of the story on your appearance before the Chicago Today Quarterback Club which I had rewritten for the late editions.

I am sorry about the earlier version. It was simply a case of bad judgment by a very talented reporter who was trying to be funny.

See you on the hill at Iwo Jima, and I will furnish the cokes this time if you come up with the broads.

Regards,

Cooper Rollow
Sports Editor/Chicago Tribune

One week in the life of Howard Cosell.

Chapter IV

JACKIE,
YOU TAUGHT US ALL

---

*"So much accomplished,
so much to be done."*

There are certain people in American sports who are now valid figures in this nation's history books. Jackie Robinson is one. Muhammad Ali is another. The Joe Namaths of the world are meaningless. They come and go, fleeting figures of passing glamour. You'll find them in the sports tomes but not in the history books.

You'll find Robinson there because of the bloodless social revolution he created. Now, as a consequence of the case of the *United States* vs. *Muhammad Ali,* you'll find Ali there. Curt Flood's attack on baseball's reserve clause will place his name in the lawbooks as well as in the history texts.

I do not weep for Jackie Roosevelt Robinson. But I mourn the injustices imposed upon all of the great black players who have come into baseball since he pried open the door. And of course I equally mourn the superb black players of another era like Satchel Paige, Josh Gibson, Buck Leonard and all of the others consigned for so many years to languish in the old black leagues.

Robinson's emergence took place 26 years ago, years of sweeping and dramatic changes in this country, and still we hear that they are looking for a "qualified" black to manage.

Now, anyone who is over the age of 12, who has ever been exposed to the sports scene, who has ever met a major-league manager, knows that this is pure and total hogwash. Any 12-year-old knows that all they do is play musical chairs with a bunch of anonymous mediocrities as managers. In fact, the longer you are around baseball and the more conversant you become with their hypocrisy in this area, the more you begin to get the feeling that there are certain preeminent qualifications to managing a major-league baseball club: You must be white and either a heavy drinker or a cardplayer. The most regaled manager I have ever known was at least two of the three.

Now that's not true in all cases. There are exceptions. Fred Hutchinson was a great man. Gil Hodges was a fine man. Ralph Houk is a strong, astute individual. Others could be named. But in general, as a class, baseball managers have been notoriously inept. What an absurdity to try to tell the American people, in the year 1973, that they are still searching for a qualified black.

Jackie Robinson came upon the scene in 1947 and they haven't found one yet. Good Lord. Forget the fact that they seldom hire qualified whites. What are they trying to say? That Bill White, who played for the Cardinals and the Phillies, who made the dean's list at Hiram College, isn't qualified? Or the articulate and voluble Maury Wills, immensely personable and attractive and terribly bright: a black Leo Durocher, but with more character. And Frank Robinson, a man who has studiously prepared himself to manage by performing that job in the Puerto Rican winter leagues. Only white managers, it seems, require no experience, can be anointed right out of the playing ranks.

I don't happen to think that a manager is a significant influence in major-league baseball. For the most part managing a team is a farce. One wearies of their studied idiosyncrasies, the spitting of the tobacco, the hitching of the belt, all the rest of the nonsense that goes with conducting a game that's juvenile enough to be totally understood by eight-year-olds in the Little Leagues.

Yet there are those in major-league baseball who will tell you privately that the "problem" is not the *hiring* of a black manager but rather in the *firing*. Their implication is clear—that they fear, in the event of such a firing, adverse reaction by black pressure groups that would do undue harm to the "game." Equally clear is the fact that this is the cheapest kind of cop-out, an alibi that could be used forever to stop a black man from becoming a major-league manager. One might note in this regard that when Lenny Wilkins (the black, former player/coach of Seattle in the National Basketball Association) was released from his job, the matter went almost unnoticed. The same was true in the American Basketball Association when John McLendon, another black head coach, got the gate. Clearly baseball is guilty of witting avoidance on this issue, all protestations to the contrary notwithstanding. (The National Football League is similarly guilty, for that matter, in the light of the absence of a black head coach.)

One major-league operator was on the verge of a breakthrough with a black manager, but it never came to pass. He was Michael Burke of the Yankees, and the time was the summer of '72. The Yankees were floundering, and the fans were booing Ralph Houk (possibly the best manager in baseball) mercilessly. Burke told me that if things didn't get better he would have to let Houk go. His first choice was Billy Martin who was managing the Tigers. If he couldn't get Billy he planned to bring in Frank Robinson. The Yankees did a turnabout, got into the pennant race and, quite properly, Burke signed Ralph to a new three-year contract. But the Burkes are few and far between, and Mike, in the immortal words of presidential press secretary Ron Ziegler, has been rendered "inoperative" by the new Yankee ownership, which took over in late 1972.

So I don't feel the injustices of the last quarter century for Jackie Robinson alone. I can recall how the two of us talked for hours upon hours about the lack of a black presence in the managerial ranks and in the front offices of baseball. And what do you have today? You

have Monte Irvin in the commissioner's office as a kind
of token. A token of what? I'm not derogating Monte
Irvin. I think he's a decent man, a man of character.
I was once his lawyer. But who is major-league baseball kidding?

Yet during all of those years I did not find Jackie
Robinson to be embittered. I would describe him as
realistic. In my opinion Jackie had as much capacity
to be a great manager as any man who ever lived. His
achievements as a human being, not just as a baseball
player, are recorded now for all of history. He was an
extraordinary man whose mere presence filled a room
wherever he went. He was straightforward, outspoken,
honest.

I remember standing in front of the church in Brooklyn on the day of Gil Hodges's funeral, a block away
from where my grandmother lived when I was a child.
And one by one the "boys of summer," as Roger Kahn
called them in his superb book of that name, appeared.
Pee Wee Reese had arrived. And Roy Campanella, Carl
Furillo, Don Newcombe and Joe Black. But not Jackie.
The crowd watched them all come in, and there were
ripples from the youngsters and from the older people
of my generation. And then, suddenly, around the corner, walking so painstakingly that it was hard to believe
that body had once been so taut and quick, hanging
onto the arm of Ralph Branca, came Jackie Robinson.
You could hear, abruptly, the whispers. The thing that
struck me first was that it was youngsters, kids under
15: "There's Jackie Robinson. . . ."

And then, incredibly, the noise began to swell—and
the applause—and the cheers—and "Hey, Jackie," and
it was almost as if you were back at Ebbets Field and
Number 42 was swinging around first in that wide turn,
tantalizing the outfielder: Does he throw to second or
does he dare throw behind Robinson to try to pick him
off? No, he daren't, because surely Jackie would take
second. But is he going to take second anyway? Is he
going to try and make it with the unexpected burst of
speed and that evasive, sweeping slide?

That's the feeling you had. You could see the whole thing telescoped right in front of your eyes, as he went heavily up the steps, hanging onto Ralph Branca's arm, in front of the church on the day of Gil Hodges's funeral. For a fleeting moment it was my entire young-adult life coming back to me, an age when baseball mattered as a sport in this country and, more importantly, when it symbolized to all the world that America could cope with its most terrible of all problems—the problem of race. This was what Jackie Robinson symbolized. He helped inspire the image that this nation was capable of racial amity instead of racial anguish, and that was the best thing that ever happened to baseball.

In later years, to my shock and consternation, when Jackie retired some wrote blithely about what he owed to baseball. Good Lord! What this man went through. What he did for the sport is impossible to measure. He gave it the only good and honest image it has in the United States of America today. What has been its image since Jackie? Carpetbagging across the land, pretending to be the national pastime, deserting the nation's capitol for little Arlington, Texas. Who is kidding whom?

The refrain against Jackie went like this: (1) He owed it to the writers to give them the story, and (2) How could he knock baseball? *Look what the game did for him.*

What did baseball do for Jackie Robinson? I'll tell you. It tortured him, tormented him. What he had to live with was the greatest debasement of a proud human being in my lifetime. But he gave baseball the appearance of being a democratic business—that's what he did for baseball—and he gave it a place in American history by his mere presence. And one of the great tragedies of American sports journalism is that often you read in the other way—that Jackie Robinson left a debt to baseball.

The circumstances as I know them were these. When Robinson quit he had a commitment to *Look* magazine to announce in its pages the details of his retirement. He was counseled in this matter by one of the shrewdest men I've ever known, Martin Stone. Originally a lawyer, Martin Stone became a preeminent television packager, originating such shows as "Howdy Doody," which alone made him a millionaire when he sold it for a capital gain. He packaged "Author Meets the Critics," among others. He was very deeply involved with Jackie. He loved him very much, almost as a brother.

A number of the sporting press pilloried Robinson as being dishonest in the way he left baseball, because he did not give the story to the men who covered the Dodgers. This was the end of 1956, Jackie's last season, and he had confided to me the simple truth. For anyone to accuse Jackie of being a hypocrite was absurd.

At that time, on my late-night local radio show, he told how he had agreed to a proposal from *Look* magazine that would produce large moneys for him if he would give them the exclusive story of his retirement, money he would need for the security of his wife and his three children upon his departure from baseball. He knew he was getting too old to play, and on the advice of Martin Stone he accepted *Look*'s terms, which prevented him from informing even the Brooklyn Dodgers of his decision.

In the meantime, the trade had taken place that stunned the fans of both teams, the trade that would have sent Jackie across the bridge to the New York Giants. I gave Jackie a forum. Privately I agreed that what he had done was right, but as a reporter I was not disposed to take an editorial stand at that time. But such was the nature of his integrity and character that Jackie, after much private torment, met with Chub Feeney and Horace Stoneham of the Giants and probed his own conscience for some way to return to baseball, to give the Giants one year of his service. But he simply couldn't do it. He had to take care of his own life. He had made a commitment and he honored it.

He was a very important figure in my career. When Gil Hodges died, Jackie knew ABC was doing a Monday-night special on his old teammate, and so we had arranged for him to drive back to Manhattan in a limousine with me, with a camera crew in the front seat. We did the last interview we ever did together—and, assuredly, I did over 100 interviews with Jackie Robinson in his lifetime. We sat in that car and we reviewed his life. One eye was completely gone, the other eye was milky white. He had diabetes, high blood pressure and had survived two coronaries. He had suffered through the problems of Jackie, Jr.—crime, rehabilitation, Vietnam, drug addiction, rehabilitation. He exulted in the superb work by the youngster at the Daytop Drug Rehabilitation Center in Seymour, Connecticut—the very work the youngster was doing for the center on the night he was driving home, exhausted, at two in the morning, when he lost control of his car, crashed and was killed.

While I was in the car we reviewed every one of those things, and I asked Jackie if he felt that God had singled him out for the most untoward adversity I'd ever seen befall a man. He said that he and Rachel had talked about it often. His wife is a glorious lady. She was an utterly beautiful woman who, quite frankly, has been ravaged now by the weight of events. But she remains a remarkable lady who was on the Yale faculty as a clinical psychologist. They both felt, said Jackie, that, yes, he had been given a cross to bear.

My last question to him, in this last interview, was how would he characterize his life.

He looked at me with those eyes that could hardly see and he said, "Oh, we've had a great life." And he wasn't being heroic. It was just an interview in the back of a limousine. "We've accomplished so much," he added.

As long as I knew him he never said "I." It was always "we." Without Rachel he was nothing and he knew it. He said, "We've accomplished so much, there's so much more to be done I guess we'll not have the chance to do it. Oh, what a great life we've had."

Jackie Robinson was a remarkable man. The day he was admitted to the Hall of Fame we sent a camera crew to his home in North Stamford, Connecticut. I was doing a special on him, called "New Man at Cooperstown." We sat on the steps of his church, a Presbyterian church some 400 yards from his property, a classic old New England church. We talked about religion—how he viewed his place in the society—what it meant to him. We went into his billiard room and shot pool and we talked about his origins in baseball, the black leagues, his relationship with Branch Rickey.

We walked down by his lake, and we talked about the neighbors who did not want the Robinsons in that plush section. We talked about his children and how they were reacting to all of the hardships they had faced. You know, it is a great hardship for a child who is *white* to be the son or daughter of a famous father. Translate that into what it means to be black and the child of a famous father and you begin to understand what had happened to Jackie Robinson, Jr. The same name. The high expectations. People never left him alone.

I don't think there was anything about life that we didn't talk about that day. I think there is only one word that describes Jackie Robinson. Unconquerable. He was the most unconquerable human being I have ever known. I loved him.

Of course, we had our run-ins. I'm a volatile man, and so was he. One of our disagreements was the result of a "Wide World of Sports" show I had to do after Ali's fight with Ernie Terrell. It was not an easy one to do because Ali, in my opinion, had behaved very badly in that fight and had, indeed, turned on me in the ring interview afterward. He turned on everyone. He knew— he later admitted it to me privately—that he had been needlessly cruel to Terrell. So there he was, three days later in the studio, and three or four New York writers were present.

It was a tense scene in that room because I knew I had a job to do and, quite frankly, I was upset at always being the one who had to do the tough shows, the issue shows that would produce a great diversity of reaction. I also knew that was my forte and that it was what was making me a well-known broadcaster. In fact,

I started that day by turning to the writers and saying, "Look, I'm not going to do this show. I want you fellows to take down this statement." As they started to take down my resignation I thought better of it and said, "Wait, knock it off. I'm going to do this damned show." And I did a very tough show with Muhammad Ali. It was later characterized in a profile of me in *Sports Illustrated* as a shouting contest. It wasn't that, but it was a very hard-hitting show, and subsequently I got flooded with mail. I was no longer a nigger-loving Jew bastard as I usually was in any adverse mail that reaches my office. I was the black-hater. I actually got, for the first time in my life, a letter signed by a whole dormitory in Michigan State telling me I was antiblack.

None of which really mattered. What did matter was an angry phone call from Jackie Robinson. "Howard," he said, "that just wasn't you. What's happened to you?"

I said, "Jack, we're just not going to see eye to eye on this." I explained my position to him, and he said, "I just don't agree with you."

I said, "Jack, I'm sorry, but that's the way it is. I think I'm right. You think you're right. I did what I had to do in my mind and my heart as a journalist. I don't apologize for a bit of it." So there was some coolness in that conversation. We had others like it.

When Goose Tatum, the legendary comic figure of the Harlem Globetrotters, died, I decided to do a commentary on his life. So I called a man who knew him intimately, Walter Kennedy, the commissioner of the NBA. Walter Kennedy had been the publicist for the Globetrotters and had traveled the world with Goose. He described how Tatum had worked and worked and how his lifelong dream was to own that yellow Cadillac. He finally got it, and his greatest pride was to drive it and honk at the other players as they waited for the team bus, and Walter told the story on the air.

Another call from Jackie Robinson. "You have got to be ashamed of yourself."

"Why, Jack?"

"That Old World trash, the Negro servile, the yellow Cadillac and so on."

I said, "Jack, here you may have a point. Unwittingly I was telling an anecdote about the man, that one of his closest friends best remembered. It was not in any way so intended, but I can understand the stereotype of the black with the watermelon and the Cadillac and all of the rest. I'm sorry. I didn't intend it that way, and the story was just a true story."

It was just a glimpse of the man. Jack was a fighter. He had a point to make. He had a point to make every day of his life and he made it loud and clear. I respected that.

For a brief time Jackie and I worked together as part of ABC's broadcasting team for the major-league "Game of the Week." Few remember that the first time a black man appeared on a sports network as a broadcaster was with ABC, and that Roone Arledge did it. We had Chris Schenkel, Leo Durocher, Keith Jackson, Jackie and myself. I remember flying home one day with Chris and Jackie, and I was discussing something he had said on the air. In my usual tactful way I began, "Now, Jack, I think you should have—"

"Howard," he stopped me, "you're not the greatest man who ever lived, and I can remember when you weren't so darned good. I admit I'm not . . ."

It was a flash of insecurity about his performance. Well, I hadn't intended it that way at all, but I had not been subtle enough in the way I expressed my criticism to him. Yes, we had differences, but it had nothing to do with the basics of our friendship and our mutuality of respect. Jack would come over to my house on a Saturday afternoon to play gin with me and Eddie Russell, Sig Shore and Marty Nierman—all friends of mine—and Jack was not the world's best gin-rummy player. But losing would enrage him. In that respect he was like Vince Lombardi.

I don't think there is any need here to embellish *The Boys of Summer*. But it is true that the Brooklyn Dodgers were all of baseball to all of the world. When Greta

Garbo did *Ninotchka* with Melvyn Douglas there were jokes in it about the Brooklyn Dodgers. In movies about the Marines, or the Army, or whomever, the jokes were about the Brooklyn Dodgers. They were the tradition, the color, the excitement, the failure, the success of baseball at a time when baseball personified America at play.

But as curiously important as all that was then, the Brooklyn Dodgers became the American dream when Jackie Robinson joined them. And so the *Brooklyn* Dodgers have a place unique in the history of sports in the United States. I think the whole thing was epitomized when I was doing "New Man at Cooperstown." I wanted to return Jackie Robinson to where Ebbets Field had been. That endearing little ball park, with all of its intimacy, with its zany fans like Hilda behind third base, like a man named Jake, whose last name I never knew, a Pittsburgh Pirate rooter who would go to every Dodger game and go to the bleacher section and make speeches about why the Dodgers stank and the Pirates were great.

That was baseball, and I wanted to go back with Jackie because they had torn it all down and were building a housing development. Jackie parked the car on Bedford Avenue, across the street from where the centerfield exit had been. Now there was nothing but steel girders and workmen on those 15 stories up in the air. I think back to it now, about how natural it was, just the way it happened. From 15 stories up, one of the workmen looked down, saw the pigeon toes and the white hair and sang out—you could hear it loud and clear— "Hey, Jackie, wait till next year."

Once Jackie Robinson came to Brooklyn we didn't have to wait till next year. We had it this year. And so did the whole country, because the Brooklyn Dodgers were a national institution.

Jackie and I walked into the project. It was a skeletal thing then, and we walked to the area where second base had been. They had marked off a place where a plaque was to be implanted. The words were written out: "Jackie Robinson stood here." (I'll go back there someday, to see if they ever did put the plaque in.)

At that time they called the project The Ebbets Field Apartments. Now they are called The Jackie Robinson Apartments.

At the end of the 1956 season, the signs were there to be read by anyone willing to examine them. The Dodgers and the Giants were leaving New York and going west. Early on I started calling the Dodgers the Los Angeles Dodgers on the air. At that time I was doing a late-night local sports show on radio, 15 minutes, right after the eleven o'clock news. Almost every night I would go in and excoriate Walter O'Malley for the impending evacuation, and I'd keep calling them the Los Angeles Dodgers. This continued through 1957 and soon it began to take hold with the public. I base that judgment on a phone call I received from O'Malley, a man I didn't like but for whom I had great intellectual respect. I knew his shrewdness. He invited me to come over to Brooklyn and have lunch with him and his three assistants, Buzzie Bavasi, a man I have great affection for, the late Fresco Thompson, a man with a sweet sense of humor, and Arthur Patterson.

So I went over, and Walter took me to a private dining room he used at the Bossert Hotel. Having grown up in Brooklyn I remembered the Bossert Hotel with some fondness, because it was at the Marine Grill on the Bossert roof, in the era of the big bands, that Freddie Martin made his debut with a song called "Dancing on the Ceiling." It became his theme.

Anyway, there we were, and O'Malley spent the whole time, as we downed one martini and then another, rendering me malleable under his suasion. This was a very easy thing for O'Malley to do, because he is a terribly bright and clever man, affable, with that tomato-shaped face and those Sidney Greenstreet jowls. He was assuring me that he wanted to work out everything to stay in Brooklyn and that it would be in the best interest of the community and so on.

I kind of sailed away on a cloud of martinis and returned to the ABC Studios on Sixty-sixth Street convinced in my own mind that, by God, Walter O'Malley was a dedicated public servant and a guardian of the public trust. By the time I opened the door at Sixty-sixth Street I realized that I had been had. None of it was credible. So I went back on the air that night and I teed off on O'Malley again.

Whereupon he called me the next day in a condition that can best be described as shock, disbelief and outrage. How could I have done that to him? He thought we had a rapprochement. Well, I explained to Walter as best I could that at the time I did feel receptive to his arguments but that I had changed my mind on the way back to the office and I just didn't agree with him. I just couldn't believe him.

There was an instant decline in our relationship until the final meeting at Gracie Mansion with Mayor Wagner, Nelson Rockefeller (not yet elected to his first term as governor) and O'Malley. Rockefeller was interceding in a last public attempt to keep Walter in Brooklyn, and by now everyone was aware that a very real possibility existed that the Dodgers would flee to California. I went there to do my last telecast interview with Walter, and it was really quite a triumph. I was still a young broadcaster, and it was only 1957, and right there at Gracie Mansion I placed the microphone in front of his massive jowls and said, "Well, Mr. O'Malley, are you prepared to finally tell the truth that you are leaving? . . ."

And O'Malley smiled thinly and said, "Well, we've come to know you, Howard, and you think you're the Mike Wallace of sports. . . ."

We played the interview just as it was done. I took his remark as a matter of high praise. Mike Wallace was then coming into his own. He had "Night Beat," the local show that brought him fame, and now he was getting a network-television interview show with ABC that would make him a feared and powerful newsman. I decided that if he likened me to Mike I must be getting somewhere as a reporter. There has never been any affability between Walter and myself since then, although up to the present day Buzzie Bavasi and I are very good and close friends. I always loved Fresco Thompson, and the last time I was at Dodger Stadium, for ABC, Arthur Patterson could not have been nicer. He even wanted an autographed picture for someone in his family.

So in sports you really don't hold grudges. Not on a personal level. I don't hold any grudge against Walter O'Malley, and I doubt that he would take me seriously enough to really have a grudge against me. But if you're in journalism it's not a matter of grudges, it's a matter of issues, and I have never let my listening or viewing public forget that the worst evidence of carpetbagging in the history of baseball was the flight of the Dodgers from Brooklyn. They were the most profit-producing club in the National League and, at the time of their removal, the only club in the league to have drawn a million or more people every year for the preceding 13 years, including the very year they were planning to defect.

None of this, I hasten to add, is relevant to the question of Los Angeles deserving a major-league team. Obviously they were entitled to one and should have gotten one by way of expansion.

In the entire incredible series of events then being played out behind baseball's closed doors, the guy I enjoyed most was Mayor Christopher of San Francisco. He was plotting to capture the New York Giants and he didn't deny it. The mayor was in New York for a meeting with Horace Stoneham, a meeting that O'Malley engineered. Later there was a press conference at the Essex House, and with newsmen all around him he turned to me and said, "Hey, you're on the ball. Your questions are very good. Yes, I'll admit it. I expect the Giants will be moving with the Dodgers and we'll maintain the same rivalry in California that you've had in New York."

That was the first real admission of what was happening. We jammed it on the air immediately.

Nor did Horace Stoneham lie. He conducted himself like a gentleman, and if anyone had a reason for bailing out it was Stoneham. The Giants had declined as a team and weren't drawing. There is no municipal obligation to support a bad product, but neither is there a law that says a businessman must go broke.

But those were years of betrayal in baseball. The abandonment of Brooklyn by O'Malley—the pointless charade over the hiring of a "qualified" black manager—the shameful failure to offer a place within the game to Jackie Robinson after his playing days were over; he had confided to me in the late Fifties that he would have managed, given a chance. I have the feeling he might have outdone the immortal Kerby Farrell.

You know, baseball was important once in this country. But Frank Merriwell doesn't live here anymore. Jackie Robinson still does.

Chapter V

LOMBARDI:
ASK HIS PLAYERS

---

*"If he says everyone swims the Fox River
to practice, I swim the damned river."*

I have never known a man who left more of himself
in those close to him, whose lives he touched, than
Vincent Thomas Lombardi. The men who moved in
his orbit—the players and the coaches and those, like
myself, who were merely passing through—were equally
influenced by him. No man has ever had a greater impact on me.

Looking back, it is odd that it turned out that way.
On the surface we seemed to have little in common.
Lombardi was a political conservative, an establishment
man. He was also a man of discipline and maxims, of
principle and unbending character, with the mind of a
classical scholar. He had—and this might surprise some—
a gift of humor. He liked to drink, to play cards. He
cared deeply about people. He cared about excellence,
about winning, and he cared about being remembered.
He had a positive obsession about being the first coach
in the National Football League to win three championships in a row. The fact that those championships would
encompass two Super Bowl victories was incidental.

I'm not certain why Vince and I hit it off so well.
But I respected his values. He trusted me, and I believed
in him. When he left the Packers and joined the Red-

skins, a Washington writer asked him why he allowed me into his training camp with my film crew when he would not allow others. "Howard is a moral man," he replied, "he would never break his word." Family meant everything to Vince, apart from football, family and loyalty to old friends.

So Vince was basically a simple man, just as his football teams played simple football. "Don't give me any fancy offenses or new tricks on defense," he would bark. "You block better, you tackle better than the other guy, you win the football game." And Lombardi, as no other coach in the history of professional football, made that dictum work. Every other team knew what was coming when the Green Bay Packers played them. The power sweep, with either Hornung or Taylor carrying, with Jerry Kramer and Fuzzy Thurston leading the charge. They knew it was coming but they couldn't stop it. That was the key play in "the Green Bay offensive category," as Vince put it, and it set up every other play in the Packer offensive scheme.

I knew Vince slightly when we were at college, he at Fordham, as one of the Seven Blocks of Granite, and I at NYU. Both schools were big time then in college football, and in later years Vince and I would talk often about the two great upsets of the mid-Thirties. In 1935 NYU was unbeaten and headed for the Rose Bowl. Until Thanksgiving Day, that is. On Thanksgiving Day, Fordham beat NYU 21–0. With that great raucous laugh of his, Vince would recall that game with relish. "We had it all the way, once Maniaci threw that option pass to Paquin." Lombardi loved the option pass play, maybe because Paul Hornung was so great at executing it for the Pack. But when I would remind Vince of 1936 he would groan. Fordham was headed for the Rose Bowl that year. NYU was mediocre, had been crushed by Ohio State in its opening game by more than 60 points. But on Thanksgiving Day a little back named George Savarese took a hand-off and slipped in for a touchdown. NYU converted, and then an end named Howard Dunney kept Fordham at bay the whole game with quick kicks into the coffin corner. Final score: NYU 7, Fordham 6. When I would vocally savor that game with Vince he would mutter, "Why don't you forget that damned fluke? Never saw a guy so lucky with his kicks." Neither Fordham nor NYU ever got to the Rose Bowl.

Though we had known one another to nod to while at college, we never became friends really until 1964. On occasion I would see him at West Point when he was on Colonel Blaik's coaching staff, and later when he was the offensive coach of the Giants. In those days he never had the security, the command presence that later became one of his trademarks. But even then you could see that he was something special as a football coach.

He literally worshiped Colonel Blaik and patterned himself after him. Until he died, the friendship between them was a beautiful thing to see. Blaik had been pictured by many as a martinet, a dictator and a tyrant, unapproachable and cold. Never mind Blaik's successes as a football coach, they would say, look at him as a man. He's mean. In later years, at the peak of his coaching career, Lombardi would hear the same things said about himself.

I suppose some of my early affection for Lombardi stemmed from my feeling for Colonel Blaik. Back in the late Fifties when I was doing a nightly network sports show, Blaik was holding forth at West Point. I hardly knew him. I was a nobody trying to become a somebody. I felt it would be a feather in my cap if I could get an interview with him. I mentioned this to Lombardi, who was then with the Giants. "Call Joe Cahill at the academy," Vince snapped. "I'll bet the colonel will see you."

I called the late Joe Cahill, a fine man who was the sports information director at West Point. Joe told me the colonel rarely did anything like this—I had told Joe I'd like to interview Blaik in depth—but he would ask him. To my amazement Cahill called back and said that Blaik would be glad to do it. We made a date for the next morning at the Battle Monument on the Plains. I have wondered ever since if Vince called the colonel.

When I would ask Vince about it, his eyes would twinkle and he would say, "Never did a thing. The colonel just respected you." The colonel, as I said, hardly even knew me.

In any event, when I got to the Point the next day, there was Blaik, right on time and cordial to a fault. I was scared to death. The man is the image of the late General Douglas MacArthur, the two were best friends, and as the story goes, Blaik did not introduce two-platoon football at the academy until he got clearance from the general who was then on duty in the Philippines. I asked the colonel about his relationship with MacArthur, and then I asked him all the direct, personal questions about himself: the unbending image, the stern authoritarianism. Blaik couldn't have been more responsive. When we got done he said, "That's a fine interview, young man. I've been wanting to do that for a long time." I left West Point on cloud nine. Ever since then, Blaik and I have been good friends. When his book *You Have to Pay the Price,* written with Tim Cohane, was published, I received a copy in the mail. It was inscribed, "From this old pro with respect for a great pro in his own field, Earl Blaik." To this day I'm as proud of that inscription as any I have ever received. And I know that my feeling for the colonel carried over to Vince Lombardi. A matter of instinct.

Shortly after the Blaik incident Vince moved on to Green Bay as head coach. I was then doing color on a six-game pro-football package that ABC had acquired. It consisted of four preseason games and two regular-season games. Green Bay was playing in one of the preseason games at Bowman Gray Stadium in Winston-Salem, North Carolina. I talked with Vince before the game. He was right on. "I've got a tough situation. Long way to go. McHan will be my quarterback as of now, but I want to look at this kid Starr. He may have something." Starr sure did. Under Vince he became the winningest quarterback in the contemporary history of professional football. And Bart would be the first to tell you that he could never have done it without Lombardi.

There were little incidents like that, where Vince was always helpful to me. Then, as I have noted, we became close in 1964, and that was because of a fine writer named W. C. "Bill" Heinz. I have characterized Bill Heinz elsewhere in this book as the greatest boxing writer I have ever read. I should have said he is one of the greatest writers I have ever read. Boxing, football, cancer surgeons (he did great writing in this area), you name it. Bill Heinz worked with Vince on Vince's book— a classic now—*Run to Daylight*.

I was at Bill's house in Stamford, Connecticut, along with Red Smith and Vince, the night the book was entitled. Bill wanted to call it *Six Days and Sunday*. That sounded fine to me, but Betty Heinz, who had read the text, said, "I like that phrase 'run to daylight.' "

Vince jumped in and growled, "So do I." And that was it. Immediately it became Vince's idea.

We had a marvelous evening. Talked football for hours. Emmy and I left with a positive glow. "I told you he was a great guy," I said as we were driving home. "And what a job he's done with the Packers." (The Pack had won three straight division titles and two league titles from 1960 through 1962.)

Emmy said something perceptive then. She remarked, "Never mind the football. He's got a great sense of humor and a fine mind. Not at all the way he's so often written about." No, not at all.

Lombardi's book was published and it was a hit. This was at a time when I was producing documentaries for WABC-TV in New York. It was at a time when professional football was entering its golden age, with Lombardi the golden figure. It was at a time when Paul Hornung was coming back from a year's suspension for betting on games. Topically, there could not have been a better time to adapt Vince's book to television. And wonder of wonders, the publishers, Prentice-Hall, agreed. Vince also agreed, and so I made a deal with them for next to no money. Money didn't matter to Vince. Quality did. I have no illusions as to why they agreed. They agreed because of their faith in Bill Heinz, who would write the adaptation. Bill was the heart and soul of "Run to Daylight," and I owe him as much for that show as I owed to Vince himself.

I have never been so excited about any show before or since. I would be allowed to shoot Lombardi as he greeted the rookies, as he oversaw the medical exams, as he addressed his men for the first time, as he consulted with his coaching staff and as he lived his professional life. Bill Heinz had mapped the whole thing out. He had a complete shot list prepared, and he had scheduled Vince moment by moment for shooting purposes over a four-day period. Bill himself got to Green Bay a couple of days before I arrived with my director and my crew. He was waiting for us at the airport and he was as excited as we were. Bill is a great storyteller, and he speaks in a clipped, staccato way with physical movements accompanying his speech that heighten the dramatic effect of what he says. "Vince is in a good mood," he said, "but he's a little nervous. He's never done this kind of thing before—he's really a shy man— and he's worried about the way it's going to turn out. I just hope he doesn't change his mind."

Bill and I drove directly to a little town outside of Green Bay where Fuzzy Thurston has a steak house called The Left Guard. Fuzzy is a fun-loving guy, short for an offensive lineman, who made it the hard way. He failed with a number of other teams before Lombardi got him. Under Vince he not only made it but became a star. So he is one of the many who loved Lombardi. When we got to The Left Guard, Fuzzy greeted us and said, "The coach is upstairs, doing his thing."

"His thing" was gin rummy. Vince, in a private room upstairs, was enmeshed in a game, one of a quartet. As we walked in he looked up and said, "Ho, ho, Howard's here—fine." And he laughed that laugh of his. "Why don't you just get yourself a steak and a drink while I give these guys a lesson. It won't take long."

So I got a drink and stood behind him while I was waiting for some food. Vince was getting beat. He was playing lousy. He knew I was a pretty good gin player and he saw me kind of cringe when he made certain plays. Finally he whirled around and said, "Dammit, get the hell over to that bar. I know what you're thinking." Do you know what I did? I got the hell over to the bar. Then I began to worry about whether or not the show would be done. So did Bill Heinz. Thank God, Vince wound up winning. We had a drink together, and then Vince said, "See you in the morning."

The next morning, right on schedule, we were at Vince's office and started doing audio tape with him to adduce some of the very lines that were in *Run to Daylight*, magnificent, descriptive lines on Paul Hornung, Bart Starr, Dave "Hawg" Hanner, Henry Jordan and others in the Packers' coterie. Lombardi could not have been more cooperative, more thoughtful, more winning in his considerateness. After that we moved out onto the campus of little Saint Norbert's College, in West De Pere, Wisconsin, where the Packers live during training. There we shot the opening scene of the show, Lombardi walking down a tree-shaded mall, thoughtful, alone, and then bumping into two of the nuns on the faculty, greeting them, continuing on. He did it so naturally, I thought to myself, "The guy's an actor, too."

We went from there to the steps of Sensenbrenner Hall, the dormitory where the team lived. The rookies were due to arrive. This was when I saw how absorbed Lombardi could be, and how nervous he could get. He kept talking to his personnel man, Pat Peppler, and kept reciting the names of the expected rookies over and over again. Finally a bus arrived, and out poured the youngsters, who were far more nervous than Lombardi. They formed a line and announced their names to Vince, who shook hands with each of them and got off a little quip relating to each of their personal backgrounds. One was Tom Brown, who was to become a strong safety for years with the Pack, a stickout player. "We've waited a long time for you, Tom," Lombardi roared with that gusty cackle. Brown had been a baseball bonus baby for a year with the Washington Senators and now was switching to football.

Now the line was done, and Lombardi turned to Peppler and chortled, "I didn't flub once. It went fine, just fine." He was in high gear.

After lunch came the physical exams. Watching Lombardi with his players—some of the veterans were already in, including Hornung—you got caught up with the way he regarded his young men. The running back, Tom Moore, for instance; Lombardi smacked him on the shoulders, put his arm around him, and as Bill Heinz wrote it, "You could see him remembering that big run against the Lions." Around and around the room he went, a word here, a word there, the memory uncanny. The rookies frightened, respectful, almost in awe. The seasoned ones glad to be back but knowing the moments of laughter would be few.

Dinnertime came, and the hazing of the rookies began. One of the amazing things about pro-football training camps is how men can become boys. Lombardi himself did. He loved those rookie hazings. "It's good for them," he would say. "Embarrasses them a little, but relieves them a lot. Makes them part of the group." After dinner he delivered the first address to the troops.

I am not a man who normally believes in pep talks. I think the time is past, generally speaking, for the Knute Rockne approach with young people. They don't grow up the way they used to. But I must admit I was taken with Lombardi's speech. So much sincerity. So much thought. Even philosophy. And most interesting of all, the reaction of the veterans—not the rookies, the veterans. Later Starr told me, "I never get tired of it. Always something new."

Hornung said, "The old boy never loses his touch."

That touch was the ability to communicate with young men to a greater degree than anyone I had ever seen. I left the room with the maxims ringing in my ears:

"You've got to give everything you've got, on every play, because any single play can determine the outcome of the entire game." "You can't play fatigued. Fatigue makes cowards of us all." "Sure I want to win. I'm here, you're here, we're all here only if we win. If we lose, we're gone. And we only want winners."

I left there thinking, "He makes it work. He believes in what he says, and with that personality, that force, he makes it work. They leave there ready to do battle." That, I suppose, is why so many thought Lombardi was another Patton, insanely driving, almost sadistic. But no, that was only one part of him.

Two-a-day practices began the next day. We were there bright and early with our cameras. The work began almost instantly. Calisthenics and more calisthenics. Mobility drills. Breakdowns into units for the respective coaches. Lombardi everywhere. Watching. Shouting. Criticizing. Applauding. The field commander in action. On the surface like all other coaches—except for one thing: Almost uncannily he would register with each and every man. His mere being brought respect. You wonder why that can be so with an individual, what there is in such a man, why it is lacking in others. Whatever the quality, Vince Lombardi had it. I was there. I know.

Our cameras were out on that practice field, in blistering heat, taking tight shots of the faces of the men as they were working. Suddenly I heard Lombardi screaming, "Get the hell out of here, will ya! Get out of here with your damn people. You're all the same, give you an inch, you want a mile. Get out of here."

I realized he was talking to me, and I said to Bill Heinz, "That's it, I'm getting out of here. This man's crazy. I won't take that from anybody."

I told the crew to start packing up and I was getting ready to leave when Lombardi came over and said, "What the hell's the matter with you? What are you doing?"

I said, "Vince, that's not part of our deal. I can't accept from you what you just did."

He said, "What are you talking about? What did I do?"

I told him. And then he said, "You know better. I get so absorbed, I don't even know what I'm saying. Don't leave now. Anything you want is yours, you know that."

I realized that the man was so totally lost in concentration that he wasn't the slightest bit aware of what he had said. Football chewed him up. For him, football was work and preparation. It was all-consuming. From that moment on, Lombardi was just incredible in the way he cooperated. What was equally astonishing was the way his players cooperated. Hornung ran the steps of the stadium for us again and again. Willie Davis, Dave Robinson, Hawg Hanner, Jerry Kramer and Henry Jordan couldn't do enough. Nor could Jim Taylor and the awesome tight end, Ron Kramer. They wanted to do it for Lombardi, they wanted to show how they felt about him, they wanted people to know what kind of man he really was. And I thought about all the trash I had read, how they called him, like Blaik, a martinet, a tyrant, a dictator. Hogwash.

There was a day when I was in Hornung's room. Hornung said, "Want a lift? I'm driving over to practice." Sure, any time.

A few minutes later Bart Starr popped his head in. "Coach says everybody in the bus in five minutes."

Hornung got up from his chair. I asked him where he was going. "To the bus," he answered.

"But I thought you were giving me a lift."

Hornung then said, "Didn't you listen? The coach wants everyone in the bus in five minutes. I'll be in the bus. If he said everyone walks to practice, I walk. If he says everyone runs to practice, I run. If he says everyone swims the Fox River to practice, I swim the damned river."

That's the way he felt about Vince, and as much as I like Paul I have often wondered how he could have hurt Vince so when he was betting on games. On the other side of the coin, Paul was Vince's all-time favorite, even after he came back. Vince would say of Paul,

"Inside the twenty-yard line he becomes the greatest football player I have ever seen. He smells the goal line."

Vince's widow, Marie, is a splendid lady, and Emmy and I are very fond of her. We see her often. Once, in an interview, she told me that, deep down, Vince would have liked to have been Paul Hornung. As I said, there was a lot of fun in Lombardi, and a little bit of the rogue, too. Yes, he wanted to be Paul, with that golden-boy charm and that life-is-a-cabaret outlook, but he wanted to be what he was much more.

What he did have was a streak of sentimentality. He would cry easily. When I was shooting "Run to Daylight," it was clear that Jerry Kramer was unwell. His weight had dropped steadily, and he suffered internal pains. Still, he was trying to play. Lombardi talked with me about it. He was enormously distressed. At first he thought Jerry had been faking. Now he knew better. The feeling was that Kramer had cancer.

When I left Jerry at Green Bay I didn't know if I'd ever see him again, a once huge, beautiful guy who couldn't stay away from the field even if Lombardi didn't want him there. "I don't know what it is," Lombardi mourned. "I'm afraid of the worst. But you can't tell the big guy to stop."

They finally opened Kramer up, found slivers from an old accident on a ranch that had been undetected in prior surgeries, and Jerry got well again—well enough to make the most famous block in football history on Jethro Pugh of Dallas, the one that Bart Starr followed into the end zone to give the Pack another title and led to Jerry's book *Instant Replay*. But too soon after the operation Jerry went hunting for polar bears. Vince had a fit.

Kramer was one of the last people I spoke with when I left Green Bay. We had done a radio show together. "Now maybe you know the truth about Vince Lombardi," he said.

Lombardi was sorely tried when he had to let a player go who was not good enough to make the team but who had given everything he had in his effort to make the team. He sat with me along the bank of the Fox River and he said, "When a kid has given you the best he has to give, and you have to tell him it wasn't good enough, that's when you ache inside and think maybe there's a better way to make a living, maybe football isn't worth it. But when you tell a man he's through, and you know he has the talent to stick but hasn't put it to work, then you don't feel sorry at all. He's got it coming. Maybe the worst of all is when you have to give the word to a veteran, a man who's been with you for years, a man who's given you everything, who's part of you. You can't face him, you don't know how to tell him, but you have to. I've had to do that, and I don't mind telling you, I've cried." Anybody who has ever said Lombardi was a cruel man didn't know him.

When I left Lombardi in Green Bay in 1964, his final words were, "How do you thing it'll come out?" I told him I thought it would be a good show but we'd only know when it had been edited. "I hope it's a good show," he said. "But above all, make it an honest show. Show me as I am. Don't try to make me look good as long as you don't try to make me look bad. Just show me as I am." I think we did. "Run to Daylight" may still be the most highly regarded sports documentary yet done.

After I left Green Bay I didn't talk to Vince until the show had been completed. The plan was to screen it for the press at Toots Shor's. I called Vince and told him that I thought we had a good show. Then I asked him to come to the screening. "How can I do that?" he screamed. "It means leaving the team, and we've got a preseason game the next night. I've never left my team. You know that." I suggested—never believing he would do it—that he make an exception and come on in. He did it. That night, before we screened the show, I spoke to a huge gathering. I did not introduce Vince. He sat there unobtrusively. I wanted him to see the show first. We viewed it. The crowd was enthusiastic. Then I brought Vince on. He said quietly that he was very proud of the show, that it was the story of the Green Bay Packers. That was enough for me.

In later years Vince and I did a number of shows together. We did a half-hour interview called a "Self Portrait." After the interview he said, "Boy, you sure did put me on the spot. But you were right to do it." I had probed him about Jimmy Taylor, who was playing out his option; words had grown harsh between Vince and Jimmy. Then we did a "Super Bowl Analysis" of the Jets' victory over the Colts, and that's when I first knew how much Vince would have liked to coach Joe Namath. We did so many shows together, in fact, that once Lombardi said, "I'm making you famous."

I told him, "You're beginning to sound like Muhammad Ali." Vince didn't like that.

In January 1970, the year Kansas City beat Minnesota in the Super Bowl, Emmy and I were at Pete Fountain's in New Orleans. Vince and Marie were at a nearby table. Pete saw me and introduced me to the crowd. Then he spotted Vince and introduced him. As we left we went past Vince's table. "See what I mean about making you famous?" he growled.

In February 1969 ABC Sports had a luncheon honoring Bill Toomey as our "Wide World of Sports" athlete of the year. After that luncheon Bill and I and Roone Arledge walked over to Mike Manuche's on West Fifty-second Street, a favorite hangout of sports people. Lombardi was there, and I introduced him to Toomey. You would have thought he had discovered another Paul Hornung. He literally bounced with enthusiasm and praise for Toomey. "Young man," he boomed, "I watched you in Mexico City. You have no idea how thrilled I was. You are the world's greatest athlete. Yes, you are. Every one of us is proud of you."

"What do you mean the world's greatest athlete, Vince?" I asked. "Bill's not a football player."

"Football player? What the hell's a football player. This man did it in ten events. In two days. A football player plays once a week." There was no stopping Vince.

And for Toomey, who never played football but knew the Lombardi legend, it was an exultant moment.

I have mentioned Lombardi's loyalty to friends. Nobody was closer to him than the Mara family. The Maras had started him in professional football. Once he went to Green Bay he would never return to football in New York unless it were for the Maras. I know. Sonny Werblin, when he was still running the Jets, asked me to call Vince and see if he was interested in coaching the Jets. A ownership percentage was also involved. Much as Marie wanted to come back to New York, and maybe Vince, too, Vince simply said no. He would never come back to New York in competition with the Mara family. The Maras had gone to Fordham, and they had been lifelong friends. One had to wonder why the Maras never asked Vince back to New York to coach the Giants. According to Marie Lombardi they did, shortly after Vince had gone to Green Bay, but, again according to Marie, Vince was too early in his commitment to Green Bay to leave.

In the beginning Lombardi never gave any thought to becoming a football coach. He wavered between law and accounting and wound up in law school. But he decided law was not for him and quit law school. He didn't let his father know until he had a job, and he grabbed the first job he could get—teaching at Saint Cecelia's High School in Englewood, New Jersey. The football coach at Saint Cecelia's was an old friend, Andy Palau, who had quarterbacked the Fordham team with the Seven Blocks of Granite. One night there was a knock on the door of the Lombardi apartment. It was Palau. He had been having a romance with a girl from North Carolina, and the love affair was in danger of busting up. Palau told Vince, "I'm going to North Carolina. Here's a bottle of gin to celebrate. You're the new coach at Saint Cecelia's." With that he shoved the bottle of gin into Vince's hand and left. And so Vince's coaching career began, and that's how he got the bug.

Years later Vince would remember that. He would

remember how when he was courting Marie they would sit on a park bench and talk for hours about the future, and never once was coaching discussed. He would remember those things when he stepped down as the head coach of the Green Bay Packers.

It was no surprise when Lombardi quit as Packer coach. More surprising was the fact that his sensitivity to sportswriters was one of the factors that caused him to quit. This man, who was supposed to be so tough, really was vulnerable to the adverse things written about him. This was particularly true of a piece in *Esquire* magazine written by Leonard Shecter. One again, I know, because Vince spoke to me on the phone about it. It upset him terribly for two reasons. The first was that he didn't believe the piece was accurate and he felt it was maliciously inspired. Second, his mother had read the piece and had called him in an emotional state saying, "This is not my son, this is not my son. What are they doing to you?" It was during the phone conversation with me that Lombardi told me he had had about enough, that he didn't want to go through this kind of thing anymore.

In the Shecter piece there was an implication, at the very least, that if you crossed yourself you made the team. There was also a story of how Vince abused Marie in front of a thousand people at the practice field. Here is Marie's recital of what actually happened and what appeared in *Esquire:*

I rode up to the field and I parked my car in back of Vin's, and there used to be quite a crowd that would come up there and watch the practice. Now the crowd had left, and Vin came charging across the field. He said, "Get the car out of the way. I have to go to a meeting." I said, "O.K. Don't get excited." I was in a Thunderbird, and they die if you gun them. I gunned the car and it died, it stopped. He didn't see that and he thought I went and he moved his car and he bumped into me. Well now he's livid; he's furious. So I slowly got out of

the car and I went over to him and I said, "Do
you see what you did to my car?" I said, "Are you
insured?" By this time he's laughing, the cop standing there is laughing, there were a few coaches there,
they were laughing, we were all laughing. Now
Leonard Shecter wrote in that piece that he abused
me in front of a thousand people, and that was the
incident. It was a very funny incident.

As one who has had his share of vilification from
certain sportswriters and knows very well how it can get
under one's skin, I still have never really understood
Vince's susceptibility to them. I know how it hurts when
you feel that something written about you is untrue.
I know how it hurts when you compare your own background, your own qualifications, your own experience
and your own character against the writer's version of
it, and you think to yourself, this is unfair, it is wrong.
But then you think: How can you reach the people the
writer reaches without lowering yourself and at the
same time helping him by merely acknowledging him?
I know all about that. But Vince had a place in the
society given to few—especially to one in sports—and,
in retrospect, it seems absurd that he let them reach him
so, even if he never did show it publicly.

It would be equally absurd to conclude that Vince
stepped down as coach only because of the writers, and
in particular because of Shecter's piece. He was tired.
He had worked relentlessly. He wanted to play golf, to
stop driving himself. Still, five minutes after he announced
his retirement he knew he had made a terrible mistake.
He wondered almost instantly what he was going to do
with himself, how he could stay away from the field,
how he could get along without his players. That's what
Lombardi's life was truly all about, how he felt about
his players, how they felt about him.

During the year he was general manager but not coach
of the Pack, his whole personality changed. Marie told
me he was miserable. He would watch the team work
out from an office window and he would be engulfed

by a desire to go down there, to say things, to do things. The Pack was dying without him, but there was nothing he could do. There was no way he could intrude upon his old and faithful assistant, Phil Bengtson, who was now the head coach. When the field was empty he would sometimes go down, walk around it, touch the goalposts. You could almost see his mind at work. Why did I do it? Why did I quit? It was a year of sadness, a year of torment for a still dynamic man who suddenly found himself bereft of everything he wanted, everything he lived for.

At the end of the year he got offers. While in Miami for the Jets-Colts Super Bowl game, I was with him at the Kenilworth Hotel when Bill Sullivan, president of the New England Patriots, arrived. He was meeting with Vince to make a tremendous offer to get Vince to take over the Patriots—again, not just a salary offer, but a partial ownership offer. Vince turned him down. Then came the offer from the Washington Redskins. By this time Vince knew he had to get back on the field, had to work with the young ones, had to live by those damned yard markers and yard lines. Washington appealed to him. The national capital. Close to New York. The people in Green Bay were wonderful, but Marie had never found the climate tolerable. Washington had years of gridiron futility behind it. It seemed a whole new challenge, a whole new stimulus. He couldn't go back— or so he thought—to Lambeau Field and oust his former aide, Phil Bengtson. He still had a contract with the Packers though. What about that? Well, through the years he had resisted other offers, kept his loyalty to Green Bay, and what a job he had done for them. The Pack was the most glamorous team in football, Green Bay was the football capital of the nation—indeed, not just Green Bay, but Superior, Racine, Ashland, Sheboygan, Madison, Milwaukee, the whole state. Lombardi had fulfilled his mission, had paid his debt and then some. He spoke to the Packer president, Dominic Olejniczak, and to the board members. He got released from his contract and went with Washington. He had a chance to live again.

And then he got it. He got it from a whole group of writers, the very men he was so sensitive to. Lombardi, the man of principle, had a double standard, they wrote. One for players, another for himself: Players should be bound to contracts, but not coaches. Was that Lombardi's philosophy? He had no right to leave the Pack. Vince grew sick over this, literally sick. In his mind he could not have acted more honorably. But he had to take the punishment. He faced up to it. By the time he began working with the Redskins at Dickinson College in Carlisle, Pennsylvania, he almost had it beat—almost. He would never completely defeat it despite the tough exterior, not with that soft Italian sentimentality.

When Vince started training camp with the Redskins I was there, along with my crew. He was a man reborn, perhaps more joyous than I had ever seen him. As always he was all over the practice field, yelling here, cajoling there. When I interviewed him his manner could not have been more hearty. Did he realize, I asked him, what he had to live up to in terms of the record he had created? "Yes," he answered, "but I'm too young to be a legend, and I never was one really." The conversation moved along, covering the new team he had taken over. I asked him about tight end Pat Richter's broken nose. He became Lombardi, vintage '66, put back his head, and roared, "It's nothing at all, Howard. I broke my nose seventeen times when I was playing."

Later, when I spoke with Richter, Richter told me, "The coach is right, it's nothing. What matters is, he makes us all feel like men."

It made me think of Henry Jordan's classic remark when we did "Run to Daylight." That's when Henry told us, "Coach Lombardi treats us all the same, like dogs." That was a great line by Henry, but it was uttered in jest. Lombardi treated 40 men 40 different ways. He would chew Hornung out. But he would baby Bart Starr. He knew the differences in the makeup of people.

He had something else: a sense of proportion, a sure

instinct for the things that mattered. He preached discipline and lived by it. But some things were more important than rules. Quality for instance.

He watched approvingly as the Redskins reported to him for the first time in training camp. Sonny Jurgensen came in. Charley Taylor arrived. And then a car pulled up and out jumped a mod kid with hair down to his shoulders and a guitar under his arm. Lombardi looked at him with suspicion and spat out to his assistant, "Who the hell is *that?*" The assistant said, "That's Jerry Smith, the tight end."

Lombardi, who had been studying Redskins' game films all winter and spring, nodded. "He can play. Let him keep the hair and guitar."

That was typical of Vince. So was the sequel. Later, as he attempted to motivate Smith on the practice field, he screamed at him: "Smith, you're out of shape. You need to lose weight. [Pause] Why don't you cut off some of that hair?" (Jerry, in point of fact, may be the lightest tight end in the NFL.)

During that interview at Carlisle, the pride in Lombardi was busting out all over. Sam Huff had come out of retirement to play for him. Vince remembered Sam. Sam, along with the old Giants kicker Don Chandler, had left the Giants camp when they were rookies. He and Don thought they couldn't make it. The man who caught up with them, stopped them before they left town and brought them back was a fellow named Lombardi.

One other thing sparked Lombardi in that interview. "Don't forget, Howard, I've got the quarterback. A real, first-class, National Football League quarterback." And with that his eyes wandered over to where Sonny Jurgensen was hunched over the center, eyes scanning the defense, barking the signals, backpedaling and releasing the football. This would be different for Vince from Green Bay. With the Pack he had to take an unknown youngster, seventeenth-round draft choice from Alabama, and mold him, patiently, tirelessly, into the Bart Starr who will be a Hall of Famer. But Jurgensen came packaged, ready-made.

Finally, the key question. What about the newsmen, some of whom were already firing the old darts at him. For the first and only time Lombardi made a public admission about them. "I know what they're writing," he said, "and I know it's not true. You know, as well as anyone, that what they used to write was one of the reasons I retired from coaching at Green Bay. But that won't happen again. I'm back where I belong, and as far as I'm concerned, they'll never get to me again. If you really want to find out, ask my players about me."

I did. It was like Green Bay all over again. Jurgensen, Charley Taylor, Bobby Mitchell—trying to hang on—one after another, including Tom Brown, the old safety whom I had seen report to Green Bay as a rookie. However trite it may sound, Lombardi produced more than allegiance in his players. Somehow he produced love. Once when he spoke of his Packers he said, "There is love on this team." It was the truth.

Lombardi was color-blind. From the beginning, with the Pack, black lived with white. Nobody ever wrote about it, talked about it. It was routine. Jerry Kramer and Willie Davis began it as roommates.

Lombardi's first year with Washington was successful. The Redskins finished above 500 in the won-and-lost percentages for the first time in years. The second season would be even better; the foundation had been laid. But for Vince it never came. Something else did. Cancer. Increasingly he had been having those pains. Then loss of weight, almost imperceptible. Marie never knew how sick he felt. He kept it from her. Then, finally, to the hospital. And three days later she knew. There was no hope. He had the surgery and came out of the hospital. It was hard to look at him. His players knew. The NFL players were on strike then, but the Redskins were practicing on their own, at a local Washington field. Vince struggled out to look at them. Pat Richter told me, "We looked over at him on the sideline. We tried to work the way he wanted us to work. When he left we stopped and cried."

The last game he saw, and he never should have gone,

was between the Redskins and Colts rookies. He almost passed out going up the steps of the stands. He went back to the hospital, and Marie told me that no man should have to suffer the way he suffered. He would prepare himself for visits, because the way he was, he had to prepare. He didn't want his players to see him cry. But he did. He couldn't help it. You don't always measure a man's strength by the toughness of his talk. Sometimes you can measure it in tears. Paul Hornung would visit Vince and then go to a local pub to drink it off. "I can't stand seeing what's happening to him," he said. And off he would go in tears.

They had the funeral services at Saint Patrick's on Labor Day 1970. There was a black player sitting in the row in front of Emmy and me. He had his head in his hands and was trying to cover his eyes. He lost his battle with himself. The tears poured out. Emmy asked me his name. I told her it was Larry Brown. Larry Brown. An eighth-round draft choice from Kansas State. Nobody ever heard of him. Lombardi found him at the Redskins camp. Looked at him closely. Thought he had ability. But something was wrong, Lombardi found out. He was hard of hearing, couldn't catch the signals quickly enough. So a hearing aid was installed in his helmet. There is no finer running back in football than Larry Brown now. And Brown will ever forget Vince Lombardi.

I got a call in April of this year in my office. It was from Larry Brown. I was surprised. I knew him only superficially. He asked if he could see me, said he had some personal problems he wanted to discuss with me. I said sure, come on up to New York. But why me? Lombardi, that's why. He trusts me because Vince did.

The funeral services ended, and the overflow crowd dispersed. I went to have coffee with Emmy. Not a word between us. My thoughts went back to the previous Friday night. Vince had died, and I had to put on a memorial special on his life. It was like the Jackie Robinson show. Scenes from "Run to Daylight" and from Carlisle,

Pennsylvania. Statements from his great stars at Green Bay.

Paul Hornung said: "He saved my life."

Jerry Kramer said: "He was one beautiful man."

Willie Davis said: "He was all the man there is."

Bart Starr said: "He meant everything to me."

I thought about these young men and about Vince. About how they had grown because of him. About what has happened to so many of the Packers who played for him. As a group they are the most successful alumni I have ever known in sports. Willie Davis runs a vastly successful beer distributorship in Los Angeles. Jerry Kramer is a multifaceted businessman and probably a millionaire. Paul Hornung is another widely diversified businessman. Jimmy Taylor is prosperous in Louisiana. Henry Jordan is the recreation head in Milwaukee. Bart Starr has a pair of automobile distributorships (and could have been a head coach in the National Football League had he wanted to). Fuzzy Thurston and Max McGee own a chain of thriving restaurants in Wisconsin.

What Lombardi taught them about life—not about football but about life—how he helped to mold them, has to be part of the reason.

I thought about Lombardi. About how in his later years he tried to relate his whole philosophy about football to the full sweep of the society itself. About how he came to understand that even for him football was not everything. About how overjoyed he was when for the first time the American Management Association asked him to address them. ("Maybe I'm not just an Xs and Os guy," he said.) About how much he wanted to do that kind of thing, to reach more and more people and to evidence the simple fact that he was a whole man, educated, sensitive and caring.

Like Jackie Robinson he died before his time. But he went knowing that he had become more, much more, than a football coach; that in his latter years government had sought him out, and industry, and educators; that he had proved, in a strange way, that some of the old virtues are infinite—like honesty, hard work and loyalty;

and that his fundamental credo was correct: "Individual commitment to a group effort, gentlemen, that's what makes a team work, a company work, a society work, a civilization work."

And he went knowing that a lot of us loved him.

Ask his players.

Chapter VI

THE UNMAKING OF
A BROOKLYN LAWYER

---

*"Please, dear, have him go back
to the profession."*

Arrogant, pompous, obnoxious, vain, cruel, persecuting, distasteful verbose, a show-off. I have been called all of these. Of course, I am.

I think it's hard for any man, introspectively, to dissect himself. I suppose Robert Burns put it better than anybody when he wrote::

> Would'st some power the giftie to gi' us
> to see ourselves as others see us.

I am asked about my drive. I do work very hard. I always have and I always will. A couple of days off for me is like poison. I go stir crazy. Surely a lot of my drive stems from the way I grew up—in Brooklyn, during the Depression, Jewish, fighting a group of Studs Lonigans and running away from them, to get to school safely; to get home safely. That was part of life then.

It was the age of Hitler, and that hovered over anyone who was Jewish. And times were difficult for my dad. I remember the electricity being turned off in our house for nonpayment of rent and my dad fighting with the janitor to try and get it turned back on.

And so I guess that growing up this way, with all

of the insecurities attendant to it, you develop a drive
or you simply cease to exist. I think your basic instinct
is for financial and emotional security. That is your quest.
You don't *ever* want to have happen to you what you
have seen happening in your home.

I remember my dad going to the bank every three
months to renew the loan that sent me through college
and law school. Indeed, that's why I majored in law even
though I never wanted to be an attorney. I owed it to my
dad, because of everything he had done for me.

My father, Isadore Cohen, was two years old when his
parents emigrated to the United States. They were flee-
ing the pogroms of Poland and Europe. My dad traveled
most of his life, as an accountant for a credit clothing
chain. They were living in Winston-Salem, North Carolina, when I was born on March 25, 1920. It is a
piece of biographical data I now find curious; no one
thinks of me as a southerner. We were in Raleigh briefly,
then moved, before my third birthday, to Brooklyn. We—
my brother Hilton and I—were raised basically by my
mother; dad was always on the road. My mother made
sacrifice after sacrifice, and it told upon her health.

I am a hypochondriac today, no doubt, because my
mother, for as long as I can remember, was either sick,
on the verge of being sick or thinking about being sick.
My brother contracted tuberculosis at a time when it
was a dreaded thing. We didn't know if he would recover. Hilton, four years older than I, spent endless
months flat on his back. He never went to a sanatorium.
He got up only to go to the doctor to take a pneumo-
thorax treatment (a procedure in which the infected lung
is collapsed, then, gradually, the lung is allowed to come
back). It took years, but today he's fine.

And that was the atmosphere in which I grew. I became determined to succeed in the material sense. Later
I realized that material success is only one kind of success—the American kind, I hate to say. But if you have
a mind and an education, some degree of culture, of
literacy, of sensitivity, you discover early on that money
is not the answer. You discover early on that there is

a great deal more that you want out of life. You discover that life is in your home, your family. And that's where I've been successful.

My marriage to Mary Edith (Emmy) Abrams was undertaken under adverse circumstances, she being Protestant, the daughter of a very well-known industrialist who wound up in the Eisenhower administration, and I being Jewish, though not formally reared as such, not even Bar Mitzvahed. But my folks recoiled at the thought of their son marrying a *shikse*.

So it wasn't easy. For two years my wife and her father did not speak. Her mother sneaked into Brooklyn to visit us. And suddenly, for the first time in her life really, Emmy came upon prejudice and rejected it. All of which probably bound us more tightly together in the very beginning. There had been unhappiness in my home. My mother and dad didn't have the best marriage in the world. Not the worst, either, for when people suffer together something does develop between them, and there was a bond, a reliance. I wanted desperately for my own marriage to work. Fortunately I found the right girl.

In this day and age this kind of talk can sound maudlin. I'm aware of that. But Emmy's my life. She has been for 29 years. I go nowhere without her. I wouldn't do "Monday Night Football," I wouldn't travel, I wouldn't cross the Triboro Bridge without Emmy. We've been very fortunate in our two daughters, Jill and Hilary. Jill is married to a fine young man, Peter Cohane, the son of Tim Cohane the writer. They have two lovely sons—our Justin and Jared. And Hilary is a very much with-it girl, very liberal, a highly intellectual young woman. She does her thing. We know she's an independent but family-oriented girl. So we're lucky.

This may sound like the scenario for one of those World War II movies they turned out like sausages in the early Forties, starring June Allyson (whom Emmy resembles). It so happens that we met—and courted— in the Army. Together.

I had enlisted as a private. In two and a half years I was promoted to major, one of the youngest in the

Army Service Forces in World War II. In fact, my initial recommendation for promotion to the field-grade rank of major was balked by the War Department on the grounds that I was being advanced too rapidly, for my age. Air Force officers could become majors, or higher, when very young. (The standing gag: "Twenty-two, and *only* a major.") But I wasn't flying a plane. That objection was surmounted, and I got promoted.

I enlisted in the Army a few months after Pearl Harbor. I was assigned, by God, to Brooklyn. I commuted every morning on the Sea-Beach Express; I was a Sea-Beach commando. Within a few short months I went from private to technical sergeant and applied for Officer Candidate School. My parents were beside themselves. They thought it was an invitation to death. But I wanted out of Brooklyn, I wanted more from my military experience. And the neighbors were complaining; their sons were going off to Europe and the Far East. They felt it was all political, that my family had fixed somebody. At any rate, it was a bad scene.

So I went to OCS, to the Transportation Corps School at Mississippi State. I got down there in time to see Chuck Conerly and Ole Miss beat State College. I finished OCS, and, I'll be damned, they sent me back to the Brooklyn docks, to the New York Port of Embarkation. I never left there the entire war except for the three months I spent at Mississippi State.

I well remember how the Minsky widow (her husband had been the burlesque king) couldn't stand the sight of me coming home every day, first with a gold bar, now with a silver, now two silver bars, now a gold leaf. I could understand this. She had a son serving in the Marines on Guadalcanal.

The New York Port of Embarkation was the largest stateside command post in the Army. It had five terminals, five staging areas and three ammunition backup points. I was in charge of all manpower, including a pool of 50,000 civilians. I was 24.

Emmy came into the Port with the first contingent of WACs. She was assigned as a secretary to a major

named Bob Lewiston, and I'll never forget the first day
I saw her. I was walking past Bob's office and I saw this
cute, pudgy blonde. I did a double take, an about-face,
and went in, presumably to engage in some badinage with
Lewiston, but all the while I was looking at her and
putting on a show in my own way, playing the big man.
I saw a twinkle in her eye and for weeks I wanted to
date her. I knew she was interested.

Finally I went to the commanding general and got
written permission to date her. We began to see each
other, and I knew I was in love with her. She wrote
a "Dear John" letter to the Kentucky squire she had been
engaged to, and we got married. Her parents were at the
wedding; they were shocked, as were mine. We were married by a judge, in chambers, and moved immediately
into a studio apartment in Brooklyn Heights. It was
charming and overlooked the harbor. We ignored the
constant threat of mice and roaches.

All too soon Emmy had a clash with her dad. You
see, Norman Ross Abrams was an Old World Republican. He believed that everybody in America could begin at the bottom and work his way to the top. That's
what *he* did. He left World War I as a lieutenant and
then was a laborer. He labored in a Congoleum-Nairn
plant and finally became its foreman. Then they moved
him up to the general headquarters at Kearny, New
Jersey, and ultimately, he was the company's executive
vice-president.

He left to join the Eisenhower administration. He
was a deputy postmaster general under Arthur Sum-
merfield and, in effect, ran the postal reform. The
Abramses were a distinguished family, a mixture of
Pennsylvania Dutch and Welsh, whose men won fame
in industry. Emmy's cousin Frank was chairman of the
board of Standard Oil in New Jersey. And Norman's
brother James—they're both dead now—was a bigshot
at Weston Precision Instruments.

In the beginning Norman just didn't want me in the
family. He was respectful of my Army accomplishments,
I think. He was proud of his own Army career and had,

in fact, persuaded Emmy to join on the grounds of patriotism. But when I left the Army and no longer had the rank, he became coldly indifferent. Emmy quarreled with him. Nasty things were said, and they went two years without talking.

It was very difficult for Emmy, because her father had exercised a great influence on her. He was handsome, a fine golfer and tennis player and, within *his* frame of reference, devoted to her—a hard daddy to reject.

The war ended. The guns grew quiet. The troops came home. And I thought the world was waiting for me to come out of the Army, that I would immediately become the biggest man in industry, or in labor relations. I got the shock of my life. They didn't credit my military experience as being worth a tinker's damn. I had juggled a working force of 65,000—civilian and military. I had negotiated with the International Longshoremen's Association. But it wasn't industry. And I had nowhere to turn. I had Emmy and a baby daughter, Jill. And I had a law degree. So, with the encouragement of Emmy, I opened my own law office—up the establishment!

We went heavily into debt. It has long since been paid back, every cent, but we struggled. I was a lawyer, living and working within a few miles, a few minutes, of the neighborhood where I had spent most of my years. Was this all there is?

The day after I got out of the Army I arranged to meet a fraternity brother from my college days at NYU. His name was Stanley Kramer, like me fresh out of the service, destined for a brilliant career as a motion-picture producer. We spent a weekend in Philadelphia, one night watching Ray Bolger in *Three to Make Ready,* when he introduced the old soft-shoe routine; the next night watching NYU beat Temple at Convention Hall, in what was then the big challenge for both teams. We were rabid NYU fans.

We were at dinner that first night when Stanley announced, "I'm gonna make movies. I can make them cheaper and better than anybody in Hollywood." Kramer was already thinking ahead. "What do you think I ought to do?" he asked. "Arthur Laurents' *Home of the Brave,* or *Focus* by Arthur Miller?"

Automatically I said, *"Focus,"* which had an anti-Jew theme.

Stanley shook his head. "No way," he said. "They've already made *Gentleman's Agreement.* I'm gonna make *Home of the Brave,* but I'll make the Jewish boy black and I'm gonna deal with the great problem of America to come. The black problem." And that's what he did.

I grew up on *Studs Lonigan* by James T. Farrell. It was light reading—until the age of Hitler. And then, *then* you began to take it seriously. As young as you were you knew, by God, that you were Jewish, and you knew every restrictive boundary and every thoughtless slight.

It was a different kind of time. It was a different age, an unsophisticated age, a wrong age. All that was wrong seemed to be exposed by the Wall Street crash and the subsequent destruction of the American economy. Only then did the real and overpowering problems begin. And they have lived with us ever since.

Sports was the one luxury you had. I attended PS 9 in Brooklyn, the most important grade school in New York, the perennial track-and-field champion. It was at Vanderbilt Avenue and Sterling Place, 15 blocks from Ebbets Field. School was dismissed at 3:00 P.M. The Dodger games began at 3:15. I'd run the 15 blocks, lie flat on my stomach on Bedford Avenue, peek under the center-field fence and watch my hero, Johnny Frederick, who set the team's pinch-hit record.

They didn't have numbers on their backs then, but you *knew* your ballplayers. It was as Roger Kahn wrote so gracefully in *The Boys of Summer.* I lived on Eastern Parkway and I'd hear the roar of the crowd and I would shout to my brother, "God, Hilton, Camilli has done it again." And you knew, you just knew by a certain kind of roar, that it was Dolph Camilli who had hit the homer.

And, of course, it was the age of Red Barber.

I grew up with all that, together with the Catholic

kids from Saint Theresa's parish. Running from them, hiding from them; they were always after the little sheenie. Years later Emmy and I found ourselves in a restaurant on Franklin Avenue in Brooklyn. I was now a major, and there at another table was the very kid who had been at me again and again and again, in that same restaurant, in a private's uniform.

And you know what? I began to sweat with fear because I didn't want to make a scene while I was wearing the uniform of a field-grade officer. And then the fear turned around. Maybe he's still going to come at me and he's only a private. Then what do I do? Because now I was a grown man and I was six-one and a half, and do you know how big he was? Five-seven. He was a runt, a midget. I could have killed him. But it all ran through me, the whole background, all of it, sitting in that restaurant in Brooklyn. I won't ever forget it.

The "Jewish Problem" was the major social trauma in this country up to and through World War II. And then it was supplanted by the "Black Problem," as Stanley Kramer so astutely foresaw. I thought back often to that conversation with Stanley in Philadelphia as through the years I watched his talent ripen, saw his reputation established with *Home of the Brave* and, later, with *Champion*, starring Kirk Douglas. (Ever since Kirk made that movie he thinks he knows more about boxing than anyone in the world.) And then Stanley brought Marlon Brando to Hollywood and made *The Men*.

But what of my own career? The future seemed to offer little excitement. I was in law, in debt and in the home of my parents. Living with them was a disaster, but apartments were scarce and beyond our budget.

Those were difficult times. Finally Emmy did make up with her parents, and ironically I became a major factor in my father-in-law's life.

He had always been a sports buff. After he became important in industry he almost bought a piece of the Philadelphia Athletics. He was friendly with Connie Mack. He had been a semipro pitcher, and in him was the kind of willful spirit you read about in children's sports books. He forced my brother-in-law to become a southpaw—he had hopes for him as a pitcher—and ultimately the kid rebelled against his father.

But after he retired from public life Norman bought a home in Fort Myers, Florida, where the Pittsburgh Pirates trained. The team was managed by Bobby Bragan, with whom I have enjoyed a special kind of friendship. Danny Murtaugh was one of his coaches, and Danny had broken into baseball through the efforts of my father-in-law. Danny wanted to play in the Pennsylvania Industrial League, the same league that had spawned Mickey Vernon, another of Norman's protégés. He went to Norman for a job. Norman helped him get one with Sun Oil, and Murtaugh was on his way.

So in the spring, when my Florida rounds would take me into Fort Myers, I would bring them over to see him, Bragan and Murtaugh and the Pirates. He was in sportsman's heaven, now that I was a broadcaster and nationally known. When he died in 1969 I had become very important to him. It was a total about-face.

But my own father never recovered from his disappointment at my decision to abandon the law. I was just beginning to get somewhere as an attorney, just coming into money, when suddenly came this freakish radio opportunity.

A radio career had been on my mind the moment I got out of the Army. Emmy and some friends went with me to WOR for an audition, and shared my hurt at being told there was *no* way; I didn't have an announcer's voice. I could understand that, with the nasal twang, the Brooklyn nasal twang. So I gave up any idea of it.

Now I was making nearly $30,000 as year as an attorney, when that was a helluva lot of money, what with different tax rates and almost no inflation compared to what we have now. And of course my income was growing every year.

So what did I do? I accepted a network offer from ABC Radio to do ten five-minute sports shows a weekend for $25 a show. Less than scale. It began, in the most curious way, with a Little League panel show that

I had moderated without pay. (I had drawn a charter for Little League baseball in New York, and ABC asked me to furnish the kids to interview athletes.) Even with that show we made news.

When ABC offered me a six-week deal—by God, what security, six weeks!—I told Emmy I wanted to give up my law practice and go into broadcasting. Me, the one without the voice, who had already been told he couldn't make it. Emmy, ignoring the fact I was finally providing a decent living, told me to go ahead. As always, she was stalwart.

My father was horrified. Right down to the day he died, in 1957, he would say to Emmy, "Please, dear, have him go back to the profession." It meant so much to him for his son to be a professional man, a lawyer.

But I was infected with my desire, my resolve, to make it in broadcasting. I knew exactly what I wanted to do, and how. Not having a name or a reputation, I knew that I had to have the biggest names I could get. I needed name value. I intended to bring to radio the actuality of sport—people in the news, as they were making it, explaining it. My first weekend I had Eddie Arcaro; it was the weekend of Nashua's last ride. Phil Rizzuto had quit baseball—no, Stengel had fired him— and I interviewed Rizzuto. I was probably the first reporter to carry his own tape recorder everywhere he went. The damned thing weighed 30 pounds and I wore it on my back. I must have looked like Edmund Hillary carrying his knapsack.

There were frequent days, in those years, when I would begin in the early morning with a fighter at his training camp—a Floyd Patterson—then hurry out to the racetrack to catch an Arcaro, and then wind up at Ebbets Field. Or the Polo Grounds.

I'd go to spring training and cover every camp in Florida in five days, still lugging that tape recorder. Some of the local announcers laughed at me. But not the professionals. I learned quickly that they respected a man who worked. "You're like shit," Ralph Houk told me, "you're everywhere." That line, I can say with certain mixed feelings, has survived to this day.

That tape recorder became my trademark. Keep in mind that the compact models so popular today were not then available. My first recorder was a Magnemite, a brute of a thing. I replaced it with a Nagra, one of the first made, another heavyweight. I paid $480 for it out of my own pocket, and it went with me to virtually every dugout, clubhouse and racetrack in America.

I was putting into practice my theory of what the sporting public wanted to hear. That was the era of the rip-and-reader—the sportscaster who would tear copy off the wire machine and read it verbatim:

For the Dodgers: six runs, twelve hits, no errors.
For the Braves: five runs, ten hits, and one error.
The winning pitcher: Clem Labine, who came on in the eighth in relief of Don Newcombe.

That was their idea of a sportscast. Not mine. I had my own notion about the business. I felt that the field was wide open for anyone willing to develop the sources and get to the scene. I wanted to bring to sports broadcasting the idea of developing a story in depth; I wanted to explore the issues. The world of sports was about to explode in America. Great changes in technology were coming; an increase of leisure time; the exodus to the suburbs to escape from the great cities. The whole pattern of society was changing, and sports would become ever more important. The influx of black athletes had begun. A whole new set of smoldering problems would emerge. Could we keep giving the country line scores as news?

There was nothing being done in depth, a total absence of commentary and little in the way of actuality. I had the background for it. First, the legal training, which gives a man the ability to interrogate, to bring out things in an orderly manner. One develops an orderly mind when one studies law. I had another advantage— a basic feel for language. In high school, at NYU and

on the NYU Law Review, I honed my reportorial instincts. At Alexander Hamilton High, in Brooklyn, as
sports editor of *The Ledger,* I wrote a column called
"Speaking of Sports"—an augury of things to come.
I quickly developed a technique that enabled me to interview in such a way that even years later I could go back
to a tape and pull out a part of the interview and apply
it to another show. The abstract interview, replete with
provocative questions concerning human personality, produces answers that are timeless. Good yesterday, good
today, good next year, good forever.

When I came into the business, one of the people I
admired was the writer Walter "Red" Smith. I got to
know him, and he gave me two words of advice: "Be
there." Ralph Houk's line in Florida indicated that I
was trying.

I made it a point to be there. I established friendships
and connections that became news sources, without which
a reporter is useless.

The first network interview Jimmy Brown ever did
was with me. And Paul Hornung. And Alex Karras. In
1955 Karras was a big, heavy, pudding-faced kid out
of Iowa visiting New York as a member of *Look* magazine's All America team. Nobody suspected that he had
comic potential. He told me, with honestly moist eyes,
the story of how he had quit school and returned to
his home in Gary, Indiana. He was too fat and too slow
and they had booted him off the Iowa team. His mother
threw him out of the house. "You go back there and be
a man," she ordered. "You get that weight off and you
play football."

It was one hell of an interview. Alex hasn't forgotten
it either. Today he's a smart-assed broadcaster and
movie star. Alex has come a long way from the fat kid
who was afraid of his mother.

By 1958 we had moved to Pound Ridge, and almost
every morning I drove into the city with Giant defensive
end and defensive Captain Andy Robustelli, a neighbor
in North Stamford and the newly appointed Director of
Operations of the Giants. We didn't drive in alone; we

were joined often by another fellow then with the Giants, a defensive coach named Tom Landry. He had created something called the 4–3 defense. We would talk about it driving in, about how Tom had the front four blocking to the outside, giving the rookie middle linebacker a clear shot at the ball carrier. The rookie linebacker was Sam Huff, and that maneuver made Huff famous out of proportion to his ability. Sam was a fine player, but, in truth, Landry's defense allowed him to make the tackles while the others were doing their job.

I once did a radio show in which I explained exactly that point. Sam heard it, and he didn't resent it; he respected it. That's one lesson I've learned in sports. Some want only to hear the good things. But the real men, the people who matter, accept the truth.

It can be a severe problem for the reporter, trying to deal objectively with the people he likes, is close to and involved with. I think I whipped it just by a mutuality of respect. In nearly all of my relationships, the connections you need to be a good reporter, they understood right on top that I was the kind of a guy who was going to speak out.

I am, of course, an incurable needler. And one's reputation does get around. In 1969 I was in the home of Don Klosterman, then the general manager of the Houston Oilers, after his team had lost to Oakland, 17–13, in the season opener. Al Davis called, a nice gesture, just wanting Don not to feel badly about the loss. He told Don that they—the Raiders—were lucky to win. Klosterman signaled for me to pick up the extension. That really isn't polite, but in this era of the wire-tap it seems permissible among friends. I heard Klosterman say: "Well, that isn't what Cosell said. He said you should have won by twenty points or more, that you've got the best personnel in football."

Davis exploded. "So what the hell does Cosell know? Who gives a damn what he thinks!"

I cut in. "Davis—"

"Who's that?" he said. "Who the hell is that?"

"Davis," I said, in measured tones, "this is Cosell."

"Howard—what the hell are you doing there?"

"I'm telling Klosterman how he lucked out only losing by four points to you."

"Are you still giving me that crap? Why, we're nothing. We—by the way, I didn't mean what I said to Klosterman. You know that, Howard. You know that. I'll admit it. Hell, we didn't play up to standard."

Early on, as I broke into local television, I did half-hour specials with Wilt Chamberlain, Lombardi, Brown, Houk, Pancho Gonzales, Julie Boros, Tony Lema. They were kind and cooperative, and each, in his way, became important to me. I came to admire a man like Del Crandall, the catcher who had good seasons with the Braves. He had retarded children, and his life was a study in strength and love.

You make news contacts by being on the beat, by meeting people in their very beginnings, taking an interest, showing them you care, being willing to listen to their problems and never, not ever, forsaking their trust. You can't replace integrity.

In 1965 I found myself in the dressing room of the Washington Senators, talking to their manager, Gil Hodges. I was fed up with the Mets, as many were, as more should have been. "Gil," I said, "the situation in New York isn't right. You should be managing the Mets."

He said, "Howard, I'd love to."

That was all I needed to hear. When I got back to New York I called Bing Devine. I knew the Mets were planning to make a move soon on Wes Westrum, who had succeeded Stengel. I told Devine of my dialogue with Hodges. "I would love to have him," said Bing, who in his brief tenure did as much as anyone to rebuild the Mets. It was under Devine that they brought in their young pitchers, including Tom Seaver.

Devine called me some weeks later. "Tell your friend," he said, "we want him. Tell him he's got to make the move to call us."

I phoned Gil. "Gil," I said, "you can have the job. All you've got to do is pick up the telephone."

"I can't call him. I won't call him. I can't ethically do that. Bing knows better. They'll have to go to my employers because I'm not gonna do that to them."

The net result was that Bing Devine went to the Washington management, and within days Gil Hodges was manager of the Mets. I had little or nothing to do with his getting a job for which he was so perfectly aimed. But the point is, there was trust. And sometimes, given that trust, you can help the news along.

And so it began by seeking out the story, by interviewing the people involved in making things happen. I still have those early tapes, as part of a personal tape library that numbers in the thousands.

The people at ABC liked what I was doing. It was the first time they had ever gotten personal, incisive actualities on the radio in sports. Now it's the accustomed thing. And now, of course I've moved more into the field of commentary.

Still, I was terribly insecure in those early years. Don Durgin, now a top executive at NBC Television, ran ABC Radio at the time and he was convinced that I was a poor risk. He went along with me only because of a man named Ray Diaz, the program head for the radio network. Durgin was convinced that I couldn't make it because of what he considered the nasal abrasiveness of my voice. But I believed in the content of what I was doing, and slowly I saw that I was having an impact. I learned, not by accident, how to use my voice, as an actor does, with variety of tone and mood.

We were living now in Peter Cooper Village, along with a rather creative group of young Army veterans. The group included John Forsythe, Karl Malden and Tony Randall. We were all friendly, all sports fans. I'd take them to some of the events I covered. It was a good place to live and dream. Down the street a young lawyer named John Lindsay lived at Stuyvesant Town, a less expensive apartment complex.

Karl Malden was already a superb actor, appearing in

The Desperate Hours and in *Streetcar Named Desire*. John Forsythe, who had grown up with me in Eastern Parkway in Brooklyn and had been for a time the public-address announcer at Ebbets Field, was beginning to make it. He was starring in *Teahouse of the August Moon*. I watched John take lessons to develop voice variety, because in those days everyone casted him as a lower-case Henry Fonda. He had no identity of his own. By osmosis I learned something about the use of the voice: the gradations of the decibels, when to speak loudly, when to cut back.

So I lost some of my insecurity, and my career began to proceed apace. But, of course, I do not now—and never will—feel totally secure. Nothing in my life has conditioned me for it; certainly not in broadcasting. It is a colossal jungle. No one is ever safe in it.

Chapter VII

UP THE CORPORATE WALL

"Have you fired Cosell yet?"

For five years, beginning in 1959, I was locked out of network television. Five years stolen from a career that started late. Five years at the peak of one's ambition.

Blacklist is a harsh word. Put it this way: When the man who runs the company thinks you can't perform, he has every right not to put you on the air. The man's name was Tom Moore. The company he ran was ABC.

Tom Moore comes from Mississippi. Originally he sold cemetery plots. He was good at it. Then he got into television, and was good at it. At ABC he was, successively, head of sales, then programming and, finally, president of the entire television network. He is smart and he is an unceasing worker. Now he has an outfit called Tomorrow Productions. They have made some good movies for television.

Moore became important at ABC when the network was struggling for attention, striving desperately to escape the tag of being "the third network." We were, in fact, the third network. We came into being as a spin-off from NBC, pursuant to a government antimonopoly edict. With television in its early stages in this country, CBS and NBC were there before us and had locked up the best stations in the big markets. Even worse, certain cities had only two television stations. Thus, ABC had a circulation problem—how to get affiliate stations of major stature and how to get into two-station markets.

A network is like a newspaper. Advertising rates for
newspapers are based upon readership. Time rates for
networks are based upon viewers. In each case the key
word is "circulation." If you can't place your product
before the viewers, you lose the very foundation for the
conduct of your business. So, yes, ABC was the third
network.

But when Moore came in, ABC was beginning to
make waves, competitive waves, in the industry. Shows
like "The Untouchables," "Maverick" and "77 Sunset
Strip" were bringing attention to the fact that ABC
did indeed exist. But Tom Moore had another idea.
The quickest, most direct way to make inroads with
major stations was through sports. If you could buy the
rights to sports events, you could then offer stations—
even those affiliated with CBS or NBC—a monopoly on
the viewership of those multimillions in this country who
are addicted to sports. Moreover, you could package the
sports event with some of your other shows and thus cut
into the competitive circulation. That, friends, is called
leverage.

Tom Moore was a bald, round-faced man with a Mississippi drawl and a quick laugh. He was all energy.
And he knew exactly whom he wanted to run his sports
operation. A young man named Edgar Scherick. Scherick
had grown up with the business side of sports at Dancer,
Fitzgerald and Sample, a leading New York ad agency.
He worked on the Falstaff Beer account, specifically, on
the CBS baseball "Game of the Week." Scherick is an
extraordinary man, with a fine, creative mind, who today
enjoys fame as a motion-picture producer. His two most
recent successes are *Sleuth* and *Heartbreak Kid*.

But at the time, nobody knew Ed's name. He told me
then—this was the late Fifties—that he would make ABC
Number One in sports. He did. He left the ad business,
formed his own company called Sports Programs, Inc.,
and opened a tiny office in an old and unfashionable
building on West Forty-second Street. When I would
visit him there, the furnishings were so sparse that I
thought he was living in a world of fantasy. Here he was

telling me how big the operation would become, and all I could see was a couple of old desks and chairs, plus two assistants, Chet Simmons and Jack Lubell. A pocketful of dreams, I thought.

All the while, ABC was still nowhere in sports. Oddly I had been on the television network with a nightly strip for 18 months, which represented the only continuing sports coverage ABC offered at the time. The name of the show was "Sports Focus," and there is a story in how I got the chance.

Jim Aubrey, a famous name in broadcasting—later known in the industry as "The Cobra," the prototype for a fictional hero in a novel by Jacqueline Susann—was the president of the television network. John Charles Daly, of "What's My Line" fame, was the head of ABC News and Sports. Daly did the nightly network news report, and it was agreed that a sports strip should be adjacent to it. Aubrey wanted his old friend, Number 98, Tom Harmon, to do the show. Daly fought for me. He had become impressed with the contacts I had developed on the radio side and with the kind of topical impact I was making. Daly won.

I thought about this later in my career, when Tom Harmon replaced me on the radio network. Tom and I, by the way, are good friends, and I usually see him when I'm on the West Coast. The fact is that in the cycles of the broadcast business you live in a political jungle, and ups and downs are inevitable. You simply don't hold grudges. It's all part of the game, and at some point, somewhere, you are liable to find yourself working with—or for—the man whose job you took.

A nightly sports strip had no place in ABC's new programming ideas under Tom Moore. So "Sports Focus" was doomed, and the truth is it should have been. It had gone on the air as a summertime replacement for "Kukla, Fran and Ollie" and had long outlived its purpose.

The whole situation was complicated at this time by an internecine political hassle. Jim Riddell, then the executive vice-president of ABC, was a great supporter

of mine. I have never had a better friend in the industry.
He is a sports buff who gladly traveled the sports beat
with me. Riddell respected my ideas and approach to
sports broadcasting. He wanted an internal sports operation, with me at the head of it, rather than the independent company run by Scherick. This created an
uneasy situation between Moore and Riddell, and an
intolerable position for me. Years later Moore was to
tell me, as he drove me home to Pound Ridge, that he
thought "I was out to get him." I was thunderstruck at
the time. The statement revealed an insecurity in Moore
that I had never suspected. He was running the network,
and I was a relatively unknown sports announcer, a
nobody.

Ultimately Riddell moved to the West Coast and ran
the ABC operation out there. Moore had clear sailing
to develop the sports structure with Edgar Scherick. In
every move he made, Tom Moore was absolutely right. I
was in no way as qualified as Scherick to run a sports
department. He had acquired experience on the business
side that I was totally without. He knew how to negotiate for rights. He knew how to budget shows. He
knew the nuts and bolts of the sports-broadcast business.
It didn't take him long to prove it.

ABC bought the rights to college football. ABC made
a deal with the American Football League. ABC got a
major-league baseball package. And, then, in a master
stroke Edgar Scherick and Tom Moore conceived a show
called "Wide World of Sports." The success of that
series is now history. Scherick built a staff while all this
was going on, and again his wisdom showed. He hired
a young man from Columbia University who had been
the director for the "Shari Lewis Show" on NBC. His
name was Roone Arledge. When Scherick sold "Sports
Programs" to ABC—for a tidy capital gain—and then
moved into the company at a top executive level, Arledge
succeeded him as sports head.

Arledge has become a legend in the industry. He is
a man of impeccable program taste and sensitivity. He

combines aesthetic qualities with a toughness that is utterly concealed by a low-key, mild personality and a warmth and humor difficult to resist. He has reddish-blond hair and a pink face and a faint resemblance to Jack Nicklaus, a comparison that always delights him.

Thus did ABC Sports develop to the point where it became and is, Number One. But I was a sideline observer. No place to go. I visited with Ed Scherick, and he was dead honest with me. Tom Moore didn't want me on the air. I wasn't his kind of image. So I had to find another route.

The avenue that opened began with a young man named John Gilbert. Gilbert was brought in from Detroit in 1962 to run WABC-TV, the network's flagship station in New York. At the time, I was doing a nightly local TV show. Gilbert's background was strictly in radio. He wanted to make his mark quickly, especially because his boss, Ted Shaker, had not picked him for the job; Simon B. Siegel, the executive vice-president of the entire ABC operation, had brought Gilbert in. (If you have a little problem keeping track of the players, imagine what it is to work there. ABC is a polyglot in terms of divisions.)

Gilbert and I had become friends when he was running WXYZ Radio in Detroit. He was an enterprising man, personable, charming, aggressive. He wanted to make things happen. His first move was to ask me to produce a television special, which he wanted to play in August 1962. This is how it came about.

I was lunching at Toots Shor's with an old friend, Roger Kahn, now famous for his previously mentioned best seller, *The Boys of Summer*. I took a call from Gilbert, who said he needed to see me right away. I suggested he join us for lunch. This was in July, which gave us precious little time to put together a half-hour show, the content of which had not yet even been discussed.

Gilbert had never heard of Roger Kahn. But Roger grew visibly interested when John mentioned that the date cleared for the show was August 18. Roger knew something about August 18. He had recently written a magazine story entitled "Babe Ruth: A Look Behind the Legend," and that date, coincidentally, was the fourteenth anniversary of the death of the most famous name baseball ever knew.

Roger suggested we do a show on the same theme—in fact, with the same title: "Babe Ruth: A Look Behind the Legend." Gilbert bought the idea. Instantly we went to work. We brought in Horace McMahon, the late actor, then starring in "The Naked City," to narrate. A great sports fan, McMahon was the very face of the "naked city" where the Babe had played.

Then I lined up the key people in the Babe's life: his widow; the pitcher Waite Hoyt, perhaps his closest friend; wild man Joe Dugan, the third baseman with whom the Babe caroused; Larry McPhail; and, of course, Leo Durocher. Leo was involved, presumably, in a locker-room theft of the Babe's wristwatch. We touched every base just as Roger Kahn wrote it, with truth, with irony, with warmth.

So we produced the show. And I'll never forget what happened. We invited the press in to preview it. Keep in mind that this was one of the earliest sports documentaries ever attempted; as opposed to the usual stereotyped action-highlight shows. No one quite knew what the reaction would be. Among those who previewed the show were Red Smith, then the most distinguished sports columnist in the country; Bob Considine, the Babe's biographer; John Shanley, TV critic of the *Times;* Kay Gardella, TV critic of the *News*. Gilbert's boss, Ted Shaker, was there. After the show played and the press had vacated, Shaker told Gilbert that the show was not airworthy. He didn't want it played.

Gilbert was shaken. It was his first big venture. I followed him to his office, and, sure enough, the phone rang. It was Shaker again, telling him how bad the show was. Gilbert was beside himself. "Well, Howard, Shaker says it's a bomb."

I leaned over his desk. "John," I said, "it's not a bomb and it will get great reviews. It's different. It has something to say. It's the writer, the writer who counts. Something television doesn't know and probably will never understand. Roger Kahn is a great writer. He tells a great story. We tell it through the people. It doesn't have a lot of needless, phony pictures. The show belongs on the air."

"What should I do?"

"It's your decision. You've got to make it."

Gilbert was torn between two emotions. He was intimidated by Shaker, but he desperately wanted to make good. "Well," he said finally, "I have no choice, I think, but to go ahead and play it."

By midnight on the day the show aired, the reviews had appeared in the bulldog editions of the *Times* and the *Daily News.* Roger Kahn and Horace McMahon called from a phone booth at Times Square. Roger proceeded to read to me what Red Smith had written. The column was a rave. It talked about maturity in television and it talked about truth. In the *Daily News* the headline over Kay Gardella's column was: "BABE RUTH HITS ANOTHER HOME RUN."

Before I went to bed that night I called John Gilbert. I told him of the reviews. "You're kidding," he said. I assured him I was not. He whistled, and he chuckled, and I assumed he slept the sleep of the pure of heart that night.

I grabbed an early train from Stamford, Connecticut, the next morning and was at my desk at eight o'clock. By 8:45 Ted Shaker, the man who didn't want the show on the air, was in Si Siegel's office with the reviews.

Oh boy! Everything was beautiful. This was what *he* could do as head of the ABC-owned television stations. Shows like this could be produced under *his* leadership. It was that very day that Shaker said to me, "Hey, you're a great producer. Production is your bag. We've got to have more shows." Like Tom Moore, you see, he didn't feel I should be on the air as a performer.

But the main point was, he had *discovered* the show.

The day before, he said it shouldn't even run. You could understand Shaker. He was a CBS type. The proper dress, the button-down collar, the right residence (Darien), two yardsticks for sports announcers: either the mellifluous voice or the gentleman jock—neither of which I conformed to. A New York City boy, reared in Brooklyn; a New York City *Jewish* boy, if you will. The nasal twang. It all added up to the wrong image in the eyes of Ted Shaker and Tom Moore.

Having produced that show I stayed on local television in New York, but until the day he left in 1971 I lived with the certain knowledge that Ted Shaker did not want me on the air. Still, there was the production bag, as they put it, going for me. Another special to be done—this time, the death of the Polo Grounds, a show called: "The Polo Grounds: Requiem for an Arena." Again narrated by Horace McMahon. This time Toots Shor's was the scene of the preview. A couple of hundred people there. Rave reviews and still another production credit for the one who shouldn't be on the air, Howard Cosell.

For all of the great moments that had created the legend of the Polo Grounds, I brought in the people who lived them: Jack Dempsey, to talk about the Firpo fight; Ralph Branca and Bobby Thompson, to talk about *the* home run on October 3, 1951; Sleepy Jim Crowley, to talk about Grantland Rice and the naming of the Four Horsemen of Notre Dame; Ken Strong, talking about the famed "Sneakers Game" when the Giants beat the Bears for the title; and the late Frank Frisch, reliving the days of John McGraw.

My next special was "Run to Daylight," which I have dealt with at length in the chapter on Vince Lombardi. At the press preview for that show, Tom Moore appeared. After the screening, Moore came to me and said, "You're a helluva producer. I want you to get with Roone Arledge. We've got a show in mind and I want you to be involved in the production." I did get together with Arledge, who by now had succeeded Scherick. The show never did eventuate. Something else did. Roone told me that he believed in me as a performer and wanted to use me on the television network.

A five-year dought was about to end. I began to appear regularly on "Wide World of Sports." It was there that my series of dialogues with Muhammad Ali began. It was those appearances that first brought me to national attention.

Then I was used on the major-league baseball package in 1965. At the same time, whenever news stories developed that were appropriate to "Wide World," I covered them. But even then I had more bricks to climb. I had been used on boxing, but only as the color man. Then, in September 1966, I was assigned to do the fight between Ali and Karl Mildenberger in Frankfurt, West Germany, by myself. The telecast went very well. Chet Forte, the producer, still feels it was the best fight telecast we have ever done. And, wonder of wonders, when I got back to New York, Tom Moore congratulated me. Roone Arledge later said, "Would you believe Tom Moore loves Howard Cosell?"

Naïvely I thought the cycle had gone full swing. I did a series of Ali fights, and then, after Ali had rejected military induction and was barred from boxing, the World Boxing Association initiated a tournament that ABC carried. I thought that in the wake of all I had done with boxing and with Ali I would automatically be assigned to the tournament. I was wrong. Chuck Howard, Roone Arledge's production head, wanted to bring in Don Dunphy to do the blow-by-blow of the first two fights. They were to constitute a double feature in the Houston Astrodome, Ernie Terrell against Thad Spencer, and Jimmy Ellis against Leotis Martin.

I couldn't believe it. Don Dunphy is a fine, veteran boxing announcer, and for years we have had a fine relationship. But Dunphy was the voice of Madison Square Garden, and they were in conflict with the WBA, whose fights we were committed to cover. As a matter of fact, Joe Frazier was fighting for the Garden and had

refused to enter the WBA tournament. I felt Chuck's
position was antithetical to the best interests of the company, and a blow to my own pride because of the job
I felt I had done.

I had lunch with Chuck Howard and Chet Forte, and
we reached a compromise. Chris Schenkel would do the
blow-by-blow of the two fights, and I would do the color.
I accepted this because I had lost five years out of a
career, and because Chris Schenkel is a close friend and
part of the ABC broadcast team. The compromise worked,
the proof of which is the fact that from then on *every*
ABC fight was done by me—until the summer of '73,
when ABC Sports began a series of Saturday-matinee,
low-quality fights from the Felt Forum in the Garden.
My total broadcast commitments had brought me far
past that kind of assignment.

But a new crisis arose in 1968. I almost fell, forevermore, from my climb up that corporate wall. The reason:
I picketed my company.

The staff announcers had gone on strike. As a member of AFTRA, I had to observe that strike. Moreover,
I was in sympathy with it because when I first came to
ABC the announcers had been great to me. These were
the working announcers, the voices that become familiar
to many but whose stars seldom rise. Since they had
been so kind to me I felt I owed them support. At the
same time there was a dichotomy in my position. I had
become director of sports on the radio side and thus
I was a member of the ABC executive echelon. With an
absolute absence of tact and common sense, there I
stood, in my trench coat in March 1968, picketing in
front of the building with news commentators Peter
Jennings and Murphy Martin. That was all Ted Shaker
had to see.

It was also all Simon B. Siegel had to see. This man,
Siegel, through all the years had been wonderful to me—
almost like a father. While he would never interfere with
the operation of any division in the company—on my
behalf or anyone else's—I knew he liked me and re-

spected me and had gone out of his way to praise my work.

Now he felt I was evidencing disloyalty and violating my obligation to the company. I got wind of this and called him. My calls weren't returned. I tried to see him. He wasn't in. I thought, "This is it." Later I learned that Ted Shaker had spoken to him about my being on the picket line. Then I was told that Jim Conley, who worked directly under him, got a call from Shaker. "Get rid of Cosell," he ordered Conley. "I never wanted him on the air anyway. I've cleared it with Siegel." Conley never moved. Later I was also told that when Siegel's anger cooled he sent the word down to hold the orders. A sullen Shaker apparently called Conley back: "Have you fired Cosell yet?"

"No."

"Then don't."

Finally a chance arose to discuss the matter with Si. I told him that I understood his position but that I felt I had to show my active support for men who had helped me so much at the beginning of my career.

"But did you have to do it," Si asked, "in front of the main building?"

I admitted he had a point. If I had it to do over, I agreed, I would have picked a less conspicuous post on Sixty-sixth Street, where the newsmen worked, not the bosses.

Another crisis hurdled. And Shaker never did get me. But he did, in a way, get John Gilbert.

He had been on Gilbert's back from the beginning. But John's life in the company was prolonged by Si Siegel, who moved him upstairs to become head of affiliate relations at the network. His assistant, Dick Beesemyer, took over at WABC-TV. Before Gilbert left I had continued to produce specials for him, including the series called "Self-Portraits," hour-long interviews with the most topical figures in sports—Jimmy Brown, Wilt Chamberlan, Pancho Gonzales, Ralph Houk, Whitey Ford, Mickey Mantle, Vince Lombardi.

The Mantle show made news. For the first time,

publicly, he talked about his fear of early death. Mickey's
grandfather, his father and two uncles had all died at
39 and 40 of Hodgkin's disease. He spoke unrelievedly
about himself and his life, in terms never heard before or
since. This kind of show, and this kind of approach,
brought dramatic new results to sports television.

Even while Gilbert was still running the local station,
and Roone Arledge had given me access to the network,
still another production avenue opened for me. This time
the open road was paved by an old friend, Edgar
Scherick. By now Scherick was running his own business
and looking toward motion-picture production. But he
wanted to do a one-hour television documentary on
sports, and recruited me to work with him as his co-
producer. Frankly, I was thrilled at the opportunity.

The pro-football merger had been consummated. The
first Super Bowl game was to be played in January
1967 in the Los Angeles Coliseum. We decided to do
a show on the merger—the inside of it, the politics of
it, the grubbiness of it. Scherick had been with the
American Football League from the beginning. He was
well versed in the whole sordid history of "baby-sitting,"
"kidnapping," double-signings, girl procuring and piracy.
The show was written by Jerry Izenberg, whom I had
brought into television with a special entitled "Johnny
Keane: The Yankee from Texas." Izenberg is not just a
gifted writer; he has a sense for television and he is also
one of the best reporters around. Nobody can buy him
and nobody can shake his objectivity. He was right for
the job.

It was a helluva show to do. It centered around Sonny
Werblin, who was the overriding cause of the merger
even though he deeply fought it. In fact, we called the
show "Pro Footballs' Shotgun Marriage: Sonny, Money
and Merger." Sonny cooperated 100 percent. And I'll
never forget the night it was shown on the ABC Television Network.

After the show had played I called Sonny at his home
in Golden Beach, Florida. I asked him how he liked it.
"You made me look like a fool," he shouted. "And why

the hell would Namath say the things he did? Has he gone crazy?"

It was no time to talk to Sonny. I racked my brain trying to think of what Namath had said that was so terrible. I still don't know. What it got down to, in my mind, was what Sonny said on the phone: "All you did was show me in that damned booth biting my nails." We had used about five minutes of footage showing Werblin's reaction during an Oakland-Jets game.

But Sonny's wrath was not long-lived. The next morning Arthur Daley's column in the *New York Times* was entitled: "Sonny, Money and Merger." Daley said that the show was exceptional, a vivid journalistic insight into the man who had single-handedly changed the face of professional football.

Bill Wallace, reviewing it for the TV section of the *Times,* praised it lavishly. Ben Gross, critic for the *Daily News,* called it "a revelation."

At ten o'clock that morning, some 12 hours after I had called Sonny, the telephone rang in my home. It was Sonny. His mood had undergone a startling change. He had read the reviews in the New York papers. "Dammit," he said, "that was a helluva show last night. It told the damned truth. I'm the biggest man in football. Congratulations on a *helluva* show." It was as if we had never talked the night before.

"Sonny, Money and Merger" was a critical success, and still another brick had been scaled in my climb up the corporate wall. But down to the deadline it had been touch and go. We had hired actor Kevin McCarthy to narrate the show. He is a fine dramatic actor who had played Biff in *Death of a Salesman.* We thought we had scored a ten-strike. We were in for a surprise. There is a fine line between narration and acting. McCarthy, as good an actor as he is, simply had no feeling for the subject. Although we spent hour after hour working with him, it was clear that he couldn't cut it.

Finally, in despair, Irv Wilson, Scherick's assistant who had worked with me night and day on this job, went to the phone to give Ed the bad news. "Ed," I heard Irv say, "we've got to fire McCarthy."

Scherick's words came sputtering through the receiver, loud enough to hear. "What? What? What do you mean?"

"He can't talk. He can't do the narration. You can't understand him."

"Goddammit, Irv, are you crazy? The man's an actor. A fine actor."

"I know, Ed, but it's his mouth. The words just don't come out. It has to do with the way he talks."

"But the man is an actor," Scherick was screaming, "a great actor."

"I know, I know," Irv was saying, "but we got to get rid of him now, before it's too late."

All this time I stood there, shouting in Wilson's other ear, telling him to tell Scherick to get his ass over there and hear it for himself. Finally Ed suggested that I take McCarthy through the script and show him how to do it. I tried. I ran through it. And Kevin looked at me plaintively and said, "Howard, you're magnificent. You should do the narration yourself."

Kevin was a pro. He knew it wouldn't work, and he gave us the out we needed. I quickly brought in Murphy Martin from ABC News. He gave it the Westbrook Van Voorhis treatment and knocked off the narration in an hour and a half.

What I liked most about the merger show was simply this: It gave me my first *network*-television credit as a producer.

I produced another documentary that touched my social and creative instincts. In a way it challenged the whole industry. It was about a black, southern college called Grambling. It was called: "One Hundred Yards to Glory." The show was the brainchild of Jerry Izenberg, who had researched the school for a magazine story.

This little college at Grambling, Louisiana—where the trains don't stop unless you flag them down—has produced pro rata an incredible number of professional football stars. The man responsible is the coach, Eddie Robinson, and Grambling College was his story.

I presented the idea to Dick Beesemyer, who had succeeded John Gilbert. Dick had the same feeling for the show I did, and he authorized the budget moneys to produce it, which took guts on his part. Once again, Ted Shaker didn't like the idea, and admittedly there was a commercial problem. It didn't seem likely that one could sell, in New York City, a show on a small black southern school.

During this time Beesemyer was having his own problems with Shaker. One day Dick and I were having lunch. He said, "I sure hope this show is good, Howard. I'm under a lot of pressure." And then he leaned across the table and asked, "Is Shaker trying to get me fired?"

"How the hell do I know?" I answered. "I've got my own problems. He's been trying to fire me for six years." Shaker brought nothing but security to the people who worked for him.

Jerry Izenberg did a brilliant job. As in every documentary I have ever produced, the writer was the key. When I screened it for Beesemyer and his sales staff they loved it. Then we screened it for Ted Shaker and Jim Conley. We weren't six minutes into the show when Conley, a perceptive, sensitive man, asked, "Howard, who wrote this show?" I told him. Jim never said a word, but I knew that the show was reaching him.

Shaker fidgeted throughout. Later he gave me a perfunctory "Okay." I learned from Beesemyer, as I had learned so often from Gilbert, that Shaker wasn't hot for the show.

All the show did was win the Golden Eagle Award, presented by the Council on International Non-Theatrical Events, the highest award in television journalism. The day after the show my old friend Tom Moore came to me and told that the president of McGraw-Hill had called him right after the show had aired, and said it was one of the most touching he had ever seen. Later the network bought the show from Beesemyer, and Grambling College was seen from coast to coast.

One more brick.

I guess the cycle catches up with everybody. It did with Ted Shaker. But before it did, he fired Jim Conley, one of his oldest friends, a man he had personally brought over from CBS and one of the most decent men I have ever known. He was more than that; he was a first-rate executive with a sophisticated broadcast mind.

A man named John Campbell succeeded Jim Conley. He was another of the imports from Detroit. Campbell was all man. He wouldn't take crap from anybody. After a period of time he had his fill of Shaker. He quit. Si Siegel called him on the West Coast and tried to persuade him to return. No soap. Campbell had made up his mind.

This was perhaps the final stroke that caused Si Siegel to take a hard look at his executive structure. Elton Rule had been named president of the Television Network, and Shaker had wanted that job. Siegel decided that Shaker was dispensable. As you might have guessed, Tom Moore had already been rendered dispensable. He was the man Elton Rule replaced.

When Tom Moore was fired I got a call from him. Could we have lunch? We did. Tom Moore asked me to go into the television production business with him. (The spiral spins.) But I declined the offer.

Beesemyer is still with ABC. He is the head of affiliate relations. He succeeded John Gilbert, who is gone.

In the myriad of events, I had yet another turbulent labor experience. The engineers' union (NABET) went on strike, and the executive board of AFTRA—my union—voted to respect the picket line. I had been forewarned of the strike by a man named Don Conaway, who was then the key executive of AFTRA. Conaway lived in Stamford, and we commuted together every morning. I told Don that if the union supported the engineers' strike, it would create a problem for me because of my dual role as an executive on the radio side and as a performing talent on both radio and television. He led me to believe that I could continue to broadcast if I did not cross the picket line. This was possible for me in radio because I had a network line from my home in Pound Ridge and could do my shows from there. This is what I did during the course of the strike. I also did a Benvenuti-Griffith fight from Shea Stadium on television. Again, no picket line was involved.

It didn't help me. Subsequently charges were leveled against all of us who continued to perform, whether we crossed the lines or not. One of the most vociferous dissenters from the AFTRA action was John Scali, now our ambassador to the United Nations, then an ABC News commentator. I'll never get over John. In our meetings he'd be fiery. He had a lot of us all charged up. And he wound up getting a paltry $2000 fine, while I was assessed a record $17,500, one of the highest, if not *the* highest, in AFTRA history. There was even a story in that. Everybody in the sports department waited with bated breath to see whether Chris Schenkel would be fined more than I, or vice versa. It was generally considered that the size of the fines would reflect the size of the salaries, a source of continuing gossip in the television industry. I beat Chris by $500.

Later the fines were appealed, and to this day not one of us has paid a cent. But at least this time I was a hero with Si Siegel, not a villain.

Another brick climbed.

But there are bricks to climb on the radio side, too. Generally speaking, throughout the 1950s my radio career prospered. One of the major reasons was the support of a man named Bob Pauley. He had come to the ABC Radio Network as a salesman and took a great interest in the kind of shows I was doing. Later he became president of the Radio Network and continued to evidence the same interest. It wasn't easy for Pauley to back me. I created a problem. I was a hard sell. Not commercial. No name. Nasal twang. And, finally, it happened.

I had been doing, for a number of years, the nightly network-radio sports strip. One day I called Jim Duffy, head of Network Radio Sales at the time and a very close friend. I asked him what was new. He replied casually, almost too casually, "We've got the deal with Delco for Tom Harmon."

The bottom fell out from under me. It meant just one thing. Harmon's show would replace mine.

That, of course, is what happened. Ironic, isn't it? I had gotten a television job that Tom hadn't gotten, a few years earlier. But even here I had come out of it lucky. Pauley decided to initiate a morning network-radio show, and that's the one I still do on the American Contemporary Network. It is the most listened-to sports broadcast on radio. Harmon's nighttime show is gone. In fact, the old radio network is gone. In the uncertain and changing face of broadcast, ABC now has four radio networks, each geared to service stations around the country according to the special programming needs of those markets. For example, stations carrying popular music for young audiences are serviced by the American Contemporary Network; stations carrying mainly news are serviced by the American Information Network. The whole new structure of ABC Radio has been a tremendous success.

Back in 1962, when Jim Duffy gave me the word— and remember, I was not then on network television—I thought my broadcast days might be ended. My income had shrunk to next to nothing. In the brief interval before I got the new morning show, all I had was weekend radio.

Jim Duffy, by the way, helped me a great deal. I remember when Jim first came to New York. He had been our radio sales head in Chicago, and now was to take over as the radio sales head of the network. We had a lot in common. He is a rabid sports fan, a tall, redheaded Irishman, good-looking, with a winning smile and an equally winning personality. This is a guy who could sell you the Brooklyn Bridge.

I'll never forget Jim's first night in New York. Nor

will he. We were standing in front of the Warwick Hotel at Fifty-fourth Street and the Avenue of the Americas. Suddenly I saw Cus D'Amato, the boxing manager, coming toward us with his dog. Cus was then the manager of Floyd Patterson, then the heavyweight champion of the world. That dog of his had always frightened me. He was a big, mean-looking German shepherd who always appeared ready to pounce if you so much as smiled at him. Jim never even noticed the dog. He was too elated over meeting the manager of Floyd Patterson.

The three of us—and the dog—walked around the block, and Jim ate up every word Cus spoke. He was getting the inside of boxing, and he couldn't contain his excitement. Neither could the dog. He urinated all over Jim's leg. Jim never even noticed it. It was then that I knew that in the natural order of events Jim had every qualification to become the president of the ABC Television Network. That is the job he holds today.

One more irony—one more brick. After Jim Duffy had moved from radio to television, and after my morning show had gotten under way, I was suddenly advised that I was going to lose the morning show; the sponsor didn't want me. He would accept Keith Jackson, the man who would be replaced years later on "Monday Night Football" by Frank Gifford. Strange world.

I went into Bob Pauley's office and fought for my job. "Bob, it isn't fair," I argued. "They took the other show away from me for Harmon, and now they're trying to do this." Pauley felt I was right. He stood up to the sponsor and kept me on the air.

Pauley himself was fired a couple of years later. Do you know what he's doing now? He is involved in a new corporation that hopes to provide an independent news service to television stations around the country. With him in the enterprise is John Gilbert. They are the two top men in the new company—past victims of the corporate wall. One other victim of the corporate wall is back. John Campbell is the head of ABC's nonbroadcast facilities.

I once told Myron Cope, the writer, when he was

doing a profile of me for *Sports Illustrated,* that my greatest accomplishment has been my mere survival. I'm not kidding myself. I don't think I ever will get up that corporate wall. But I don't think anybody else at ABC will either.

Chapter VIII

A HOLE IN THE SUBWAY

"It's wrong to hate the way I hated."

There is a quality about boxing that attaches to no
other sport. Well, maybe not boxing; maybe the men
who fight, rather than the science itself. They are the
most interesting of all athletes, for they seem to have
the deepest feelings about life. Theirs is a lonely sport,
at times ugly, brutal, naked. You have to get inside a
ring to appreciate how small it is. You wonder how men
can ever escape.

Boxing has been infested with corruption and gang-
sterism from the day it began, yet it engages our basic
emotions like no other athletic activity. Somehow it
touches the men of letters and art and culture. When
great writers are drawn to sports they turn irresistibly
to the ring. Ernest Hemingway did. Budd Schulberg did.
So did Norman Mailer.

It is also a fact that while movies with sports themes
almost invariably fail at the box office, the exceptions
have been movies with a boxing plot. John Garfield was
memorable in *Body and Soul*. Kirk Douglas burst into
public prominence with *Champion*. Jack Palance was ac-
claimed in *Requiem for a Heavyweight*. And, of course,
there was *The Harder They Fall*, Budd Schulberg's opus.

I have discovered that sooner or later the great writers
who turn to boxing fall in love with a fighter. For Mailer
and Schulberg, for instance, there were Muhammad Ali
and José Torres. For Roger Kahn, unaccountably, it

was the momentarily glamorous Swede, Ingemar Johansson. Which only proves that each writer romanticizes in his own way.

My own interest in boxing developed because of three men: Floyd Patterson, Cus D'Amato and Bill Heinz.

In my view Heinz is the greatest boxing writer who has ever lived. He had a feeling for the sport like no one I have ever known, and it showed itself in the way he wrote. Somehow he could get inside a fighter's head—and his heart—from the champion to the lowliest pug, and there would emerge an earthy insight into the whole being of the fighter.

He loved the smell of the gym. The old Stillman's on Eighth Avenue in New York City held an unending fascination for him. He would go there, watch the fighters work, talk with the trainers and managers, and for him every one was a story. Stillman's was so much a part of Bill Heinz that once, after the tragic death of his older daughter, when he and his wife Betty parted temporarily, Bill rented an apartment in New York in a new building on the very plot where Stillman's Gym had been. A homing pigeon.

It was Bill Heinz who would sit and talk with me about Lew Jenkins. (His piece on Lew in the *Fireside Book of Boxing* may be the all-time boxing classic. Bill, incidentally, edited that book.) He would take me back to Fritzie Zivic, stir my memories on Maxie Baer, Jack Sharkey, Max Schmeling, Joe Louis, Archie Moore and Rocky Marciano. His writing is marked by a superb ear for dialogue, much in the manner of another great writer, the late Frank Graham, and he tells a story the same way, colorfully, humorously, so that you get totally caught up in it. I remember back in 1955, when Moore was about to fight Rocky Marciano in Yankee Stadium, Bill whispering in my ear, "Rocky better watch out. Old Archie has studied him closely and he thinks Rocky can be hit with that quick, short, sneaky counter-right."

Sure enough, that's what Archie threw in the second round, and down went Rocky. To this day Archie will tell you, if you gave him a chance, that Referee Norm

Kessler gave Marciano a long count. "Otherwise," says Archie, "I would have been the heavyweight champion of the world."

The more Bill Heinz talked, the more fascinated I became with boxing. And then it was the age of Floyd Patterson. Bill liked Floyd. He never thought he was a great fighter, but he liked him. In fact, in those days I didn't know anybody who did not like Floyd Patterson. He was a sociologist's dream, and a psychologist's guinea pig.

Many people know Patterson's background. A product of the Brooklyn ghetto. One of many children in the family. No clothes of his own to wear. A ludicrous figure in outsized garments of his father's. Overly sensitive, overly shy as a result, he turned ever inward and found a nest, a hole in the subway where he would sit, alone, afraid, watching the trains go by. Little wonder he became a disturbed child.

He wound up in the Wiltwyck School, then located in Aesopus, New York, a school for disturbed children. Oddly, at about the time Floyd was there, a documentary film was made about the school. The film focused mainly on one introverted black youngster. It was called *The Quiet One*. It could have been named after Floyd Patterson.

At the Witwyck School Floyd discovered the countryside. He fell in love with it for the rest of his life. He loves quiet, he loves peace, he loves to walk alone, to hear the birds, to pick up a twig, to throw a stick in the air, to watch the ripples in the stream when he tosses a rock in. Wiltwyck School was right for him. It was there that Floyd Patterson began to emerge from his shell.

He came back home and attended a special school in Manhattan. This kind of school was called a "600" school. It was programmed for young men with the kind of background Floyd had.

How odd that one with such a background should wind up in a profession of violence, a profession where, notwithstanding one's own sensitivity, one seeks to im-pose pain upon another. But strangely, in apparent contradiction of his whole personality, Floyd Patterson did.

The "600" school he attended was not far from Fourteenth Street—Union Square if you will. Almost just around the corner, upstairs in a seedy, broken-down building on Fourteenth Street, was a place called the Gramercy Gym. What it really was was a fleabag. Nobody in his right mind would visit there. It was stark and empty except for the fact that in the middle of the floor—it was an old-time loft—there was a boxing ring. And over in a corner, there was a cot. There was also a dog, a vicious-looking German shepherd, always muzzled, and there was a man who lived there, slept on that cot—a man with a vigorous body, crew-cut white hair, a man who spoke in an educated fashion, the sentences grammatically correct, the speech interestingly literate. The only problem was that he spoke in terms of mystery, of devious plots against him, suspicious figures lurking everywhere who were out to get him. The plain truth was, you could never tell what the hell he was talking about. His name was Cus D'Amato, and he was a boxing manager.

Whether or not you could understand Cus when he talked about his "enemies," when he talked about boxing it was another thing. On this subject he was clear and explicit. And he could get young fighters to come to his gym. Two of Floyd Patterson's older brothers would go there. And Floyd, at age 14, would leave the "600" school and go there to watch his brothers. It was inevitable that he would start to train, to learn how to fight. And so Floyd's dream was born early: to become a professional fighter and use the money he would make to help his family.

Floyd was a natural. He won the Golden Gloves as a middleweight and again as a light heavyweight. In Helsinki, Finland, in 1952 he won the gold medal as a middleweight in the Olympics. He was Cus's boy, with a special style of fighting that Cus had taught him, the "peekaboo," the gloves up high, in front of the chin, to afford better defense and yet be so positioned as to be able to deliver blows with greater quickness than the opponent. At least that was the theory.

He came back from Finland, and his professional career began, under Cus's careful tutelage. He became a young hero at the Eastern Parkway Arena—those were still the days of the local boxing clubs—and his career enjoyed spectacular growth. Only one setback: a hotly disputed decision to Joey Maxim, which most onlookers thought he had won.

Those were the days when I became friendly with Floyd and Cus. Those were my early days in radio. Repeatedly both of them guested for me. I developed an almost fatherly affection for Patterson. And I was sympathetic to Cus's drive against the IBC—the International Boxing Club—an octopuslike organization, headed up by the late Jim Norris, that controlled boxing and, as was later documented, was gangster influenced.

I would go up to Greenwood Lake, New York, and watch Patterson train. I had begun to learn much about boxing, and it was clear that Floyd was an exceptional young fighter. He had enormously swift hands, swift feet, and was a surprisingly powerful puncher. His left hook could take out a man, any man, and his right was almost equally punishing. The one drawback seemed to be his size, or the absence thereof. He had become a heavyweight, but looked to be more like a light heavyweight. Cus said I was wrong. "He strips heavy," he would tell me.

I became absorbed with Floyd—with his personal life, his softness, both of manner and voice, the way he would express interest in a variety of things—religion, family and hobbies. He converted to Catholicism and seemed utterly at peace with himself. He was that way then as a fighter. "If Cus says I can win, then I can win," he would say.

And he kept winning. Until finally, on November 30, 1956, Patterson knocked out Archie Moore in the fifth round at the Chicago Stadium to become the heavyweight champion of the world. He was only 21, the youngest champion in history. When I went to Chicago to cover

that fight I visited with Floyd and Cus at their training
camp. It was at Sportsman's Park, an old deserted racetrack outside of Chicago. They were camped in the
jockeys' room, and when I went there I thought to myself: "This can't be. The Gramercy Gym was one thing
in the early days, but now they're fighting for the title.
They should have better facilities than this." But that
was Cus's way, and so, of course, it was Floyd's way.
The place was so barren, so unattended, I left there
feeling sorry for them.

When Floyd got in the ring, I was no longer sorry for
him. He won the title on a Friday night. The following
Sunday at ten in the morning our doorbell rang. We
were living in Peter Cooper Village then, at First Avenue and Twenty-third Street in Manhattan. I went to the
door. It was Cus D'Amato, ebullient, enthusiastic and
eager to savor the fruits of victory. He brought with
him a bottle of 100-year-old Armagnac brandy as a
gift. "Take it," he insisted, "you've been with us all
the way." We sat and talked for a couple of hours, and
Cus told me his next move would be to hold a press
conference and announce that Floyd would not be fighting in any fights promoted by the IBC.

That press conference was held shortly thereafter. The
people at Madison Square Garden pretended indifference.
They had no choice. A new era was presumably to begin
in boxing. Control of the heavyweight champion was
almost tantamount to control of boxing.

In the hectic days that followed that press conference
I would get phone calls from Cus D'Amato at all hours
of the day and night. I remember one, when he whispered
into the phone that he was in a phone booth on the
Merritt Parkway and that his life was in jeopardy. His
enemies were after him. "If anything happens to me," he
told me, "you'll know who did it. Tell the truth."

I never had the foggiest notion of whom he was
referring to, except that he would try to relate everything
that was happening to him to the IBC. There was never
a shred of evidence—at least not perceptible evidence—
to back up what he was saying. In fact, when you would

pursue Cus with a lawyerlike interrogation, you would wind up befuddled, meandering through a maze of unnamed persons who somehow were occupied with spending their lifetimes trying to destroy Cus D'Amato.

He was right about one thing, though. The IBC was bad for boxing.

Once he became champion, there was no tangible change in Patterson. He was as quiet as ever, as shy as ever. He had a home in Rockville Centre, Long Island, was married to a girl named Sandra, and they had a baby daughter named Seneca. My own daughters, Jill and Hilary, were crazy about him. They worried every time he fought. Emmy was much the same way. Floyd had become a personal thing. Out of nowhere he would drop in to visit us in Pound Ridge. Or we would visit him in the isolation of his training camp and watch him work out.

I found myself no different from the writers. I had fallen in love with a fighter. So had my family. Part of his charm for all of us was his apparent vulnerability. Even when he was champion he was somehow a figure of sympathy, which he had been in the public mind ever since.

As for boxing, Cus was more than cautious with Patterson's career. Floyd faced one stiff after another. Names like Pete Rademacher. Roy "Cut and Shoot" Harris. Brian London. Tom McNeely. I remember Cus coming into my office when he was setting up the Rademacher fight. "It'll be the biggest thing in boxing history," he trumpeted. "Just think of it, the pro champion against the amateur champion."

To tell you the truth, I didn't want to think of it. It seemed absurd on its face. Finally, there was to be a championship defense in New York against Ingemar Johansson, a Swedish heavyweight who had knocked out Eddie Machen in the first round in a bout held in Sweden. Everyone remembered that Johansson had been disqualified in the 1951 Olympics for "not fighting." Everyone thought that Ingemar was just another handpicked patsy for Floyd to beat.

The Paterson-Johansson fight was the first I ever broadcast. It was in June 1959 and it was to be broadcast on the ABC Radio Network. It would also be seen on theater television and would set the pattern for many major heavyweight-championship broadcasts to come—radio network to the home, and theater TV for those who wanted to see it. Our broadcast was being sponsored by United Artists and the Mirisch Brothers to promote a new movie of theirs called *The Horse Soldiers*. The stars of that movie were John Wayne and William Holden, and they were to work the radio broadcast with me and Les Keiter.

Holden came into town several days before the broadcast, and I visited both training camps with him. Paterson was training in Summit, New Jersey, but wasn't even there when we appeared. That finished off Patterson as far as Holden was concerned, despite every excuse I made for Floyd. Then we went to visit Johansson at Grossinger's, in upstate New York, and because he was there, and was most amiable, Holden responded to him instantly. As a matter of fact, Ingo, who has always had a good eye for the buck, was on tenterhooks waiting for Holden. Ingo thought he should be in the movies and that Holden could help show him the way. Bill did nothing to discourage him. Holden's eyes had fastened upon Birgit Lundgren, Johansson's fiancée, who also nurtured Hollywood visions and who hardly seemed antipathetic to the vision of Holden himself. It's altogether possible that Bill could have been reciprocal to Birgit's apparent interest, but a look at Johansson in fighting trunks deterred him.

On the way back to New York, Holden said, "Howard, Johansson will beat Patterson."

With grandiose self-assurance, I laughed at him. Bill then spent the rest of the ride telling me about his place in Kenya and describing to me the positive delicacy that was filet of eland, a dish he had come upon in Africa and learned to treasure. I asked Bill, "What the hell's so special about that? We have it over here every day." It broke him up.

We got along very well. He was a first-rate, down-to-earth guy, and so for that matter was John Wayne when he joined us the day before the fight. The two of them really enjoyed the fight, which proved to be one of the big upsets in boxing history. Holden led the cheering as Johansson's right got to Patterson in the third, and Patterson went down *seven* times before they finally stopped it. At that moment Ingo had made believers out of all of us. Suddenly there was truth in what his manager, Edwin Ahlquist, had told us all at a press conference a week earlier. "Dere is toonder in his right. You vill see."

We had all laughed.

In the ring after the fight Cus D'Amato said to me, "Floyd Patterson will become the first heavyweight champion ever to regain his title." Having lost the fight, Patterson went into seclusion at his home in Rockville Centre. My daughters had stayed up to hear the fight, and Jill, who was 13 at the time, cried all night. The next morning she wrote Floyd an impassioned letter, begging him not to give up and telling him that he would be the champion again. She still has Floyd's reply.

A few days after the fight I got a call from Cus. He told me that Floyd was still in a deep depression and that he was worried about him. He asked if I would go out to see him to try to cheer him up. I said, "Sure, but why don't I take Jackie Robinson along?" I knew that Floyd, though he had never met Jackie, respected him enormously. Cus thought it was a great idea, cleared it with Floyd, and the next morning at nine o'clock Jackie and I were at Floyd's house.

From the outside it looked unoccupied. All the blinds were drawn. We rang, and rang again. And again. Fially Sandra appeared and let us in. Floyd was unmarked, but he tried to avoid looking us in the eye. I could only suppose that the terrible shame he felt derived in some way from his whole background. It was as if he were sitting in that little hole in the subway all over again.

Robinson talked to Floyd at length. He told him about his own life, about the comebacks he had had to make and how Floyd could do it more quickly than Jackie had ever done it, because he was so much younger. Patterson seemed visibly encouraged by the time we left. This, by the way, was the beginning of a long-term friendship between Patterson and Robinson. Years later Robinson was to go to Alabama at a time when Bull Connor, the sheriff, was turning the dogs loose on the blacks of Birmingham. Patterson went with him. There was a time when the two were in the deep South, when Patterson, no longer diffident and sheepish, would in the presence of southern whites go up to the two water fountains in the center of town, one marked "black" and the other "white" and deliberately drink from the fountain labeled "white." Then he turned around, faced the whites and said, in his quiet, laconic way, "Tastes like the same water."

There was a rematch clause; Patterson was to fight Johansson again. The training camp selected for Floyd was in Newton, Connecticut, on an obscure estate owned by the onetime famous bandleader Enric Madriguera. Floyd was a recluse as he prepared for the return fight. Some reporters would come, but they were not welcome. It turned out that Floyd himself was not welcome. The place was infested with rats. They didn't like Patterson, and he didn't like them. Once, when Emmy and I were up there visiting, he told us the story.

"This place is terrible," he said. "Nothing but rats. I complained to the owner, and he said there were no rats in the house. I got a gun, shot three rats and hung them up on the line in front of the house where he lives. Now he's gonna do something about the rats."

The day before the fight—it was June 19, 1960—I was alone with Patterson taping the prefight show. It was then that I could see the fury in the man. For a whole year he had been seething inside. He didn't like Johansson and he had for the first time in his life felt hate. It was amazing that he had been able to disguise his feelings so well. He told me that he would nullify Johansson's right and beat him with his left hook.

June 20, 1960, made boxing history. It was at the old Polo Grounds, and in the fifth round Patterson hit Johansson with as strong and as clean and as pulverizing a left hook as I had ever seen. Johansson lay there on the canvas, unconscious, his right foot twitching, blood pouring out of his mouth. I interviewed Patterson briefly and then went over to where Johansson still lay, on the canvas, still out cold, the blood still coming out of his mouth. Whitey Bimstein, his trainer, was leaning over him.

"For God's sake, Whitey," I said, "is he dead?"

Whitey, a colorful relic of boxing's heyday, looked up at me and answered, "The son of a bitch should be. I told him to look out for the left hook."

Two weeks earlier Whitey had been my guest on a local television show and had proclaimed the greatness of Johansson in his best New Yorkese. Whitey had assured me on that show that Johansson "had the mind of a Tunney and the punch of a Dempsey." This was no Tunney, nor Dempsey. What he was in that ring, on the canvas that night, was a demolished fighter. There was bedlam in the Polo Grounds that night. The ring was in the middle of the field, where second base was. I had to keep the broadcast going while getting from the ring some 200 to 300 yards to the clubhouse steps, then up the steps to the Patterson dressing room to talk with him again. Crowds of people blocked my way, and at the steps the police wouldn't let me up.

One man got me through the crowds, and through the police—Jackie Robinson. When I reached Patterson in the dressing room, I asked him about the fact that nearly all the writers had picked Johansson to knock him out again. "I'm looking at their faces now," he said.

That was the zenith of Floyd Patterson's career, but only the beginning of the vicissitudes in our relationship that were to follow.

I realized Patterson was not an outstanding fighter after his third bout with Johansson, which came a year later in Miami. Johansson was overweight, out of shape, bloated, had virtually no movement in the ring. Yet

Patterson was defenseless against Ingo's right and went down several times. Ingo finally went down one more time than Patterson and stayed there, so Floyd retained the title. But he had made it utterly clear that he could not defend against a right hand and that he went down with unbecoming ease. The more I listened to Floyd talk after that fight, the more I began to wonder about him. On the surface he was still the same—diffident, almost timid. But things were happening. He had broken with Cus D'Amato, the very man who had made him, who had carefully selected his opponents and who, even though D'Amato never would admit it, knew Patterson's limitations as a fighter.

It seemed to me that, forever after, Patterson was helpless without D'Amato. Yet his public image was never higher. He was the "good guy" and Sonny Liston, the "looming threat," was definitely a bad guy. And always, somehow, Floyd got you involved in his personal psychiatry. He could not be vicious against Johansson in the third fight, he said, because he had been so vicious in the second fight and he never wanted to be that way again. "It's wrong to hate the way I hated," he said.

Then the new tack started to develop. "I keep getting knocked down, but I keep getting up. That's the test." As if it were now the mark of a champion to be knocked to the canvas even by a Tom McNeely, as long as one managed to regain one's feet. I mentioned some of my doubts about Floyd to my family, but Emmy and the girls wouldn't hear of it. Floyd was still their hero. More than that, he was as thoughtful and considerate as ever. He would keep popping up in our lives. From Sweden suddenly came a set of sterling iced-tea spoons. Also from Scandinavia an ashtray. With another foreign postmark a dinner bell. And, always, cards and letters from wherever he might be.

I often wonder what Cus D'Amato would have done about Sonny Liston, whether he could have kept Floyd away from Liston. After Patterson broke with him I continued to see Cus down through the years, but only intermittently, because of the strange and private life he led. I did see him every day during the 19th Olympiad at the Mexico City arena. Cus watched every fight in the boxing competition, studied every fighter. He was at his positive best in the process. Cus never wanted anything more from life than to work with fighters, train fighters, watch fighters and analyze fighters.

The last time I saw him in Mexico City he was sitting in a kosher delicatessen eating a hot pastrami sandwich. It may have been the most out-of-character scene I have ever witnessed.

But Cus D'Amato or no, the pressures were building on Patterson to meet Sonny Liston. The newspapers were headlining Liston's successes, speculation was rife as to when the two would meet. Even at the White House President Kennedy in a meeting with Floyd inquired about a fight with Liston.

So the fight was set, for September 1962 in Chicago. I was certain it would be no fight at all. In my talks with Floyd I sensed a preacceptance of defeat. On my prefight show he openly said, "I wonder how it will be when I come out."

Yes, he wondered—but not too much. Remember, he had a disguise ready, which he adopted to escape town. The fight lasted 2 minutes and 11 seconds. In the ring after the fight Patterson told me, "Sonny started too fast for me tonight." My instinctive feeling was that he was relieved that it ended so quickly.

Patterson became a recluse again, ashamed and alone, but there was to be a rematch the following year at Las Vegas. In the buildup for that, the word was that Floyd had fought Liston's fight the first time, that he had gone at Liston and should have used his superior foot speed, moved around and outboxed him. This time it would be different.

The day before the return bout Emmy and I visited Floyd at a ranch outside Las Vegas which was famous because Liz Taylor had stayed there. We spent an hour with Floyd, and, frankly, I was uncomfortable. There was no profession of strength, no expression of confidence. There was the same sweet little boy, the underdog, the hangdog air that seemed to have become his trademark.

When we left, Emmy said, "I get the feeling he's already beaten."

"He is," I answered.

This time it took 2 minutes and 16 seconds. And Liston told me in the ring, "I said it would be a rerun."

It was at this point that Liston looked down at ringside, picked out the young Cassius Clay and pointed, "You're next, big-mouth." It was the summer of '63.

Now my own relationship with Floyd Patterson was undergoing a subtle transition. Emmy and the girls remained emotionally tied to him. So did I, but only because of the past. And that tie was growing weaker; not because he was losing as a fighter but because of his constant excuses, constant escapes from society. At some point—especially when you have been the heavyweight champion of the world and have achieved in this society—you have to get out of that hole in the subway.

Patterson's next big fight was in the fall of '65, against Muhammad Ali, who had become the champion. Floyd insisted on calling him Cassius Clay, and I didn't like that one bit; it seemed to me a deliberate attempt by Floyd to cast himself in the role of the good guy. He did something else in this fight. He went into it with a bad back, a fact he never disclosed, and he should not have been in that ring that night.

In one of the strangest scenes in boxing, Patterson's trainer, Al Silvani, would lift him off the floor between rounds and try to pop his back to relieve the pressure. During the rounds, Ali would torture Patterson. After the fight, and after the broadcast had ended, I was working with a film crew at the Las Vegas Convention Center when Patterson was being, in effect, carried out of the arena. He was wearing jeans and a cap with the brim upturned. I thought, "It's amazing. He still hasn't changed that much. The thin lips, the shy little face. Almost like a kid from an *Our Gang* comedy." Floyd caught my eye. He wanted to be interviewed, even at that time. I found it bizarre. But I did the interview, with his aides propping him up as I did it. The excuse was ready-made. "It was the back." They carried Floyd out, and suddenly I felt terribly sorry for him. Where would he go from here?

A few days later, in New York City, I did a "Wide World of Sports" show on the fight with Muhammad Ali. It was during the taping of this show that Ali admitted that he *carried* Floyd Patterson. According to Ali, he "didn't want to kill him." Also according to Ali, he was damned if he did and damned if he didn't. "When I knock a man out I'm cruel. When I don't I can't punch."

At the moment when Ali confessed that he carried Patterson, I stopped the taping. I asked Chuck Howard, the producer, and Lou Volpicelli, the director, to come down from the control booth. I wanted them to be present while I advised Ali of the implications of what he had just said. I said, "You might lose your license to fight because of what you are saying. In effect you have admitted that you didn't put forth your best effort."

"I don't care," Ali retorted, "it's the truth and I want to say it."

It wasn't long after that that an article appeared in *Esquire* magazine, by Floyd Patterson, with Gay Talese, the writer. Gay had been close to Floyd for as long as I had. Indeed, Floyd was one of the principals in a book by Gay called *The Overreachers,* so Talese was very familiar with the singular quirks and fancies of Floyd Patterson.

In the piece, Patterson wrote in effect that "Howard Cosell, who used to be my friend," had gotten Ali to say that he had carried him. In the first place, that was untrue. In the second place, a ventriloquist couldn't put words in Ali's mouth. In the third place, friendship has nothing to do with reporting.

The next time I saw Floyd Patterson he couldn't look me in the eye. I challenged him about what he had written, and he tried to avoid the subject. More and more, as the years passed, Floyd would be receptive to those who had most recently written or spoken well of him.

Patterson's boxing life had now formed a pattern. In the World Boxing Association tournament, which began in 1967 to anoint a successor to the unfrocked Ali, Floyd was paired against Jerry Quarry in California. I did that fight, and in my opinion and in the opinion of most ringside observers, Patterson won it. In the peculiar California scoring system, Floyd won on rounds, but Quarry on total points.

Later, in the ring, there was Floyd again, the perfect gentleman, the gracious loser. There is no question that this posture continually appealed to the public; it had been working successfully for five years. But equally in my mind there had become no question that it *was* a posture, and this was confirmed for me forevermore in 1968.

That year the scene set was Stockholm, Sweden. Patterson was to fight Jimmy Ellis. Under the Swedish system the scoring was to be done by just one man, the referee—in this case a man named Harold Valan. Again, in my opinion and most of those at ringside, Patterson won convincingly. It was the best fight I had seen him make in years. Among other things, he broke Jimmy Ellis's nose early in the fight, which hampered Ellis throughout.

Valan gave the decision to Ellis. There was almost a riot in the arena. Valan had to be escorted out of the place by a cortege of Swedish police. I watched them sweep past, this frightened little man in tow.

Moments after the fight ended, Patterson—on the air—was again the perfect gentleman, the gracious loser. I looked at him. I knew he felt he had won the fight. Yet he wouldn't say it. The next morning the Swedish newspapers were filled with the story of how Patterson won the fight yet lost the decision. They wrote about me, about how I had made it clear that I thought Floyd had won. Emmy and I read those write-ups at breakfast in the Grand Hotel. We were to catch a plane for New York in about an hour and a half.

Suddenly I was paged. It was Floyd Patterson on the phone. He had to see me. Within minutes he was at the hotel. He personally carried our bags to the trunk of his car and drove us to the airport. He had about him a sense of elation. He admitted to me, now, that he indeed thought he had won the fight. I asked him why he wouldn't say so in the ring. He shrugged that little shrug of his. When we got to the airport Floyd carried our bags to the ticket counter. The Swedish people looked at him with love. Some would reach out and touch him, softly, gently, as he would bow his head.

Weeks later—after finding that the sympathy of the American public was on his side—he called my office. He wanted to go on television with me. We did the show, and he stated that, yes, he felt he had won the Ellis fight; he was sorry now that he hadn't said so in the ring, *but he hadn't wanted to look like a poor sport.* It was exactly what the fans wanted to hear, and Floyd instinctively knew it. He always did know how to appeal to the public.

The impact he had made upon that public reached its apex on the night of March 8, 1971. Madison Square Garden. The fight of the century. Perhaps the most extravagant sports event of the age. *Frazier* versus *Ali.* One by one the great champions of the past were introduced: Dempsey; Louis; Tunney; Sugar Ray; Archie Moore. Then another name echoed from the loudspeakers: Floyd Patterson. People stood, heads swiveling. They screamed his name. They searched for him. They gave him the loudest ovation of the night.

He wasn't even there.

It was a perfect tribute to a man whose career had been a fantasy.

But that was all the opportunists at the Garden had to see and hear. They realized Floyd was still box office. Quickly they promoted a match for him with Oscar Bonavena, which Paterson won on a disputed decision.

And that led to a rematch with Ali, who was now fighting anyone and everyone as he waited, and existed, to meet Frazier again. I was preparing to leave for

Munich and the 20th Olympiad when the match between Patterson and Ali was announced. I went on the air to say, unequivocally, that the fight should not be licensed.

I was in Munich, in the center of every controversy, when a press release from the Garden appeared one morning in my mail slot—carefully timed, I suspected, to coincide with the anti-Cosell publicity I was receiving in the States. It quoted Patterson as saying that he intended to "show the Cosells of the world." And to my disbelief he resurrected his old claim that I had induced Ali to say he had carried Floyd in their last fight.

Patterson had allowed himself to become a witting dupe to the cheap publicity cranked out by the Garden's boxing department. I thought, ironically, back to our last meeting. He had dropped by our home, some weeks after his loss to Ellis, with his second wife, an attractive blonde whom Emmy had never met, and their two young daughters.

When I returned from Munich I learned that "Wide World of Sports" would be carrying the Ali-Patterson fight. I was assigned to it. It was just what I expected—a grotesque mismatch. For five rounds Ali did nothing, absolutely nothing. In the fourth he had held his hands at his sides the entire round and merely bobbed and weaved and slipped punches; poor Patterson could do nothing with him. Then in the sixth Ali went to work, and, in nothing flat, blood gushed from a cut over Patterson's eye. They had to stop the fight, of course.

In the ring interview Floyd told me he was going to make his move in the next round. He said he wanted a rematch, "if the public will buy it."

That speaks for itself.

To this day I give Floyd Patterson credit for this much: His love of boxing, I'm convinced, is sincere. It gave him a place in society that he never dreamed he could possibly have. He has a tremendous gratitude to the sport for that. In an interview with me after he had visited the troops in Vietnam, he put it in a quite moving way:

"It's like being in love with a woman. She can be

unfaithful, she can be mean, she can be cruel, but it doesn't matter. If you love her, you want her, even though she can do you all kinds of harm. It's the same with me and boxing. It can do me all kinds of harm, but I love it."

We—my family and I—had made a commitment of the heart quite early to Floyd Patterson. With the passing years I grew ever more disillusioned and disenchanted, until I discovered what I felt was an ultimate truth about this strange and moody and complicated man, that he lives off self-martyrization and sympathy. Emmy and the girls to this day are touched by him. They believe that he has spent a lifetime trying to be understood.

I think I understand him. It took a long time.

The bridge between Patterson and Ali was pugilism's gift to literacy and culture, Charles "Sonny" Liston.

The character of Sonny Liston seems to have improved in death as it never could have while he was alive. He was a thug with a record of more than 20 arrests including a number of felonies—really serious crimes—to his credit, or rather discredit. He was a cheap and ugly bully without morality, and I had no use for him. It's just too easy a cop-out to say that Liston was a product of a society in which the black is a second-class citizen. Sonny was simply a bad apple.

In my dealings with him I found him unlike any other man I've ever encountered in sports. The first time I met Sonny—I mean *really* met Sonny—was in September 1962. He was getting ready for his first title fight with Patterson and was training at Aurora Downs, a broken-down old racetrack some 40 miles outside Chicago. I was doing a radio broadcast of that fight with Rocky Marciano, who had never met Liston either. We drove out to tape our prefight show, accompanied by Oscar Fraley, who had coauthored "The Untouchables" and who was then the feature sportswriter for United Press.

When we reached this seedy old place we were stopped by a barbed-wire fence, behind which patrolled as tough-looking a henchman as you would ever want to see. A pistol jutted out of a holster strapped to his belt. The whole place had the appearance of an armed camp. By a vote of two to one we agreed that Rocky should get out of the car and talk to the guard. Rocky went, reluctantly, and spoke to him through the wire for about three minutes. We could see the guard shaking his head. Finally he jumped into a jeep and drove toward the main house. It took about ten minutes and he was back. Wordlessly he swung open the gate.

At the steps to the clubhouse—where Liston trained— we found Jack Nilon, Liston's manager. He told us we couldn't go in; Sonny was in a violent mood; seeing no one. I told him: "Look here, Jack. You know as well as anyone that we [ABC] paid a lot of money for the right to carry this fight on radio. And that includes a prefight interview. Liston gets his share of the money. We need that interview and we need it now."

Nilon said, "You go in at your own risk."

And in we went.

The ring had been set up in the middle of what had been the clubhouse. The floor was littered with losing horse-race tickets, and all the betting windows were smashed in. The place was so ramshackle as to be almost beyond belief. The whole scene was eerie. When we entered, Liston was in the ring, shadow boxing to a recording of "Night Train." There were five or six other people there, but no one would make a sound. No question about it, Liston was a fearsome-looking man. You somehow got the impression that he had one eye in the middle of his forehead.

Suddenly, from an upper level, Liston's wife Geraldine, dressed in slacks and a lavender cashmere sweater, came down the stairs and, without a word to anyone, without looking at anyone, walked straight toward the ring and climbed in. And then she and Sonny started to do the twist to "Night Train." And all this time no one said a word. I tell you, it was *weird*.

I pulled Marciano aside and said, "Look, as soon as the Listons finish dancing, the smart thing for us to do,

Champ, since you were the greatest, is for *you* to do the interview."

Rock looked at me and croaked, "Knock it off. You're the professional announcer. I'm just a washed-up, out-of-shape ex-fighter. I want no part of it. You think I'm nuts?"

So I turned to Fraley, and before I could say anything he wailed, "Let's get the hell out of here. I feel like I'm on the set of 'The Untouchables.'"

They finally stopped twisting. Liston scowled at us in that baleful way of his, and Nilon went over to him. We heard Sonny shout, "Goddammit, I ain't talking to no one! No one, you understand?"

We understood, but we had to get that interview. When his workout was over, Marciano and I hesitantly approached Liston. Rocky started to stammer, while I held the microphone, "Uh—Sonny—uh—just a—just a couple of words and—uh—"

Liston snapped, "I ain't talkin'."

I took my life in my hands and stepped in. I said, "Now look, Sonny, you're going to be the heavyweight champion of the world and it's not going to take you long. You're going to have to present a whole new image to the American people, because you have a lot to make up for. I don't give a damn if you hate me; I don't like you either, and I just met you. But you gotta do this interview."

To my astonishment Liston responded with a big, slow smile. Suddenly I realized that at heart he was just a big bully. And he finally did a quiet acceptable interview. When we left they were playing "Night Train" again.

My first meeting with Sonny Liston. And once should have been enough. But there would be more, many more, for Liston was interwoven with the early saga of Muhammad Ali.

He came quickly, and passed quickly. Charles "Sonny" Liston, real age unknown, died under mysterious circumstances in Las Vegas, Nevada, in January 1971. I know of no requiem for this particular heavyweight.

Chapter IX

HIS NAME IS MUHAMMAD

---

*"I saw the punch,
and it couldn't have crushed a grape."*

PART 1:

The Rise

The first time I met him he was a brash, lippy kid from Louisville, Kentucky. He was a descendant of slaves, and his very name bespoke the fact. Cassius Marcellus Clay. His namesake had been a Kentucky senator, a relative of Henry Clay, and a slave owner. I had no reason then to suspect that he would become a dominant figure in my career, and an historical one in sports.

This was August 1962, about a month before Liston was to meet Patterson for the title at Comiskey Park in Chicago. I did my first interview with the young Clay, then engaged in a long-range campaign to draw attention to himself. It was very easy to be charmed by him, and I was no different from anyone else. He was attractive, outgoing, full of nonsense. (In the interview he picked both Patterson and Liston to win.) He didn't know who Howard Cosell was. Nor did he care. He knew me only vaguely as the guy who did the fights on radio. There was an appealing gaiety and irresponsibility about him.

In the weeks after that I had little contact with him other than to follow the pace of his career. He was going through a series of beginning bouts as a pro, coming off his gold medal at Rome as a light heavyweight. One had no way of judging his worth as a fighter. But some months after that first meeting I went to see him oppose Sonny Banks at the Garden. Banks (who some years later was to die from a blow in the ring) knocked him down. With me, Clay was suspect as a fighter because of that.

And then I watched him gradually develop under the shrewd handling of Angelo Dundee, beating poor old Archie Moore and then taking on Henry Cooper in England. As director of sports for ABC Radio I arranged to have the fight carried in the States. It was deliciously broadcast by a pair of British commentators. Clay won, but in the process was decked by Cooper, an inferior fighter who had been described by the British press as having "a great capacity for public suffering." Ali's defenses were not then refined to the level of precision they would reach within two years.

When Clay returned to New York I had him delivered straight from the airport to our studios, where he went on live with me on a local television news show over Channel 7. This, I think, really touched off our whole relationship and the series of dialogues yet to come.

I happened to know that he was waiting for an advance from Madison Square Garden and I asked him about it. He was startled. "Gee," he said, "you really know this boxing business, don't ya?" I did not disagree. Then we went on the air and we kidded back and forth. By this time, of course, Liston was the champion, and all Clay wanted, he kept insisting, was "the Big Black Bear, the Big Black Bear."

I needled him: "Cooper knocked you down. What's Liston gonna do to you?"

He said airly, "No contest, not a chance."

That interview attracted some notice. There was an instant rapport between us, not just because I found him a natural entertainer but because instinctively he sensed that the two of us made a very good pair in reaching the public.

Finally he was signed to fight Sonny Liston in 1964 in Miami. I distinctly remember a show I did on the radio network the day before I was to visit Clay in the Fifth Street Gym where he trained. In it I described what Liston would do to him, how Clay had to be frightened of him and how he was trying to cover with a youthful kind of braggadocio that would vanish when he stepped into the ring.

So I got to the Fifth Street Gym the next morning and at the sight of me Clay broke into a grin as broad as Atlantic Avenue. A feigned stricken look then contorted his face, "I'm gonna—just gonna collapse when I get into the ring against that Big Black Bear!" And I knew he had heard the show. "There is no way, no way," he went on, "that young Cassius can fight that man . . . he is a terror."

He made a mockery of everything I had said on the air. I surrendered. He wasn't angry, just having a great deal of fun with it, and instantly I began thinking, "My God, maybe it's not false bravado; the guy really thinks he can beat Sonny Liston. . . ."

I was one of the many who subscribed to the Liston mystique. The baleful stare, the huge head wrapped in the towel, all the rest. At that point I opened my tape recorder and explained to Clay that this was for the prefight show, that no one would hear it until he was in the ring; he could speak freely. I said, "Now, I want you to assume that you're about to leave the dressing room. You start walking toward the ring. What do you think your mental processes will be as you make that walk?"

He nodded, and in a voice that was barely above a whisper he began: "I'm leaving the dressing room, about to go against the Big Black Bear. This terrible man. Cassius Clay is frightened. Cassius Clay is ready to run. I keep walking toward the ring and, all the time, even while I'm so frightened that I'm almost afraid to look

at him with that terrible look he gives you, I'm thinking—
YOU POOR OLD MAN!"

I left there still not giving him a chance to win but
now convinced that the guy was totally unafraid. I
learned early in the game that Cassius Clay is one of
the most confusing men in the world; just being in his
company one can undergo a series of conflicting impressions. He has the instinct of a honeybee, darting from
flower to flower, always looking for the pollen.

The next day came the famous scene at the weigh-in,
like something out of the Mad Hatter. Sugar Ray Robinson, restraining him. Drew Brown, one of his handlers,
who called himself Bundini, restraining him. All the
while, Clay going through this act of apparent insanity,
gesturing and screaming at Liston, leaping around the
room. The blood pressure was way up. Everyone who
saw him wondered if he had truly popped his cork out
of fear.

So now what did I think about this curious young
man? I had been with him the previous day when he
manifested nothing but assurance. Now I saw this crazed
behavior and I thought, "Well, he fooled me yesterday
. . . the guy *is* scared to death." But somewhere deep
in the cabinet of my mind I began to understand that
here was one terrific actor. He had never trained for
the Group Theater or the Theater Guild or the Mercury
Players but he was nonetheless a born actor.

This was utterly confirmed when I arrived at the
Miami Beach Convention Hall that night to do the fight.
While the preliminaries were on, as I mixed with friends
in the crowd, I suddenly discovered Clay standing in the
semidarkness in the back of the hall. His brother was
about to fight in the next prelim. He motioned to me.
"You watch Rudy," he whispered. "He'll show you
something."

I did a double take. He was the most composed guy
in the place. "Wha—what was all that this afternoon?" I
stammered.

He looked at me, winked and said, "I wanted Liston

to know I was crazy. Only a fool isn't scared of a crazy man. You'll see tonight."

Now the fight began. We got to the third round. Clay was boxing Liston all over the ring, and Sonny couldn't get to him. The Liston left arm that used to seem as long as a lamppost couldn't even reach him, because Clay was circling steadily, swiftly, to his left, staying out of range. And he did it so quickly, so continuously, that he was always free to respond with his own combinations, beginning with the left. Liston was slow and ponderous, and suddenly I was in the process of seeing the Big Black Bear exposed.

Later a lot of people wanted to know if I thought the fight was fixed, if Liston just quit or what. They still want to know. To a degree Liston did quit, but he was a beaten old man, and in my opinion the fight was completely legitimate. To explain how I became totally convinced of that, I take you back to the third round. In those years Clay had a technique of turning his punches at the moment of impact, and it would be almost like a knife. It would just slit a man's face open. He once described it to me as "being like a fly swatter," which I though was a pretty vivid description. It was one of the skills I felt he lost in the three and a half years he was away from the ring.

But he sure had it then, and with it he slashed the left side of Liston's face. Now, Sonny had a flabby face, except that no one ever noticed it because he was so all-powerful. After all, he had the two quick first-round knockouts of Patterson, the sinister history, and people were petrified of him. Except for one blow by Cleveland Williams, he had never been really hit hard enough to stagger.

Now out of nowhere the left side of Liston's face was just slit from the eye down to the lip. It was like a zipper, and out gushed the blood, which he tasted. Rocky Marciano, who was doing the fight with me, leaned over and said, "Jesus Christ, Howie, he's become an old man."

Clay was in complete command and appeared to have

the fight won. But no, in Liston's corner some liniment was picked up on the gloves, got into Clay's eyes and temporarily blinded him. It is true that he would not have come out for the fifth round if Angelo Dundee hadn't pushed him to the ring. But there was nothing Liston could do, because Clay instinctively kept moving his legs, circling to the left. And then, as the eyes cleared, it was all over.

Did Liston hurt his shoulder? Was his arm gone? Yes, in my opinion it was completely gone. But more than that was gone. His spirit had vanished, because he was just a big bully anyway. He was a completely battered and broken guy.

In the ring afterwards. in my interview with him, Clay went berserk. He taunted the writers at ringside. "I told ya, I told ya," he laughed at them, "I'm the greatest, the Big Black Bear, I'm the greatest, I told ya . . ."

The next day the mood suddenly, almost melodramatically, turned somber. He appeared at a press conference as the new heavyweight champion of the world. And he told them, defiantly, "Yes, the rumors are true. My name is Muhammad Ali. I'm a Black Muslim now."

Everyone had heard the rumors. Everyone knew that Malcolm X and Clay had been meeting. Perhaps what some didn't know was that Rudolph Valentino Clay had *already* become a Black Muslim and had a major influence on his brother's thinking. It meant nothing to me because I felt it was the man's own business. I was amused by the fact that it mattered so much to the Old World sportswriters who have their own vision of America, which is planes flying over a stadium at half time and raising the flag and singing the anthem.

It was the same old refrain: The Old World writers wanted him to live by their code, the same mythological sports legend that through all of the years these non-contemporary men had been propounding; that every athlete must be a noble example, in accordance with their concept, of shining manhood; that he is pure—doesn't drink, doesn't smoke, doesn't try drugs. And there they were, in the 1960s, with the Vietnam tragedy already under way, with drug abuse raging across the country, with all the realities of life, and they wanted him to be another Joe Louis. A white man's black man. This young spirit couldn't possibly be that. There was nothing in his makeup that would allow it. He was completely a part of his time and he couldn't wait to tell them: "Look, I'm a Black Muslim. My name is Muhammad Ali."

Not only that. If the writers thought about it at all, *he* was the one who didn't drink, didn't smoke, didn't try drugs. Paradoxically he was the one who was pure. But he had taken the wrong religion, a different name.

I said that I was "amused" at the reaction of much of America and in particular some of the writers. I was— at first. Later I grew angry and finally furious. Didn't these idiots realize that Cassius Clay was the name of a slave owner? What intelligent proud black in the 1960s would wish to bear the name of a white Kentucky senator who, before the Civil War, bought and sold black flesh? Had I been black and my name Cassius Clay, I damned well would have changed it! The insinuations and objections of whites, in particular the ones that appeared in the press, can best be called racist snarls. What should I say about the likes of Patterson and Ernie Terrell? They didn't know any better.

This was 1964, and now the dialogues between us really began. We would tape virtually every Ali fight, bring him into the studio, talk over the film and have our conversations. And I would challenge him, as no one else would, because reporting was still involved in our exchanges. Invariably he would bang back. The fans argued over whether we were friends, enemies or what, a confusion that exists to this day. Some expected Ali, at any moment, to punch me in view of the cameras. If he ever had, of course, I would have broken every bone in his body.

Muhammad Ali immediately knew that I was on the side of justice. Only one person in the media called him by the name he had adopted. I did this instantly. I could not have cared less what the public's reaction would be toward me, and in some corners of the country I was already labeled a "White Muslim." I'm born and raised at law, and under the law a man is entitled to be known by the name of his choice, unless by that change of name he seeks to avoid payment of lawfully inculcated debts to creditors.

How selectively we apply our righteous indignation. Nobody calls Betty Perske by that name. She's Lauren Bacall. Cary Grant was a stilt walker at Coney Island named Archie Leach. Ever hear anyone call him Archie? As part of the sickness of the decade, and as part of the dugout mentality of a certain portion of the press, they would ceaselessly refer to Ali as Cassius Clay. But he knew my position and respected me for it.

(Coincidentally, I wonder how many people would know Howard Cosell as Howard William Cohen? And for the record, Cosell—once spelled with a K—*is* the family name. It was changed back not for show-biz reasons but by the family, to comply with the wishes of our late father. As a Polish refugee, my grandfather had been unable to make his name clear to a harried immigration inspector. The official simply compromised on Cohen and waved him through. So I understood, better than most, that names are not necessarily engraved on marble tablets, never to be disturbed.)

The only time we clashed even mildly on this was during an interview at a restaurant in London, before the second Henry Cooper fight. I began by introducing him as "Muhammad Ali, also known as Cassius Clay...."

He stepped back, very seriously, a hurt quality in his voice, and he said, "Howard, are you going to do that to me, too?"

I said, "You are quite right. I apologize. Muhammad Ali is your name. You're entitled to that." And I began the interview over.

As a practical matter, there is propriety to the "also known as" approach. Even today the *New York Times* occasionally refers to him as "Muhammad Ali, also known as Cassius Clay." But I don't think it is morally right to do so. As a matter of fact, it was sickening to me intellectually, and to the students on the campuses I visited, that people would actually make an issue over my calling this man by the name of his choice.

However, that was part and parcel of my association with Ali. Did it attract hate mail? Of course. But one cannot live by the reaction of such people.

Ali knew now that I would back him. Whenever he came to New York he would either call or just walk in on me unannounced. He'd get a kick out of strolling down the street with me, and he reacted to the stares we attracted. Our kidding would be very racial. He would say, "Call me nigger in front of these people. They'll think we hate one another. . . ."

By early 1964 it was clear that he was totally under the control of the Muslims. The syndicate of Louisville businessmen who gave him his start was now an object of the past. It should be said that the Louisville group did well by Ali; started a trust fund for him, were sincerely concerned for his long-term well-being, and then faded out rather gracefully. Now Ali couldn't make a move without Herbert Muhammad, the son of the Grand Prophet, Elijah Muhammad. This wasn't an easy situation for Angelo Dundee, but he kept trying to do his job.

So there was a suggestion of tension around Ali, leading up to what was to be the rematch with Liston and the famous hernia scene in Boston.

He was training at the Boston arena, and I arrived there one afternoon to interview him. Sam and K. C. Jones, of the Celtics, were in the crowd. I was outside at the front entrance with a camera crew when Ali drove up. The place was mobbed with fans waiting to catch a glimpse of him. He got out and raised a hand and announced, "Stop, everybody, I want you to know that this is Howard Cosell. And I'm gonna whup him. He thinks Sonny Liston can beat me."

That's when he started his "I'm-gonna-whup-Howard-Cosell" theme and made it a part of the act. That was also about the time that Bundini began supplying him with poems:

Bet on Sonny,
Lose your money.
Float like a butterfly,
Sting like a bee,
Bet your money,
Bet on me.

Now he took me aside and asked, "What do you think this time? What do you think is gonna happen to the Big Black Bear this time?"

I said, and I half meant it, "I still think he can beat you."

He was stunned. "You what? You kidding? You must be kidding. I'LL WHUP YOUR HINEY. You hear that? You folks hear that? Howard Cosell . . ." And he started all over again.

A few days before, I had interviewed Sonny Liston in a magnificent place called the White Cliffs of Plymouth, which looked for all the world like England's White Cliffs of Dover. You could see Hyannis Port in the background.

Sonny had heard—or been told about—my recent radio commentaries in which I had referred to him as, among other things, a congenital thug. He greeted me stonily, with the words, "You ain't my friend."

I agreed, and proceeded to lecture him about the necessity, in this life, of working with people whose company one did not enjoy. I told him I had a job to do, just as he did. The next thing anyone knew, we were walking along a deserted, windswept beach, under gray and forbidding skies, while the cameras rolled and I asked Liston the key questions relating to their first fight: Had he thrown the fight ("No"), and was he owned by gangsters ("No").

Later Rocky Graziano was incredulous, as he frequently is. "You gotta be nuts," the storied ex–middleweight champ told me, "to ask Liston questions like dat. I couldn't believe it, dat last scene, when da two of youse started joggin' up da beach, arm in arm."

I had to admit, it was a helluva piece of film.

I had never seen Liston look so formidable. He was just in superb condition, as though he had willed himself to atone for everything that had happened in Miami. I found myself thinking—in spite of all that had developed in my relationship with Ali—that given the shape Liston was in, it would still be a man against a boy. This time Liston would surely destroy him.

This was on a Thursday. On Friday night I got a call from the mysterious Cus D'Amato. He was at a Boston hospital. Ali was undergoing surgery. A hernia. That's how I learned about it. Cus was telling me on the phone that if they handled the operation right the fight could still take place—on Monday. Even as they were wheeling Ali into the operating room, D'Amato was holding court before a pack of reporters and explaining the nature of the surgery to them, and how the fight could still go on as planned. "Would you believe it?" Jerry Izenberg, covering for the *Newark Star Ledger,* told me later, "Some of them were actually taking notes."

The next morning I made arrangements to fly to Boston to update the story. There was a press conference on the Commons with Liston, and, to my shock, he had grown old again. There were bags under the eyes. Lines in the face. The sharpness I had seen at Plymouth had vanished. Overnight, it seemed, a physical and emotional debilitation had taken place. I left there convinced, at last, that he would never beat Ali. I had now gone full cycle in my impressions of this fight.

It was, of course, canceled in Boston and eventually held in Lewiston, Maine, which would become as famous in its way as a boxing landmark as Shelby, Montana. Ali resumed training at Chicopee Falls in Massachusetts, and when I arrived there to interview him two things were on his mind: a new camper bus he had bought and driven up from Florida—and a new wife.

He had married this sexy ex-model in Chicago, and she was due to land momentarily at the Hartford-Springfield Airport. So he wanted to talk to me and kid around on the one hand, but on the other he was impatient and kept muttering, "My wife, my wife." He had recently discovered women. At the same time he was worried about her nonadherence to the Muslim rites and the Muslim faith. So Ali was a confused young man, and Liston was hardly even on his mind. "There can be no talking," he decided, "until Sonji gets here."

Finally his bride appeared and all was well. He was free to do the interview. He asked me what I thought, now, about the fight.

I pointed to his scar from surgery and said, "It all depends on how much the knife took out of you."

He started to laugh. "That's my man," he roared, *"Howard Cosell!* All right. Let's use that, because I'm gonna kill this guy. Let's make it look like a fight and we'll talk about my rupture." He patted himself on the stomach.

The last recollection I have of Chicopee Falls was Ali telling me, "You gotta come for a ride in my bus." So I had to get on the damned bus, and he was just unbelievably proud of it. When we parted he said, "Remember, no contest. *No contest!"*

Then came that curious night in the ring at Lewiston, and to this day people ask me, "Was it fixed?" I still don't know. Was I suspicious of it? I was then and I am now. I never saw the knockout punch. The reports from ringside were mixed. Jimmy Cannon, the veteran boxing writer, said he was situated exactly right when the knockout occurred. He told me later, on the air, "I was sittin' right there. I saw the punch, and it couldn't have crushed a grape."

We may never know for certain what happened. My most vivid memory of the whole episode was of Jersey Joe Walcott, the referee, staggering around the ring and the late Nat Fleischer stopping it when the count had reached about 24. The entire moment was surreal. The kids from Bates College were pouring down the aisles and screaming, "FIX—FIX—FIX." It was an unbelievable scene in this little Saint Dominick's Arena in Lewiston, Maine, and I can't forget the two fighters leaving the ring. There was a look of absolute relief on Liston's face. I don't think I ever saw Sonny appear so content in his life, and I wondered about that. Was he glad just to have it over? Or just to be alive? There had been wild talk about rival Muslim factions and possible gunplay directed at either fighter, or both. Cannon had kept the story bubbling. Jimmy is the last of the Damon Runyon era of Broadway sports columnists, and melodrama was his meat. He had murder-by-implication hanging in the air. He dwelled eagerly on the presence of Muslims in the crowd at Liston's camp. It lent even more strangeness to the occasion, and it lent credibility to the rumors—that Liston's life was threatened, that he lay down, that it was fixed.

I can't explain the expression of total release on Liston's face when the fight ended. Or Ali, leaving the arena, spotting me and winking. Was it a dump? That was not then and is not now provable. If there is a secret to the story of Lewiston, Maine, it went to the grave with Sonny Liston.

We showed the film of the fight in stop-action on "Wide World of Sports." It was more ludicrous than ever, the mistiming of the count, the confusion in which it ended, the phantom punch. I brought in Rocky Marciano and Jimmy Cannon as part of a panel to review the footage. Rocky insisted he never saw the punch. Cannon made his public declaration that it wouldn't have crushed a grape.

Ali called it his "anchor" punch, and claimed that he had gotten it from Stepin Fetchit, the old, shuffling, black character actor. That was something I never understood about Muhammad. He included in his entourage this comic figure who symbolized all the old darky stereotypes, all the things Ali himself did not represent. It was a poetic turn, I thought, when Ali announced that the invisible punch was taught him by Stepin Fetchit. The fight was a fiasco.

I ended my show that night with the statement, "If boxing can survive this, it can survive anything." And it has, more or less.

*   *   *

The next public moment was the Patterson fight, and I began to get an index to the fact that Mohammad Ali could be a terribly cruel man. He didn't like Floyd. He considered him an Uncle Tom. He resented deeply the fact that the public loved Patterson and that he himself had become controversial because of his Muslim position. He did not respect Floyd as a man. He said to me, curious, "You like Patterson, don't you?"

I said, "Yes, very much," and I explained why, how I had become interested in him.

He shook his head. "He's not a good man and he's no fighter at all. I can do what I want with him."

I had the awful sense then that he was really planning to punish Patterson. He did so, savagely, needlessly, to my total disgust. But at the same time I had begun to grow uneasy about Floyd Patterson—the two embarrassing bouts with Liston, the departure with the beard, the constant humility, the obsession with saying the right thing to please the most number of people at a given time—so my own feelings were confused about the two men. Nevertheless, there was no need for Ali to have dealt so contemptibly with him. He just tortured him.

And so, for the first time, I went after Ali in a "Wide World" interview, establishing that he had, indeed, been needlessly vicious. He could have finished him at any time, but he kept Floyd on his feet. This was when he admitted that he carried Patterson. As it turned out, there were no repercussions from the New York State Boxing Commission, or any other.

Public disapproval of Ali had not yet reached the stage of hysteria, but it would shortly. His draft board suddenly elected to reopen his case. He was reclassified as 1-A. Ali greeted the news with the deathless words, "I ain't got no quarrel with them Viet Cong." It was an attitude many in this country would come to share, but not then, not in 1965.

He signed to fight Ernie Terrell in Illinois, but the commission there no longer wanted it. Not a state in the Union did. He was suddenly poison in his own country. Instead he fought George Chuvalo in Toronto, Canada.

The only memorable thing about it was that Ali could have gotten water on the knee, from where Chuvalo was throwing his punches. Later on, on "Wide World," Ali showed off his protector, the metal cup fighters wear to defend their manhood. "Look at his," he said proudly. "I needed that protector." It had dents in it. The referee in that fight could have been Errol Garner.

Ali was now forced to fight overseas. In May 1966 he traveled to Britain to meet Henry Cooper. I found him a moodier young man but still open and receptive to the love the British people lavished on him. He was a hero in another land. It was at this point that he came to understand that he was a world figure, unlike any other American athlete.

I doubt that he had ever, at the beginning, anticipated what would happen to him in America, between his public embracing of the Black Muslims and his resistance to the draft. Now he was getting a taste of it. Yet through all of the troubles he would endure in the next five years he was, in one sense, the most extraordinary human being I have ever known.

Outwardly, at least, he was totally untouched by it. I'm convinced he was unafraid of whatever the future held. His behavior convinced me of his total sincerity in the action he had taken. No man could have walked around with no apparent change of mood or humor if he were less than sincere. I observed him on college campuses, I was with him at all different times of the day and the night, in different atmospheres, and he never exposed the slightest vestige of fear. Not ever. Not over his future. Not over the threat of jail. Nor of his shrinking financial prospects.

He grew homesick in England, troubled by the uncertainty about when he would fight again in America. But the homesickness soon disappeared. Everywhere he walked on the streets of London, the crowds knew him and surrounded him. He had a taste of what it was to be an elegant, almost foppish figure of means. Once he even affected the top hat and tails and striped diplomat's trousers. He made a speech in Hyde Park. He could hardly have been in a gayer mood.

To open the telecast of the fight, producer Chet Forte had prepared a half-hour show, a film creatively done of Ali in various London scenes, all laid against the lyrics of Roger Miller's tune: "England swings like a pendulum do, bobbies on bicycles, two by two. . . ."

ABC was to carry the fight live by satellite, and we had rolled about five minutes of the film package when Jimmy Ellis knocked out his opponent in the first round of the last preliminary. Under the British system the fighters were to enter the ring within two minutes of the prior match, but if they did, our half-hour show on Ali would be down the drain. So we were in serious trouble. Chet screamed at me, "Howie, you gotta hold up the fight."

Chris Schenkel was calling the blow-by-blow. I was to handle the color with Rocky Marciano. Everyone turned toward me. I retreated a step, raised a hand and said, "Look, I'm in a foreign country. I couldn't do it in America, much less England. There must be another way."

Chet said, "No there isn't, Howard. You know Ali. You gotta get him to hold up this fight."

There was no time to argue. I leaped from my seat and started racing toward the dressing rooms. I really had no idea what I would say when I got there. At ringside Emmy was startled to see me go flying up the aisles. She must have thought I had suffered an attack of dysentery. "I'll explain later," I shouted over my shoulder.

The entire ABC staff was in an uproar, except for Marciano, who had no idea what was going on. I got to the dressing-room door and the bobbies wouldn't let me in. I screamed at them that I was Howard Cosell, and of course that made no impression at all. Just as I was about to give up, Herbert Muhammad stuck his head out the door. "Herbert," I pleaded, "tell them who I am. I've got to get in there."

He cleared me. I ducked into the dressing room, knowing that at any second the ring attendants were coming for Ali to make his entrance. Ali was sitting on the training table, relaxed, ready to go. He was telling stories to the bobbies, amusing them—and himself—with charming yarns about his boyhood scrapes with the police in Louisville.

Angelo Dundee looked up and said, "What the hell are you doing in here?"

I tried to catch my breath. "Angie," I panted, "hold everything. You can't send him out yet."

His jaw dropped. "What the hell is the matter with you, Howard? Are you crazy? My man's got a title defense. The other guy ain't a bad left-hooker. He knocked him down once. Cooper can do a job, ya know. Get out of here before you upset—"

Ali heard us arguing. "What's the matter?"

I said, "Muhammad, remember the great footage we shot of you walking around London—the way the people here feel about you—how much you want the people in the United States to see this now, with all your troubles?"

He nodded. I said, "It's on the air right now. Just started. We won't be able to show it if you go out there now. They're going to be coming in for you any second. If you go with them there's just no way we'll get the whole show on. It's critical."

He was thinking this over when they knocked on the door. A British ring official stuck his head in the doorway: "Aw right. It's time to go."

Instantly Ali was on his feet, shadowboxing. "How much time you need?" he asked me in a whisper. I told him 18 minutes would do it.

He started dancing around the room, bobbing and weaving. "I won't be out for eighteen minutes," he announced. "Nobody tells the champ when to go."

I patted him on the shoulder. "Great work, champ." And out I went, tearing back to ringside to report to Forte. "I don't know what's going to happen in this arena, Chet, but he isn't coming out for another eighteen minutes."

By now the place was in total darkness, and the

crowd was just sitting there. Three minutes passed and you could physically *feel* the impatience and the restlessness that spread across the arena, Arsenal Stadium, in Highbury, London. The fans started that rhythmical handclapping familiar to American baseball crowds. They stamped their feet. They screamed. The sound rose and carried. They must have heard it for miles. It was almost ghoulish, all of us waiting in this unlighted, outdoor stadium, like some kind of mass séance.

It was incredible, but Ali held fast. And finally the time passed. Abruptly a white spotlight cut the darkness and out came Cooper, who had refused to appear until Ali left his dressing room. And, at last, here was Ali. He had held up a championship fight for 18 minutes—long, labored minutes—in order for the American public to see a film we had prepared of him moving about London.

The fight began, and Ali quickly sliced Cooper to ribbons. It was over, and a riot broke out. The fans stormed the ring, some climbing over Chris Schenkel's head and shoulders. And I was desperately trying to get into the ring to interview Ali. Jimmy Brown, the football player turned actor, was there and he helped bodyguard me through the mob, along with our assistant director, Joe Aceti, a tanklike guy who later worked on "Monday Night Football" with me. I climbed into the ring, catching an occasional ricochet from some of the wildly swinging fans. But I was basically protected, and I proceeded to interview Ali.

He started off by thanking everybody in the world, and he began to go through his litany about the Muslims and the Grand Prophet.

I cut him off. "We've been through all that before, Muhammad," I said. "How about thanking the president of the United States?"

And he said, "Oh, yes, yes. Him, too."

I would recall that moment with irony in the months to come—as Ali took on the weight and power of the United States government—as I would later reflect on so many of our meetings and exchanges and stages shared.

What were my feelings then and now about Ali? What kind of man, at bottom, did I find him to be? These are the questions I have been most often asked in my lifetime in sports. I'm not sure they can be answered in the abstract.

He is a chameleon—a man of many moods. Open, expansive, gay and charming. Full of fun and mischief. Gregarious. Born to perform. But sullen, petulant and sometimes cruel. Without formal education but with native brightness and vocally quick. A very short attention span. A practical joker. A man of inordinate courage; how else to explain the willingness to have a career destroyed, to give up millions of dollars, to defy the authority of the United States, to risk the abuse of multimillions of people? A man of unquestioned sincerity in his religious belief. A man with an inborn need for that belief. A man who does not hate whites, but a man who would rather not be with them. A man reluctant to discuss his religion with whites. A mercurial man, impenetrable, a man who will always puzzle and confuse me. But, always, a salesman.

I was present at what I would regard as his denouement, against Ken Norton, when in the throes of inexplicable defeat and humiliation and pain, his only words to me were a final attempt at humor. To the end, he played a part.

PART 2:

The Limbo

"Howard Cosell . . . why don't you take the step?"

The summer of 1966 marked the beginning of what, in retrospect, would be the last sweet days of Muhammad Ali as a fighter. He would soon enter a three-and-a-half-year limbo in which Uncle Sam would be his only opponent. It was a battle that would cost him dearly and erode his great skills, which now, I felt, had only begun to mature.

How good was he, at his best? Who can say with authority? The judgment of any athlete, I think, must be related to the period in which he competed. It is absurd to talk about a Louis, Dempsey, Marciano and Tunney without relating them to their time. One can only surmise that a champion in one era would be a champion in any. Except for this: With every passing generation it is my own conviction that the athletes get better. The civilization around them makes it so. They enjoy better nutrition, better conditioning practices and equipment, their bodies are generally larger and stronger.

So I am of the opinion that the finest fighter of my life was Muhammad Ali—until, to all intents and purposes, his career was terminated by 42 months of enforced idleness. He was a picture fighter. Watching him in action I got a sense of watching an artist work with oils, hearing Beverly Sills sing an aria, listening to Rubinstein at the

201

piano. First of all, Ali had that superb size, that marvelous body. Second, while not a one-punch knockout fighter, he had the blow that could slit open a man's face. Third, few could touch him—not even with his hands held mockingly at his sides. His speed, for a heavyweight, was not approached by any fighter who has yet lived. And he had that same speed with his fists. He could land combinations with such swiftness that an adversary—any adversary—could only wonder where the punches were coming from. He was an extraordinary athlete. Lombardi once told me he would have made the perfect tight end in football. I have seen him on the Madison Square Garden court sink basketballs like Jerry West. He was a natural. But the skills vanished—as they had to—at the very peak of his boxing life. In so sedentary a sport as baseball, Curt Flood could not make it back after being away for one year. How then, in the most demanding sport of all, could Ali recapture the old skills after three and a half years?

There was no way. He was, after all, human.

In August 1966 he was still, in effect, in exile, driven abroad to earn the living that was denied him in America. He had to keep fighting; the legal bills were beginning to look like the budget for the Pentagon. So it was back to England for a quick joust with Brian London, at an historic London arena called Earl Lord's Court.

Shortly after my own arrival I learned that the motion picture *The Dirty Dozen* was still being filmed on location 30 miles away. To alleviate the impending boredom—everyone knew how the fight would turn out, including Brian London—I went with Ali and Arthur Daley, of the *Times,* to visit the set of the movie, whose cast included the ex–Cleveland fullback Jimmy Brown, Clint Walker, Lee Marvin, Charles Bronson, John Cassavetes and Telly Savalas. There hasn't been so much acting talent in one place since the last time Henry Kissinger sat down to lunch alone.

All shooting came to a standstill when we arrived. Ali took over instantly, captivating them with his stories. Finally Lee Marvin blurted out, "The son of a bitch ought to be in this movie. He's a better actor than any of us."

It was obvious that Ali had his head everywhere but on the fight. He was far more interested in ABC's plans for the telecast than he was in the match itself. He remembered the soft mood, the scene sets of the show we ran prior to his bout with Cooper, and he wanted to know if this one would do him justice. I assured him that the show would be five times as good. "We are going to open," I told him, "with Frank Sinatra singing 'A Foggy Day in London Town.' And we'll film you all over the city in conformity with the lyrics."

So we did. You heard the opening lines of the song as the camera caught Muhammad, alone. Then:

> *. . . had me low and had me down . . .*
> *And you saw him looking glum.*
> *. . . I viewed the morning, with alarm . . .*
> *And you saw him looking up at the sky.*
> *. . . the British museum has lost its charm; how*
> *long, I wondered, can this thing last . . .*

Now the camera cut a tight shot of Brian London's face.

> *. . . and, suddenly, I saw him there . . . in foggy*
> *London town the sun is shining, everywhere . . .*

And then you saw Ali with a big, self-satisfied grin.

A few days before the fight I still had to do an interview with Brian London, who was training at a beach resort near his home in Blackpool. I flew up in a chartered Lear jet with Joe Aceti and waited for London for hours at the beach club. He never showed. So Joe and I drove to London's home, and his wife suggested that we might find him at a British air base a few miles away. We drove past some of the most beautiful countryside I've ever seen, and then the base appeared off in the distance. I turned to Aceti: "My God, Joe, I feel like Dean

Jagger opening *Twelve O'Clock High* and going back to the scene."

When we reached the base, London was inside a hangar, playing squash. I whispered to Joe, "Let's get some shots of this. The guy is a better squash player than he is a fighter."

Shortly we explained who we were, and that we needed an interview with him. London was mumbling, but he agreed to do it. So I led into it, gently, by telling him, "Brian, they say you're a pug, a patsy, a dirty fighter, that you have no class, that you're just in there for the ride and a fast payday and that you have no chance against Ali. Now what do you say to that?"

London's eyes widened. "I say flip you, I ain't answering the bleeding qustion."

Joe Aceti rushed over. "You don't understand, Brian. Howard isn't saying those awful things about you. He's saying that this has been written and hinted at. You know all that, Brian, and the only way to meet this sort of thing is head on."

He said, "Oh, I didn't understand. All right. I'll do it."

So I went through the same opening. And this time he listened, and reflected, and shook his head. "I still don't like the bleeding question."

On the third attempt he answered it, we got our tape and returned to the city.

The fight itself was noteworthy largely for what happened in the ring afterward. Ali had knocked London unconscious in the third round, and he began our interview once again by spouting his gratitude-to-the-Muslims speech. I cut him off: "Awright, Muhammad, I think we've been through that enough, once and for all, do you understand? Now back to the fight."

The one-sidedness of the bout was illustrated by a curious vignette that occurred later in the week at Blackpool, which is the Coney Island of England. A courier rode up on a bicycle to the front door of Brian London's home. He knocked. Brian's wife answered. The courier asked if Brian was there. She said no.

"Well," he said, handing her an envelope, "I've got his purse from the fight."

"Oh," she blinked, "you mean they're giving it to 'im?"

I flew back to New York the next morning with Ali and Herbert Muhammad. Ali started right in. "Do you know what you said to me in the ring last night? When I was talking about Elijah and Herbert?"

"Yeah, I know what I said."

Herbert broke in: "Howard was exactly right. He had to say that. You've just got to stop doing that."

Photographers and reporters were waiting when the plane landed at Kennedy Airport. And that was when Roger Sharp, the ABC correspondent, asked him: "After what he said to you in the ring last night, when are you going to fight Howard Cosell?"

Ali answered, "Why, Howard Cosell is my man. We ain't never gonna fight." Pause. "No, on second thought, I'm gonna whup him."

Ali was now taking on every match he could get. He was a man running out of time, trying to squirrel away a few nuts for what would be a long winter. His third opponent in four months would be the German southpaw Karl Mildenberger, at Frankfurt. It was to be a fight of many diverse and intriguing elements. It would be the first color telecast of a sports event to be transmitted by satellite, and the first fight I had ever done alone. We filmed a dramatic interview with Ali on the banks of the Frankfurt am Main River, with boats and whistles as the backdrop and German urchins waiting around to get Ali's autograph. The night of the fight would witness the reunion of Max Schmeling and Joe Louis at ringside.

So September 1966 was to be a memorable time. Yet I didn't feel easy as I flew the Atlantic for my first visit to a country that, after all, had created an Adolf

Hitler. As I walked into the lobby of the Intercontinental Hotel in Frankfurt, the first person to spot me was, of course, Muhammad Ali. It developed that he was not altogether at peace with Germany either. He actually embraced me and said, "No porter. I'm taking your luggage. Where's the room?"

He couldn't wait to talk with me. So we sat in my room for half an hour, just chatting and needling each other. After a while I asked Ali if Jimmy Brown, who had been acting as an advisor to him, planned to be at the fight.

"He's here now. Upstairs."

"Good, I want to see him." I studied Ali's face for a moment. "You know," I said, "Brown became famous on his own. When you stop to think of it, I did, too. But you, Muhammad, without me you're a nothing. Nobody would know your name."

He wasn't sure if I was kidding. "What you talking about?" he said, frowning. "I'm the one that made *you*. I made you an international traveler."

I leaned closer. "I'll tell you the honest-to-God's truth. Not even Brown made it entirely on his own. He'd be the first to tell you. I *helped* make him. But I *made* you. Do you understand that? I *made* you. Nobody would know your name."

His personal photographer, Howard Bingham, was with him. "That's ridiculous," he broke in. "Everybody knows Muhammad Ali."

I shrugged. "Ask Jimmy Brown. He knows something about publicity. Where would you be without all the shows, without 'Wide World of Sports,' without me doing your fights, without the interviews in the ring? Yes, I made you. And everybody knows it."

Ali got to his feet and dismissed the conversation with a wave of his hand. "Ahh, I'm going downstairs." And he left.

An hour later I met Jimmy Brown in the lobby. "Hi, Jim. Good to see you. Muhammad check it out with you?"

"Check what?"

To "Pudgy"
With All My love
Howard

This is how I looked at 21—when I had my own hair.

Here is my daughter Jill and son-in-law Peter on the day they were married in 1968.

This is not Frank and Dandy—but Justin and Jared, our two grandsons at three and eight months.

My wife, Emmy, at the Olympic Village in 1972.

My younger daughter, Hilary Jennifer.

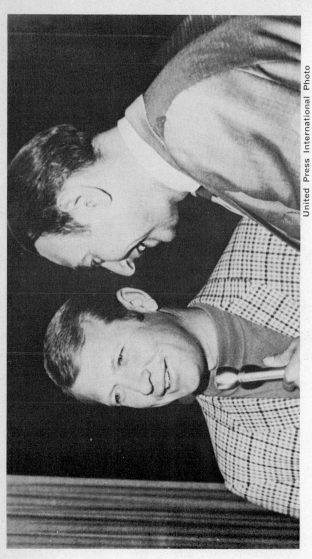

United Press International Photo

Mickey Mantle, the day he finally had to call it quits in March 1969.

The triumvirate who changed the living habits of millions of men and women.

Johnny Unitas, the second Monday night ever when I was at my lowest.

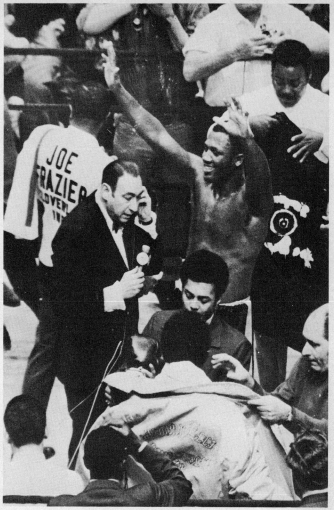

Joe Frazier at his peak after knocking out Jimmy Ellis
in February 1970.

Sea World, San Diego, California

Sea World in San Diego when I trembled in the presence
of a killer whale.

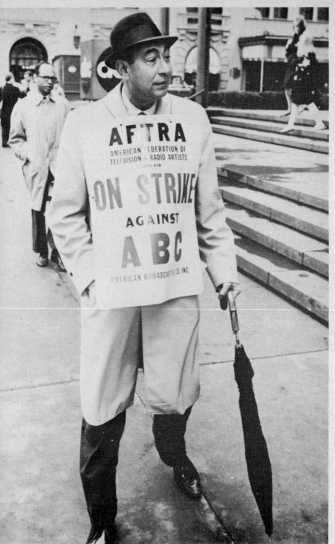

American Broadcasting Company

Up the corporate wall.

At work at Der Boxhalle in Munich, West Germany.

Ali, uncomfortable, at the United States Military Academy in August 1972 at the Olympic boxing trials.

Testifying before the Senate Commerce Committee in 1972 in favor of an amateur sports bill.

Gil Hodges after the Mets miracle World Series victory in October 1969.

World champion racing driver Jackie Stewart at the Grand Prix of Monaco in 1973.

"The fact that I made him."

He flashed a grin. "Oh, yeah."

"And did you tell him the truth?"

"Well, he asked me if you made him, and I said yeah. Then he told me that you said you made me, too, and I told him you were a goddam liar."

Over the years I have become friendly with Jimmy Brown. I can't say that we're "good friends" because on one occasion he explained to me that we were not—we could not be as long as black was second best in this country, as long as color prevented him from being a first-class citizen.

"But you and I are friends anyway," I pressed him.

"Only to the degree that our society will allow," he replied.

Jimmy Brown, one of the greatest runners football has ever produced, has been controversial in the past because of two highly publicized brushes with the law. Frankly, I never discussed them with him and I don't want to. I believe he is long out of that wild and admittedly unattractive phase of his life. As a person he is known to few. I like Jimmy and respect him but find him hard to understand. He is not an ardent revolutionary, but he is a proud black. He believes in blacks working together to better their job opportunities and economic growth, and toward that end he started the black economic union with offices on Euclid Street in Cleveland. "Only through economic equality can we achieve real equality," Brown says. When outstanding football players leave the game, they are asked if they will miss it. Almost all of them say yes. Jimmy Brown said no, and I am convinced he hasn't missed it at all. In the first place, he quickly developed a splendid new career in the movies. Secondly, he has a fine dimensional mind. He turned that mind off football and focused on the actors and writers and other stimulating people in his bright new environment.

Incidentally, Jimmy's ties with Muhammad Ali were based on more than his respect for Ali as an athlete and the warmth of their friendship. Jimmy had a financial interest in Ali in the television area.

I became convinced at Frankfurt that Ali is the most profligate man I've ever known. He has never understood the value of money and really doesn't give a damn. He discovered a jewelry store in the lobby of the hotel and, impulsively, bought a diamond-studded wristwatch for a figure over $2000. Now, even in a foreign land, if you're looking for a bargain the ideal place is rarely the lobby of a luxury hotel. But Ali couldn't wait to show me his terrific purchase. "Isn't this a beauty?" he kept repeating, and he fondled that watch as a man would fondle a beautiful woman. Then he added, "I've called all the jewelry stores in Frankfurt. They're all sending a man over to show me their best watches."

One by one they paraded in, until I lost track. He would look at their watches and nod. Then he'd pull out his own and ask, "What do you think of this?" And each would say, no, no, his watch was better. All had one thing in common: They were expensive. A Swiss elf could not have told them apart. But Ali went through all of them and when the last jeweler had left he said, triumphantly, "See, I got a good buy."

Ali needed 12 rounds to knock out Karl Mildenberger, who was tough and game and put up the fight of his career. Ali fought badly. He completely ignored the instructions Angelo Dundee had given him. Instead of fighting his normal fight and circling steadily to his left, he worked it out in his mind that because Mildenberger was a southpaw he should circle the other way. He just got himself totally fouled up.

In Chet Forte's room after the fight, Dundee joined us for a card game. He was so disgusted with Ali's performance he refused to discuss it. The famous card-player's lament, "Shut up and deal," could be heard until four in the morning.

* * *

Ali had now effectively cleaned out the European heavyweight division. As his date with the Army—or the federal attorney—drew closer, a few promoters emerged who were willing to risk the wrath of the super-patriots in return for the fat box office that Ali's presence assured. The likeliest shelter was the Astrodome, in Houston, where ironically his draft case would be decided. Ali wasn't exactly playing with a cold deck. Bob Arum, one of his attorneys, and Fred Hofheinz, whose father operates the Astrodome, were partners in Top Rank, a closed-circuit television company.

So Ali signed to fight Cleveland "Big Cat" Williams under the vast acrylic bubble on the night of November 16, 1966. Williams is a story in his own right, a once powerful puncher of the kind the contenders always avoided, gunned down by a Texas deputy and apparently finished, then managed by a man named Hugh Benbow, the Elmer Gantry of boxing. Benbow owned a farm at a town called—so help me—Yoakum, Texas, a half hour from Houston, and Williams trained there for his comeback against Ali. In those years we always filmed a fight preview for "Wide World of Sports," and so we—myself and Chet Forte—chartered a small plane to fly us from Houston to Yoakum.

We got there and couldn't find the damned airstrip. Finally, the pilot spoted it and we landed. It was about 100 yards long, in the most isolated place this side of the Amazon River. A car was supposed to meet us but there was absolutely nothing in sight, except one pole with a pay telephone on it. Forte walked over and called New York to get the point spread on the pro football games.

There we were on a Sunday morning in Yoakum, Texas, getting the line on the pro games at this remote airstrip in the heart of nowhere, when at last a car appeared, and we drove to Benbow's farmhouse to meet the great evangelist. Incredibly he had people pouring in from the wide-open spaces to actually watch Williams train. And the only interesting thing about the Big Cat was the gunshot wound in his belly.

We came out of it with a remarkable film piece. We moved in close on the scar and had Williams tell his story: how he was stopped on a dark country road, ticketed for speeding, shot and nearly killed when, in a panic, he tried to get away. We used Benbow's speech to the crowd, how Williams was going to upset Ali.

Of course, the fight lasted only three rounds and Ali destroyed him. Williams was no real opponent, but it was vintage Ali, probably the best anyone will ever see him. He chose this night to introduce a move he called the "Ali Shuffle," a kind of dance step that was right out of vaudeville. It was almost a quick foxtrot, a sleight-of-foot movement that, against the helpless Williams, worked. Later, on "Wide World," he demonstrated it on me. I found it as bewildering as had Williams.

Three months later he returned to the Astrodome—on February 6, 1967—to meet tall Ernie Terrell, who had won the World Boxing Association title in a process that can best be compared to a secret ballot. Ali couldn't wait to reunite the two halves of the heavyweight title.

We needed to film Ali for a prefight show on "Wide World," and we shot footage one day as he sparred with Jimmy Ellis. Ali was taking it cozy with Ellis, and Herbert Muhammad wasn't pleased. He came over to me afterward and said, "Look, are your people planning to be filming tomorrow?"

"I hadn't planned to," I hold tim. "This will serve our purposes."

He shook his head. "I'm not happy with it. The champ wasn't sharp. Come back tomorrow and I'll give you good footage."

So we returned the next day. The fighters came out, and within a matters of moments poor Ellis was defenseless. He was being beaten to a pulp. It was a savage thing. Dundee jumped into the ring screaming, "That's enough. What the hell's the matter with you?" He tore Ali away from him.

Dundee understood what had happened. He was upset. He was mumbling, "Dammit, I'm training the fighter."

He knew that Herbert Muhammad had told Ali, privately, to lay into Ellis. Poor Jimmy. Some years later, when Ali was making his comeback after being reinstated, they fought for money in Houston, and the line went that Ellis had a chance, sure, because he had worked against Ali and knew his style. I thought back to that day as he trained for Terrell, when he made it so clear that he could handle Ellis at will. And you had to wonder again about the whole farcical world of boxing.

The Terrell fight was Ali at his ugliest, a throwback— and more—to his performance against Floyd Patterson. He despised Terrell, thought him a whiner and a complainer. Ernie had been critical of Ali's stand on the draft and persisted in calling him Cassius Clay. Ali taunted Terrell all through the fight. With each shattering blow he challenged him with "What's my name? . . . What's my name?" The question was clearly audible at ringside. It was a mean game that Ali played that night. I felt there was lust in the way he tortured and humiliated Ernie Terrell for 15 rounds. At times he laughed out loud.

The moment the fight ended I was in the ring to interview him. He turned on me with a meanness I hadn't seen before. "I'm sick and tired," he bellowed, "of talking to you and taking your stuff . . ." He kept up a tirade until we went off the air. I walked away without comment.

The next morning I again saw the contradictory nature of Muhammad Ali. I was with him at the Hotel America in Houston, and he said, almost sheepishly, "I was really bad last night, wasn't I? With you—with everything."

I said, "You sure as hell were. You made an ass out of yourself."

He said, "Well, when I go into the press conference I'll make up for it."

A few minutes later he faced a roomful of reporters and could not have been more charming. This is the most vacillating man, in terms of mood, I've ever known. He complimented Terrell and appeared rather contrite.

Two days later he was in New York to appear with me on "Wide World." That was when we did the show that I have described earlier, a tough, hard-hitting show in which Ali said to me, "You know, you're not as dumb as you look."

Yet, a week later Ali flew to New York to announce the signing of the Zora Folley fight, and he chose that moment to say: "I want the people of America to know that Howard Cosell was very fair to me on our 'Wide World' show last Saturday."

The man was now completely penitent. There was simply no anticipating his moods or whims.

It was during this period—March 1967, a week before the Folley fight—that I saw Ali at his absolute comic best in a show with Wilt Chamberlain. The story was then gaining currency that Wilt wanted to fight Ali. And he really did. He saw the possibility of a quick million or two, and he actually did believe that his mere size and strength would give him a chance against the champion. Wilt had meetings on the matter with Cus D'Amato, and D'Amato reinforced his confidence.

Se we decided to do a segment on "Wide World" with Ali and Wilt. Wilt got to the studio first and sat quietly, waiting for Ali and Dundee to arrive. The next thing we heard was the voice of Ali, arriving: "Where is he? Where is this big basketball player who wants to fight the heavyweight champion of the world? This is ridiculous! Is this Howard Cosell agitating again? I would kill that man. A basketball player ain't no fighter."

And with those words, into the studio sailed Ali. Chamberlain rose and looked at Ali amusedly. Ali looked up at Wilt, all seven feet plus of him and for a moment looked startled. But just for a moment. Then the bluster started again as we prepared to do the show. We ran a "tale of the tape," putting the two men back to back, with Dundee and Bundini measuring the reach of the two men and all the other vital statistics. Ali looked like a pygmy next to Wilt; the mere picture would entice speculation about a fight between them.

All the while, Ali kept up a steady line of chatter:

"He would have no chance. I'm the heavyweight champion. This must be Howard Cosell, trying to make me look bad."

All Chamberlain ever said was: "Just sign the contract, baby. Then we'll find out."

Finally Ali, rising even further to the occasion, whirled and faced Wilt. "Size don't mean nothing. Reach don't mean nothing. I'm a fighter, the greatest." And then he leaned into Chamberlain, touched his beard and said: "Besides, you gotta shave that beard. I ain't gonna fight no billy goat."

With that he stormed out of the studio in a mock rage, content that he had done his thing. Wilt and I walked out after him, and found Ali already ensconced in Wilt's waiting limousine, which was to take "The Stilt" to Philadelphia. Ali looked at Wilt and said, "The champion should have the limousine. Take me to my hotel."

Wilt, ever the cool cat, smiled that sardonic smile of his. He casually got into the car, looked at Ali and said, "I'll take you there. Maybe I'll knock your block off on the way." The car drove off.

The fight, of course, never took place. Thank God. The NBA needs Wilt Chamberlain.

Around the country, speculation was now building over what Ali's response would be to his draft call. One by one his attorneys had lost their appeals to have his status reclassified. Would he accept induction and serve his time in the kind of soft, cushiony, showcase job the military had found for Joe Louis and others in the last war? Or would he refuse to serve, risking the contempt and abuse of his countrymen and even jail?

Ali's last fight before his moment of public decision was set for March 22, a month after his baiting of Terrell. He would meet Zora Folley in Madison Square Garden in an odd fight in which he would have little interest and little spirit. He knew he could beat Zora, a man he liked and for whom he could work up no anger. So the scene was set for a routine, dull exercise that saw

Ali knock him out with regret. It was quite a contrast from the Terrell fight.

Later, well after midnight, I sat in the Warwick Hotel bar with Roone Arledge and observed one of the oddest incidents of my career.

Who walked into the bar, carrying a little brown bag under his arm, alone, looking so remote from all of life that it was spooky? Who but Zora Folley. I motioned to him. "Zora, come on over and sit down." I asked him what was in his sack. He said a sandwich from the Stage Delicatessen.

We sat at the table in silence until I said, "Well, how do you feel, Zora?"

He said, "Fine. I feel just fine."

"Did he hurt you?"

"No, it was quick."

He had a drink with us and then off he went. I turned to Roone and said, "It's not real, is it? Unbelievable. It was as though he had never fought, as though he went into the thing to be put away, a matter of routine, an operation."

It was to be the last time I ever saw Zora Folley alive. Some years later he died, tragically, in a weird accident in Arizona. He fell into an empty pool.

Now the odyssey of Muhammad Ali drew Ali back to Houston, to 4800 San Jacinto Street, the Federal Customs Building—and a confrontation with the United States Army.

The date was April 28, 1967. I arrived in Houston the night before and went directly to Ali's room at the Hotel America (now the Sonesta). My assignment: to live with him through the induction—or rejection—process, with a film crew, and be back in New York the next night with the footage. It was to be the basis for a special we were doing with John Scali, then one of our ABC correspondents and now the U.S. ambassador to the United Nations. The special was to be entitled, "The Champ: Count Me Out."

I found Ali lying in bed watching the Johnny Carson

show, the bed sheets tucked under his chin. I began to probe. "What are you going to do, Champ? You going to refuse to take the step?"

"Can't tell you a thing. Can't tell you *anything*. I'm under orders not to talk to nobody. I only let you into the room because it's you. But I can't talk."

"I understand. I know the whole picture. But I have a camera crew and I have to spend the whole day with you and I must have assurances that you'll talk to me."

He shook his head and pursed his lips. "I'm under orders. Talk to nobody. You won't get a word out of me."

"What if I get a crew over here right now. Champ? Just shoot you on the night before—"

"No. Absolutely no. Not a word."

I had pleaded all I could. "Look," I said, "this is crazy. It's not going to do you any good, the Muslims any good, or anybody else. I think you ought to pick up the phone and call Herbert Muhammad right now and let me talk to him."

"Okay, let's see what the boss says." He picked up the phone, dialed Herbert Muhammad and said, "Howard's here."

He kept nodding his head. I could see it was not going well. So I said, "Here, let me talk to him." I grabbed the phone and got as far as "Herbert, I think—"

And he cut me off. "Absolutely not, not a single word. It's Elijah's dictates and that's it." End of conversation.

I hung up, watched television with Ali for a moment and took a few minutes to study this complicated young specimen. The astonishing thing was that the man was as untroubled as ever. During all of these days, and all of the years of turmoil that followed, I never observed any single evidence of weakness or loss of faith on his part. I consider that utterly remarkable, and, in its way, a testimony to the strength of his belief in his religion.

Finally, I got up to leave. "I'm going to bed," I said. "See you tomorrow. Maybe tomorrow we'll be able to do something." Ali nodded and continued to stare at the TV screen.

The next morning I took a camera crew to the Federal Building to shoot whatever footage we could get. Ali arrived, climbed out of his car and started moving quickly up the steps. I was right behind him, a microphone in my upraised hand and the camera crew at my heels.

"Are you," I yelled after him, "going to take the step, Muhammad? Are you going—to take—the step?"

In spite of all his orders, and all his intentions, and all his denials, just as we were about to enter the building he flashed me a quick grin and said, "Howard Cosell—why don't *you* take the step?"

"I did," I snapped back. "In Nineteen forty-two."

So now we moved through the crowd and proceeded to an assembly room upstairs, there to wait for that symbolic moment when the recruiting officer asks the inductees to take one step forward. The moment came. Ali stood fast. Within seconds he had been whisked into a private office, where a federal marshal read his rights to him. He reappeared, passed out a statement prepared by the Muslims and would not say one word to the press.

In the meantime I had been interviewing his attorney, Hayden Covington, and establishing what the legal defense would be. It was going to be *Dickinson* versus *the United States,* he told me, a famous case involving a Jehovah's Witness, in which Covington had been involved. I thought he had a strong basis for sustaining Ali's position.

Dickinson versus *the United States* was decided by the Supreme Court. In essence this was the case: Dickinson was a radio/TV technician who derived his income from repairing sets. But he spent only five percent of his time in this craft. The remainder he spent distributing the *Watch Tower* pamphlet and propagating his faith in the hope of achieving converts. The Supreme Court determined that the ministry was his primary occupation.

Covington intended to make the same argument on behalf of Ali. He felt he could establish that although boxing accounted for all but a fraction of Ali's income, it consumed no more than five percent of his time, the bulk of which he now claimed to be spending in the Muslim ministry.

Indeed, I suspected that they were laying the foundation for this argument when the press was invited to hear Muhammad preach a sermon at a mosque in Houston. I recall that the reverend addressed his flock largely on the inherent evils of eating pig. He explained that the sizzling sound that arose from the frying pan was actually "the maggots being cooked alive." I found his sermon persuasive. I have not felt truly comfortable with a slice of bacon since.

Covington soon passed from the picture, as Ali went through a succession of lawyers. Ironically, when the Supreme Court ruled on his case it would be simply on the sincerity of his religious conviction as a Black Muslim.

As Ali left the Federal Building I fell in beside him. "Look, Muhammad," I said, "I want to drive back to the hotel with you. I'll have my crew follow us. We'll sit in the lobby of the hotel. I will read your statement on the air and I will bluntly say, 'Muhammad Ali, in the protection of his rights, has been advised to make no statement other than that which appears here in writing.' And I will read your statement. Will you do that?"

He hesitated. "You'll get me in terrible trouble."

I said, "I think you should do it. I mean, it's just ridiculous for you to go on this way."

He said, "I'll do it."

We went back to the hotel lobby. His face was as stern as a mask. He can put that on, of course, whenever he wants. I read the statement. He sat there, said nothing. As the very end I asked, "Is there anything else you want to say at this time?"

"No."

"You're satisfied that this is a fair representation of your position?"

"Yes."

Later, after we had finished filming, he said to me, "I may have talked too much."

I said, "If you did, Muhammad, it will be one helluva scoop."

I flew back to New York and we did the special. The details of that day are with me forever.

Within a matter of minutes after Ali chose not to step forward, Edwin Dooley, the politically appointed boxing commissioner of New York State, stripped him of his championship and of his license to fight—in short, of his right to earn a living.

Mr. Dooley, a former congressman, was doing the popular thing. But there had been no arraignment, no grand-jury hearing, no indictment, no trial, no conviction, no appeal to a higher court. And, in a matter such as this, with the Supreme Court likely to hear the case, there had been no appeal to the court of last resort. In other words, due process of law had not even been initiated, let alone exhausted. Under the Fifth Amendment, no person may be deprived of life, liberty or property without due process of law. Yet every state in the Union adopted the action of the New York Commission. Now here was Ali: unable to fight anywhere in America; stripped of his right to leave the country, hence unable to fight overseas either.

Yet during the years of his idleness, New York and other states were licensing men who had been deserters from the Army. Ironically two of the major stories of 1972 would involve the boxing career of convicted murderers: Ron Lyle was pardoned to become a professional fighter; Bobby Lee Hunter, through special arrangement with his warden, emerged as a sentimental favorite while fighting.

But this unsettling, confusing, sometimes arrogant young man was dealt with, punished, locked out, while an overwhelming majority of the press and public gloated.

We were still in contact during the troubled months and years ahead, and still I found him utterly unperturbed. I saw him on the campuses and in New York and during his rehearsals for an Off-Broadway play called *Buck White,* part of a wave of black-relevant productions then developing in stage and film.

I attended his opening night. Who should be sitting next to me but Floyd Patterson, exercising again his habit of appearing unannounced at the unlikeliest of times. For reasons of his own—curiosity, perhaps—there he was at Ali's opening night. At the end of the show, as Muhammad was on the stage taking bows, he looked down and included in his final lines a welcoming quip to me. I pointed to Patterson, and a flicker of surprise registered in Ali's eyes. "My friend, Floyd Patterson," he said gently, "has come to see me."

And suddenly they were enemies no longer. At least for a time.

It was during this time that James Earl Jones had revived the legend of Jack Johnson in a Broadway hit called, aptly, *The Great White Hope*. Ali identified with Johnson, who in an earlier time had been persecuted and hounded for a life-style white America could not accept. He saw the play and, emotionally, went backstage to visit Jones, who had portrayed Johnson. "That's me," Ali told him. "That's about me."

He also recounted an anecdote that had been passed down to him by his grandfather, who had seen the old champion in his heyday. Johnson, driving one of the long, sleek fast cars he favored, was flagged down by a country sheriff as he roared through Kentucky. He asked how much the fine was. "Fifty dollars," he was told.

Easily, he peeled off two fifties and handed them to the surprised lawman. "I'm coming back," he explained.

It was all symbolic to Ali. He almost reveled in it. To many it now seemed certain that he faced imprisonment. I never thought so: I contended from the first that the courts would uphold him. But I often wondered how people could ask me, during these years, if he was really sincere. My God, the man gave up three or four million dollars. He was pilloried by ignorant fans and sportswriters and politicians. He gave up a deal offered by the federal government that would have made him a hero, a deal even cozier than Joe Louis had had. I was advised by Army sources that if he would agree to be drafted,

Ali would spend 30 days overseas entertaining the troops, and then return to the States and a rematch against Patterson, with a fortune in money for him and a chunk of the receipts to charity.

It is possible that if he had never fallen under the wings of the Muslims Ali might have bought that kind of deal. But I'm certain of one thing: There is no way this young man could ever have assumed the behavior pattern of a Joe Louis or a Floyd Patterson. It was just not in him. He was of a different time, a different nature, a different color. One way or another, whatever the reason, there would have been rebellion in him. Ali bent neither to pressure nor friendly overture. At one point the most famous black athletes in America gathered in Cleveland, at the behest of Jim Brown and Bill Russell, to meet with Ali and attempt to persuade him to accept some kind of compromise with the Army. Immediately after the meeting, by prearrangement, Jim Brown called. I asked what happened.

"No soap," he said. "The man is sincere. He's going to do his thing. He's ready to take whatever comes."

Every few months during this period a rumor would surface that a boxing commissioner somewhere had sucked up his nerve and was about to license Ali to fight again. But time after time, pressure from the American Legion or the Boy Scouts or local politicians would send everyone scurrying under their rocks.

One such instance occurred in Texas, and I tracked Ali down to a college outside of Dallas where he was to make a speech. At the time I was doing a series of shows called "Instant Sport Special," dealing largely with fast-breaking news. If a story broke we would commandeer air time from "ABC Evening News" and in a matter of minutes I'd go on with the "Special."

So I induced Ali to drive to our studios at WFAA in Dallas, and we talked about the prospect of his comeback, what it meant, how he felt about having the state of Texas license him. It never happened. The license was withheld, and he remained a man in exile.

But as one result of that television appearance, and

his expressed wish to return to boxing, Ali was sus-
pended by the Muslims. He was accused of acting without the approval of Elijah Muhammad in discussing his
plans publicly. The next time we met he shook his head.
"Can't talk to you no more," he said, "not without Elijah's permission."

This was simply further evidence of the degree of
control the Muslims exercised over him.

It was during this period of inactivity that a subtle
change in national sentiment toward Ali began to occur,
tied to the growing frustration over American policies
in Indochina. Ali had become the continuing story of a
man adrift; a latter-day Philip Nolan; a man who could
not find a friendly port. He was, in a way, tormented by
hope and anticipation and promises. Austin. Detroit.
Seattle. Las Vegas. Pittsburgh. Tampa. Hot Springs. In
town after town promoters hustled to make him offers
that could not be fulfilled.

During all these days, subtle and at times high-placed
pressures were brought to bear on Ali and those who
trafficked with him—including ABC. There came a time
when we were to telecast an amateur boxing tournament
between the United States and Russia in Las Vegas. It
promised to be a colorful event, with overtones of strong
national fervor. Roone Arledge wanted to use Ali—a
past Olympics champion, a still highly visible figure—on
the color commentary. Ali was delighted to accept.

On the morning of the matches the telephones were
suddenly and repeatedly jangling from New York. The
word had come from Washington that the "government"
did not view kindly the appearance of Ali on national
television in an international sports event that would
reach millions. Arledge would not back down. He made
just one concession: Ali was not to appear in an ABC
blazer.

So only a matter of hours before the telecast we had
to scurry around and rent tuxedoes. With his unending
cool, still serene in the face of all the furor around him,
Ali cheerfully climbed into his rented tux and preened
in front of the mirror in my hotel room. He studied him-

self from every angle, cocked his head and announced,
"No man can wear a tuxedo like The Greatest."

The show went on. Ali did his thing, taking special
note of the U.S. heavyweight, Ron Lyle. The cause of
democracy did not seem noticeably to suffer.

His draft-induction case was moving laboriously
through the corridors of justice. Would he go to prison?
Would he ever fight again? Would he have any skills
left if he did?

Meanwhile, Ali's attorneys had initiated their own
action to have his boxing license restored in the state
of New York—a case totally unrelated to the federal
government's pursuit of him. This separate action by Ali
came before the Southern District Federal Court, in
October 1970, in the very state where his persecution
had begun.

Judge Walter Mansfield determined that Ali had been
denied his rights under the Fourteenth Amendment of
the Constitution, which provides equal protection under
the law. The judge explained in his decision that the
New York State Athletic Commission had been granting
boxing licenses to deserters from the military. How, then,
could Ali's license be denied constitutionally?

So Ali now had his license back. But he had lost a
commodity no one could restore. He had lost time. Now,
three and one-half years later, he began a frantic comeback that would lead him ultimately into the ring against
Joe Frazier, the inheritor of his title. His first tune-up
would be with Jerry Quarry, in Atlanta. Those negotiations had been in progress and the promoters insisted it
would be held. Now the federal-court ruling by Judge
Mansfield gave the fight new momentum, even though
Governor Lester Maddox had declared the occasion a
"Day of Mourning." How fortunate the people of Georgia
were to have a governor able to react so forthrightly to
an emergency.

Ali's return to the ring represented a victory for truth
and order. In a way it also meant a return to games.
What had been a serious, vital, meaningful issue so

basic to the rights of man was to be replaced once more by the burning question: Who has the better left hook?

Yet still unanswered was the most vexing question of all: Would he go to prison?

PART 3:

The Fall

"I guess I'm not pretty any more."

Judge Walter Mansfield's decision, which in effect restored Ali's license to fight in the state of New York, was warmly greeted by that astute protector of civil rights Edwin B. Dooley, the chairman of the New York State Athletic Commission. With a magnificent gesture of hypocritical largesse, Dooley piously intoned that Muhammad would be welcomed back into the ring in New York. This from the man who carefully licensed Ali to fight Folley in New York just one month before he rejected military induction, when almost everyone knew Ali would do exactly that. This from the man who one month later stripped Ali of his title and his license to fight within minutes after Ali refused to take the step—and before due process of law as guaranteed by the Fifth Amendment had even begun. Dooley's cycle of cheap expediency had run full. If this doesn't teach you something about boxing, nothing will—and about politics in sports.

But Ali's mind was now on Jerry Quarry. One had to wonder how wise it was to have selected Quarry as the first man to go against after the long layoff. As a fighter Quarry is many things, mostly bad. But he can punch, he can take a punch and he is always unafraid. As a matter of fact, Quarry is one of the more interesting fighters around. He is an extremely attractive, well-spoken and personable young man with many of the tools

224

to be a good fighter but cursed with a rare capacity for defeat in all his important fights. He lost the WBA title to Jimmy Ellis. Frazier knocked him out. Unaccountably, so did George Chuvalo, and that takes some doing. He fought Patterson twice, really lost to him both times, but under the peculiar California scoring system Quarry got a draw in one and won the decision in the other.

But Quarry has a number of things going for him. He is white. He has an effective way of alibiing his defeats. He occasionally looks impressive. And always, there is the Madison Square Garden Boxing Department. They will keep Jerry alive. The best evidence was when Quarry outpointed ponderous Ron Lyle, a former convict who, at age 31, with only 19 professional bouts behind him, was ill equipped for the occasion. Yet after the fight Harry Markson (head of Garden boxing) said, "Quarry could have beaten any fighter in the world last night," thus setting up another match for Jerry some time in the future.

This, then, was the man Ali was to meet, fighting for the first time in three and a half years. What a marvelous situation for Quarry, if he could pull it off.

Atlanta, Georgia, was a happening the night they fought. The soul people came in from everywhere. Their clothes were a knockout, the costumes so garish, so colorful, that the artist LeRoy Neiman had a field day. It was like Van Gogh discovering the vineyards. They came to rejoice. The king was back. Long live the king.

The king looked like his old self in the very first round. He did not look so good in the second round. But Ali did open a severe cut over Quarry's eye, and they stopped the fight after the third round. Few noticed that Ali, after the first round, did not do much; that the old hand and foot speed seemed diminished. Few conjectured about what might have happened had Quarry not been cut.

But Ali did. Whatever he lost in boxing skills during the long layoff, he lost nothing in the way of promotional ability. Cunningly he told me after the fight that Quarry was entitled to another chance, that the cut eye was just a stroke of bad luck for Jerry. In fact, on "Wide World" that week we set up a split-screen phone conversation during which Ali promised Quarry another chance. This was October 1970. Quarry would get his other chance in June 1972.

But now step number one on the road to Joe Frazier was out of the way. Step number two would be the clumsy Argentine heavyweight, Oscar Bonavena. This fight would be held in New York, at the Garden, and, perhaps symbolically, on Pearl Harbor Day, December 7, 1970. One could almost see in the mind's eye Commissioner Dooley approaching the arena with the American flag held aloft.

It was while Muhammad was preparing for the Bonavena fight that the changes within him became visible. They were mental as well as physical. He no longer had a taste, even an urge, for training, the way he once did. His preparation was slovenly. His body seemed flaccid. And it showed in the fight itself; he was sluggish throughout. Often Bonavena would bull him about the ring. But clearly Ali was on his way to a decision, when suddenly, in the last round, he connected with a left that finished Bonavena. Ali, ever the instant promoter, grabbed the microphone from me in the ring and pronounced, "I have done what Joe Frazier couldn't do. I have knocked out Oscar Bonavena. Now where is he? I want Frazier."

And so the scene was set for what would be the biggest money bout in history. Joe Frazier had come into his own. During Ali's long absence Joe had become the recognized heavyweight champion of the world. He had beaten everyone, and he got championship recognition when he literally pulverized Jimmy Ellis, the WBA champion, with a series of devastating left hooks.

The Ali-Frazier fight was set for March 1971 at the Garden. The fighters were to share an incredible five-million-dollar guarantee, four and a half million of which was put up by Jack Kent Cooke, the West Coast sports entrepreneur who owns part of the Washington Redskins and all of the Los Angeles Lakers and the

Los Angeles Kings—plus his own sports arena in Los Angeles, the Forum. The whole deal was put together by an unknown to sport, a Hollywood agent named Jerry Perenchio, who represented such talents as Burt Lancaster and Andy Williams. There were multimillions potentially to be made from theater, television and the public—the general public, which had waited so long for this fight—would be virtually shut out from viewing it. In the name of free enterprise.

This was a fight that needed no promotion. But it got it. Every day, or so it seemed, Ali would spout off. He was going to do this to Frazier, he was going to do that to Frazier. Frazier said little. He was training as he had never trained before. Ali was not. Angelo Dundee was working as hard with Ali as he could, but Ali was not running in the mornings, the way he should have been; he was not conditioning his body for 15 rounds, the way he should have been; and there was telltale flab about his midriff. I asked his doctor, Ferdie Pacheco, about this and he shrugged and said, "He'll be in the best shape possible for a man his age who lost three and a half years of fighting."

I watched Ali closely during this time, and I became more convinced than ever of two things: first, that he could not recapture the old speed; second, that he took Frazier too lightly, that he thought he had more than enough left to beat Joe.

After an incident at Miami Beach in January 1971, I became absolutely convinced of the latter point. I was down there for the Baltimore-Dallas Super Bowl game. Ali, of course, was training at the Fifth Street Gym. There came a day at the Americana Hotel, where Emmy and I were staying, when, lying at poolside, we suddenly heard Ali approaching. He was screaming, attracting everyone's attention. "Where is he? Where is he? Where's that white fella who gives me so much trouble? Where's Cosell?" And then, his new jingle: "When I'm finished with Frazier, at the sound of the bell, I'll jump through the ropes and take care of Cosell."

He got to where Emmy and I were. The group around

us included, among others, Arthur Daley of the *Times* and the late Milt Gross of the *New York Post*. Ali's attention was diverted from me when he spied Arthur. "You pick Frazier," he said accusingly to Arthur. "I read your column." Arthur blushed, then laughed, and kidded Muhammad back. The truth was that Arthur was both complimented and impressed by the fact that Ali had indeed read the column.

Then Ali turned to Emmy and said, "I want your husband. I want to take him with me. I want to show him it's only fifteen minutes from heaven to hell." To my sore chagrin, Emmy said, "Take him. He's yours."

I protested. Ali insisted. "I know what you've been saying about me. I'm not in shape, my speed is gone. Well, I'm gonna take care of you." And off we went to his car.

Driving across the Seventy-ninth Street Causeway to Miami, Ali said, "I'm going to take you to the ghetto, to meet my people. You'll see what life is really like."

"I've seen Harlem and I've seen Watts," I told him. "It won't be news to me." And then with a quick grin I added, "After all, remember what the vice-president said: 'If you've seen one you've seen them all.'"

Then Ali grew serious. First he talked about the fight, explained why Frazier was no match for him, how he would box his ears off. After all the years I had spent with Ali I knew when he was talking honestly about a fight. There was no question of his confidence. I cautioned him about taking Frazier too lightly. He laughed it off. I cautioned him about his physical condition and his training. He laughed it off.

And then, in that mischievous way of his, he jumped suddenly to another topic. "Listen," he said, "there's something else I want to talk to you about. It's that football business you're involved in. And this guy who works with you. What's his name? Dandy? I think you're making too much of him. You gotta remember that we're the number-one act in sports."

I was utterly astonished. Here the man had less than two months to go before the biggest fight since Louis had fought Schmeling for the second time, and he was occupying his mind with matters like these. I looked at him and said, "You know, you're a nut. Besides, I probably won't even be calling the fight."

That set Ali back. He was dimly aware that Perenchio, whom I had never even met, had made statements to the effect that he didn't want me to do the fight. As a result I unwittingly became part of the publicity before the fight. Perenchio's star was to be his client, Burt Lancaster. Don Dunphy would do the blow-by-blow, but Lancaster would be the focal point of the advance promotion. I think Burt served very well in this regard. And he brought me into the picture. He went to Philadelphia to watch Frazier train. An entourage of writers was at the scene, and Lancaster started telling them how the telecast would be done. "Not like Cosell," he said. "He talks too much."

I'll say this for Burt. When he did the telecast he didn't talk too much. But that's about all I can say for him. As a matter of fact, we have become friendly since that bout. We've had dinner together on a couple of occasions and we have laughed about the promotion and the ploy in my direction. He's a hell of an actor and he has no illusions about his broadcast of the fight.

One interesting sidelight to this whole announcer situation was a talk I had with Jack Kent Cooke just a few days before the fight. He bluntly told me that he felt Perenchio had screwed up the promotion. To this day Jack will not state how much money he made on the fight, and the guess is he made much less than was estimated. He and Perenchio parted company when it was all over. Subsequently Jack made a verbal deal with me to do the Ali-Frazier rematch. There's no telling how much money Cooke lost by the failure of the fight ever to take place. And as for me, I'm in my fifties now and I couldn't care less whether I do an event or not. I learned long ago that sometimes you prosper by not doing something—you might even be missed—and that life doesn't begin or end with a telecast of a sports event.

But back to the automobile ride with Muhammad. By

now we had gotten to the Miami ghetto. His first stop
was at a pool parlor. We jumped out of the car and
went in, with Ali yelling, "Here he is, here's the white
guy who gives me all that trouble on television."

It was a dingy, smelly place filled with what were
doubtless habitues. The shades were drawn, the only
lights those above the tables. The scene looked like one
of those dust jackets on books about junkies.

"Knock it off," I whispered. "These guys might take
you seriously." But nothing would contain him. He kept
egging them on as they gathered around him and me,
and I began to get more and more nervous. Then,
abruptly, in that manner so characteristic of him, he
threw an arm around my shoulder and said, "I'm only
kidding. He's my friend." And then he leaned into my
ear and said, "Call me nigger." No way. I may have a
few years left.

From the pool parlor, we went to a barbershop which
he had frequented years earlier, in his early professional
boxing days when he lived in Miami. Unlike the pool
parlor it was clean and cheerful, a place to go and
shoot the breeze. A very big guy—he looked like a fighter
himself—started throwing not-so-soft punches at Ali.
Muhammad blocked and slipped the punches, dancing
about, laughing, never hitting the other man. He handled
what might have become an ugly situation with his usual
extraordinary grace.

But then he turned and grabbed me, forcing me down
in a barber chair. "Let's give Howard a haircut," he
laughed. "Howard needs a haircut bad, don't he?"

"Lay off me, Muhammad!" I was squirming to get
out of the chair. "I have little enough hair as it is."
I wasn't wearing my toupee.

The next stop was out of the ghetto—the house he
had lived in those many years before. He introduced me
to the people with whom he had lived, and once again
performed his act. Finally we were on the way back to
the Americana. His last words to me were: "It's no
contest. No contest." Then he added, "I'm glad you met

my people. But you gotta do the fight. We gotta fix that. It's no Muhammad Ali fight without Howard Cosell."

Emmy was waiting for me in the hotel room. "What did he want?" she asked me.

"It was strange," I answered. "Somehow he felt he wanted to be with me. Maybe because he's coming up to the fight of his life, and because we've been together so long. Maybe because he feels kind of lonely, with so many writers picking Frazier. And he did want me to see the ghetto, where he had hung out when he first came under Angie's wing. But he said another funny thing." And then I told her about Dandy, and how Muhammad felt that Meredith was displacing him as my number one broadcast sidekick.

"As long as you know him, you'll never really know him," she said. As usual, she was right.

The days moved swiftly leading up to the fight. Ali came up to New York, and so did Frazier, but it was Ali who was the source of news. Reporters clung to him as flies are attracted to a wet jelly bean. The braggadocio never ceased, nor did the crowds as he walked the streets. Finally it was just too much. People so pressed in on him that Dundee became concerned about his physical safety. Suddenly, in the week before the fight, Angie took him back to Miami Beach. The final couple of days Ali would train away from the crowd.

I was with Ali in the Fifth Street Gym for his last training session. It was a Saturday. The fight would be on Monday. I was doing a last-minute preview of the fight for exhibition that very afternoon. I had already video-taped Frazer, who was as tightlipped and determined and physically ready as any fighter I have ever seen. I watched Ali intently in this last workout. I didn't like what I saw. He didn't seem in any sense to be the old Ali. He seemed tired. In one respect he was unchanged: His self-assurance looked to be as high as ever.

We did the show after he finished the workout. Later, when Emmy and I got to the airport, we found Muhammad and Angie and the rest of the Ali retinue. On the

flight to New York he seemed positively joyous, kidding
with the stewardesses, moving up and down the aisle
and having fun at the expense of everyone around him.

I picked Joe Frazier to knock out Muhammad Ali
somewhere between the tenth and twelfth rounds. I had
been saying this on the air continually from a month before the fight until the day of the fight. Ali knew it. All
he said was, "Cosell, you're wrong. You're always wrong."

I suppose no matter how old you get, no matter how
long you've been around, the tension of an event can
get to you. In this case it got to me and it got to Emmy.
It even got to Don Klosterman, the general manager
of the Baltimore Colts, who was our weekend guest and
was going to the fight with us. New York City was alive
and it, too, was tense. You could feel it everywhere. We
went to the Rainbow Grill the night before the fight and
Louis Prima talked about the fight more than he blew
his horn. There wasn't a saloon in town where the arguments weren't taking place. There hadn't been anything
like this since 1938, when Louis did away with Schmeling. My mind kept going back to Bob Considine's superb
write-up of that fight. He told how the sweat was on his
hands, how the typewriter keys wouldn't work, how the
mind was numb. Here the Ali-Frazier fight hadn't even
taken place yet, and I had some of the same feeling.

The day of the fight seemed to take forever. First, the
weigh-in, with the usual Ali act, and with Frazier just
snarling that he was ready. Finally there was dinner,
which Emmy and I had with Don Klosterman and Elton
Rule, president of the American Broadcasting Companies.
He was ill, but was going anyway, because he didn't want
to miss this one. Later he learned that he had hepatitis,
and nearly everyone in the company was scurried for
gamma-globulin shots.

We got to the garden. In my lifetime there has never
been an event like it—for atmosphere, for tension, for
anticipation. The preliminaries dragged on. At last
the main event was on tap. All over the arena there were
nothing but celebrities. Sinatra was taking pictures for

Life magazine, and Lancaster was duly posted at ring-side. The crowd could not be still. When Frazier was introduced there were thunderous cheers and boos. When Ali was introduced there was the same admixture, but trebled in volume. Referee Arthur Mercante gave the fighters their instructions, and it was under way.

The rest is ring history. It was a great fight, a truly great fight. As always in Ali fights there were curiosities: the way Ali would rest against the ropes, gloves together in front of his face, expecting Frazier to punch himself out; the way Frazier came ceaselessly at him; the way Ali would show flashes of what he once was—an utterly superb machine; the way Frazier seemed, with that non-protecting style of his, a human punching bag. For ten rounds Ali amazed me. I had him ahead at that point. In the eleventh Frazier got him with a left hook, and Ali wandered aimlessly about the ring. Some still think he was playacting. I don't. I think that blow in the eleventh turned the fight for Frazier. I believe Joe won the twelfth, thirteenth and fifteenth, when he floored Ali. I scored the fight 8-6-1 for Frazier.

But the punishment Joe took was unbelievable. His manager, Yancey Durham, and his handlers virtually carried Frazier to his dressing room. His face was a hideous pulpy mess. And then Emmy and I waited in the aisle as Muhammad walked out. *Walked out.* His right jaw was swollen, as if he had an apple in it, but he had all his senses. As he went past he spotted me—and he winked! He actually winked. He would never change.

They talked about that fight for weeks. The following Saturday Frazier and Ali were to be on "Wide World" with me. Only Ali came. Frazier was in the hospital. He didn't get out for three weeks. Ali had taken the defeat the night of the fight with good grace. He had told the press, as he held his jaw, "I guess I'm not pretty any more."

But on Saturday he began his new campaign. He was the real winner of the fight. That was his line. He was declared the loser only because of his religion and his

attitude toward the draft. Look what he had done to
Frazier. In the succeeding weeks, with Joe still in the
hospital, he developed this theme repeatedly, for all
who would listen and for all who would write. And
people began to believe him. He called himself "The
People's Champ," and somebody manufactured buttons
with Ali's picture and those three words "The People's
Champ" on the face of the button. But Frazier was the
champion. Ali could be the propaganda champion, but
Frazier held the title.

I look back on the fight often. I have studied the films.
Under the circumstances it may have been the greatest
fight Ali ever fought. Why? Because he was going against
a very good, very tough fighter. He had lost three and
one-half years at the peak of his skills. Those skills were
no longer supreme. His physical condition was not what
it had been in those earlier years. Only on rare occasions
in the fight could he move with the speed of yore. He
had to rest against the ropes, to conserve himself, in
order to go the distance. Yet he did go the distance, and
in the process he inflicted untold physical damage upon
Frazier, who ever since that day has shown no sign of
being the very good fighter that he had been. In my view
the Frazier fight was an authentication of Ali's greatness
as a fighter.

Now all the talk would be of a rematch. But, in the
first place, there could only be a rematch if Ali were
available. The government's action against him was before the Supreme Court. He had been convicted in the
federal district court, and the circuit court of appeals had
upheld the conviction. If the Supreme Court of the United
States upheld the conviction, then jail beckoned. Ali
remained unperturbed. Whenever I was with him he
would talk only of fighting again, and of fighting Joe
Frazier again. His battle with the government hardly
seemed to be on his mind.

The Supreme Court ruled on his case in May 1971.
It was now as much a conservative court—based upon
Nixon appointments—as a liberal court. But it didn't
matter. They all voted alike. By a count of eight to noth-

ing the conviction was reversed. The court simply decided that Muhammad was sincere in his religious convictions. And so Ali was a free man. I spoke to him on the phone immediately after I heard the news. He was quiet, almost humble. He had always been certain, he told me, that it would turn out that way. And he said he had no bitterness. "The people who were against me thought they were right."

Of course, they thought they were right. But that hardly excuses their willingness to ignore due process, to accept violations of constitutional guarantees that they hardly understood. The case of the *United States* vs. *Muhammad Ali* was duly processed at a time in this country when people were understandably clamoring for law and order. The only problem was that many of the people doing the clamoring understood law and order only in terms of a policeman with a billy club hitting some bum in the street. Law and order, in a government of laws, begins with the fundamental law of the land, the Constitution and its multiple amendments. When due process of law, as guaranteed by the Fifth Amendment, had been finally exhausted, Ali had won the biggest fight he would ever fight. This is why he is a figure for the history books, not just the sports-history books. His case proved again the truth of the old adage: What is popular is not always right; what is right is not always popular. But nobody could give him back the three and a half years that had been taken from him. Nobody.

Later Ali would confide to me that the decision was a load off his mind. It had to be. Despite all the cover, all the bluster, he is human, and the specter of incarceration had to have taken its toll on him.

So it was back to fighting, to stay in shape for the return match with Frazier. Ali's next bout would be against Jimmy Ellis, his former sparring partner, in June 1971. While I knew that Ali was no longer a great fighter, I couldn't believe this one. My mind went back to the time, before the Terrell fight in 1967, when Ali, at the behest of Herbert Muhammad, simply destroyed Jimmy during a sparring session. I went on the air and disclosed that incident, and I took the position that the fight should not be licensed.

Ali heard what I was saying. He sent word to me: "Tell Cosell that I'm going to whup him next." Then came the inevitable buildup that is part and parcel of boxing. Ellis would be a tough opponent. He knew Muhammad's style of fighting better than anyone else from the long years of sparring with him. The Frazier bout had taken much out of Ali.

This was all hogwash. Ali put him away in laconic fashion.

Next was the fiasco in the Houston Astrodome in November 1971—Ali against Buster Mathis. Muhammad did virtually no training for this one. He was woefully out of shape, sluggish and had actually made a quick trip to South America for an exhibition within two weeks of the Mathis fight. I arrived in Houston to do the fight for "Wide World" and I was appalled by the proceedings. Ali did little or nothing in the ring. Mathis did even less. The disaster was leavened only by the "Ali Shuffle" from time to time, whereupon Mathis would counter with his own version of the shuffle. In the ring after the fight Ali said to me, "You said this fight shouldn't be licensed. Mathis was a tough opponent. He fought a great fight." Actually Mathis went down from sheer fatigue, the fatigue of trying to move his huge body around the ring for 12 rounds. So Ali won by a knockout.

When I got back to New York, Roone Arledge and Jim Spence met with me. They did not feel that the fight was worthy of being shown in its entirety. We discussed at length the approach to be taken. We had paid a lot of money for the broadcast rights to the fight, but that didn't matter. What mattered was that the highest standards of professionalism had not been observed by Ali in his preparation for the event, and we wanted the public to know it. So we took selected rounds of the fight and showed it for what it was. When Ali and Mathis shuffled we used as accompanying music the song "Shuffle Off to Buffalo." When Mathis was stumbling about the ring we played Johnny Mathis singing "Help Me Make It Through the Night."

And that was the way the show played. I also did a commentary explaining our position, what we felt the obligation of Muhammad Ali, or any fighter, was to the public, and where we felt he had failed in that obligation. An uproar followed. Some sportswriters took the stand that we had an obligation to show the fight in its entirety, that we had advertised it that way. Actually we had not. But they were entitled to their thinking.

What was interesting was that Mathis's owners and Mathis himself threatened ABC, Roone Arledge and me with a libel suit. Mathis called me "a cruel man." That threat died aborning. When the writers called Ali for his comments about what we had done with the broadcast, Ali said, "That's their right. 'Wide World of Sports' has been very good to me." He then added, "I'm gonna whup Cosell." (What else?)

After Mathis, Ali finished off the likes of Jürgen Blin, Mac Foster and, believe it or not, George Chuvalo again. The bum-of-the-month club was back.

In June 1972 it was Jerry Quarry's turn again at Las Vegas, Nevada. Ali's body looked better conditioned than it had for a long time. He really gave it to Quarry this time. Some of the old foot movement was back, and the hands seemed quick again. Quarry is a sucker for a left. Immediately after he delivers a right he drops it and is wide open for the opponent's left. For Ali it was a matter of target practice. He battered Quarry at will. Between the fifth and sixth rounds he leaned over the ropes in his corner and said to me, "So I'm washed up, am I? How do you like the way I look tonight?" I had to admit that he was putting on quite a show and I began to wonder if I had counted him out too soon.

Mercifully they stopped that fight in the seventh. After Emmy and I had left the arena I was accosted by a woman who screamed at me, "Why did they stop it? Jerry was still on his feet. He could have beaten that bum."

We looked at her as if she were crazy. "Who are you?" I asked.

"I'm Jerry's aunt," she replied.

"Do you want him to get killed?" I asked her. And we walked away, disgusted.

In August 1972 I was doing the finals of the Olympic Boxing Trials at West Point. Arledge hired Ali to do the color with me. It was an interesting experience. I went to the academy with Wally and Ginny Schwartz. It was a glorious summer day, the Hudson looked as beautiful as the Rhine ever did, and a percentage of the cadets were on the grounds. We got there early, before Ali arrived, and were on our way to the Officers' Mess for lunch when a limousine approached us. Ali was in it. He asked where I was going. I told him. He wanted to go with me. He was strangely discomforted, and I sensed immediately what his difficulty was. Here he was, the man who had rejected military induction, visiting the heart of the military, the very place where our Army officers are incubated. I represented security to him. I told him to go down to the field house, report in to our producer, Ned Steckel, and advised him to join us right after that. He never did catch up with us. The cadets were friendly to him, and with his confidence restored he bantered jovially with them for the rest of the day. But the minute the program ended—we were going live— he was gone. Just a wave good-bye. He wanted to get out of there.

That was the day he saw our Olympic heavyweight, Duane Bobick, for the first time. Never one to miss a trick, Ali started to promote him at once. A new "White Hope." A terrific puncher. You would have thought the youngster from Bowlus, Minnesota, was ready to fight for the heavyweight title. Ali was counting the potential gate two years hence. He was too optimistic, in light of what happened to Duane at the Olympics.

Another interesting sidelight occurred that day. Muhammad had signed to fight Floyd Patterson again at the Garden in September. "You're saying that this fight shouldn't be licensed, aren't you?" he asked me.

"Yes," I answered "I don't want you to hurt him."

"I won't hurt him," he promised. "But Patterson's broke, he needs money."

"What? I thought Floyd, of all fighters, had kept his money. I thought he was in good shape for the rest of his life."

"No," Ali told me. "His taxes were all mixed up and the Internal Revenue has got all of it." I was astonished, and lated called Bob Arum, Ali's attorney and, incidentally, a good tax man. He confirmed what Ali had told me. So there may be another factor in why Floyd keeps fighting.

After Patterson came Bob Foster and Joe Bugner. Foster cut Ali over the eye, and Bugner survived 12 rounds—both facts not very subtle indexes to Ali's decline as a fighter. Still, at the time when Ali fought Bugner, many believed that Ali could defeat the new heavyweight champion, George Foreman, who had destroyed Frazier at Kingston, Jamaica, in January 1973. One of those who thought so was the famous oddsmaker, Jimmy "the Greek" Snyder. I did a show with Jimmy in March wherein he said he would make Ali a six-to-five favorite over Foreman if the two fought within the next year. This was just a couple of weeks before Ali fought a man named Ken Norton in San Diego, California.

When Emmy and I landed in San Diego on the afternoon of March 30, Jerry Gross, a San Diego sports announcer, was waiting at the airport to do a news spot with me. "What do you think of the fight, Howard?" Jerry asked me.

"What fight?" I answered.

He laughed. "Ali-Norton," he said.

"It's a farce," I said. (I never go out on a limb.)

The truth is, I had seen Norton in sparring sessions with Joe Frazier. I considered him a club fighter and I still do.

I got my first shock that evening. We went over to the hotel where Ali was staying. A party was being held

for the benefit of sickle-cell anemia victims, and I
wanted to stop by. Downstairs in the coffee shop Ali
was holding court. H saw me coming, jumped up and
started the usual twaddle. "Here's Cosell, the man who
gives me such trouble," etc., etc.

I looked at him. In the six weeks since the Bugner fight
he had ballooned terribly. He looked flabby. But I
never gave it a second thought; there seemed no way he
could lose to Ken Norton. Angie Dundee had told me
all about Norton. "He's tailor-made for Ali," Angie had
said. "He's wide open for a left, he has no right, kind
of chops with it, his only good punch is a left hook
to the belly, and he has an open stance and drags one
leg." With that assessment from Angie one couldn't expect any kind of fight at all. And obviously Ali didn't.
It was the night before the fight and he was all over
that coffee shop, laughing and talking, here and there,
swarmed over by people. Not a moment's rest. However it was only about eight o'clock then.

Emmy and I paid a visit to the party, and then, together with Dundee and Yancey Durham, Frazier's manager, we went out to dinner. We never even talked about
the Norton fight. Throughout dinner the talk was about
Dick Saddler, Foreman's manager, and how Dick seemed
to be avoiding Durham. Saddler had been in San Diego
but left before Yancey arrived. Yancey was, of course,
pursuing Saddler because he wanted a rematch with
Foreman for Frazier. Saddler, however, the day before
Durham arrived, had met with Bob Arum and Herbert
Muhammad, Ali's attorney and manager, to discuss an
Ali-Foreman fight. This is the kind of inner sparring
that takes place in the formation of championship
matches. You can't really believe or trust anybody. But
one thing was certain: Ken Norton did not exist, not
for Durham, not for Dundee and not for Dick Saddler.

After dinner we went back to the hotel. It was now
about eleven o'clock. Emmy waited in the car while I ran
into the hotel to see about tickets for the next day. Ali
was still up, still holding court. It was as if there were
no such thing as a fight the next day. I was incredulous.

When I got back to the car I told Emmy. "The man's crazy," I said. But I never gave a thought to his losing.

I had to go back to the hotel the next morning to get the tickets. It was about 9:45. The scene hadn't changed. Ali was on center stage, regaling 15 or 20 people around him with story after story. He saw me and came over. "Look," he said, "I want you to know this for the telecast. When we're both in the ring, being introduced, I'm going to start waving my hands in front of him, slowly, like this, as if I'm hypnotizing him. You'll be able to explain what I'm doing for the people at home."

"Fine," I told him. I went off and got my tickets, thinking to myself that I had never seen him so sure, so unconcerned about a fight—any fight. Norton did not exist for him either. The hypnotism business he talked about related to the one peg they had for the promotion of the fight. Norton has a hypnotist who presumably has had a major impact upon his career. Norton told me that the hypnotist had reduced him from being overconfident to just confident. Honest.

The fight was to begin at 2:30 in the afternoon. I was to tape an interview with Ali in his dressing room at 2:15. This was not uncommon; we had done this on many past occasions. But this time an odd situation developed. The lights were out in Ali's dressing room, and the guard told us he was sleeping and could not be disturbed. This was just 20 minutes before the fight. Three minutes later I got the guard to let me in. We were fighting a desperate time problem. The room was pitch-dark, and I called to Muhammad.

"I'm not ready yet, Howard," came the voice. "I'm having an important conversation with Herbert."

All that time Ali had not been sleeping! He had been talking with Herbert Muhammad about heaven knows what. What a time for a conference. Suddenly the whole situation seemed eerie. Outside of Ali's dressing room I found Dundee. "Do you think Muhammad and you are taking Norton too lightly?" I asked him.

"Not at all," said Angie. "He's tailor-made."

Two minutes later we were allowed in. Quickly I did the interview. Ali no longer seemed at ease, no longer was he so casual. He seemed strangely tense. Yet Dundee showed me the inside of Ali's glove, where Ali had written, "KO 3." He would knock Norton out in the third round.

The interview done, I scrambled back to ringside to open the telecast. Ali came into the ring late. He never did do the hypnosis thing he had spoken to me about that morning.

The fight began. I had Yancey Durham sitting to my left, Joe Frazier to my right. In the first round Ali seemed transfixed. He showed no movement of any kind. Virtually no blows were struck by either fighter, but of the minimal scoring there was, Ali had the better of it. At the end of the round Durham leaned over to Frazier and said, "Ali's too strong for him."

In the second round Ali did absolutely nothing. Norton began to land some blows. None seemed in any sense damaging, but clearly Norton had won the round.

In the third round—the round marked down in Ali's glove for the knockout—Ali came out dancing. He was all over the ring, Norton couldn't even find him, and this was the first sign of the Ali that everyone expected. He didn't come close to knocking Norton out but he won the round easily.

At the end of the round Durham said, "He'll put him away in the next round."

Ali did nothing the next round. All movement stopped. Norton won the round, again with blows that seemed to do no damage. During that round, on microphone, I asked Dundee what was wrong with his fighter. "Nothing," Angie assured me. "It's going according to plan. He's just letting Norton punch himself out."

Durham agreed with Angie.

The fifth came and went, and so did the sixth. Nobody was doing much of anything, though in the sixth I felt that a Norton right had hurt Ali. It landed on Ali's left jaw. I asked Dundee again what was wrong with Muhammad. "Nothing at all," Angie said again. "Look at the way he's fighting now."

That's exactly what I was looking at. It was inexplicable.

"What round is coming up?" Durham asked me.

"The seventh," I said.

"He'll put Ken away in this round," Durham predicted.

Nothing happened. But Frazier was openly rooting for his old sparring partner, saying on the air to me that Norton was a good fighter, very much underrated. This discomforted Durham. He knew that if he couldn't pin Saddler down to a rematch with Foreman, he could sign a rematch with Ali. He didn't want to see a second big payday go down the drain, the way the first one did when Frazier fought Foreman instead of Ali and wound up losing his title.

But Frazier didn't care. As Ali sloughed around the ring, Joe leaned over and said to me, "Maybe they'll talk now about how much I took out of him, instead of what he took out of me." Make no mistake about it, Frazier despises Ali.

The eighth round came. This was when I detected that Ali's mouth looked curious, twisted. And I spotted just a little bit of blood at the left corner of his mouth. I conjectured in my commentary that he might have a loose tooth. I put the microphone in front of Ferdie Pacheco and asked him what was wrong with Ali's face. "Nothing, nothing at all," Ferdie told me. And then he added, "No breaks of any kind. No fractures." He shrugged his shoulders. At that time I thought he was saying, in effect, "The fighter's out of shape. He's not fighting at all." Later I attached a different meaning to his sudden introduction of the question of whether anything was broken.

The fight droned on. Suddenly, in the eleventh, Ali showed the movement he had shown in the third. He won the round easily.

Going into the twelfth I asked Durham and Frazier how they scored the fight. Each had it even.

Norton beat Ali all over the ring in the the twelfth. In this round he hit him on the left jaw, hard and clean,

at least twice and maybe three times. Ali was clearly
hurt. Norton had won the fight.

The whole thing seemed like a fantasy. Frazier was
exultant. Durham was anything but. I jumped into the
ring.

The decision took an interminable length of time.
While I was waiting, Dundee ran over to me and said
that Ali's jaw had been broken in the first round. I
was thunderstruck. I couldn't remember a single right that
had landed on Ali's left jaw in the first round. But I
had no time then to question Angie; the telecast was
on the verge of running over into "The Reasoner Report."
But I did briefly think, "How could Angie and Ferdie
have insisted throughout the fight that their man was
fine?"

Then I interviewed Norton, who said, "What do you
say now?"

I replied, "Like most of the country, I was wrong."

Ali came over. He looked terrible. His jaw was broken,
but somehow he muttered, "Cosell, you're always wrong."
Some writers mistakenly thought that Norton had spoken
the line that Ali uttered. One couldn't blame the writers.
It seemed irrational that at such a time Ali would
try to come up with a gag. But that's Ali.

We left San Diego for the National Football League
annual spring meeting at Phoenix. It was good to get
away. Remembering Ali as he had been, at the beginning,
in his prime, remembering the way he had held together
during the three and a half years of inactivity, remembering the classic bout against Frazier, remembering him
for the artist he had been, it seemed such a shabby way
to go out. I recalled one day when he looked at me
and laughed, "When I'm done, you won't even remember
who I was. I'll be just another ex-champ." Not in my
book. Never. He was special.

No one will ever really understand that fight, or when
Ali's jaw was broken. Ali, Dundee, and Ferdie Pacheco
were supposed to appear on television with me the following Saturday. Ali's jaw was wired, and so they can-

celed out. Instead we brought in Dr. William Lundeen,
the chief attending physician at ringside. We played the
key rounds of the fight, at regular speed, and some in
slow motion. Dr. Lundeen drew the conclusion that Ali's
jaw was definitely not broken in the first round. It could
have been, he deduced, in the second, fourth or sixth.
Finally we agreed that it had probably been in the sixth,
and that certainly the break had been intensified in the
twelfth.

There was also a story after the fight about Ali's ankle.
Apparently he had visited the trainer of the San Diego
Chargers football team for treatment of a sprained ankle
about a week before the fight. The films showed no
evidence of Ali being hampered by such a sprain. As
Dr. Lundeen noted, Ali showed real foot movement as
late as the eleventh round.

There were many stories, truthful ones, about how
Ali hadn't even trained for the fight. Later Dundee
amended his story. The jaw, he said, was broken in the
second round.

Muhammad Ali is already fighting again. He and
his people are busy propagating the notion that the first
Norton fight was a "warning to him from God"; that
he now stays in hard training; that he will again become
the old Ali. People will pay to see him. He is box-office
magic. I think it is unfortunate, even sad. Watching
him now will be like listening to Sinatra when Frank
can only croak.

I don't know how much money Ali has. As I've said,
he is a terrific spender. He owns a home in Cherry Hill,
New Jersey, and property near Reading, Pennsylvania,
where he has built a training camp. He recently sold a
second home in Philadelphia, the proceeds of which he
applied toward the purchase of a new home for his
mother in Louisville. He also owns automobiles, sometimes more than you can count, and has owned two
Rolls-Royces at one time, plus a 1901 Oldsmobile, a
colorful antique that Ali loves to drive around the neighborhood. Bob Arum tells me that Ali has no tax prob-

lems, that they have managed to save about $300,000 for him. Bob also says that, contrary to popular opinion, the Muslims have not taken his money. "He just spends it," says Bob. "It was all we could do to put aside the three hundred thousand."

Muhammad may need it.

But he will never look for help, not this descendant of slaves who stood tall and proud, even against the government and against most of the people. He will look at those around him, long in the future, and he will say, "I was right, and I won. Ask your grandchildren. They read about me in American history. My name is Muhammad Ali."

Epilogue

The two richest money fights in boxing history never came off. After all the talk and all the excuses and all the postmortems, that's what it boiled down to for Ali, Frazier and Foreman. What the business boys call the bottom line.

I want to take you back to January 1972. The place: New Orleans, Louisiana. Dallas was to face Miami in the Super Bowl. But the night before the game, Joe Frazier was to fight a college student named Terry Daniels. Like so many fights of this ilk, it was hard for me to believe that this fight could be licensed. It was a disgraceful mismatch. But the promoters were hungry, the New Orleans boxing authorities were hungry, the whole state was hungry to make it a big-time sports weekend and to reap the rewards that were in the offing.

It was, in a boxing sense, a time when people were clamoring for a Frazier-Ali rematch. Everyone seemed to want it but Frazier. He had some coming back to do, after the physical punishment he had taken from Ali. Yancey Durham thought the best way to do it was slowly, carefully, by matching Joe with setups almost as if he were beginning his career all over again.

Nobody was even giving George Foreman a serious thought. Foreman had been building a long victory string against soft touches, also-rans, washed-up fighters, and youngsters even less ready than he appeared to be. Still, the general notion was that Foreman was anything but a polished fighter and he wasn't considered to be in the same league with Frazier and Ali. One man thought otherwise—his manager, Dick Saddler. I know. Saddler came to me two days before the Super Bowl game. I was lunching at the Royal Orleans Hotel when Dick arrived with Foreman in tow. He got me aside and said, "George is ready and I've got to get him a big fight. We can't keep going the way we're going. Assuming I could get either Ali or Frazier, which do you think we should fight?"

"Without question," I told him, "Joe Frazier. His style is exactly right for George. George will kill him. He might have trouble even finding Ali in the ring."

Saddler looked at me and said, "That's exactly what I wanted to hear you say. I agree with you one hundred percent."

That was our conversation in a nutshell. George and Dick took off, and I thought no more about it. I couldn't believe that there wouldn't be an Ali-Frazier rematch before anybody even thought of George Foreman. This was my mistake. I underrated the deep dislike that Frazier has for Ali, a dislike that would ultimately cost him multimillions of dollars. Frazier went his own way. He did away with poor young Daniels. He even fought a pitiful stiff named Ron Stander in Omaha, another fight that should not have been licensed. This one reminded me of the rape of Shelby, Montana, when Jack Kearns and Jack Dempsey took 100,000 silver dollars out of that tiny town after Dempsey had done away with a man named Jess Gibbons. Only this time it was a rape of Omaha and Council Bluffs.

Joe Frazier is not a difficult man to understand. He is a decent, honest man, one who wants to be liked. No—put it another way: He is a man who wanted to be popular and yet never achieved great popularity as the heavyweight champion of the world. He was deeply hurt by all of this and, quite understandably, he blamed Ali for it. In my lifetime I have never seen a man work harder, train harder for a fight than Joe Frazier did for Muhammad Ali. Next to Ali, Frazier is a small man, though his biceps are huge.

His managers, his handlers, even his attorney all knew what a difficult job Frazier had before him. Nobody knew it better than Frazier. But for Joe, beating Ali had become a matter of fierce necessity. He had spent all his years in Ali's shadow. While he had knocked out the Quarrys and the Ellises of the world to achieve championship eminence, he lived with the knowledge that the public still viewed the idle Ali as the real champion. It became an ugly, festering sore within him.

In a way I had helped foster this notion—both in the public mind and Frazier's. During Ali's exile I had cut a network-radio promotional spot that went: "This is Howard Cosell . . . if you don't believe Muhammad Ali is the heavyweight champion of the world then *you* get in the ring with him." Ali loved it. He ate it up. Everywhere he went he began to mimic me saying that. But for Joe Frazier it was just one more twist of the knife. Joe also felt that I favored Ali over him, despite the fact that I picked Joe to knock out Ali. But Joe is a direct man. It is one of the things I admire most about him. He came up to me one day and said, "I've got all the respect in the world for you, and for all you've done. But I think that sometimes you mislead the public about Ali."

I told him that I thought he was dead wrong. I added that I had a vast personal respect for him, Joe Frazier. But the wound was deep in Joe. After he beat Ali, as I have pointed out already, Ali actually convinced much of the public that he had won the fight and had been robbed by the decision against him. This was unbearable medicine for Frazier to take. He would go on tour with his rock group and there would be nothing but empty seats. This clean, decent man, who had never invited any public disfavor by any action of his, simply was not being accepted by the public in anything like the manner to which he was truly entitled. Little wonder that he could not bear Ali, and this had to be a primary reason for the long negotiations for a rematch—negotiations that were never consummated.

Instead, Frazier signed to fight George Foreman in Kingston, Jamaica. His manager, Yancey Durham, did not want that fight. He made that clear before the fight took place. Frazier wanted it. First, he regarded Foreman lightly, and second and more important, he wanted Ali to wait and wait and wait, though his public cry was always to the effect that he would fight Ali anytime, if he got the right money deal. There may have been *some* truth to this but, in my opinion, not a lot.

Kingston, Jamaica, was an extraordinary experience. It was a whole new and utterly illogical scene set for a heavyweight-championship fight. Kingston is a poverty-stricken, as ghetto-like a city as I have ever seen. At sundown the atmosphere is sick with an uneasy feeling. There is enormous tension between black and white in the current restive political situation that exists there, clearly the result of years of exploitation of the natives by the British. One rarely sees a white out alone at night.

Into this situation came two black fighters and a horde of white sportswriters and tourists. One of the remarkable things the Jamaican government did was set up a wall of security the night of the fight that gave everybody a feeling of relief upon arrival at the stadium.

In the days before the fight I spent much time with both fighters. I was frankly shocked by Joe Frazier. I went down there picking Foreman to win, to knock Joe Frazier out, because I had meant what I had said to Dick Saddler. My faith in Foreman was very secure. I had believed in him since the 1968 Olympics. I had been with him often since, and indeed for a brief spell he sat next to me and added comments during the boxing competition in the Munich Olympics. Foreman is the American dream. He lives clean and he thinks clean and he has a sense of values. He has a true, deep and abiding concern for young people. He's a man of strong religious bent. He is also one of the most powerfully built young men I have ever seen and quite possibly the strongest puncher I have ever seen, including even Joe Louis. He is not a polished boxer and probably never will be, but you don't have to be a polished boxer to fight Joe Frazier.

I was shocked by Frazier because he seemed to have taken none of this into account. I visited with him at length in his suite and found him almost contemptuous of Foreman as an opponent. Also—and he was quite ready to talk about it—Frazier didn't like some of the things that Foreman was saying. This was not the usual boxing buildup. Frazier thought that Foreman was being personally insulting in the way he characterized Frazier himself. And Joe spoke to me about it openly in the prefight interview I did with him.

Another thing surprised me. Even though it was clear that Frazier thought he could beat Foreman almost at will, he was very edgy. Ali was still on his mind. And if he wasn't, the writers would put him right back there by questioning Frazier about the rematch. Once while I was with Joe in his suite he got a call from Mel Durslag in Los Angeles. Mel asked him how soon there would be a rematch with Ali after he was done with Foreman. This was representative of what Frazier was facing every day in Kingston.

I remember leaving Frazier's suite with Harold Conrad, the press agent, and saying to Conrad, "I feel sorry for Joe. He doesn't even know that he's going to get murdered."

One morning I walked with George Foreman for the better part of an hour. Nobody was paying any attention to George, and it didn't matter to him at all. He just went his cheery way, totally confident that he would surprise the world, but not himself. The morning I walked with George I had just left Frazier, and both visits were being covered by an NFL film crew, which was doing *a cinéma vérité* documentary about me. So they filmed and recorded both visits. During the Foreman conversation I began by telling him that Frazier was edgy but seemed to be taking George lightly. Foreman just laughed. "To tell you the truth, George, I don't think Joe likes you," I said. He laughed again. Then I talked to George about the years I had known him, about my faith in him and how I thought he would knock out Frazier. He chuckled delightedly.

When I finally left George, I bumped into Red Smith, the famed columnist. The NFL film crew was still with

me and still shooting. I asked Red how he thought the
fight would be. "Might be pretty good," he said, "for
seven rounds or so." The inference was that Frazier
would clearly have his way with Foreman. Then he
asked, "What do you think?"

I grinned broadly. "I think Foreman may kill him,"
I said. "Literally, may kill him."

During the fight, brief as it was, that thought surfaced
as a very real fear—that Foreman might kill him. He
manhandled Frazier with astonishing ease. His punches
had all the power I suspected they had, and more. One
actually lifted Frazier off the floor. When the fight was
stopped I jumped into an incredibly wild ring scene.
In that ring George Foreman came to me and said, "I
won this fight for Howard Cosell, and for all the others
like him who believed in me. I knew I could win it when
you told me I could."

What was happening at ringside, and on the periphery
of the fight, heightened the drama. Bob Arum, Ali's
attorney, was there to press Durham on the rematch.
Angelo Dundee, Ali's trainer, sat at my elbow as the
night unfolded. Dundee, in fact, had a portent of what
would happen. He even picked Foreman to win. When
Frazier went down again and again, for the fifth and
sixth time in the second round, Dundee was on his
feet, screaming at the referee to stop it.

Bob Arum and Dundee were pale when it ended. They
knew that Frazier was not the only loser; millions of
dollars had vanished in the night. Arum was a dazed,
stunned figure, wandering aimlessly through the crowd,
seeking to salvage what he could. He and Dundee were
consoled by one thought: Another potential bonanza
might be created by an Ali-Foreman confrontation. The
Frazier riches were gone forever. This is the nature of
boxing; it feeds off its own energy. Another deal, another
angle, is always around the corner.

Their concern at that point was keeping Foreman
alive and unbeaten until a match with Ali could be
arranged. It was clear that Foreman's handlers wouldn't
rush into it. And no one could possibly anticipate that

the clinker would come not from Foreman but from Ali's carelessness in preparing for Ken Norton, and the debacle that followed.

George handled himself superbly, with grace and modesty and cool assurance. At last the American boxing public had a way to go: Those who could never tolerate the attitudes of Ali—who could never understand him, actually—and those who could never get excited over stolid Joe Frazier now had a place to turn, a hero out of the classic mold. A kid up from the streets, out of the Job Corps, who isn't a thug, who likes youngsters, who feels a genuine debt to his country, to his sport, to the people who helped along the way.

George himself saw his victory as reflective of the uncertainty and inconstancy of boxing. "Nobody holds the title very long," he pointed out. "Someone else will come along to take it away from me. It was Ali's turn and then Frazier's and now mine. I intend to honor it while I have it."

Yet even in the case of wholesome, appealing, storybook George Foreman, a question exists: Can he avoid being obscured by the sheer personality of Ali? It may be that in the public view Foreman doesn't have, and isn't likely to acquire, that mystical quality called "charisma."

Ali, for one, doesn't think he can. He delights in telling how he had to introduce George to people in San Diego when the young champion appeared at the scene of the first Norton fight. Ali paraded him around, testing strangers' recognition of him, creating a scene wherever they stood. "See," he would bellow, "nobody knows who you are, George. They think I'm still the champ." Foreman watched Ali do his act and walked away, laughing.

And that's Ali's problem. Where Joe Frazier cared, George Foreman doesn't give a damn. He gives a damn about other things, such as appearing for Eunice Shriver and Ethel Kennedy on behalf of the Joseph P. Kennedy, Jr., Foundation for Retarded Children. He cares about the things that count, yet strange things are happening

to George Foreman. His marriage appears imperiled. He
has broken with Dick Saddler. One must begin to wonder
what is in store for George Foreman.

But I remain convinced that Ali will never touch
George Foreman, vocally or otherwise.

February, 1974

When Muhammad Ali was awarded a unanimous
twelve-round decision over Joe Frazier on the evening
of January 28, 1974, all I could think of were Emmy's
words to me after my sojourn with Muhammad into the
ghetto of Miami prior to Super Fight I: "As long as you
know him, you will never really know him."

It should have been all over for him after the debacle
with Ken Norton. There should have been no rationale
for Ali ever climbing into a ring again. Even with
Muhammad's uncanny instinct for promotion and publicity, there remained not one shred of logic behind the
continuation of his career. What with the losses to Frazier
and Norton, the advancing years, and the debilitated
skills, he should have been through.

But they kept him going. A split decision over Norton
in their second fight set the stage for the rematch with
Frazier, a sort of elimination match between losers to
see who would next challenge the reigning champion,
George Foreman.

If, as I have previously suggested, boxing is a sport
that feeds on its own energy, then Super Fight II established irrevocably that what energy is left in the sport is
provided in overwhelming measure by Ali. That is why
the fight was viewed by over a billion people, and what
should have been no more than a mediocre gate has
grossed out to some eight million dollars. The man is
a constant source of amazement to me.

For Muhammad Ali, the fight with Frazier is important
for two reasons, both of which deal with financial security for himself and his family. Of the 2.6 million dollars that both fighters grossed from Super Fight II, Bob

Arum says that Ali has agreed to bank up to $750,000. On the strength of that alone, he has gone a long way towards securing his future.

The second reason, of course, is the obvious bonanza that will be made when he fights Foreman sometime within the next year. With that added fortune put away, whether he loses to Foreman or not, I believe that the career of this remarkable man will finally have come to an end.

He says that he can beat Foreman, and he makes you want to believe that he can reclaim those skills that once would have made it seem likely.

Among the many things that I have learned from and about this man through the years, more than anything else I have learned never to count him out. But, when you really think about it, one has to wonder what may happen to him when he fights George Foreman. For the sake of all that he is, I hope that the ending is one of dignity.

Chapter X

THE REVOLUTIONISTS: THEY DIDN'T PLAY THE GAME

*"In the same sense as Tommie means it,
I'm a militant, too."*

A major distinction between the athlete of today and those of yesteryear is that the old jocks rarely read books. Today, some even write them.

One of the amusing things about the sports establishment, which includes commissioners, owners and what I call "Old World" announcers and writers, is its expressed shock at those athletes who turn rebel. Leaving aside Jimmy Bouton and *Ball Four,* which was just a kiss-and-tell book designed for popular sale, there are the new breed of philosopher-militant, the David Meggyesys, the Bernie Parrishes and the George Sauer, Jrs. Also, Jack Scott, author of *The Athletic Revolution,* now director of athletics at Oberlin College. And in a separate compartment—Joe Willie Namath.

The shock of the establishment at such people stems, of course, from its careful adherence to the grade-school notion that no matter what happens in the society around them, no matter how habits change, no matter how much more sophisticatedly young people grow up, no matter how the social patterns of life advance, nothing that happens in real life can ever happen with athletes. Naïve, isn't it? But true.

Dave Meggyesy is typical of many young Americans

today—not atypical. He is not now and never was a man of high scholastic accomplishments. But his instincts are good. He tried desperately to grow in an intellectual sense. He was aware of the life around him, aware of hypocrisy and injustice, aware of racism and aware of drugs. He has used them. He was also, as a football player, intimately aware of big-time-college-football corruption. He was part of it at Syracuse University. He knew something about the innards of professional football because he was a fairly good linebacker with the Saint Louis Cardinals.

So what did he do? He wrote a book, *Out of Their League,* after he left professional football. In the book he described factually, specifically, the nature of the football system at Syracuse: how the football player, as long as he could produce on the gridiron, got paid under the table; how some got exam questions in advance; how those who stopped producing good football were quickly shunted aside; all this and more—and all of it reflecting the corrupting evil of big-league college sports. Syracuse has never answered Meggyesy's statements, and neither has the NCAA. What did he do wrong? He told the truth about the system, just as David Wolf did in his fine recital of the life of Connie Hawkins, a Brooklyn boy who, with a sixth-grade reading level, wound up with a baskeball scholarship at the University of Iowa.

Meggyesy also wrote about racism on the Saint Louis Cardinals football team. He wrote the truth. It did exist. What Meggyesy wrote upset the establishment. The question is why. He also wrote that some athletes use drugs. This also upset the establishment. Again the question, why? Does the establishment really believe that athletes are not human, that sports is not part of life? Sports is human life in microcosm. You can go to Ames, Iowa, or Kansas City, Missouri, or Birmingham, Alabama, choose your place. Wherever you go, you will find users of drugs, from "good" families as well as ghetto families. Why then the shock when an athlete does it? Only

because of the insular perpetuation of the sports syndrome by the establishment.

In my view, the issues about which Meggyesy wrote
would be far better dealt with by the establishment if
they confronted the truth and bluntly said: "These things
are wrong, but let's face it, it's part of life today. You
find it everywhere. And just as society is trying to correct these things, so must we." At least, you'd have
honesty, not hypocrisy. And the recognition of a problem can be the beginning of correction.

I don't write of Meggyesy by hearsay, by the way.
I spent much time with him, did an hour talk show
with him and had him to our home. Dave is a Falstaffian
man who will probably run to fat, as he has already
begun to do. The hair is long, the face bearded, which
bespeaks a man who quickly adopted a commune-type
philosophy about life. He wears an expression of pain,
as though he has been through much more than he has
actually endured. Indeed, when he inscribed his book to
me, he wrote, "Yours in struggle."

I do believe that David has struggled within himself,
but I think he takes that too seriously. I find him without
much humor, a condition that makes any man unhappy.
None of which, however, dilutes the truth that appeared
in his book.

There was one area, however, in which I felt he was
on weak ground. This was when he discussed homo-
sexuality in the National Football League and half implied that it was a frequent thing. While it's a hapless
subject to write about in the first place, as one who has
been closely connected with the beat for 17 years I have
found scant evidence of it. I could name a case or two,
specifically, but that's all, and it would be utterly pointless to do so. If Meggyesy were going to bring up the
subject in the first place, he should have had a far
firmer evidentiary basis for it.

When George Sauer, Jr., quit professional football,
some of the establishment reacted: "What a fool. So
much good football still before him. And look what
football has done for him." Sauer was, of course, one

of the finest wide receivers in the National Football League. He was a star in the Jets' Super Bowl upset of Baltimore. So one could understand the reactions cited above. But that is surface understanding only. George Sauer, Jr., is a very bright and educated young man. Blond, attractive, with a pale, almost delicate face, he had in his bearing—and his mien—an air of the 19th Century romantic. You would take one look at him in the locker room and you would wonder what he was doing there.

Even before you talked to him you could sense that George wanted to be a writer, which he is trying to be now. Such a man, understandably, could not forever subscribe to the regimentation that he later denounced. He always seemed a quizzical young man. You never knew what he was thinking. He always looked at you questioningly. Financial success and football were never really what George happened to want. They were what his father, George Sauer, Sr., wanted. The father was one of the greatest football players of all time, a Hall of Famer. He wanted his son to emulate him, and he got his way. There were early signs that his father influenced him. He passed up his senior year at Texas to turn pro and sign with the Jets, whose personnel director was then, curiously, George Sauer, Sr. Junior became, in the narrow term of sports parlance, "a great one." Once he did, he reached a point where he took a look at himself and his life and he said, in effect, "That's it. I've had enough."

In his late twenties, with a mind that was seeking new outlets, he rebelled against the life he had led for the sake of his father. There is nothing unusual about this. It happens in homes every day. Children rebel and go off. The difference is that George Sauer, Jr., was not a child.

Young George may yet change his mind and come back to football. I doubt it, but if he does, it will be his decision, not his father's. When he left he said some harsh things about the sport. He challenged the regimented atmosphere, the standardization of thought, the dehumanization of it. And so, some called him an ingrate. "Look what football has done for him." I have always thought that life is a two-way street. I labored under the illusion that George Sauer, Jr., did something for the Jets. Namath's ailments have not been the only reason for the Jets' decline in recent years; Sauer's absence has been an important factor.

It is true that George had a kind of martyr complex that led him instantly, instinctively, to rally to friends in real—or imagined—need. He was among the first to appear at Bachelors III the morning of Joe Willie's memorable, if temporary, retirement from pro football. Proudly George told me, "I'm leaving, too. They can't strip a man of his rights."

Namath, of course, is the most famous figure in professional football today. And together with Muhammad Ali he is one of the two foremost symbols of the anti-authority motif in sports. Namath did his own book, ghosted by Dick Schaap, called *I Can't Wait Until Tomorrow 'Cause I Get Better Looking Every Day*. The book will never appear next to the works of Alexander Pope or Jonathan Swift in any library. But then, it wasn't intended to, and Joe couldn't care less.

For reasons not entirely clear, I find myself identified in the public mind with Namath. Probably it's because I, too, am considered antiestablishment. Possibly it also has something to do with my home base being New York, where Namath plays, and with the fact that I praised Namath on the very first "Monday Night Football" game ever telecast. I noted that Joe had led the Jets up and down the field for more than 500 yards, albeit in a losing effort, against Cleveland. This was taken by much of middle America to betoken my particular prejudice in favor of Joe Willie.

I want to make it clear that I am not nearly as friendly with Namath as most people think. I do not see him often, and our life-styles are hardly parallel. He simply does not swing with grandfathers. Nonetheless I was the first to interview him when Sonny Werblin brought him to New York. I have done many shows with him. I have been in his company all over the land. And I like him and respect him.

The odd thing about Namath, when you stop to think about it, is that he *is* the symbol of antiestablishmentism, when, unlike the Meggyesys of the world, he's never fought for a cause in his life—except the cause of Joe Namath. His whole image relates to life-style—booze and broads. Namath is a bachelor and he does like to drink. He also likes to go out with girls. Strangely, I've often had the feeling that he doesn't really respect girls, only uses them. I say that because I have seen him on occasion when his treatment of them can only be described as contemptuous.

On the other side of the coin, I have never seen a more devoted son, his manners with older women are exemplary, and he is a positive Old World southern gentleman, out of Beaver Falls, Pennsylvania, when he is with them or with girls much younger than he. He will do things that are totally unexpected and totally nice. He sent flowers to my mother-in-law when her husband died. One night, at his Bachelors III in Fort Lauderdale, Florida, he spent the entire evening hosting my younger daughter, Hilary, manifesting a real interest in her college career, her ambitions and her interests. I almost got worried!

I also respect Namath for his loyalty. He will stick by a friend, do anything for him. And he will stand up to anyone if he thinks he is right, just the way he did to Pete Rozelle when he "retired" from football. Namath is more than just loyal; he is dead honest. He will tell you what he thinks, when he thinks it, and he'll never recant or back off. Now, there may not seem to be any virtue in admitting that you were out until three o'clock in the morning. But there is a lot more virtue in that than there is in the hypocrisy of many of the great names in sports who are married, who cheat, and then maintain the public pretense of being All-American boys. Sadly, there are many such men whom the public idolizes, and if I were mean enough to identify them, thus hurting their wives and children, the public wouldn't believe it anyway.

But the public can be sure of this: They'll never read in any scandal sheet about Namath being with another man's wife. He has a moral code—despite all the adverse publicity—far better than most.

As a football player Namath came to the pros with more ability to play the quarterback position than any man who has yet lived. This is not my statement alone; it is the consensus of the most expert minds in football, and they make their judgments on the basis of such yardsticks as poise, quickness in setting up, quickness of release of the football, ability to read defenses and leadership quality. But he came to professional football with the terrible disability of his knees. And so he has missed almost two seasons and he will never have the durability to rank with men like Unitas, Starr, Waterfield, Van Brocklin and Bobby Layne. Yet he is better known in his time than any of the others in theirs. Why? Because he is Joe Namath.

Why should Arnold Palmer be a legend, when he never saw the day that he could be as great a golfer as Jack Nicklaus, who will never be regarded by the public with the worship that Palmer receives? Star quality, an intangible thing, a presence that captivates people. Personality. Big personality. That's what makes Joe Namath.

There's nothing new about all this. Sonny Werblin, a master of show business, the smartest promoter I've ever known, saw it in Joe instantly. Sonny did nothing to dilute the booze-and-broads bit. In fact, he embellished it. As long as Joe could do his thing on the football field, Sonny didn't give a damn what Joe did off it. He just wanted people to know Joe Namath quarterbacked the New York Jets.

Has it ever occurred to you that Namath has won only two big games in his professional career? The one against Oakland in December 1968 that carried the Jets to the Super Bowl, and the one against Baltimore in the Super Bowl on January 12, 1969, that changed the face of professional football. That, by the way, was the finest quarterbacked game I have ever seen. Namath was totally disciplined that day as he has never been before or since.

He has two major problems now: He continues to defy defenses constructed to stop the long ball—and interceptions too often result; and when Namath is inside the opposition 20-yard line, his bad knees strip him of the added threat that mobility provides, making it difficult for him to put the ball in the end zone. Still, Namath, with a team with a seven-and-seven record, was all-pro in 1972.

Namath doesn't complain about his pain. He doesn't seek sympathy. He doesn't want it. He has thought many times about quitting football. He can't do it—not because of the money but because he loves football. As a matter of fact, even though he has done every major variety show on television and every talk show, Namath doesn't hang around with show-business people. He likes the show-biz routine but he picks his own friends. You'll find him with people the public never heard, of, like Bob Skaff, or his two lawyers, Jimmy Walsh and Mike Bite. Even they are an index to Namath. With all his big money deals—and they have been numerous— Namath never has gone to a big-name attorney. He is more comfortable with two old friends. I think that says something for him.

Another index to Namath is the way other players respect his ability. John Hadl of the Rams says, "I think I'm a helluva quarterback. Until I see Joe. He's off by himself."

O. J. Simpson was about to graduate from USC. His publicity and his fame were overwhelming. I interviewed him on his plans to go into pro football—would he play for Buffalo, which was the big question then. After the interview we went over to Bachelors III in New York. Namath came in moments after we arrived, and I said, "O.J., here's Joe Willie. I'll tell him you're here." O.J. caught my sleeve. "Howard," he said, "don't ever rush the great ones."

In 1971, after missing ten weeks because of a broken bone in his passing hand, Namath returned to action

against a fine San Francisco team. Among the curious
was John Brodie, the 49ers' gifted quarterback, who had
been engaged in repartee with Don Klosterman, now the
general manager of the Rams but once a key figure in
the old American Football League. Klosterman had made
a big money deal with Brodie to jump to the AFL. The
merger canceled the deal, but John still collected from
the war chest—to the tune of nearly a million dollars.
Understandably he is fond of Klosterman. He enjoys
needling him. "What's all this talk about Namath being
so great?" Brodie would tell his friend from the AFL.
"I just can't see him."

So the 49ers and the Jets met for the first time. The
49ers had to hang on for a shaky 24-21 win, as Namath
came off the bench in the second half to hum three touch-
downs through one of the NFL's finest secondaries. A
few hours after the game Brodie got a brief wire from
Klosterman. It read, "NOW YOU HAVE SEEN JOE
WILLIE."

Later Dick Nolan, the coach of the 49ers, told me,
"The guy scares you when he just walks out there."

Al Davis of Oakland, one of the smartest men in football, puts it another way: "Let's face it. As long as they
have Namath, they're a football team."

Namath has often said to me, "No matter what they
write, I've never done anything off the field to hurt my
team or my football ability." I don't think that's true.
I don't think it could be true, because, with the hours
he keeps, his body has to feel the abuse. I often wonder
what kind of quarterback he would have been under
Vince Lombardi. Vince once said to me, "I'd give anything to be able to coach that boy. All that talent . . ."
And then Vince's voice trailed off. Would Namath have
gotten more out of himself under Lombardi discipline
than he has? Would he have been malleable to it? I
think yes, because he bent to the discipline of Bear Bryant at Alabama and to this day regards Bryant with a
respect I think he gives to no one else. At the same time
it may be that his present coach, Weeb Ewbank, is exactly right for him. Weeb is the opposite of a taskmaster

and is content to let Namath do his thing as long as Joe is ready on Sunday—or Monday night. And I know Namath respects Ewbank's knowledge of the game.

It's hard to believe that a kid from Beaver Falls, Pennsylvania, who started out as an athletic hick, could wind up at ease on the air in concert with the finest performers in show business. But he did. He is a rare one, a natural-born performer who uses those big, soulful eyes and an immense sex appeal to draw attention to himself. He is quick with a line, and instinctively his reactions are good. He is loaded with confidence, and yet at the same time uses a pretended shyness to good effect. Thus he can kid with a Dick Martin and holds his own. Martin once told me, when I was doing "Laugh-In," that Namath was the only athlete they ever had on the show who really drew mail and had a discernible impact on the ratings. We know about that. He doesn't hurt a bit when the Jets are on "Monday Night Football."

Although he doesn't talk about it, or show it, I think Namath has grown up a great deal, does more thinking about life, about where he's headed, about what's in store for him. He is very alert to what he can't do. He tried a couple of movies, and they didn't work for him. Even though he's a natural talent for variety shows on television, being an actor is a different thing, and Namath realizes this as a result of his movie tribulations. So he's not at all sure that show business is his long-term future. Nor does he necessarily want it to be.

The happiest I have ever seen him is when he's away from the booze-and-broads bit, and that's in Tuscaloosa, where he went to college and where he goes for a number of weeks every spring. He likes being back with the "Big Bear" and with the kids on the football team. He opened a Bachelors III in Tuscaloosa, and quite significantly it's the only one he still has a financial interest in.

He loves to needle and he can take it when you give it back. As long as I've known him I've needled him, and he has needled back—which he did in the book he wrote. When I was with him at Tuscaloosa I really had him. We were walking across the football field in front of 35,000 people—it was the day of the spring intrasquad game in May a couple of years ago—and the spectators suddenly started to stand and chant, "Sock it to 'em, Howie." I laughed, turned to Namath and said, "See that, Joe? Even down here where you played, you're nothing next to me."

Namath answered, "Damn, I wouldn't have believed it." I'll never let him forget it.

When Namath had his own weekly syndicated television show, he used to do it at a studio right around the corner from the ABC News Studios. I made it a habit to go over there almost every week. Namath got a kick out of doing the show. "Learning anything?" he would ask.

"Only gossip," I'd answer. "I had no idea Anthony Newley was dating Charlotte Ford." (Newley was his guest one week and he came to the studio with her.)

Namath often needles me about certain sportswriters. After his last knee operation they held a big press conference at the Lenox Hill Hospital, where he spends as much time as he does at his plush brownstone apartment on East Eighty-second Street. Joe was wheeled in, looked around, saw me and said, in front of everybody, "Hey, you still covering football? The way some of these guys write about you, I thought you'd be fired by now."

So I said, "Perish the thought, Joe. If I leave, they've got nobody left but you to take apart."

Namath himself is very susceptible to the sportswriters. "The terrible thing is," he says, "a lot of people really believe those guys." Yet there are sportswriters he likes and respects, perhaps most notably Dave Anderson of the *New York Times*.

There is another trait to admire in Joe. He is color-blind. Black or white doesn't matter to him. He looks at the man.

So does a fellow named Jack Scott.

Jack Scott has had a major impact upon athletes like

Meggyesy and Sauer. He has talked with them, studied them and counseled them. He did not seek them out; they sought him out. He first came into public notice in the Bay area and was on the faculty at San Jose State. His talks about sports, his writings about sports, were unorthodox in the view of the establishment. Unorthodox because, consistently, Scott would consider the athlete an individual, a human being, not chattel. He took cognizance of the changing times. He related sports to society, examined the role of sports in society and talked of "democracy in sports." Regimentation was repugnant to Scott. It still is today.

I am not at all sure that I agree with everything Scott propounds. Indeed, I am quite sure I don't. But I respect him very much because he was one of the first to recognize that the football players of today are, in the main, sensitive, educated men, with minds not to be abused and aspirations not to be negated, and that the baseball players of today are not to be equated with some of those of the past, tobacco-chewing "toughies" who would hurl profanities at a man because of the color of his skin, or go out of their way to maim a man with their spikes for the very same reason. In his book *The Athletic Revolution* Scott makes his views clear, and in the basic principle that sports today invades every aspect of life, the law, politics, economics, sociology, I agree with him wholeheartedly.

Scott is now director of athletics at Oberlin College, where he is seeking to put his ideas into practice. Only time will tell whether or not they will work, but I think he has gone to the right place. First, his very appearance suits the Oberlin College campus. He is a smallish man, mild of speech and mild of demeanor, the exact opposite of what you'd expect a revolutionary to look like. Take a second glance at him and this man who has so influenced a whole new group of athletes could be mistaken for Mr. Peepers.

Oberlin is right for his experimentation. It is one of the finest colleges in this country. The first white col-

lege to admit black students. The first to become co-
educational. It has one of the finest college conserva-
tories of music in the United States. Its emphasis is on
education, which is what a college or university is supposed to provide. The first thing Scott did was hire
Tommie Smith, of the black-power incident in the Mexico
City Olympics, as his assistant. Most recently Oberlin
allowed the football team to interview candidates for the
head coaching job. Though the faculty retained a veto
right, they approved the selection of the team, a young
black named Cass Jackson. I did a network-television
show at Oberlin, because I think what they're trying
deserves encouragement. As I said, I don't know if it
will work, and one must question whether it could *ever*
work at a big-time sports institution, where the whole
quest is for winning, the whole attention is on recruitment of athletes.

While at Oberlin I asked Tommie Smith if he is still
a militant, and after a vocal exchange in which I described the word in terms of what he did in Mexico City,
he looked at me and said, "I am still a militant."

Later I asked Jack Scott about Smith's characteriza-
tion of himself, and Scott said, "In the same sense as
Tommie means it, I am a militant, too. The desire for
improvement in the existing structure, the treatment of
all athletes, regardless of color, on an equal basis. If
that's being a militant, I am surely one." Come to think
of it, so am I.

Bernie Parrish is a different matter, and I have come
to disrespect him as much as the establishment does.
Parrish was a good defensive back with the Cleveland
Browns. Nobody could knock him as a player. What
they did was knock him as a player who was involved
with things in which the establishment did not want him
involved. Like player associations, like unionizing the
players, getting the players more and more benefits.
Generally speaking I was much in sympathy with what
Parrish seemed to be trying to do. Then, after he was
out of football, he started working with Harold Gibbons

in Saint Louis. Gibbons is the man who runs the Teamsters Union, and Parrish hoped to bring the NFL players under the Teamsters' umbrella.

One day Parrish called me at ABC, asked if he could see me. I told him I'd be delighted. He wanted to talk through player problems with me, let it "all hang out." He came to my office. I found his thinking utterly disorganized, or, if it *was* organized, his ability to speak was not. Nonetheless he wanted to talk and he wanted a forum. I agreed and led him upstairs to a radio studio to do my weekly talk show, "Speaking of Everything." As I questioned him on the ills of professional football, and as I tossed names at him he presumably wanted to "expose," he broke down completely and said, "I guess I'm not ready yet. I don't have my thoughts in order." He sure didn't, and he had been working on his thoughts for a couple of years, since he had left football. I found him strange, erratic in his behavior.

Subsequently his book *They Call It Sport* was published. I found it no better. As far as professional football was concerned I found it an exercise in McCarthyism. Scattershot accusations at owners like Modell of Cleveland, Rosenbloom of Baltimore (then; now of Los Angeles), no documentation of merit, in my opinion as an attorney, and even veiled implications that the Jets' victory over Baltimore in the Super Bowl was manipulated. Again, not the remotest documentation.

After the book was published I went on the "David Frost Show" with him, and despite Frost's total absence of knowledgeability of the book, and of the whole subject of professional football, it was still possible to make clear that Parrish had not done his homework. I reminded Bernie on the air of the opportunity I had given him when he came to see me at ABC, and of how he had cratered in our radio interview. His answer was to hurl an insult. Bernie should have remembered that he was good at knocking down passes, not throwing them. He flunked out. Proving that the establishment is not always wrong.

Chapter XI

THE ESTABLISHMENT: ONCE YOU CROSS THAT RIVER, EVERYTHING IS BRIDGEPORT

"I'm like Macy's, in competition with Gimbels."

Wellington Mara, the owner of the New York Giants, cloaks himself in the piety of Saint Patrick's and behaves as if his ownership derives from the Vatican. He is so sincere in doing this that his defiance of the public interest assumes a holy aura. And make no mistake about it, his forthcoming evacuation from New York City in favor of the swamplands of East Rutherford, New Jersey, is a defiance of the public interest. More than that, it symbolizes the cheap expediency of many owners in professional sports and emphasizes the hollow hypocrisy of many sports operators as they continue to propagate the idea—in the year 1973—that sport is a world separate and apart from real life; a Camelot where everyone is concerned only about serving the public.

I will go further. I think the National Football League will be tarnished by the Giants' removal. It will align the NFL, for the first time, with the carpetbaggers of baseball. And as sickly evidence of how sports operators can do total turnabouts to advance their own private purposes, I give you the unholy alliance of Wellington

Mara and Sonny—as in money—Werblin. But let me document.

Playing their home games in Yankee Stadium in New York City, the Giants have enjoyed a remarkable prosperity. For the past 12 years they have not had an unsold seat; standing room only is the rule. Possession of season tickets to the Giants' games is a sign of social status. It makes you part of a tight little island of memory, enables you to bask at Mike Manuche's bar or Toots Shor's saloon in the delicious nostalgia of Chuck Connerly, Frank Gifford, Kyle Rote, Andy Robustelli and "Big Red" Webster.

But the Giants' prosperity does not end with ticket sales; it only begins. Incredibly, at the time the National and American Football Leagues merged, the original AFL owners by a vote of six to three agreed to pay the NFL $18 million. Equally incredible, the AFL owners did not know that ten of those millions would go to the New York Giants for "territorial rights."

The leading dissenter, let us take note, was Sonny Werblin, president of the New York Jets, who strongly opposed the merger and violently opposed paying tribute. When he later learned that the NFL was allocating ten million of the indemnity to the Giants, he screamed, "Ten million dollars? To the Giants? What for? I'm like Macy's, in competition with Gimbels." Werblin was right.

Like you and me, or anyone else in America who wants to start a business, Werblin opened a store in another part of New York City and made it a better store than Mara's. Now at this late date to pay for the privilege of doing what he had already done was an unthinkable refutation of the whole doctrine of free enterprise by which we live in this country. Put in the softest possible way, Werblin was not kindly disposed toward Mara. But years pass, and times change, and Werblin and Mara are now virtual partners in Mara's projected move to New Jersey. Werblin, you see, sold out his interest in the Jets to his partners after a bitter quarrel with them.

To this day they don't speak. And Sonny is not a man to forget.

The matter becomes complicated. Sonny and his partners also shared ownership in the Monmouth Park Race Track. Sonny sold out that interest. A hyperactive man, and a brilliant one, Sonny could not be idle for long. Always active in Jersey politics, he is a close friend of Governor William Cahill and, together with the governor, conceived the idea of a Jersey sports complex to be constructed in the Jersey swamps, the financing to come from a new issue of state bonds.

What a beautiful idea. Build a state-owned racetrack as part of the complex, pay a much lesser state tax than the competitive privately owned racetracks—Monmouth, Garden State and Atlantic City—pay to the state and use the excess income derived therefrom to help defray the interest to be paid on the bond issue. Also, build a football stadium as part of the complex, and maybe later a baseball stadium and an indoor sports arena. But the racetrack will be the big moneymaker. If this can be done you accomplish a lot of things—if you're Sonny Werblin. You've always wanted Rutgers to go big time in football. Playing in that complex they would be big time.

The new racetrack might get some good dates that Monmouth used to have, and if that hurts your former partners, so what? After all, you made the Jets what they were, they've been declining ever since you left, and by your precepts they wronged you. And you've always wanted Jersey to stand on its own, have a place in the nation as an important state. What better way to do it than with a modern sports complex? Not only that, but the blight of New Jersey, the swamplands, would be all but obliterated.

But for Werblin and Governor Cahill to sell the whole idea they had to have a peg, a franchise in hand, the most valuable kind of sports franchise in America, a professional football team committed to move into the football stadium immediately upon its completion. The obvious answer? Wellington Mara and his Giants.

At this juncture, let's examine the two men—Mara

and Werblin. Mara is a simple man to understand. He and his brother Jack, now deceased, inherited the football team from their father Tim, who was one of the pioneers of professional football. Tim was a decent man who suffered many financial adversities with the Giants before the team became successful. Too often Tim has been cheaply labeled a bookmaker—which he once had been—and too often Wellington has been written off merely as the son of a bookmaker who inherited the club. But the football team is Wellington's life. He is at his happiest at Giants' practices, garbed in a sweat suit, surveying his coaches and his players. One can almost sense that his dream is to be one of them. For him the Giants can do no wrong, and any criticism of them is akin to treachery. In his view the function of media people is to serve as an arm of the club's publicity department. Anyone who violates this notion is carefully marked off, made in many small ways to feel unwelcome. No seat in the press box. No invitation to the weekly press luncheon. Things like that. Wellington doesn't think this is wrong. He really doesn't. He doesn't think anything he does is wrong. After all, he is a religious man, a family man, utterly devoted to his wife and his children, and he owns the Giants. What more is there? Thus, his life is insular, and his social activities are limited to spending time with people who are suitably worshipful, not of him but of the team. You will find him and them at the Winged Foot Golf Club.

The net result is that Mara, though physically attractive, is socially unappealing. He has a personality like wet cement.

Sonny Werblin, on the other hand, is a dynamic man, and in some ways a genius. He is personable, he is interesting, his interests are broad, he can travel with ease and grace at any level of society, he cares about people, and while he doesn't enjoy criticism (who does?), he understands that it is part of life and he knows how to accept it. He also understands how to make money and he is a self-made millionaire. He will settle for nothing less than the best and he will spend whatever it takes to produce the best, which in the long run is the way to make the most money in sports. He is a sports lover, always has been, always will be. He owns thoroughbreds, misses the Jets terribly, resents his former partners deeply, loves his wife Leah Ray overwhelmingly, travels often, and somehow efficiently juxtaposes and commands a dozen different matters at the same time. In short, he is one hell of a guy, far too much for Wellington Mara.

Werblin proved this latter statement with the Jets. He and his partners took over a defunct organization called the New York Titans. They played their games at the old Polo Grounds where the spectators were so sparse that linebacker Larry Grantham once said, "When we were on the bench, we would look up into the stands and count the people." None of this bothered Werblin. Nor did the fact that the Giants played to capacity houses and literally owned New York bother him. This is a man who took performers nobody ever heard of and made them into stars, like Andy Williams, for instance. He would do the same with the Jets.

In making the Jets successful, Werblin—and Werblin alone—changed the face of professional football. When he bought Joe Willie Namath for $400,000-plus, he established a market level for talent that, in the words of Art Modell, president of the Cleveland Browns, "made it economic suicide to continue to fight." Werblin also negotiated a big-money television contract with NBC that enabled the American Football League to survive and to grow. Thus, Sonny, who opposed the merger of the two leagues, was in fact the unwitting chief catalyst of the merger.

Everything Sonny did took guts, cost money and took wisdom, too. I know. I believed in the American Football League and I virtually lived with Werblin through all those years. As director of sports for WABC Radio, I wanted to carry the Jets games on our station. So did my boss, Wally Schwartz. But the Jets were nothing then, and you couldn't give them away to a sponsor. Werblin understood this, but he also understood that

WABC was the number-one station in the market. He wanted the best possible exposure for his team while it grew. He took a puny $5,000 for the broadcast rights. And it worked for him, like everything else.

In 1964 his first draft choice was Matt Snell of Ohio State. A few days later the Giants drafted Snell in the NFL draft. Sonny was fishing at Islamorada, Florida, at the time. I called him and told him the Giants had just drafted Snell. "What the hell," he said, "do the Maras think they can show me up? I'll call you in twenty-four hours." It didn't take that long. Sonny called me from Columbus, Ohio, early the next day. "I've signed Matt Snell." That's when the Giants, who had made Snell a high draft choice, said they had no place for him anyway; no way he could make it in the National Football League. Thus the early love affair between Werblin and Mara.

It didn't stop there. Mara kept pretending the Jets did not exist. Werblin paid no attention. He kept doing his thing. His team needed a quarterback. He owned the future draft rights to a kid named Jerry Rhome, at Tulsa, who was setting all kinds of college passing records. Rhome's coach was Glenn Dobbs, a former pro-football great. Dobbs, who wanted to see Rhome get a big money deal, brought the lad to New York to get him some publicity and, hopefully, meet Werblin. Dobbs called me, and I did a local TV show with Jerry. Then I took the two of them over to meet Werblin for dinner. Rhome, by the way, was a smallish lad for the quarterback position, and quiet, reserved—a country boy. After dinner, as Dobbs and Rhome left us, Sonny said, "He'll never make it. Nobody will know his name." That was the end of Jerry Rhome's chances of joining the Jets. Werblin traded the draft rights to Rhome to Houston for the draft rights to a kid named Joe Willie Namath at Alabama.

Namath was to be the first-round draft choice of the Jets and the Saint Louis Cardinals in the other league. But then there were stories that, quietly, the Cardinals were prepared to deal their rights to Namath to the

Giants, if the Giants thought they could sign him. That would have meant a bidding war between Mara and Werblin. It didn't happen. Mara would have had no chance. Werblin visited Namath in Puerto Rico before the Alabama-Texas Orange Bowl game and called me from San Juan. "I've got him," he said. "I'm sure of it." He signed him immediately after the Orange Bowl game had been played, signed him formally that is.

During the days of the pro-football war the only player Werblin lost that he thought he had was Ben Hawkins, a wide receiver from Arizona State. Hawkins signed with Philadelphia, whereupon Sonny shot out to Norman, Oklahoma, to meet with a superb linebacker named Carl MacAdams. He wasn't ever going to let the other league beat him again. Once again came the telephone call. "I've got MacAdams."

Pittsburgh had draft rights to Emerson Boozer. So did Werblin. Sonny made sure. He went down to Maryland State and established a scholarship there as part of the deal to get Boozer. So Werblin was building a great football team, getting national attention, people were flocking to Shea Stadium, and he was showing up Mara. The Giants were in disarray. Their old grandeur was dissipated. They had become losers. Wellington Mara was desperate. He did something nobody else in the National Football League would even think of doing. He turned a bidding war into open piracy. He signed kicker Pete Gogolak of the Buffalo Bills in the American Football League.

This opened the floodgates. Under the canny leadership of American League President Al Davis, with the help of Houston General Manager Don Klosterman—two men whose knowledge of football personnel is unequalled— the AFL went to work. Mike Ditka of the Bears signed with Houston. Roman Gabriel of the Rams signed with Oakland. Klosterman met with John Brodie of the 49ers in Hawaii, and Brodie made a deal to jump. For the sake of a field-goal kicker, Wellington Mara had hurt his co-owners in the NFL beyond repair. And Gogolak would hardly challenge Joe Willie Namath for attention.

Mara was still the loser, Werblin the winner. Merger became an instant necessity for the NFL and with it nullification of all the deals mentioned above.

In the wake of all of the above, can you imagine Werblin and Mara getting together? But they did.

Wellington Mara became the witting foil for Werblin's gambit, gave it credibility and urgency, and once Sonny had Mara's commitment success for the project was assured. Sonny's selling points were simple: a brand-new stadium; 75,000 seats (Yankee Stadium could handle about 63,000); a better neighborhood (Yankee Stadium is adjacent to Harlem); a better deal on concessions and parking. In other words, lots more money for Wellington, as if he didn't have enough already.

As for outcries against the move from civic-minded New Yorkers, don't worry about it. Look at the trend of the society. People moving from the urban areas to the suburbs and exurbs. The old cities aren't there anymore. It's a new world, and the new word for it is "megalopolis." After all, the new stadium would be almost as close to Times Square as Yankee Stadium is. And we'll still call the team "New York."

So, Wellington Mara committed, the deed was done, and sure enough some sportswriters (mainly the ones who live in New Jersey) took helicopter trips over the swamplands with Sonny and wrote columns about "megalopolises." Mara told the Giant fans the move was in the interest of the fans. No poles in the new stadium, no obstructed views. Always, it is the fan who matters.

While all this was going on, it was baseball, for a change, that was showing integrity. Mike Burke, the president of the Yankees, did not want to move. Burke is a contemporary man, one of the best things that's happened to baseball in the last decade, and he understands the important of a sports franchise to a great city. "I'm not moving out of New York to pick up a few cheap dollars," he said, "not unless I have to." And so he worked out a deal with New York City to have Yankee Stadium renovated, modernized. And the Yankees will

stay. But sadly, Mike Burke, the man of principle, has
been heisted out of his job by a new Yankee ownership.

Suddenly the sportswriters began to write that New
York can't afford the millions to be spent on Yankee
Stadium. As if Jersey, with its terrible ghetto problems in
Newark, Camden, Jersey City and Trenton, should be
raising $200 million to build a sports complex. In the
whole maze of events, nobody asked why Mara had to
move. Nobody talked about the tax moneys, city and
state, that would be lost to New York. Few wrote that
the word "megalopolis" was irrelevant since it has no
relationship to existing city- and state-government juris-
dictions. Few wrote about all the benefits that had ac-
crued to Mara from the city through all the years. Few
wrote that the spirit and intent of the ten-million-dollar
"territorial rights" payment was for New York City, not
East Rutherford, New Jersey. Few wrote that the AFL
owners had been hoodwinked—ironically, Sonny Werblin
among them.

And then, in the total hypocrisy of the whole situation,
comes the last straw. The new stadium in Jersey won't
be ready until 1975. Yankee Stadium won't be available
for the Giants for most of 1973 and for all of 1974
while it undergoes renovation. Where will the Giants play?
Suddenly columns appeared criticizing New York City
for not deferring the renovation of Yankee Stadium and
for not making Shea Stadium available to the Giants.
As if the city were kicking the Giants out, rather than
the Giants deserting the city. Look at the rental moneys
the city will be giving up, they wrote (the city owns both
Yankee and Shea stadiums), and all the other moneys
that the Giants provide, taxes and otherwise. What a
magnificent non sequitur! It's all right for the Giants to
move out and cause the city to lose all those moneys
forevermore, but not all right to see the Giants home-
less for two years because the city would lose rental
and tax money for two years. Renovation of the stadium
must begin immediately and along with it renewal of
that whole area of the Bronx—a project critical to the
welfare of the city. Yet the writers studiously overlooked

these serious implications and were trying to find ways of helping a deserting owner at the expense of the very city he was deserting.

The saddest part about the whole mess is that it epitomizes the callous disregard of sports operators for the good of the whole society, the willingness to subvert public interest to private purposes. I wrote Werblin an open letter on all of this, and here is an excerpt:

> *... And then, Sonny, there is the matter of tradition. Yankee Stadium is rich with it, you know it, I know it, everyone knows it. Part of the life of this city would leave with the Giants.*
>
> *This is the nub of it, Sonny, and you know this too. The city and its continuing life and greatness. It is more important than the Giants, the Yankees, football, baseball and all the sports. One of the great crises of this nation is the crisis of the great cities. And New York is a city in crisis. It is being bled dry by Albany, which by your precepts is part of the megalopolis. Because of this, its problems with housing, schools, essential services, drugs are excessive. But withal, it remains the great city of this country. It is the world center of shipping and transportation, industry and communications, fashions, the arts and stage and screen. While it is in anguish, it can and must be saved. The answer is not evacuation but in renewal. The departure of the Giants would be symbolic of evacuation in the most serious terms, a damaging blow to the life stream, the pulsation of this great city. It must not happen, especially in the face of the city's willingness to renew Yankee Stadium and its environs.*
>
> *Space does not permit me to dwell on the questions affecting New Jersey. Whether a state-operated racetrack can legally compete with the already existent private tracks. Whether municipally bonded stadia ever really pay their way (remember how you complained about the state of Shea, and the fact that it wound up costing the taxpayers money?)*

Whether 200 million dollars for a Sports Complex might not be better expended in Newark, Jersey City and Camden in the order of priorities of the day. Serious questions, all. Someday, let's discuss them at your pad in the United Nations Plaza—right in the heart of New York City. But you will have to answer the core question: What single justification is there for the immensely profitable Giants to leave the greatest city in the country, if not the world?

Sonny has never answered my letter. He is much too smart. What is left is a perfect picture of how sport—in 1973—affects the politics, the law, the economics and the sociology of the society, in this case the nation's leading city. And what of the cast of characters?

Wellington Mara has his millions and will make more. But—and here is the real tragedy—he is damaging the other owners in the National Football League and the league itself. He damaged his league when he signed Gogolak. But that is nothing compared to what now has happened. After stumbling around for months, after being rejected by Princeton University, the Giants on May 23, 1973, finally announced that they would play their last five home games in 1973 and all home games in 1974 at Yale University. During all this stumbling the league was unable for a long time to even issue the 1973 schedule because of uncertainty as to where the Giants would play. And then, because of a political scandal in Jersey, there were whispers of doubt that the Jersey complex would ever be built. Many of the other owners began to get edgy. They would express their concern and resentment in private, not in public. And they especially resented the indignities to the image of their league as a result of the whole uncertain situation.

But once New Haven, Connecticut, became a definite temporary home for the Giants, an overwhelming problem presented itself to the league. That problem was the league's television blackout policy. Under former Commissioner Bert Bell the National Football League established a rule that all games played at home would be blacked out on television sets within a 75-mile radius of the home city. It is a simple fact that this policy has worked for the economic good of the league through all the years since its inception. It has been religiously adhered to by Pete Rozelle as Bell's successor, and Rozelle has been steadfast before the Congress in supporting it. Often he has faced pressures from the Congress to relax the rule, and indeed, once the 1973 Super Bowl game was sold out in Los Angeles, Pete did lift the blackout. The result was 8450 empty seats, the very specter that Rozelle and the owners fear would become a prevailing situation if the blackout policy were lifted. Empty seats bought and paid for might inevitably lead to empty seats not bought and paid for. This is why the owners view their blackout policy as the economic underpinning of their league's fiscal prosperity.

Now come the Giants with their problem. The Hartford, Connecticut, area is less than 75 miles from New Haven. About half a million viewers have gotten all 14 Giants games on television ever since the Giants began televising, because Hartford is more than 75 miles from New York. Now, if the blackout policy is adhered to, those viewers would miss five games in 1973 and seven games in 1974. Yale University officials don't want that to happen, neither do the Giants, neither do the other owners because the public outcry will be enormous. So the Giants are adopting this policy: If the games are sold out at Yale Bowl six days in advance of the contest, and if the visiting team agrees, the blackout will be lifted in the Hartford area. Such a position is permissible under league rules. But if this happens, even though Rozelle might argue that the position is taken to meet an exceptional situation that will last for two seasons only, the Congress might take a different view and demand that the whole blackout policy be relaxed. If you can relax it in the Giants' case, they might reason, why not in all cases? Obviously for a politician this position would have great public appeal.

So Wellington Mara has put Rozelle and the other

owners in a potentially perilous spot. The five opposing owners who will play in Yale Bowl have agreed to give permission to lift the blackout if Yale Bowl is sold out six days in advance. They have done so, however reluctantly, on two grounds: First, that the situation is unique and will only last for two seasons; and second, they fear the pressure of public outcry in a populous area of the country should the people of the Hartford area be deprived of what they have always had—14 Giant games. But they know in their hearts and minds that this could well open the door to congressional action that would eliminate the blackout policy that has made the NFL so economically successful. The best they can do is privately hope that the Giants don't sell out the Yale Bowl. They've got a friend in Wellington Mara.

One other thing: Since the racetrack is the key to making the Jersey complex work, Mara, however unwittingly, has in effect made an NFL franchise a front for the track, because the complex could never have gotten started without a Giants commitment to move.

The original American Football League owners provide still another wrinkle. Why don't they sue for the return of the ten million dollars they paid for "territorial rights"? The National Football League will tell you they have a rule that says territorial rights span a 75-mile radius and that East Rutherford is within that radius. Many top lawyers and judges will tell you that the spirit and intent of the indemnity payment was for New York City, and the Giants would lose in court if the old AFL owners sued them. If Werblin weren't involved with the Jersey complex, you could bet your bottom dollar he'd be leading the lawsuit.

But now, in his new role, Sonny Werblin surveys all from United Nations Plaza. The same Sonny Werblin who told me in an interview in 1966, "Let's face it, Howard. Once you cross that river everything is Bridgeport." Which is exactly why Sonny lives where he does. The last time I saw Sonny I reminded him that I still have the tape. "Why don't you burn it?" he growled.

Then he flashed a grin and said, "I never did say what river."

On June 25, 1973, the Werblin-Mara rapport reached its apex. In a burst of insensitivity, the New York Chapter of the Football Writers Association bestowed upon Wellington Mara an award for long and distinguished service to professional football. The man who made the presentation to Mara was David A. Werblin. A fitting finale to a sordid saga.

Walter O'Malley, the owner of the Dodgers, never did agree with Sonny Werblin. Once you cross that river, he reasoned, there is Los Angeles, the second-greatest city in the country, and a piece of property called Chavez Ravine that he could get for nothing. So Walter O'Malley crossed that river, not quite in the manner of Lewis and Clark but like one of the great prospectors of Cimarron days, and staked his claim to Los Angeles.

All he left behind was Brooklyn. Brooklyn, with the most colorful fans in the world. Brooklyn, with the richest baseball tradition in the world. Brooklyn, where for every one of the 13 years prior to O'Malley's departure the Dodgers had drawn over a million people—the yardstick of baseball prosperity. No other team in the National League could match those attendances. He didn't want to leave Brooklyn, he said. He had no choice. All he wanted was a municipally built new stadium at the site of the Long Island Railroad Depot, the Grand Central of the borough. He wanted it there because it would skyrocket the value of the railroad, in which he had an important financial interest. This was why Shea Stadium—which he could have had—did not interest him.

When he left, there was a public outcry against him. Poor Walter. He couldn't understand it. Like any other businessman he had simply moved his business. That, he said, was his right in a free-enterprise society. Walter was absolutely correct—if one assumes that baseball is a free-enterprise business. The trouble is, baseball gets its federal antitrust-law exemption on the ground that it is not like any other free-enterprise business. Ford, Chrysler,

General Motors, Macy's, Gimbels—you name it—are
all subject to the federal antitrust laws. So is the National
Football League, the National Basketball Association, the
National Hockey League. Baseball is the only business
in the United States, other than public utilities, to be
free of the threat of a government antitrust crackdown.
O'Malley knows very well that baseball has gone before
the Congress and said, in effect, "Leave our reserve clause
alone [the reserve clause binds a player to his team
forever], we can't operate without it. We're not like
Macy's and we're not like Gimbels, we are like the phone
company, the power companies, the broadcast companies.
We are tinged with and affected by the public interest.
We belong to the public." And the argument has worked
for baseball through all the decades.

So Walter O'Malley executed the ultimate hypocrisy.
He deserted the very public that baseball says it belongs
to. Worse, he deserted the very public that provided
him with a handsome profit. And when he did, he had
the audacity to resort to an open double standard. Baseball was now free enterprise again. How the Congress
allows the reserve clause to remain inviolate in the light
of such actions is beyond me. Because O'Malley was
only the beginning.

When O'Malley departed, his last words were: "I had
to do it to compete with Milwaukee." Milwaukee, you
remember, had been Boston. Now, playing in the new
Milwaukee County Stadium, and blessed with a fine team,
the Braves were indeed setting new National League
attendance records. But the Braves were not long for
Milwaukee. Lou Perini, the owner, stopped the fans from
bringing in their own beer—this had been a long-term
custom in the Beer City—and this offended some fans.
Then the Braves stopped winning. The two factors together produced an attendance decline, but certainly not
enough to warrant moving out. So Perini got out. He
sold the club to a group of young men who used bor-
rowed money from Illinois banks to negotiate the purchase. And very shortly thereafter the new owners got
themselves a new stadium and a much better television

deal in Atlanta—where the Braves are now—all in the name of sport. The Milwaukee County Stadium, except on the few days when the Green Bay Packers played there, stayed empty for years. A simple sign in front of the stadium read, "No Game Today."

Then there is Seattle, the great city of the Pacific Northwest. They got major-league baseball. For one year. In and out, just like that, while a man named Dewey Soriano escaped with a neat capital gain. Go to Seattle and talk to the civic leaders and to the man in the street. They'll tell you about the carpetbaggers. They'll tell you how such men want new stadiums built at municipal expense, how they want the public to flock to the stadium as a civic obligation even if the product is not good, how their city was, in effect, raped. All in the name of sport.

Then there is the capital city of this nation, Washington, D.C., a city with one of the richest traditions in baseball, but a city which had not been given a good baseball team for many decades. A city vital to the game, one would think, because of baseball's pretension that it is the national pastime. How could baseball open a season without the president throwing out the first ball? Where else would baseball have its centennial all-star game but in Washington? That nonsense is all over now. The pretense has vanished. Another underfinanced owner, a fellow named Bob Short, took the Senators to the vast, sprawling metropolis of Arlington, Texas, where attendances languish even though major-league baseball is a novelty there.

In each and every one of the above cases, the public interest was defied—always in the name of sport. And still baseball is free of the antitrust laws. The only consolation is that baseball has about run out of cities. They're back in Milwaukee now, and in Kansas City, too. Remember, Kansas City was moved to Oakland by owner Charles Finley. Now Finley wants to move out of Oakland; the Minnesota Twins are making eyes at New Orleans; and the Atlanta Braves are viewing their sparse attendance with a roving eye.

And—would you believe?—major-league baseball, National League variety, is going back to Washington. The San Diego Padres, an abortive expansion experiment, have been sold to a group of Washington businessmen. Pressure from Congress to return to Washington was a factor in this, but economics was the principal element.

In fairness to the San Diego management, the last thing they wanted to do was sell out and have the franchise removed. The man who ran the Padres (and who owned 32 percent of the club) was Buzzie Bavasi, one of the smartest and finest sports operators you could find. On an attendance of less than 650,000 in 1972, he nonetheless showed a $50,000 profit on his operation. But his profit margin was overwhelmed by an annual $700,000 interest payment due on a ten-million-dollar loan to the banker-industrialist C. Arnholdt Smith, who together with his daughter owned 62 percent of the ball club. The ten-million-dollar loan was used to pay the National League for the cost of the franchise. There was no way, financially, they could keep going.

I knew the San Diego situation intimately because of Buzzie Bavasi. And as evidence of how Buzzie knew he was in a desperate spot and wanted to save the franchise, here is a letter I received from him dated February 1, 1973:

Dear Howard:

When you read this letter you will think I have a hell of a nerve and you are right. I have nerve but here goes.

Last year we held our first Old Timers Game and I am told by baseball people that it was probably the best ever held. We changed the format a bit and honored people other than the stars of the game. Last year Mr. & Mrs. Red Barber were our guests and Red was the MC. This year we would like very much to have Mr. & Mrs. Howard Cosell as our guests and Howard as the MC.

The game is to be held on July 13. We are inviting the participants to come in on Thursday and stay

*as long as they want. If at all possible, could you
let me know if there is any chance that you can
make it. We think you will add a lot to the game
and, at the same time, do me a favor* and heaven
knows I need help.

With kindest personal regards,

E. J. Bavasi

Buzzie will probably go to Washington to run the ball
club. But he loved living in La Jolla, and his distaste
for franchise removals goes back to when his former boss,
Walter O'Malley, deserted Brooklyn. With typical out-
spokenness, Bavasi blamed the National League owners
for the San Diego fiasco. "They charged us ten million
dollars for the franchise," he said. "Had they charged us
the American League price of six million dollars, we
could have stuck it out and made it work."

But the fact remains that baseball is now a floating
crap game. You can't tell the cities without a map.

And in yet another irony, things haven't worked out
for the man O'Malley piggybacked to California, Horace
Stoneham, the owner of the San Francisco Giants. Attendances have so declined there that Stoneham had to
unload the big salary of one of America's greatest fa-
vorites, the symbol of the team, Willie Mays. In the
interest of the player, of course. To complete the cycle
of hypocrisy, the Mets gleefully bought him under the
fiction that, at age 41, he would lead them to a pennant.
Again, in the interest of the player, of course. Not to
hypo attendances.

In the wake of the curious Supreme Court decision in
the Curt Flood case, one wonders if the Congress will
finally step in to protect the public interest against the
baseball owners. In the Flood case the Supreme Court
said, in essence, that the reserve clause was an anachro-
nism, a violation of the antitrust laws. But, the Court
said, it has been in existence so long it is up to the Congress to change it.

The Flood decision was rendered on the very day

that I was in Washington testifying before a Senate Commerce Subcommittee headed up by Senator Marlow Cook, Republican, Kentucky. Senator Cook is a man deeply cognizant of the manipulations of some of the professional sports operators. So he introduced a bill on the Senate floor that would have established a Federal Sports Commission. Under the terms of the bill, an owner could only move his franchise from one city to another with the approval of the commission. Thus, the public interest could be protected. No more Brooklyns, Washingtons, Seattles, Milwaukees. I testified in favor of the bill. Virtually no one else did. All of the commissioners of sport came out against that old bugaboo, government control. Anything wrong with sport should be cleaned up by us, they argued. They won. The bill was tabled. I'd like to see the day when they put their own houses in order, but that day will never come. Nor will it for the moguls of amateur sport, the U.S. Olympic Committee, the National Collegiate Athletic Association and the Amateur Athletic Union.

The U.S. Olympic Committee belongs to the aged. It is dominated by men with medieval philosophies who should have sailed around the world with Magellan. In the wake of their numerous fiascos in Munich the public has finally caught up with them. And it is the public which, through its multimillions of dollars of contributions, foots the bill for U.S. participation in the Olympic Games. The misfeasances and nonfeasances of the committee have been dealt with elsewhere in this book. Now there is an outside hope that Congress will try to do something about it.

Once again, Senator Marlow Cook is a prime mover. He has introduced a bill that would create a Federal Amateur Sports Commission to which the U.S. Olympic Committee would be responsible. Such a commission could effectuate a change in the membership of the committee, so that young people would dominate, especially former Olympians who know what the needs of our athletes are, and how best to service those needs. Such a commission could also oversee a long-term program of development of training facilities for our athletes. Those facilities are sadly lacking now. Such a committee could check on the selection of our Olympic coaches.

It is an open secret that many of our coaches are "political" appointees who are not qualified for the job and whom our athletes do not respect.

I happen to like and respect Henry Iba, our Olympic basketball coach. But the plain facts are that Henry has not been an active coach for years, his style of basketball does not suit our contemporary basketball players and the United States has dozens upon dozens of fine young coaches who are presently better equipped for the job. Everywhere one went in the Olympic Village American athletes could be heard muttering about the coaches. George Woods, the shot-putter, bluntly told me in an interview that there weren't two track-and-field coaches in the American contingent that he respected. Bob Seagren felt the same way. So did Bill Toomey, who was part of our broadcasting team.

And everywhere you went you would see our Olympic officials, pompous, bustling, wearing their badges of authority, enjoying themselves, looking forward to their cocktail parties in the evening. Unfailingly the ones neglected are the athletes, and they are the ones to be served for they are what the public is paying for.

The two prevailing bodies over the amateur sports structure in the United States are the National Collegiate Athletic Association and the Amateur Athletic Union. It is now a fair statement to say that no matter how much good they might do in matters of administration, each is motivated by a selfish power lust that is doing great injustice to the athletes of this country. The examples are many. Some of the finest American basketball players couldn't oppose the Russians when the Soviet Olympic team visited America. Some of America's finest track stars couldn't compete against the Russians in a dual track meet in Richmond, Virginia. Why not? Because the NCAA would not allow them to. Why not? Because the AAU had certified the event, not the NCAA.

In other years the AAU was guilty of doing the same

thing. Each wants total control of amateur sports. The NCAA has a mighty weapon: It can kill off a collegian's athletic career; it can penalize a young man's university. Chris Dunn of Colgate is the nation's finest indoor high-jumper. He wanted to jump against the Russians at Richmond. He was told he would never be eligible in college competition again if he competed, and Colgate was told it would face disciplinary action by the NCAA. Dunn did not compete.

In one of the most disgusting actions within my memory the NCAA sought to stop several young men of Jewish persuasion from participating in the basketball competition in the Maccabiah Games, a respected international competition held in Israel. Gymnasts, swimmers and track-and-field performers were allowed to go because the NCAA certified them. But not the basketball players, because the AAU certified them. Jack Langer, a basketball player at Yale University, with the approval of Yale, participated anyway. This was one time when God and man were truly at Yale. So the NCAA put Yale on probation. As Al McGuire, the outspoken Marquette basketball coach, later told me, "Isn't that absurd? With all the dirt in college recruitment, they penalize a school like Yale." He was absolutely right. Big-time college athletic recruitment is one of the continuing scandals in sports, and the NCAA could better spend its time policing it rather than occupying itself with the frustration of the legitimate aspirations of the athletes. Imagine how some of our Olympic basketball players felt, after their controversial loss to the Russians in Munich, when they were told they could not play against that very same team here in the United States and obtain some measure of revenge for the chaotic ending that deprived them of a victory in Munich. I was with those American players the morning after the game against the Russians. All they wanted was another shot. Finally, because of senatorial pressure at the last minute, some American collegians got a chance to play against the Russians. They sure as hell deserved it.

The feud between the AAU and the NCAA has actually

lasted longer than the American involvement in Vietnam. It has defied the peacemaking efforts of some of this country's most distinguished figures. The late General Douglas MacArthur was assigned to try to settle the matter a number of years ago, and failed. Theodore Kheel, perhaps the country's finest labor mediator, was picked to mediate, and, after many months, failed. And still it goes on.

Finally the House of Representatives could take no more. It was long past the time, as a matter of fact, for them to have taken notice. But there is an excuse: Most sports broadcasters and writers have paid little attention to the problem of the amateur athletes. One sportswriter, who had seen a whole show I had done on the Jack Langer injustice, asked me what I was so excited about. "Nobody cares," he said. "That's a nothing subject." The same writer had just devoted an entire column to whether Duffy Dyer or Jerry Grote should be the Mets' catcher. That really says it all about most print and broadcast sports journalism, and explains why only lately the Congress and the public have awakened to the plight of the amateur athlete.

Early in 1973 Congressmen Peter Peyser of New York and Michael O'Hara of Michigan each introduced bills directed at the amateur-sports mess. Peyser, in the manner of Senator Cook, proposed a Federal Amateur Sports Commission. O'Hara is proposing a more limited measure. I testified before them both. Congressman O'Hara explained that he wanted to refrain from government interference as much as possible. It was therefore the intent of his bill to correct the worst abuses while leaving the parties "where we found them, as much as possible."

I responded, "Oh, no, don't leave them where you found them, because where you found them is in the gutter."

In 1973, the Senate and the House may have finally begun action to take the amateur sports bodies out of the gutter. The Senate Commerce Commission has reported out of committee to the Senate floor a bill that would create a U.S. amateur sports board. Representative Dellenback of Oregon has placed a similar bill before the House.

The final indignity in this whole grubby sports burlesque is the way the professional sports franchise carpetbagging sets in motion the cheap political wheels. State is pitted against state. City against city. Georgia steals from Wisconsin. California and New Jersey plunder New York. Texas raids Washington, D.C. Kansas City lifts a team from Philadelphia and loses it to Oakland. And the beat goes on.

It is, I think, a sad commentary on the political structure. Senators and congressmen act with passion to defend their own special interests, but who speaks for the public good? In specific terms, I was with Senator Stuart Symington of Missouri when he charged into New York in an effort to prevent the A's from abandoning Kansas City. And that time—the destination then was Louisville—he succeeded. I witnessed the wrath of Senator Proxmire as the Braves marched on Georgia. But, curiously, no Georgia or California statesmen shared the concern of either Symington or Proxmire. Nor does Governor Cahill of New Jersey sympathize with Rockefeller or Lindsay as they attempt to protect their turf.

In circumstances like these it's hard to separate the politicians from the sports promoters.

But maybe all of that is past, in view of the new and more public-spirited kind of congressional pressure that is building—at least with respect to the amateur-athletic structure. Hopefully we can begin to get the athletes their due and the public its due. Hopefully. In the meantime one adds up the score, and this is what one finds: Power. Money. Disregard of the public interest. Retribution against old friends. Double standards at law. Desertions of the cities. Foul-ups in the Olympics. Frustration of the young athlete. Petty politics.

Makes a pretty picture, doesn't it? All in the name of sport.

And when was the last time you saw a kid peeping through a knothole?

Chapter XII

MONDAY NIGHT FOOTBALL

"Get that nigger-loving Jew bastard off the air. Football is an American game."

PART 1:

It's Going to Be a Trip

"With a voice that had all the resonance of a clogged Dristan bottle, sportscaster Howard Cosell made pro football addicts of more than 25 million viewers on Monday nights . . ."

The above quote could conceivably have originated with a television critic or a sportswriter. But it did not. It might have been the brainchild of the ABC Publicity Department. But it was not. Believe it or not, the above quote appears in the Encyclopedia Britannica Year Book—1973. In what I can only view as the ultimate in misplaced emphasis, I have been biographied in the most distinguished of all world books. "Monday Night Football" is the reason.

We are now in our fourth year of "Monday Night Football." It continues to be a television phenomenon, a sensation in the television ratings and, in financial terms, the most successful sports package in history. It is a phenomenon because it has changed the social habits of America on Monday nights in the autumn. The movie business has gone to hell on those nights. In Los Angeles, for instance, some of the movies remain dark. Some have tried to entice women. "Come see us on Monday nights," they would advertise. "Admission price only a quarter." It hasn't worked.

The bars aren't doing business either; neither are the restaurants. Some bars have tried a gimmick to induce customers. One place in Buffalo pleads, "Watch the game here with your buddies. Fight with Howard Cosell." But they can do that at home.

Many restaurants shut down on Monday nights. And the department stores complain about a sharp drop in sales. ABC does not share that complaint. In its first year, "Monday Night Football" was sold out at $65,000 per minute of commercial time. Now it is sold out at $80,000 per minute. And there are sponsors waiting on line. Onward and upward.

None of this was what John Keats had in mind when he wrote the "Ode to Autumn."

The truth is, ABC didn't have it in mind either; nor did the National Football League; nor did NBC and CBS. "Monday Night Football" has transcended the most hopeful expectations of both ABC and the NFL, and it has begun to force CBS and NBC to consider major changes in the manner in which they transmit events. In the middle of the whole thing, once again, is the invisible man, Roone Arledge. Also in the middle—in a different way—is the recipient of the biggest publicity wave (good and bad) any sportscaster has ever received—Howard Cosell.

This is how it all began.

In the spring of 1970, at a time when I was doing a nightly local television show, I got an urgent phone call. It was from Chuck Howard. Could I get right over to the National Football League Office with a film crew. I knew at once that the negotiations had been completed, that ABC had purchased the right to telecast professional football in prime entertainment time on Monday nights. I picked up my crew and shot over to interview Pete Rozelle and Roone Arledge.

How different the reaction was then. CBS and NBC quietly—no, not so quietly—snickered. CBS had twice tried pro football in prime time. It hadn't worked, not even with the Green Bay Packers of Vince Lombardi as the attraction. And, the thinking went, if you couldn't make it with the Pack, you couldn't make it with anybody. The problem, according to most industry thinking, was women. Women watched television at night. They dominated the sets in use. They would not watch football. Not with shows like "Carol Burnett," "Laugh In," the "Monday Night Movie" on the air. Their thinking made sense. Privately, some at ABC agreed. But ABC had to do something. Its ratings on Monday nights languished terribly. They were not remotely competitive to the other two networks.

Thus, when Pete Rozelle came up with the idea of "Monday Night Football"—and it was *his* idea—he found a willing listener in Arledge.

Weeks passed after it was announced that there would be "Monday Night Football" at ABC. I personally gave little thought to the idea that I would be part of the package. Then one night I did my local television show with Pete Rozelle. Subsequently, we went over to the Tavern on the Green in Central Park for a cocktail. This was when Pete said that he hoped I would do the color commentary on the games. I was frankly surprised, because while I had always liked and respected Rozelle, I did not fit his mold, nor the traditional NFL mold. That mold had been carefully stamped out through all the years of NFL telecasts: You get a play-by-play announcer, add one former NFL player for "expertise and analysis," and you've got the telecast. In my opinion, every telecast sounded like every other.

But Rozelle understood this. He felt that a new approach was needed in prime time to capture a new type of audience. However, he could only think about it. He had nothing to do with selection of announcers. Arledge had quite properly retained all authority in that regard when he made his deal with the NFL. So it would be up to Arledge.

The way Roone works, events take on an erratic flow. You may not see him or hear from him for many days. Then suddenly he is all over you, and you begin to hope that he will vanish again. Thus, out of nowhere, on a hot June day, I was lunching with friends at Jimmy Weston's, when I was paged. Roone wanted to see me immediately. I went directly to his office and, in that carefully mild, understated way of his, he said, "Hey, we've got to talk about the pro football package."

"What about it?" I asked.

"I'd like you to be a part of it," he replied. "It's a question of how we set it up."

We began to discuss play-by-play announcers. We talked about Vin Scully, and, although it never became public knowledge, Vin was actually approached. He had no interest. Not with his baseball commitments. We also considered Tom Harmon and, in fact, Roone did call Tom. For reasons that I am unaware of, there was no follow-up on Tom.

Then there were Chris Schenkel and Keith Jackson, two of our regulars on the ABC Sports team, both of whom were doing NCAA football. Chris made no secret of the fact that he would love to work the Monday Night package, but the NCAA was an insurmountable barrier to that possibility. They insisted on keeping Chris as the spokesman for college football.

Abruptly, talk of the play-by-play announcers was deferred.

"How would you feel about working with Don Meredith?" Roone asked me. "We'd use him on replays."

I said fine. I had known Don for a lot of years, only superficially, but had always enjoyed his company.

"Well," said Arledge, "Frank Gifford recommended him. And I think it's a hell of a thing because Frank wanted this job himself." The Giff was then under contract to CBS. Meredith got the job.

Then, in the days that followed, Arledge developed his approach to the telecasts. A different approach. One that would excite all kinds of press. One that would draw enormous attention to the package. He wanted three men in the broadcast booth. It was his conviction that the play-by-play announcer should serve really as a public address announcer, that he should be on quickly with the basic information, and then quickly off, as Dandy and I were to pick up with color and analysis, and hopefully some candor, some humor, and some human insight into the athletes so that they would become more than face masks, shoulder pads and numbers.

Keith Jackson was the man Roone hired for play-by-play. I was delighted. Keith is all competence, all work and all man. So that was our broadcast team.

Immediately, Meredith, O. J. Simpson (also part of the ABC team) and I went on a tub-thumping tour to set the stage for "Monday Night Football." We covered Pittsburgh, Boston and Washington-Baltimore. Keith could not be with us because of other assignments. We tried to explain what the approach would be. Some writers were skeptical. How could we possibly use three men in the booth? Wouldn't we fall over one another? To tell the truth, we wondered ourselves. But always, Arledge had one thing in mind. Football was invading prime time. New viewers, especially women, had to be attracted. The old way of presenting a game would not be good enough. He knew the other two networks were gleefully anticipating a debacle in the ratings.

Chet Forte was named producer-director of the telecasts. He was an ideal choice. This little former basketball All-American from Columbia is a volatile man, emotional, sometimes even tempestuous, but when a broadcast begins he is all business and he knows his business as well as anyone in the industry. He also knows sports— including football—inside out.

Now we were all set. We were to do a trial run. We would tape a preseason game between Detroit and Kansas City just as though it were a regular telecast, but it would never air. Keith, Dandy and I met in Detroit and the three of us drove to the Lions training camp to watch them work out and to move among the players. Dandy knew the Lions, of course. He had worked often enough against them. And I knew most of them from my coverage of the beat. So we stood together on the field chatting with a group of them, one of whom was Bobby Williams, a reserve defensive back.

Suddenly I turned to Williams, and said, "You know, of course, that Meredith has no use for you black players."

Dandy became crimson and said, "What's that?"

"Don't play the innocent line with me, Don," I shot back. "Everybody knows."

Meredith shook his head. "Man, this 'Monday Night Football' is going to be a trip—a trip with Howard Cosell. Bobby Williams, you know that this little native Texan from dear ole Mount Vernon doesn't feel that way at all about you black folks, don't you?"

Williams laughed. He enjoyed the put-on. So did Don, and that was the beginning of my relationship with Dandy the way it so often comes out on the air. There was, from the beginning, a natural chemistry between us— the Yankee lawyer and the Texas cornpone. Each putting the other on.

We did the test-run game and Don was painfully ill at ease. He wasn't really sure of his role in the telecast. Keith was first-rate. I made some observations that pleased Arledge. Not that they were anything brilliant, but they were the very kind of observations that had been studiously eschewed in the telecasting of NFL games in the past. For instance, I mentioned that Len Dawson's statistics were always better than his true effectiveness. Len has an inordinately high percentage of completions because he uses the quick sideline hitch pass so often, where the defense gives away the short yardage. He is, of course, a fine quarterback, but instead of raving about him, I pointed out some fallacies. Roone liked that.

But it was all new to Meredith, and he was not, after all, a professional. We went back to New York and studied the tape with Arledge and Forte. Roone and Chet pointed out to Don the areas where he could do better, and what was expected of him. Dandy is a sensitive man to begin with, and at the time he was struggling with a tremendous personal depression and concern. His little daughter, Heather, born blind and retarded, was about to be institutionalized. Against that, football could not have been less important.

So Don was wrestling with himself and his emotion got the better of him. He stood up and said, "Let's face it, fellows. I'm not qualified for this. I don't even know that much about football. I just know the Xs and Os that Landry taught me."

Roone and Chet made it clear that they were not being critical in a destructive sense. Both knew that Dandy was a natural, and Don, for his part, settled down. Later, before Don left for the airport to go to Dallas, I had a drink with him.

"Don," I said, "in my opinion you'll be making the biggest mistake of your life if you even think about leaving us. You're going to come out of this a hero. Middle America will love you. Southern America will love you. And there are at least forty sportswriters in this country who can't wait to get at me. You'll benefit thereby. Don't worry about me, though, because in the long run it will work for the old coach, too. You'll wear the white hat, I'll wear the black hat and you'll have no problems from the very beginning."

Dandy lifted his drink. "By golly," he said, "I'm with you, coach. All the way." And off he went to Dallas. He didn't know it then but he was only 20 weeks away from winning an Emmy. And I didn't know it then, but I was going to reach a point where I would lose my perspective, and begin to feel sorry for myself. Only in my case it would take a lot less than 20 weeks. And I would learn that I still had a lot to learn about myself and some more growing up to do.

Keith and Dandy and I did our first on-air game together in Pittsburgh. It was a preseason game that promised to have a maximum of disinterest. The Giants against the Pittsburgh Steelers. The Steelers were terrible. It was Chuck Noll's first year as head coach, with a long rebuilding program before him. The Giants were coming off a four-won, ten-lost season. About the only interest we could conjure up was the fact that Terry Bradshaw, the Li'l Abner type-character from Louisiana Tech, would be making his debut as the Pittsburgh quarterback on national television.

Arledge recognized the situation. He wanted to grab some national attention for us despite the unattractive match-up. So he suggested that we try to put a mike on Fran Tarkenton, the Giants' quarterback, who would not be playing that night because of a pulled muscle in the groin. I had misgivings about the idea because I did not want the public to think that we could do this during the regular season. But I sparked to the notion because I knew we could liven up what might otherwise be a terribly dull evening.

So I talked to Fran, who was most agreeable on the condition that his coach, Alex Webster, would agree to it. I think Fran felt that it would otherwise be a boring night for him, and Fran is an extroverted, articulate young man who may some day be doing some announcing himself. Webster, as nice a man as you would want to meet, was agreeable too. Thus we started the game with Fran wearing a live microphone.

He was outstanding. Dandy would talk to him during a lull in the action—which was almost all night long— and say, "Son of a preacher man, what do you think of that young blond-haired boy from my part of the country, that there quarterback from Louisiana Tech?"

And Francis would chuckle and then answer. I had my own series of quips going back and forth with Tark, and we all felt good in the booth because we had a whole new thing going. But overall, I was not happy with the telecast because of the way it was formatted. I opened the show on the field and interviewed Terry Bradshaw. We were six minutes into the game before I even got to the booth. And then, I was concerned about the three men in the booth, trying to feel my way with Keith and Don. I left the stadium feeling that this whole thing was wrong for me. I was now the way Don had been after the trial-run game. I did not join the others after the game, but went straight to the hotel room and to bed. Arledge called me about one in the morning and asked me how I felt things had gone. I told him I thought the Tarkenton bit was a great idea. Later we found out that the affiliate stations had loved it, and the fans loved it. But I told him I was concerned about my own role in the telecast and I thought perhaps it might be a better package without me, from my own point of view and from the company's point of view. I told him I was going to the Jersey shore the next morning to join Emmy, and that I wanted to think about it. He said it was a good idea.

I expected what would happen after that telecast and it did. The sportswriters were up in arms. There was Cosell again, breaching all the rules. How dare I wire Tarkenton? (As if I had done it without the approval of the coach and the man himself.) How dare I have the idea, the temerity to try to do it? (It wasn't even my idea.) So the New York writers called Rozelle and demanded that they be allowed to sit on the bench with the team during the game if ABC was going to put a live microphone on Giant players. Rozelle had no taste for the idea either, but he knew we were just trying to juice up our first telecast. For myself, I wondered when someone other than me would tell the truth. What right did the writers have to demand this? Their newspapers don't pay one red cent for the right to cover the games. Their writers sometimes travel and eat at team expense, thus defying one of the fundamental laws of journalism and creating a clear conflict of interest. ABC, on the other had, paid millions of dollars for the right to broadcast the games, and each announcer was paid by ABC, not the National Football League. We also slept and ate at ABC's expense, and we traveled at ABC's expense. But no, in the peculiar and often sick structure of "sports print journalism" I was to be the whipping boy. I even considered doing a commentary demanding that newspapers pay for the right to have their reporters cover the games.

So I got it from many of them, all across the country. "Cosell is at it again," they wrote. "He makes himself bigger than the event." As if a preseason game between

the Giants and Pittsburgh (which won only one game
that year) was a major circumstance in this nation's
history. Frankly, I was disgusted. But then I got mad.
I called Arledge, told him I wanted to stay on the package, and I couldn't wait to start the regular season.

The night before that Pittsburgh-Giants telecast, I had
dinner with Dandy at a restaurant situated on a cliff
overlooking the great confluence where the Monongahela
and the Allegheny become the Ohio River. Dandy looked
over toward Three Rivers Stadium and grew retrospec-
tive. He talked a lot about his former coach, Tom
Landry. Deep inside he carries with him a great wound
where Landry is concerned. He has never liked Tom.
He feels that as a coach Landry mechanized him, stifled
his creative instincts. He saw Landry as much too cold
and unemotional and unapproachable a person for his
taste. He said, "He's a cold man, Howard, with no human
understanding in him."

I think that epitomized his feelings about Tom Landry.

We were joined for dinner that night by Fran Tarkenton. It could have been a sticky situation, but it
wasn't. Not with two men like Fran and Dandy. Un-
beknownst to the general public, the Giants had contacted
the Cowboys about acquiring Meredith. The Giants'
management seemed to be buying the line that Tarkenton
was a "loser," and that the four-won, ten-lost record
of the preceding year stemmed mainly from his deficien-
cies. Thus the Giants wanted to get Meredith from the
Cowboys and talk him out of retirement. The go-between
in this situation was Dandy's close friend—and a former
Giant—Frank Gifford. Tarkenton knew of all this, but
he is first of all a gentleman, and second, one hell of a
guy. So when he met us for dinner, there was never a
word about what was going on behind the scenes. Instead, the two men spent the evening regaling me with
stories of things they had done together when they were
working for the Fellowship of Christian Athletes.

The truth was that Meredith's interest in returning
to football had been piqued by what the Giff was telling
him. The thought of playing in New York was appealing,

and Frank assured Dandy that the Giants could be a contender. "Giff says all they need is a brick here and a brick there," Don related.

I answered, "Well, Giff may be right, but his brick here and brick there, I think, amounts to a whole damned building, Dandy. But you can judge for yourself when you see the Giants tomorrow night."

The next night, with Tark on the bench, the Steelers ripped the Giants. As we were leaving the booth Dandy said, "Ha'hrd, you're right, a brick here and a brick there means an entire building." From that point on he ceased to think seriously about coming out of retirement.

Tarkenton, incidentally, had an amazing season. He led that Giant team to a nine-and-five record, and Don and I still don't see how.

Our first regular season game was to match the New York Jets and the Cleveland Browns at Cleveland. We felt that it was a break for us, for two reasons: First, Cleveland is always a solid team; and second, the Jets had the biggest draw in pro football—Joe Willie Namath. I never have been better prepared for a show in my life than I was for the first "Monday Night" game.

I was very close to the Jet players and, of course, I was particularly close to Joe Willie Namath. Meredith knew little about the Jets. He knew about Cleveland, because the Browns had always had a hex on Dallas and had defensed Meredith very well throughout the years. But to Don, the American Football League had never existed.

So I took Meredith with me much of that week preparatory to the game—to the Jets' dressing room, out to the practice field and, finally, to Joe Namath's apartment. There Joe sat with a projector and ran the films again and again for us of the Cleveland defenses. He explained the basics of what the Jets were going to do. The main element of the ground game was to go against young Jerry Sherk, a rookie defensive lineman from Oklahoma State. And, indeed, when the game took place that's exactly what they did.

Namath then explained to Don and me exactly how he would try to crack the Cleveland zone defense. Don related to Joe the troubles he had suffered through the years with the Cleveland secondary. "They're a funny kind of team," Don told him. "They bend, but they don't break. Just when you think you've got them, they'll come up with the key interception."

Namath couldn't have been more honest with us or more thorough in his evaluations. In fact, in our three years of "Monday Night Football," nobody has treated us more openly or fully. When we left, Meredith said, "I'm glad I spent this time with him. He's not at all like they write about him."

When I got to Cleveland, I spent most of Sunday with Bill Nelsen, the quarterback of the Browns. Bill is another direct guy, who told me exactly what the Browns were going to do. Not that there was any mystery about it. The key to the Jets' secondary had always been the fine strong safety, Jim Hudson. But Hudson had bad knees, which the public knew about, and also a bad back, which the public didn't know. So, obviously, Bill was going to test Hudson immediately. It would be Hudson's task to·cover one of the best tight ends in football, Milt Morin. Naturally, he would resort to other familiar aerial tactics, including his favorite play when near the end zone, the post pattern to Gary Collins. He would also, of course, balance the attack, if he could, with the running of Leroy Kelly and Bo Scott.

We arrived at the Ball park at about 7:00 P.M. on that opening Monday night. We'd had a full-scale rehearsal the night before, which was to become part of the pattern of "Monday Night Football." I was to open the show on the playing field with an interview with Namath. This had been prearranged. We were to tape Joe at 8:00 P.M., an hour before the kickoff. The appointed time came and went, but Namath didn't show. The minutes ticked by, and our tension grew. Bob Cochran, head of radio and television for the NFL, waited along with me. It grew dangerously close to game time. The teams would be coming out for their final run-through . . . and then the kickoff. So Cochran was kind enough to race down to the clubhouse for me. He came back and said, "Well, he didn't want to do it. He's uptight—it's the opening game of the year and the first Monday night game—but he's coming out." And so he did.

I started the interview when, suddenly, I heard Weeb Ewbank, Namath's coach, yelling: "Howard, I've got to have my quarterback, we're almost at game time." I knew Ewbank was right and I felt guilty as hell. But I hurried the interview. Then, I introduced Dandy to the audience. The introduction had been carefully set up in the form of a film package that Dandy didn't even know about.

We had put together a montage of Don in action, featuring some of his most inglorious moments as a Dallas Cowboy: Don getting swamped for a loss, Don fumbling, Don throwing an interception, Don missing a hand-off, Don in a variety of forced landings. It was a riot to watch, and Dandy completely understood the spirit of it. In fact, it set the stage for our whole relationship and all the ribbing to come during the course of the season. The idea had been concocted by Beano Cook, our publicity man for college football, and Roone Arledge went for it hook, line and sinker. So did I.

Forty-eight hours later we were getting letters and I was the butt of columns denouncing me for "showing up" Meredith, the man "who had played the game."

The game itself followed the very pattern that Namath and Nelsen had disclosed earlier in the week. And the badinage between Dandy and me established the pattern for the seasons to come. I quickly established that the Jets would go at Number 72, Jerry Sherk. They did, and Rasmussen, the Jets' guard, cleaned him out all night long. I said almost immediately that Nelsen would go right at Hudson, and he did. Morin had a tremendous night. As the Browns moved downfield for the first touchdown of the game, I pointed out that Nelsen liked to use the post pattern to Gary Collins. That very play produced the Browns' first touchdown.

I also went out of my way to say, the very first time that Cleveland got the ball, that Bill Nelsen's knees

were more damaged even than Namath's, but that Nelsen
didn't get the publicity Namath did because he didn't
play in New York. As the game progressed it became
clear that it was not a night for Leroy Kelly. Twenty-six
carries produced only 44 yards. I thus commented, that
"Leroy Kelly has not been a *compelling* factor in this
game." The game really turned on two things: a touchdown run by Homer Jones on the opening kickoff of the
second half, and a key interception for a touchdown by
Bill Andrews. Cleveland won it, 31-21.

The whole flow of the game tied neatly to our preparation for it. We pointed out that the Jets gained more than
500 yards, but that when the chips were down the
Cleveland defense would not break; it would only bend,
as Don had said to Namath.

In the course of the game we were each fitting into the
roles expected of us. Keith was right on. Dandy was
humorously corn pone. I was wisecracking, second-guessing and leading Dandy. Examples: After a pass interference call I asked Don to explain the rule. After a
couple of false starts Dandy nonchalantly cornponed,
"Don't know what that there rule is, Ha'rhd, but whatever happened down there was a no-no."

I also managed to slip in a barb or two, such as when
Jones ran back the second-half kickoff to score. "I
imagine," I noted drily, "that Homer's friends back in
New York observed that with some degree of interest."
Jones had been traded by the Giants in the off-season
to Cleveland.

But the line that caught the most postgame flack was
my seemingly harmless observation on Kelly's production.
I had simply pointed out that 44 yards on 26 carries
was well below his standard. From the fan and editorial
reaction you would have thought I had called him a
Communist. You see, in the spoon-fed, Alice in Wonder-
land world of sports broadcasting, the public was not
accustomed to hearing its heroes questioned.

Another highlight of the telecast was Dandy Don's
irreverent reference to the colorful name of the Cleveland

rookie wide receiver, Fair Hooker. Keith and I had no rejoinder.

So "Monday Night Football" had made its debut; a new treatment for television and professional football. A new hero had been born. Dandy Don Meredith. And a new goat: Howard Cosell.

Leaving the stadium that night, we all felt pretty good about the telecast. It had been a fine game. There had been a definite rhythm among the three of us. We were on our way. Until the next day. Then I found out that I might be on *my* way—out. Looking back now, you have to wonder about the whole seedy business, how and why there could have been such a storm surrounding me. But at the time, despite all I had told Dandy about how I would be ripped, the damned thing got to me. I felt I had fallen into all six of Nixon's crises at once—and Watergate was yet to come.

Instantly, the flood of letters began, addressed both to ABC and to me directly. Only a minimal amount of it— out of literally thousands of letters—favored me. That was the first wave of a building, critical, first reaction to my part in the "Monday Night" debut. Next, the columns began to appear, almost unanimously against me with a few notable exceptions, among them *Variety, Newsweek* and *Sports Illustrated*. Writers called Arledge to inquire—perhaps wishfully—if I were to be removed from the package. Agencies representing one or two of the sponsors called, nervously. As the clamor grew it inevitably reached the board of directors of ABC, who applied pressure on Leonard Goldenson, the chairman of the board: "What are you going to do about Cosell?"

One had to pause and reflect on this phenomenon. What was it all about, Alfie? Was football that important in this country? Was it a moral crime to introduce objective commentary to the transmission of a sports event? If so, how did we as a people get this way? Remember, this was 1970—an endless war was raging in Vietnam. The economy was in trouble. Unemployment was high. Racial problems were still in the news. The fact that there could be such outrage against a sports commentator, after one football telecast, had to be a reflection of the values of many Americans. But none of that could change the fact that the outrage was there and a broadcast network had to be concerned about it.

Carefully, ABC studied the reaction point by point. First, Chet Forte and Roone Arledge reviewed the tape of the telecast, over and over again. Then they analyzed the mail. The other elements were rather easily dismissed: The inquiries from sponsors were less than expected; the calls from the writers, and the columns, represented a reaction typical of the beat men who had felt competitive with me throughout my years of coverage of the sports scene.

In the midst of all this furor Emmy and I escaped— to Puerto Rico, where I was to do the live telecast of the lightweight championship fight between Ismael Laguna and Kenny Buchanan. This assignment came at exactly the right time. We planned to revisit the statehouse where I shot the opening scene of *Bananas,* to have lunch on the patio of El Convento where we had lunched with Woody Allen, and to try to forget the whole mess. The only trouble was I honestly couldn't. It was chewing me up inside.

Then a call from Chet Forte helped me a great deal. He told me that he and Roone had studied the tape of the telecast, and had graded me "very good." They had graded Keith similarly and had marked Dandy as "raw but very promising." Then he told me about the mail. "More than half of it, Howard," he said, "doesn't even relate to the telecast. It's about you and Muhammad Ali." I knew instinctively what he meant. It was a pattern with which I was painfully familiar: "Get that nigger-loving Jew bastard off the air. Football is an *American* game."

Then he said, "Some of it says you can't criticize the players, you never played the game."

Another refrain I had heard throughout much of my career, carefully propagated over a long span of years as an aftermath of the networks' continued use of ex-athletes as announcers. I had long had strong feelings about the policy of using ex-jocks as announcers. I think it is perfectly proper to use them limitedly, for "analysis," under the guidance and leadership of a professional. I think it is a desperately wrong thing, and a debasement of my profession, to take a man off the diamond, or off the gridiron, or off the basketball court, and put him on a news show as a so-called reporter.

The reasons are obvious. In the first place, the man has had no training whatsoever in journalism, in communications and in speech and delivery. In the second place, he doesn't begin to know the nuts and bolts of reporting, the who, what, when, where, how and why of a story. In the third place, participating in one sport doesn't remotely make a man knowledgeable in any other sport. Quite the contrary, it often inhibits his knowledgeability. In the last place, the ex-athlete is, in a journalistic sense, hampered by divided loyalties, because of old ties and old loyalties to the management for which he worked, to the sport in which he participated and to all of the teams and teammates with whom and against whom he played.

The ones to blame for this are the broadcast executives who initiated the policy. It is like saying that a music critic must be one who played the cello, a theater critic must have been a prior actor. Obviously, by such reasoning, if one needs surgery one must go not to a surgeon but to one who has undergone the most operations. And Walter Cronkite and Harry Reasoner cannot comment on the political scene; neither has ever held public office.

Thus, by my precepts, the employment of Dandy Don was exactly right. He was being used for a specific purpose, in a specific way, without any pretense that he was a trained professional. I also want to make it clear that ex-athletes of long broadcast experience must be regarded as professional broadcasters—men like Frank Gifford and Pat Summerall. This is not to say that it was right to hire them as all-purpose sports reporters in the first instance—and that's the way they were hired. But it is to say that they are highly intelligent men and, given the opportunity, have worked and studied hard through the years. This is why they are professionals now.

But the worst thing, to my way of thinking, about hiring ex-athletes as all-purpose sports reporters is the impact that the practice has on young people and the frustration it produces in them. As one who travels the campsues almost incessantly, I have been face-to-face with hundreds upon hundreds of brilliant young people who are studying communications, who want only a chance—in the American way—to grow professionally in the field of sports broadcast. They describe to me how they are negated at the local level by the practice of hiring the local hero. Thus their frustration becomes my frustration.

All of this, and a great deal more, was on my mind as we idled away the hours in Puerto Rico. I guess, in times of stress, people always tend to become philosophical. But I had made up my mind to one thing: I was going to do one helluva fight broadcast. I was going to open that show with absolute confidence in my performance. I wasn't going to let anybody, either in the public or in the press, think that I had been reached by the static crackling around me at home.

And I did just that. The Laguna-Buchanan fight was a honey. Buchanan won it, cleanly, by dominating the late rounds. No one expected that this could happen in a climate so favorable to Laguna, and with the fans overwhelmingly in his favor. The scene was both colorful and nostalgic. A blistering sun. A temperature of about 100 degrees. One could almost see Jack Johnson, lying on the canvas, with Jess Willard towering over him, in that long-ago epic fight in Havana. And then, as we waited an interminable length of time for the decision—I suspected they were trying to find a way to give it to Laguna—we were beset by one of those instant tropical torrential rains. Finally they announced that Buchanan was the new lightweight champion of the world.

I closed out the show, waved good-bye to Ned Steckel, my producer, and ran with Emmy to a waiting limousine that would take us to the airport. There was a 5:00 P.M. plane to Baltimore, the scene of the next "Monday Night" game—Kansas City against the Colts. I was ready to do battle again—if my company was ready.

PART 2:

A Monday Kind of Love

"Every plot needs a villain."

As our plane touched down at Friendship Airport in Baltimore my spirits were still soaring. The tempest I had left behind in New York five days earlier seemed an incidental part of a distant past.

But I was soon reinfected with the whole doleful situation. While I was away certain National Football League owners had objected to my presence on the "Monday Night" package. Some of my friends thought I was in trouble. I didn't need to be told this. I could read it in their faces.

We were to be met at the terminal by Don Klosterman, the general manager of the Baltimore Colts. As Emmy and I approached the airport bar, we spotted Don whispering to Jim Mahoney, a Beverly Hills public-relations man whose clients included Frank Sinatra. Klosterman and Mahoney are close friends. They share a dry sense of humor, and each can get a laugh out of an empty gum wrapper. But this time their faces were somber. I knew Don was telling Jim about the flow of events following the first "Monday Night" game. I said so to Emmy.

"Let's not go through that again," she begged. "Forget the whole thing. Don't let anyone know that it bothers you."

I said I'd try. But I could feel myslf crashing. Stop the world. I wanted to get off.

We had a quick drink and left for Don's home, where we were to spend the weekend. My mood was subdued. I was sick to death of the whole silly affair. My dilemma was: Do I quit now, tell them all to go to hell? Who needs to be bothered with petty people who live their lives in thimbles? What I had done was to bring a few decent lines to a pro-football telecast, and the reaction against me, as far as I could see, was a reflection of the whole seedy structure of the sports business and the phony sports legends. On the other hand, if I didn't stick it out I'd be giving in to everything that in my mind was wrong and unfair. I talked it through with Emmy at Klosterman's. Finally we looked at each other and laughed. I made the choice I knew I'd make from the beginning. To stick it out.

Once I had made that choice, my mood was again resilient. By late Saturday night Klosterman, one of football's champion freestyle telephone callers, was dialing his friends around the country and I was right there with him. At 2:00 A.M. he placed one to West Texas, to a blithe spirit named Bobby Layne. Shortly he handed the phone to me. I swung into my on-the-air delivery.

"Let's face it, Bobby," I barked. "There was Waterfield. And Graham. And Van Brocklin. And Unitas. Now some say Bart Starr. Others say Tittle, but he never won the big one. But for those of us who know the game, there is only one quarterback—Bobby Layne."

"Howard," Bobby replied, "you're only telling it the way it is, and that's what you're doing on the air."

I spent the next several minutes agreeing with him. Then, impulsively, I said: "Bobby, I want you to come to Baltimore. We have a game here in two days and I need your moral support. I need you to tell this town what you just said."

He promised me he would. But I never really expected him to appear. I assumed that he was overcome with the kind of emotion that comes from imbibing branch and bourbon.

A few hours later Klosterman received a call from Bobby Layne. He was arriving at Friendship Airport at such-and-such time. Meet him! That's the kind of guy Bobby Layne is. That's the kind of football player he was.

Before I knew it we were at the stadium for the second game of "Monday Night Football." Roone Arledge was quite aware of the enormous flak surrounding me and the tensions I was under. He suggested that I cut back a little, that I go easy and ride this thing out. All of which made sense to me.

I opened with a joint interview with John Unitas and Len Dawson, the two great veterans. I was pleased with the interview. It renewed my confidence, not only for what was said but because of the attitudes of the two quarterbacks. Dawson patted me on the shoulder. He had read all the garbage about me. Unitas added, "Don't pay any attention to them. They used to try to tell me how to play quarterback. Do your thing."

I had known them both since they were barely out of their teens. The first pro game I ever broadcast was when Dawson was a rookie with the Pittsburgh Steelers. It was a great encouragement from both of them.

In that interview I asked Unitas the question that was foremost in the minds of football people: He was aging, having trouble with his arm. I asked if he could still throw the long ball. He met it head on, the way he always does. Would you believe that at least 15 columns followed that interview, denouncing me for daring to ask such an impertinent question of the greatest quarterback "who ever played the game"? You see, I had never played the game.

During the course of the game I started to lay back a little as Arledge had suggested. But early on, Mike Garrett was hurt, and when he went out our camera zeroed in tight on him. I said, feeling as confident by now as I always feel on a telecast, "Dandy, there's little Mike on the sidelines." And just then you could pick up Garrett's voice on our sideline microphones, and the TV audience heard him ask a teammate, "Wonder what Cosell is sayin' tonight?"

I couldn't resist a chuckle. "Tough little cookie," I commented offhandedly. "He'll be back."

Whereupon Roone spat out from the truck, over my intercom: "There you go, Howard. That's the very kind of thing that's going to get you in trouble because they're looking to sock you. What if he doesn't come back?"

I was shocked. What if he didn't come back? So what? It was a throwaway line, a passing comment. What the heck. I had known Mike Garrett and had been friendly with him since his junior year at USC. I knew his physical capacities. It didn't really matter whether Hank Stram returned him to the game or not. I knew Mike would be willing.

Well, I then decided to just shut up. I virtually remained mute for the rest of the night. I didn't know what the consequences would be and, frankly, I no longer cared. Nobody could have been more prepared than I, nobody could have known the teams better, the people better, and if we bowed to that kind of fear . . . all right, I understood. My company deals in mass communications, and if it was their conviction that I was turning people off they had every right to dispense with my services as quickly as possible. The damned truth is I was feeling sorry for myself.

I was amused some years later when a sports writer wrote a book in which he claimed I *shilled* for the NFL by keeping quiet because the game was dull and one-sided. Kansas City won, 44–24.

As I left the press box I felt terrible. I had said virtually nothing the whole night. I hadn't done my thing. On my way out of the stadium I encountered Layne. He could see instantly that I was troubled.

"What's wrong?" he asked.

"Bobby, something is bothering me, but I'd just rather not talk about it."

"Is it something I did?"

"Bobby," I assured him, "it doesn't involve you in any way. You're the greatest."

I was upset about everything, but mostly about Arledge having snapped at me. And yet I understood. He was uptight, under pressure from higher-ups in the company with respect to me. And he had handpicked me as the key man in the package. (Incidentally, Roone was proven right. The one remark the writers did seize on from the telecast was my statement that Mike would be back! In a telecast where I was accused on the one hand of shilling by my very silence, the Garrett comment was held up as another example of Cosell's ignorance. I never played the game.)

Coming up to the third week of "Monday Night Football"—Chicago at Detroit—I was really down, more depressed, professionally, than I have ever been in my life. Everywhere I went in that damned ABC building I felt the eyes of people. I was imagining whispers about getting rid of me. Only later did I learn that Leonard Goldenson had called Elton Rule every Tuesday morning to ask, "What about Howard? What are you going to do about him?"

And Rule, even though he knew Goldenson was getting pressure from the board of directors, stood firm. "Nothing," he would say. "Howard works for Arledge."

I really respect Elton Rule. It's not just the debt I owe him. It's the fact that he's a man. Direct. Honest. Nothing phony about him. If he fires me tomorrow, at least I'll know that it was his own doing.

Along about here I began to go back to my days at law, to recapture my mind, to reexamine my own reasoning process, to get back my sense of proportion. What was this all about? Here was a man doing telecasts of football games, which in themselves have little significance on the scale of human events. To have excited this outcry . . . it was simply beyond me. I was getting nearly as much publicity as Henry Kissinger, and I never dated Mamie Van Doren or Jill St. John (which may well be the only thing Dr. Kissinger and Mr. Joe Willie Namath have in common).

The night before the third game Meredith, Keith Jackson and I had dinner at the Hotel Ponchartrain. I had worked up a good case of the blues. "I'm not coming back," I kept saying.

Jackson joined in. "I'm not coming back either," he said. "It's not worth it. I don't like this whole setup." Keith was tired of being told from the truck to stay out of the conversation; his job, they kept reminding him, was to report the game.

Meredith sat back and listened to us cry. Finally he raised a glass and said, "Aw, I'll tell you fellows something, I don't know about you guys, but the ol' Cowboy, he's coming back. I got nothing better to do that pays me so much." He had come a long way from the Warwick bar.

All this time Dandy was getting every rave in the book. He loved it. And he should have. But he saw what was happening to me, and he would put his arm around my shoulder protectively and he would say, "I don't understand it, coach. You sure helped me when I needed it. Keep your chin up."

I did a helluva job on the Chicago-Detroit game. Arledge said, "Keep that up and there's no way they can touch you." But the letters kept pouring in, fomented by the still critical columns that were appearing in papers all over the country. I made it a point to study them all. And to read every letter. The columnists would take a single line out of an entire telecast and pounce on it. Sometimes a word. There was no way I could defense that.

The mail was a different thing. A literate, cultured Miami department-store executive was critical. I took that letter seriously, because he reflected a certain common reaction: *I had never played the game.* To this man's credit, before the season ended, he wrote a letter to the president of ABC apologizing, saying, "I have learned much about football and even more about the men who played the game, from a man who never played the game."

Green Bay at San Diego was next. I couldn't wait for this game. I really couldn't. No man alive knew more about the Green Bay Packers than I did. No man was closer to the players than I was. (Remember "Run to Daylight"?) I opened the show with an interview with Bart Starr. I will never forget what Bart Starr did. He knew the travail I was going through. At the end of the interview, still on the air, he deliberately said, "Howard, I want you to know that every member of the Green Bay Packers thanks you for the remarkable memorial you paid to Mr. Lombardi when he died. Every man on the team asked me to tell you this."

Thus I started the game on a high note. I rattled off a series of anecdotes that I had accumulated in years of observing the Pack, and Lombardi, at close range. I remember Dandy leaning over and saying to me, "Where do you get all that stuff? How do you learn it?" I had told, among other things, of how Willie Wood, the incomparable free safety, became a Packer. How his college coach had filled out a form for Lombardi in which he labeled Wood "no pro prospect." How Willie had written a letter to Vince, begging for a tryout as a free agent. How Lombardi brought him to camp because something in the letter moved him. How at practice Vince, at one end of the field, suddenly saw a smallish man, under the goalposts at the other end of the field, from a standing position, jump and chin himself on the goalposts. How Vince ran the length of the field and said, "What's your name, young man?" And he answered, "Willie Wood." And how Vince turned to Norb Hecker, his defensive backfield coach, and said, "Look after this young man. He will become a great one."

That's when Dandy really flipped. Wood had intercepted Meredith in the past. The story, of course, came from "Run to Daylight."

I flew back to New York on the red-eye special with Arledge. It was just a routine working day for me. Our limo was caught in traffic on the way to the office, and at 8:20 I realized I had five minutes in which to reach the radio network and do my live morning show. I leaped out of the car, wove my way through the cabs and automobiles and pedestrians like a broken field runner. Arledge called me, laughing, an hour later. "I knew you made it," he said, "because I had the radio in the limo turned on. You were a little breathless, but you made it."

One thing Roone said to me on the flight from San Diego stayed with me. "I think," he mused, "that the country is beginning to catch on to what we're trying to do."

God knows, I hoped he was right. And there was good reason to believe he was. I began to take stock. Our ratings up to that point were outstanding, far better than we had expected. We were achieving better than 30-percent share of audience. ABC had never come close to this on Monday nights.

The press attention—good and bad—we were getting was simply incredible. I personally had been interviewed in *Newsweek, Sports Illustrated, Time* and, even, *Life* magazine. Virtually every sports columnist in the country had been writing about me, most of them calling me "abrasive," but some of them now beginning to write that I was bringing a new look to the game, that I was a perfect offset to Meredith. My byplay with Dandy was no longer a shock, an inside joke. Many people didn't really know whether we were friends or not, but they were beginning not to care. They would just enjoy it when I would say, as I looked down at Bart Starr, "Of course, Starr will be remembered for his excellence, Dandy for his futility under crisis conditions."

And Dandy would shoot back: "What would you know about that, Ha'rd? You never played the game."

Then I would say, "As Dandy so well knows . . ." and I would give a small piece of historical trivia about a reserve player he hardly even knew existed.

Dandy would then say, "Ha'hrd, where do you get that stuff? You know, I don't have a clue to what you're talking about." And the public would eat it up.

Dandy was at his most lovable at our fifth game, Washington at Oakland. In our production meeting before the game Arledge suggested emphasis upon the quarterbacks—Sonny Jurgensen and Daryle Lamonica. We really hoped for an exciting encounter, with these two in action, but any time the action lagged I was to lead Dandy into anecdotes about the quarterbacks.

The way the game went, we needed Dandy in a hurry. The first quarter wasn't three minutes old and Oakland had a 14–0 lead. The second touchdown came on a Lamonica pass to Warren Wells. With a rout in the offing I turned to Dandy and said, "Well, our good friend Lamonica really knows how to capitalize on an opportunity, Dandy."

Whereupon Dandy said, "That's right, Ha'hrd. Speaking of Daryle, that reminds me of a funny story." And Dandy told his anecdote. Only it wasn't about Lamonica; it was about Dandy himself. He related how he contracted amoebic dysentery while hunting in Africa. His story was greeted by a stony, embarrassed silence. Keith Jackson and I almost fell out of the broadcasting booth. Dandy looked at us both and muttered, "Well, I guess it doesn't sound as funny as it was."

We were very careful about future anecdotes.

I learned so much about Meredith that first year. I learned that he was not what some represented him to be, a dim-witted Texas corn pone. I learned that he's a highly intelligent, sensitive man who has gone through a great deal of personal hardship in his life. I learned that his aspirations go far beyond football. And I learned a fundamental thing—that we both look at life in very much the same way; that we both take our private relationships very seriously; that we both enjoy humor and a good time, but that we're both always very much aware of that which is going on in the world.

During that first season Meredith wasn't married. He had been divorced for the second time and, as I said before, had a little baby daughter, Heather, born blind and retarded. When he talked about her he would talk gently about what a beautiful little thing she was, and his eyes would fill up with tears over the fact that she was born with these handicaps. He carries that kind of thing always inside of him, but rarely lets you know about it. It's a very rare moment when he reveals himself. Dandy and I, through the course of that first season, did have many private, serious talks about life. Always he knew that football was just a game, and that's the way he treats it in the booth.

One night before a game he leaned back and said, "Ha'hrd, there's got to be more to life than that down there." Which from his point of view said it all.

As for our personal relationship, we couldn't believe some of the things that were being written about how we were fighting behind the scenes. In truth, we never had a single quarrel or a single disagreement. It sounds almost grade-schoolish to say it, but that's the unembroidered truth. Each accepted the other, knowing each had his own place in the telecast. It worked like a charm. When I would needle him on the air and he would needle back, I suppose it was inevitable that some people would feel there was acrimony between us. But there wasn't. We were each doing our thing and getting a kick out of it.

Except that Dandy was on a continuing upcurve. He was marching to an Emmy without knowing it. I, on the other hand, was experiencing nothing but peaks and valleys. Exultant one moment, depressed the next. I reached a positive nadir when I got to Minnesota for our sixth game, Los Angeles against the Vikings. As I have explained, I had gotten the distinct feeling that I had begun to beat back the early onslaught. But now a new wave appeared. The columnists had a new line: The chemistry in the booth was working, but it was based on the hate motif. Cosell was the "voice you love to hate."

"Every plot," Bill Cosby later told me, "needs a villain." I was elected.

I was staying at the Marriott Hotel in Bloomington, and there in the lobby I bumped into Don Weiss of Rozelle's staff. All the frustrations suddenly came gushing out of me. I had just read again that I didn't know football. I began to ruminate all over again, this time at the expense of the hapless Weiss. At that moment he seemed to represent the football establishment, which was exactly what I felt most of the football writers did with their treasured nonsense: "He never played the game."

What the hell was it anyway? Was it invented by Enrico
Fermi and refined by Werner Von Braun? Hardly. On
the contrary, except for the lexicon it has created, that
tired litany of mystical cliches, it is the same game you
played in the streets: Send the tall guy out against a
short guy, a fast guy out against a slow guy; hook to
your left at the fire hydrant.

On any Sunday afternoon, in any stadium in America,
you can capture the action with this one limerick:

> You've got two setbacks and two wide receivers and
> a zone defense,
> The tight end becomes a primary receiver in the
> crease up the middle,
> And you isolate the setback one on one against the
> linebacker . . .

It was exactly this type of presentation that we wanted
to change on Monday nights. On Sunday afternoons the
game had become a simplistic stereotype of itself. And
I was damned if I wanted to be the butt of any more
of that "hate" syndrome that was enveloping me.

So I poured it all out to Weiss, a fine, sensitive, quiet
fellow. And then I behaved badly, boyishly, monosyl-
labically all day, with Forte, with Dandy, with Keith,
with all of them.

Just before the telecast was to begin, Arledge came
to me in the booth and said, "Howard, this may be the
most important game we have yet done. It's a big game.
Two teams with a real chance for the title, Los Angeles
and Minnesota. And you've got everybody unnerved,
everybody, the way you're acting."

"Yes, sir, yes, sir, whatever you want," I said.

Arledge looked at me hard. "If you want to quit after
this game—fine. If you want to talk it over tomorrow—
fine. But give us all a break and do your thing tonight."

I knew he was right. "Don't worry about it," I said.
The telecast went fine.

But let's face it. I had become a pain in the ass. To
everyone, including myself. I had done what I had never

thought I would do; I had allowed myself to fall prey for the first time in my life to the critics. And I was riding an elevator of emotions from week to week.

One might wonder why Arledge put up with it. Why he didn't just fire me. The reason, I think, is clear. Regardless of my moods, regardless of what was going on inside me, once in that booth I was the catalyst. And it was, as Roone himself had pointed out, working.

The strongest capacity Arledge has is for program taste and program judgment. He is almost uncanny in his evaluation of how the public will react to a personality or a format. He was absolutely right about Meredith and me, and I have to believe that one reason he lived with me and backed me to the hilt that first year was his inner understanding of the fact that we were getting fantastic attention, It was almost as if "Sunday Afternoon Football" no longer existed.

The night after the Minnesota-Los Angeles game Pete Rozelle dropped by our apartment for a cocktail. Don Weiss had told him of my outburst, and Pete was concerned. He addressed himself first to Emmy. "Look," he said, "I just wanted to come here and talk as a friend and tell you that Howard is taking this thing much too seriously. He should have fun with the 'Monday Night' games. I think he has been, on the air, but deep inside apparently he's still being troubled. It's ridiculous. Howard"—and he turned to me—"just have fun with the game."

That was the thrust of it. We sat and had a couple of drinks, and Pete left. Emmy said, "He certainly does oversimplify—but, basically, he's right."

It was on to Pittsburgh and Dandy Don's turn. Incidentally, while all the publicity flack was taking place, my practice of calling him "Dandy" had come under question. It was felt by some that it was patronizing, and partly responsible for some of the disfavor in my direction. I had lunch one day with Elton Rule, and he said, "I don't think you should call him Dandy."

I felt it was like worrying over whether or not one should 'bow to Anthony Armstrong-Jones. I said, "All right," and for the next game or two I avoided calling him Dandy. Some alert reporters noted this, and one TV critic telephoned and asked if there was a reason.

I said, "Well, some feel I just shouldn't call him Dandy and so I've stopped."

She said, "That's silly. It makes no sense."

I agreed with her. It made no sense to me, either, so I started calling him Dandy again. I didn't pin the name on him, incidentally. It was a nickname given him by his brother when Don was 16, and it followed him to Dallas and through his college days. But now it was a matter of national notice and it became a part of the legend of "Monday Night Football."

Later I did a commercial with him for Gillette, where our voices were interposed. It was Meredith talking and out would come my voice. Then I'd talk, and out would come the Texas drawl. The gimmick worked. At the very end, as an ad-lib, I said to him, "Just another pretty face, Danderoo." Well, you wouldn't believe the mail that came in, approving of my reference to him as Danderoo. Today, just as a natural thing in the booth, I alternate between the two, and wherever I travel people will say, "Hey, where's your buddy, Dandy," or "Where's the ole Danderoo?"

In Pittsburgh Dandy virtually cemented his Emmy. This was a dreadful match-up—Cincinnati against the Steelers. Cincinnati had won one and lost five. Pittsburgh had won two and lost four. Shrewdly, Arledge managed to miss this one. He went to Europe. Other business.

The highlight of the telecast came when Dandy confused the teams and the linebackers. Here's what happened. Chuck Allen, the Steelers' retread middle linebacker who played for years at San Diego, moved one step to his right and made a tackle. Sensational. Over the earphones Forte said, "It looks pretty good. Let's replay it." So I led Dandy into the replay.

Well, Dandy had a massive disinterest in the game. He looked quickly at his three deeps (the charts that show the offensive and defensive lineups and the substitutes for each unit), ran a finger down the numbers and picked out Number 58. Except that he was on the *Cincinnati* side. So he picked out Beauchamp, who was also a linebacker. He recapped the whole play and said, "There's my old friend, Beauchamp, showing great lateral pursuit." He pulled out all the stops. And then sat back contentedly. Keith and I looked at one another.

Then came the voice of Forte: "You had the wrong player on the wrong team," he shouted "We're in Three Rivers Stadium, Pittsburgh, the Steelers are playing the Bengals, and don't say a word until Howard asks you a direct question."

Meredith looked at me and asked, innocently, "What's biting him?"

I answered, "He gets upset when Arledge is away."

We went to Milwaukee—Baltimore was to play Green Bay. The telecast was in its early stages and Dandy was breezing along, as he had been through the whole series. He was telling one anecdote after another. Arledge was in New York for this one. Suddenly Chet spoke to Dandy from the truck. "Dandy," he said, "Roone just called. He wants you to stop with the anecdotes. He says they're getting silly."

Meredith looked at me. "Did you hear that?" he asked. "I've had it. I'm going back to New York with you to have it out with all of them. I'm getting out of this thing."

The spiral was still spinning. Now it was Meredith who was going to quit. One or the other of us was leaving the package each week. Keith was our only contribution to sanity.

Later, when we got back to the hotel, I assumed the unlikely role of peacemaker. I told Chet he had hurt Dandy's feelings. "What was I to do?" he responded. "Arledge called and he was right. The stories *were* getting silly."

"Well," I said, "he's a sensitive guy."

Meanwhile, Dandy was off somewhere with an ice skater who had an old familiar role with the Geen Bay Packers. Two days later Dandy and I read that we'd had a fistfight under the stands in Milwaukee. I have never known a man with less homicidal instinct than Meredith.

He resolved his problem with Roone and it was back home for Dandy, back to the scene, back to Dallas. The Cowboys were to meet the Cardinals, and Meredith would come unglued. As for me, I dreaded the trip. Dallas to me was the heart of hard-core conservatism. It was the city where John F. Kennedy, whom I had admired so much, had been killed. Besides, I had been through so much trash in the first six weeks of the season, my mood was still unsettled.

But they held an affair in Dallas at noon on the day of the game and they labeled it "The Why I Hate Howie Luncheon." They had a turnaway crowd, and Sam Blair wrote about it in the next day's *Dallas Morning News,* ending with the words: "Hate Howard Cosell? Hell, no. This was a Monday kind of love."

The people in Dallas, it developed, were wonderful to me, and my reception there has grown each year. In 1971 they drew 1800 at the old Adolphus Hotel and had to open a separate ballroom to seat everyone. The guests there couldn't even see me, but they could hear, and they didn't complain.

What happened *after* the game that first year, which the Cardinals won by a crushing 38–0, was more confusing than a Japanese morality play. Meredith went wild in the booth over the performance of his old team. He couldn't understand their absolute futility and he all but exploded with personal emotions.

Later, at the Fairmont Hotel, Dandy approached me with a big, sheepish grin. He knew he had gone berserk over the ineptness of the Cowboys and now he held out a telegram he had received. It was the first of its kind he had ever gotten in the span of the "Monday Night" series and it advised Meredith that he did not deserve to be on the air because he wasn't an impartial reporter. The wire came, I think, from Memphis, where the fans root for Saint Louis, not Dallas. All of a sudden the guy wanted fair reporting. Of course. What the typical fan wants is for his own team to be treated favorably. That's fair.

I no sooner returned to New York the next day and walked into my office than I received a call from a local writer. "It's all over town," he said. "You led Meredith into the trap, you did it deliberately, you hate one another."

I laughed at him. I had never heard such nonsense in my life. But out of nowhere, I was under the gun once more, just when I thought I had broken clear. Now, Dandy and I were in it together.

Letters flooded in from Saint Louis, denouncing another of my tasteless, cruel remarks. I had pointed out that the Cardinals still had to face the Giants before they could celebrate the playoffs. The manager of the ABC affiliate in Saint Louis called the network. He was swamped with letters complaining about me. He was worried about losing the business of the Bidwells, who owned the Cardinals.

Sure enough, the Giants later trounced the Cardinals, the Cardinals collapsed, and Dallas went on to the Super Bowl.

But in the jungle of broadcast, all of this was par for the course.

I had an interesting phone conversation during the week with Pete Rozelle. At some point during the telecast I had said, bluntly, "The Cowboys stink. The fans are all over Landry." So when Rozelle and I talked he said, "You really killed Landry."

I said, "The hell I did. I never laid a glove on him. It was the Saint Louis Cardinals, thirty-eight to nothing. But as for my own feelings about Tom, you should know that after the game I went to our radio affiliate, KVIL, and I did a show in which I defended him. I praised him as the man who created the four-three defense with the Giants, where he had Robustelli, Greer, Modzelewski and Katcavage hitting to the outside, giving Sam Huff a cheap shot at the carrier."

The show was heard by Alicia Landry, Tom's wife, and she told me later how grateful she was for it.

"So, Pete," I said, "it's a lot of crap. I did a show in support of Landry. It was Dandy's old team and he was going crazy. I did my own thing. There was no way in the world I could have stopped Dandy from doing his."

Pete said, "Well, I thought you respected Landry as a coach."

"I sure as hell do," I said, "and I think I made that clear on my radio show." And that was the end of that.

Every week was now a happening in every town. The spin-offs, the reactions, the people, all formed a kind of hazy panorama. The front pages of the various newspapers would welcome us to the city. It was like a road show, and always I was in the center, as the controversial one who now was beginning to get some love, as well as hatred. And then came Philadelphia. Someday I may even be able to pronounce it.

I don't really remember much about the Giants-Eagles game that Monday night. I only really saw a quarter and a half of it. What I do remember is how cold and vicious that day and night were, and all the events leading up to the now historic was-he-sick-or-was-he-crocked episode.

I started the day feeling queasy. I had lunch with Leonard Tose, the new owner of the Eagles, and Pete Retzlaff, his general manager. Tose arranged to have a limousine take me to Franklin Field in the late afternoon to do the half-time highlights. Dennis Lewin, who was producing the highlights, went with me. We were in for a treat when we reached the stadium. The power was out. No lights, no heat, nothing. I sat there for two and a half hours in the winter chill. Finally they raised sufficient power to transmit the highlight show.

We went directly from the stadium to the athletes' lounge and dining room at the University of Pennsylvania, where Tose was throwing a party for us and the press. It was now nearly 6:30. I was beginning to feel slightly fevered, clammy, uncomfortable, with occasional dizziness. I stayed about three-quarters of an hour. Then I returned to the field to prepare for the opening interview, with Ron Johnson of the Giants, which we were to videotape. The moment I hit the open air I began to get chills all over again. It was even colder than it had been before. This was late November. The wind had razor blades in its teeth. As I started toward the field someone slapped me on the shoulder, almost knocking me down. "Hey, buddy." I heard him say. I turned around. It was John Carlos, then on the taxi squad of the Eagles.

"John," I said, "I'm freezing. It's terrible."

"Well," he suggested, "let's run, buddy."

So, like a nut, there I was, running wind sprints with the former Olympian, John Carlos, on the cinder track surrounding the field. It must have been quite a spectacle.

I finished the Johnson interview in short order, returned to the party just long enough to say my good-byes, and then Dandy and I climbed up to the press level, down a winding stairwell and across rickety wooden steps to reach the broadcast booth. The booth at Franklin Field is an overhanging one, and getting there is to take your life in your hands.

The booth was open to the cold. Keith Jackson was ready. He had bought a brand new overcoat for the occasion, and I kidded him about it as the show opened. I was really feeling a little better, from the sheer exhilaration of performing. As the game got under way I had a great time with Dandy. I was all over him that night, crediting him with statements about different players that he had never made. Dandy would wail, "Now, Ha'hrd, I don't know where you got that. I never said anything like it. I don't even know that little fellow from Bowling Green."

Arledge later said to me that the first quarter and a half of that game was our best job of the year. But midway through the second quarter I began to sink. I was beginning to sense a loss of balance, I was uncommonly light-headed and was having trouble articulating. By the half-time break they knew in the truck that something was wrong with me. My voice had become thick, I could not say Philadelphia, and all of this happened on camera. If anyone ever looked like an on-camera drunk, I did.

Immediately after getting off camera I threw up in the booth—all over Dandy's cowboy boots. Then, with the help of a policeman, I staggered out of the booth, was led out of the stadium and got into a taxi for the airport. I don't remember anything about the drive to the airport. I only dimly remembered that my secretary had told me of a late night flight to New York. When I got to the airport I staggered to the ticket counter and somehow mumbled to the agent that I wanted the late plane to New York. She told me that the flight had been discontinued.

Some things you do remember. And it's funny the way you remember them. With all the dimness of my mind, I suddenly thought, "My God, I'm going to die in Philadelphia." And then, oddly, I thought of W. C. Field's epitaph.

I stumbled out of the airport and into another cab. "Please take me to New York," I said. The driver said it would cost a lot of money. "I don't care," I said, "just get me there."

The only thing I remember during that ride was thinking, "I don't care what happens to me, as long as I'm with Emmy when it happens." I really thought I was having a stroke. Or at least I was wondering if this was the way it happens. It was a kind of three-dimensional feeling, as though it were happening to someone else and I were watching. The whole thing seemed a fantasy.

The next thing I knew, the driver was telling me we were in New York. I thickly mumbled my address to him. Finally I was home. I remember paying the driver $92 for the ride. It was about 3:45 A.M. I fumbled at the door to my apartment, and Emmy ran to meet me. She had been terrified. Friends from all over the country had called to see what had happened to me, friends like Don Klosterman, Al Davis and Jim Mahoney.

My body was still shaking with chills, as though I had the ague. I couldn't keep my balance at all. Emmy helped me into bed and wrapped me in blankets. At 6:30 in the morning I called my doctor, who agreed to come right over.

Somehow, I'm almost embarrassed to recall it today, but I even managed to mumble out my morning radio show. The show must go on, and all that theatrical baloney. Here I thought I might be dying and I had to get my last five-minute radio trick on the air.

An electrocardiograph established that my heart was okay. What I suffered from, it developed, was toxic vertigo, an infection in the inner ear that causes loss of balance and, sometimes, thickness of speech. It is a terrible thing to get and terribly difficult to get rid of. To this day I have vestiges of it. I will wake up in the morning, on occasion, get out of bed and totally lose my balance, tumbling back into bed.

During the course of that next day the phone rang incessantly. I knew I had become a whole new *cause célèbre*. As Roone Arledge told me on the phone, the whole country "thinks you were drunk last night."

"That's bullshit, Roone," I snapped, "and you know it. I've never been drunk in my life."

"I know that," Arledge answered, "and that's what I've told the brass."

The days of the week that followed were torture for Emmy and me. We went up to our home at Pound Ridge, and I just lay in bed for most of the week. I simply couldn't get my strength back, and I simply couldn't shake the damned dizziness. In the meantime the inevitable columns were appearing—all over again. Some of them mocking, some of them gloating, most of them contemptuous. A battle I thought I had clearly won was in danger of being permanently lost. Indeed, *Sports Illustrated* carried an item saying Cosell was "out."

The next "Monday Night" game was at Atlanta—the Dolphins against the Falcons. I still felt ill and debated not going. I also didn't want to face the press. I was tied up in a knot, a knot of anger, of shame and self-pity. I talked to Arledge about it, and he told me to make my own choice.

I flew to Atlanta the morning of the game. I had made up my mind to one thing: I would open that game lightheartedly and I would be myself. I wouldn't let the press know how I felt inside.

So I opened the show and I felt the comforting sympathy of Dandy and Keith. Garo Yepremian kicked off for Miami. Quickly I told the story of how Yepremian, when he was with Detroit, had kicked six field goals in one game to defeat Minnesota. And how, after that game, a scribe asked Van Brocklin, then coaching the Vikings but now at Atlanta, how he thought one could handle Yepremian.

"Tighten the immigration laws," Van Brocklin snapped.

And with that Dandy and Keith roared and we were on our way. It was a fine telecast, and Arledge and I flew back to New York together. I felt strong and clean and good.

The next week Cleveland was at Houston, but I was in New York doing the Ali-Bonavena fight. Suddenly there were a spate of columns and letters declaiming how much I had been missed on the telecast. And all over ABC the talk was the same. The life had gone out of the party. Dandy said, "I sure missed ole Ha'hrd." I missed him and Keith, too. But, in a way, not doing that game was the best thing that happened to me that season.

Our final "Monday Night" game that first year was Detroit at Los Angeles. We had a great telecast, it was a fine, exciting game, Dandy was loose and easy, singing on the air, and Keith, Dandy and I had really become a triumvirate. Each knew the other's moves, we had good timing, perfect rhythm. And we had behind us the most extraordinary and the most exaggerated series of individual experiences that the imagination could invent. We had lived through a 13-week fantasy. We had all emerged as national personalities. We had achieved a marvelous success in the ratings. "The Carol Burnett Show" would have to move to a night other than Monday on CBS. There had been talk of moving "All in the Family" to Monday night. It would now stay in its Saturday time slot. ABC had now become competitive, and then some, in Monday-night prime-time television.

I said good-bye to Dandy and Keith. Jim Mahoney drove Emmy and me to the airport. As I was getting into the car a couple of fans spotted me and shouted as we were driving off, "Hey, Howie baby. Were you really drunk in Philadelphia?"

I chuckled. And so did Jim Mahoney. Then he said, "They bum-rapped you the whole damned season, and they wound up making a star out of you. 'Monday Night Football' is the biggest hit in the country."

This from the man who represents Sinatra.

As I ducked into the plane I knew two things: There was no more talk about quitting. Dandy, Keith and I would never sit at the Ponchartrain again, looking at ourselves and cursing our fates. We had proved something, and we all wanted to come back. Two of us would.

The other thing I knew was that I had been a damned fool. I had behaved with emotional immaturity. That would never happen to me again.

The writers never laid a glove on me. And they never will.

PART 3:

We're Number One

"What do you tell them?"
"I tell them you're a son of a bitch."

On reflection, that first year of "Monday Night Football" is still a source of absolute wonderment to me. I realize it was a stroke of genius, or luck, or a combination of both, on the part of Roone Arledge to pair Don Meredith and me.

But it was a different universe for Keith Jackson. His role had been clearly defined: a straight play-by-play man. It was impressed on him time and again that he was to think of himself as a public-address announcer, slipping in and out, factually, accurately, with the vital information—who made the tackle, who threw the ball, who caught the ball, how many yards were gained, what down it was.

No one in America, in my opinion, could have done it better than Keith Jackson. He was not only a highly competent professional but a complete gentleman. During that whole year, as Dandy Don and I were reaping swarms of publicity, Keith never complained.

Keith has his own pride and his own sensitivity, and later, when he was removed from the package, he handled himself with a dignity and a purpose and a manliness that I will admire for the rest of my life. Obviously he was not being removed on grounds of incompetence.

He gave a number of interviews after that in which he said, bluntly, "I've got my own pride, my own self-respect, and it wasn't easy for me to go a whole year with two other men getting all the notices."

Keith was absolutely right in feeling that way. It was understandable. Curiously, as it turned out, Keith received more publicity and became better known as a broadcaster by the mere fact of being removed from "Monday Night Football" than he ever got as a member of the package. He had been used as a mechanic, and acclaim would never have been his.

I remember the curious way in which I first learned that Jackson might be replaced. I received a call from Merlin Olsen of the Rams, who, with Roman Gabriel, was starting a new show on the West Coast called "Man to Man." Would I come out and guest with Tom Harmon? I accepted, and later mentioned to Arledge that I was planning to appear on the show.

To my surprise Roone said, "I'd like to go with you. I'd like to fly out there with you and go on the show."

I found this strange because Roone was not disposed to do such things. I quickly called Merlin and said, "Look, Tom Harmon is a great guy, but here's a chance to get Arledge who rarely makes appearances, and he's the guy responsible for 'Monday Night Football.' "

Merlin thought it was a splendid idea, so Arledge was set to fly out there with me. On the plane he quickly cleared away the aura of mystery.

"How would you feel," he asked, "about working with Frank Gifford?"

I said, "Giff and I are great friends. It's fine with me. I've known him for fifteen years. When he won the Jim Thorpe trophy in fifty-six, he used to come down to the studio when I was just beginning and sit with me for hours, guesting every hour on the hour with me." I laughed at a sudden wisp of a memory. "Studebaker was my sponsor. I not only lost the sponsor, the car died." Then I looked hard at Roone. "But what the hell are you talking about? Where are you going to use him?"

"In place of Keith."

"Are you kidding?"

"No."

"Well, on what grounds? Keith did a hell of a job."

Roone nodded. "You're absolutely right, he did. But on two grounds. First, I want Gifford in our stable of announcers. He has great, great appeal. Research in New York indicates that he's the most popular sportscaster in New York."

I said, "Well, I don't think that's true. I don't give a damn about the research, but I agree with you that he has appeal, first, the looks, and second, the fact that he 'played the game' [to use that hated expression myself]."

"That's right," said Arledge. "I think, as an addition to our whole stable of announcers, Schenkel, McKay, you, he'd be great for us, and we'll be taking him away from CBS. Second, I think he'll be great for the football package. I'll use him in Jackson's role. Maybe he can provide little insights that Jackson can't, based upon his experience as a player."

He paused and added, "The three names together will just be overwhelming."

"I said, "Assuming you're right, Roone, what about a moral obligation to Keith, a man who did everything he was asked to do and did it very well?"

He said, "I'll make it up to Keith. He'll get more work than ever. I'll move him back to college football on the regionals, increase his pay and put him on NBA basketball."

It was clear that the decision had been made. "If you feel this is morally right," I said, "it's your business."

"I've got to do what I think is best for the whole company," he said, "and I think it's right to bring Gifford over."

"Well," I said, "if you're asking me how I'd feel working with Gifford, I can tell you I'd be delighted. He's a perfect gentleman, same as Keith, and he has been a much longer-term friend of mine. I'm not going to have any problems working with Frank."

(After all, he had passed the test of our friendship

forever, back in 1956, when my then infant daughter, Hilary, tinkled all over his lap and he handled it with impeccable grace. Not a word of complaint. But lots of paper towels.)

That's how the Keith Jackson matter came to my attention.

It would take three months for Arledge to work out all the details of a contract for Gifford—if it could be worked out at all. In the meantime, Dandy—who that winter had an urge, and a need, to make some money fast—was on a pell-mell speaking tour. He had suffered financial setbacks in his life and now he seized the chance to take advantage of his new fame. He embarked on the most grueling schedule I had ever seen, including my own. He would be somewhere in North Carolina one night, in Denver the next. He told me that every place he went, the most popular question was always: "How do you live with that guy Cosell? How do you really get along with him?" When Dandy honestly described our friendship, the reaction was always the same. He told me, "They really think we're enemies. It's amazing. They keep asking me, 'What kind of guy *is* Cosell? What's he *really* like?'"

"Well," I prodded, "what do you finally tell them?"

Don shrugged. "I wind up telling them you're a son of a bitch. Because they won't believe the truth."

In mid-January 1971, Dandy and I were back together again. We served as comasters of ceremonies at the Columbus Touchdown Club annual dinner in Ohio. Actually, we did this dinner together two years in a row, and at one of them I presented an award to Bart Starr, who followed with an inspirational talk. Dandy topped us both. After Bart had finished, Dandy got that angular body of his to his feet, looked at Starr, then looked at me, then faced the 1500 people in the audience and said, "Ha'hrd, just once before I die, I'd like to hear Bart Starr say she-e-e-et."

It was at that dinner that Dandy spoke to me about Gifford. "Won't it be great," he said, "if the Giff can join us?" Coming from Dandy this was understandable.

Remember, Frank is his closest friend, and it was his recommendation that landed Meredith on "Monday Night Football" in the first place. It was a purely personal feeling for Gifford that in no way reflected on his working relationship with Jackson.

By the end of March, Arledge had worked things out. He was at the Masters golf tournament in Augusta, Georgia, in early April when the story leaked. I was at an ABC function at Gallagher's Steak House when I was paged to take a phone call. It was the TV critic for the *New York Daily News,* Kay Gardella. She got right to the point. Were there to be any changes in the "Monday Night" announcers, and if so, who was involved?

I ducked the question. Any statements about that would have to come from the man in charge, Roone Arledge.

She persisted. "Are you involved?"

"Not as far as I know," I said.

The moment I got off the phone I called Irv Brodsky, the ABC sports publicist, and told him he had better reach Arledge immediately. Brosky said, "The impossible takes a little longer."

The next thing I knew, the story broke in both the TV and sports pages of the *Daily News.* Kay had the right story. Jackson was out. The sports page gleefully hailed the news: Gifford is in, Cosell is out. And that wasn't the only false report to appear in print. Weeks later Keith made his only public statement—that I know of—about Dandy and me. A writer in California had suggested that it was Cosell who demanded Jackson be removed. Keith was incensed. "Howard is my friend," he told an interviewer. "He's on an ego trip, that's for sure. But there is absolutely no malice in him. As for Meredith, he's just all corn pone and bullshit and that's fine, if you like it."

Part of Gifford's deal was that he would relieve me on nightly local television. Now, after 12 long years, I found myself suddenly free to do other things outside of the confining dimensions of sport. I was in demand because of "Monday Night Football." Believe it or not, I was wanted in Hollywood. The tall figure with the ferretlike face, having passed the 50-year milestone, would debut in prime-time situation comedies. I cackled all the way to Los Angeles.

"The Partridge Family," with Shirley Jones, came first. Shirley's older daughter on the series was played by a pretty young thing named Susan Dey, who it so happened was my own daughter Hilary's classmate at Fox Lane High School. When I approached the set for the first time she raced over to me, flung her arms around my neck and embraced me. I could sense the raised eyebrows around the set and I could envision the headlines in the Hollywood scandal sheets. I was disappointed when they didn't appear. Susan asked eagerly about all the kids back at Pound Ridge and Bedford Village.

After helping the Partridges save the whales—I played the part of an investigative reporter—I moved on to another triumph, this time as a biology teacher on "Nanny and the Professor." I quarterbacked the faculty football team—as Golden-Arm Taylor—and we got our comeuppance from a team of kids 12 years old and under. As a sidelight, sports columnist Jim Murray was the referee of the game. Jim kept grumbling that he shouldn't be in the show, that he was camera-shy and that he was undignifying himself. But the minute the cameras started rolling you would have thought that the name of the show was "Nanny and the Referee."

I will always remember that show with affection. I have never worked with a nicer, more considerate man than Richard Long, and Juliet Mills was a delight.

But it was back to football. Serious football.

By this time Dandy had won his Emmy—the industry's highest honor. His erratic march to this most treasured of all broadcast awards, in his first year of TV work, has to be regarded as one of the great feats of modern times. Dandy knew it. When I called to congratulate him, he said, "Ha'hrd, I don't understand it, but I'm very happy about it."

I said, "You damned well should be, Danderoo. You damned well should be."

The new trio, now consisting of Faultless Frank, Dandy Don and Humble Howard, made its 1971 premiere with the Hall of Game game—Los Angeles against Houston—on August 4. The night before, I had worked the College All-Star game in Chicago with Chris Schenkel and Bud Wilkinson. I flew into Canton the next morning on a chartered plane with Lamar Hunt, the owner of the Kansas City Chiefs and son of H. L. Hunt, one of the world's wealthiest men. We played gin rummy during the flight. Lamar lost $1.77. I still have his check—uncashed. He'll never be able to balance his account.

The game was a disaster. Players flooded in and out; you could have spent days just trying to identify them. But it was a trial run, a shakedown process for the new crew. It was an uneven performance for all of us, and by half-time we were punchy. The game lasted more than three hours.

Late in the fourth quarter Gifford solemnly intoned, "Four minutes and five seconds remaining on the clock until the game ends."

"What," I broke in, "makes you think this game will ever end?"

Right here I want to talk about Frank Gifford. Where the pressure had been on me a year earlier, now it was clearly on Frank. He is a serious-minded man—not without humor, mind you—but very serious in terms of football. It has been the major part of his life. It was asking a lot of a man like this to essay a new role, that of a play-by-play announcer, and to undertake that role in a booth dominated by a couple of nuts. On top of that, there was the Keith Jackson problem. Giff, Don and I went on a tub-thumping tour in August that took us from Kansas City to Saint Louis to Detroit and to Chicago. Everywhere we went, we would appear on television shows and we would hold press conferences. On every show and at every press conference they would ask about Keith Jackson. Frank couldn't have been in a more ticklish situation. But everywhere he went he met the issue squarely. He would say, quietly, "I am not Keith Jackson. I cannot be Keith Jackson. And I'm not going to try. Keith Jackson is a fine announcer. But I am Frank Gifford, and that's all I can be. I think I can contribute to the package."

I've known Frank for a lot of years. And I knew how nervous he was. After our preseason game between the Jets and the Chiefs in Kansas City—a game where Giff made a number of mistakes—he asked me in the booth how I thought it went. I told him that the essence of it was fine, that we had quickly established a fine mood among the three of us. That was the important thing, because we would be working together a long time. Wrinkles can be ironed out. Personal relationships can't always be.

We opened the regular season in Detroit. It was incredible how fast the months had flown by. "Monday Night Football" was back. We celebrated our new alliance the night before the game at the London Chop House. Bud Shrake, of *Sports Illustrated,* was with us. He was doing a piece on the new triumvirate and on ABC's approach to pro football. Before the season even started we were getting the same magnitude of press attention that we had gotten all of the prior year.

When Emmy and I and Dandy and Susie Dullea (now Susie Meredith) and Frank and Bud reached the restaurant, the place was mobbed. There was a waiting line all the way up the steps and out into the street. "We'll never get in," Meredith said.

"Follow me, Dandy," I blustered. "The coach will take care of everything."

I poured past the people with my entourage in close pursuit and blustered my way through the rope that had cordoned off the waiting patrons. Now we were at least at the bar, and all eyes were on us. If I say so myself, I was at the top of my game. We had a drink or two while we waited for our table, and in the process I acquainted every attractive young woman within sight with handsome Frank Gifford. "Look at him standing there,

girls," I would announce. "A veritable Greek god.
America's most famous football hero. The dream of the
American working girl. The single most sexually dynamic man in the chronicle of the male sex. He's in
room nine fourteen at the Ponchartrain."

Emmy and Susie were giggling. Meredith was uproari-
ous. Shrake was taking notes.

"The coach has hit a high point tonight," Dandy
roared. "Ladies and gentlemen, this is the coach himself. This is Howard Co-sell." He said it with the kind
of staccato mimicry of me that has become a household
habit.

All the while, Gifford was smiling pleasantly. "If I
were one-hundredth the man Howard is making me out
to be," he said, "I'd be the greatest man alive."

After dinner Frank bade us all good-night. "I'm going
to barricade my door," he announced, "and get ready for
the game."

We had a great opening game to work with—the Lions
had a fine offense, the Vikings had the best defense in
football. But the Vikes had something else going for them
that year. Or so it was thought. They had acquired quarterback Norm Snead in an off-season trade. Giff was high
on Snead. In all of our preseason talks he gave Minnesota a good chance to win it all. He thought Snead
might well become the most valuable player in the league.

For that opening night, however, Giff had one problem.
Bud Grant, the Vikings' coach, didn't agree with him.
He started Gary Cuozzo, Number 15, at quarterback.
Snead was Number 16, draped on the bench.

Detroit got off quickly and assumed a ten-point lead.
Meredith had become infected with Gifford's enthusiasm
for Snead. The Vikes were going nowhere with Cuozzo.
Dandy and Giff started calling for Snead on the air.
As Minnesota languished, Dandy could no longer contain himself. He started motioning across me to Giff that
Snead was warming up on the sideline. Frank rose to
the occasion and remarked that Snead might be coming
in.

Moments later, when the ball changed hands and the Minnesota offense returned to the game, Dandy tried to semaphore frantically that Snead, at last, was in the game. Frank didn't notice. Finally Dandy scribbled a note and passed it across me. Gifford grabbed the note and triumphantly announced that Snead was in the game. Sitting between the two of them, I was wig-wagging my arms, shaking my head, telling them both in sign language that it was still Cuozzo, not Snead! At last Giff got the message and corrected himself. Dandy then apologized to Giff on the air: "Well, sometimes it's hard to tell the difference between fifteen and sixteen."

Yes, I thought to myself, especially when 16 is four inches taller than 15.

The next day the Minnesota papers denounced Cosell for second-guessing Bud Grant and putting Snead erroneously into the game. That was when Gifford turned to me and said, "You're a regular lightning rod. You get blamed for things you don't say."

And Dandy added, "It'll be that way all year. Whatever you and I say, Howie will end up taking the rap for it."

Dandy knew that from the prior year. That first season Bud Grant had kicked him out of the Minnesota dressing room before a game against the Rams. When Dandy got to the booth he was furious. "If there was a personality contest between Bud Grant and Tom Landry," he said on the air, "there wouldn't be a winner."

It was a great line. Except for one thing. Some of the Minnesota writers attributed it to me. That's what Dandy meant in his crack to Giff.

So we were off and running as a trio. The next week Bud Shrake's story appeared in *Sports Illustrated*. It was damned good. He had caught the mood of the three of us and even sensed a little of the tightness between Frank and me—the tightness of beginning together.

Shrake's story emphasized the way our competition felt about "Monday Night Football." "It's entertainment," shouted Bill MacPhail and Carl Lindemann, the respective heads of CBS and NBC Sports, "it's not football,"

thus forever enshrining the game as one of the seven
wonders of the world. MacPhail went further. "If we
wanted that kind of stuff, we'd put Jack Benny, Don
Rickles and Bob Hope in the booth. But we're not going
to sink to that. We're not running a comedy hour."

Lindemann blurted, "We've got the best football an-
nouncing team there is, Curt Gowdy and Al Derogatis.
We don't need to bother with any of that junk that
Cosell and his buddies are handing out."

They were, of course, absolutely right, as later events
proved out. MacPhail turned to a former player, Alex
Hawkins, a simulated, lower-case Don Meredith, to
try to spark the CBS telecasts in 1972. In the spring
of 1973 Carl Lindemann did a 180-degree turn. He
utterly recanted. He was saddled with 15 Monday nights
of major-league baseball and he knew he had to attract
enough viewers for those games to induce advertisers to
pay enough money to recapture the very costs of carrying
the package. And so, Curt Gowdy and Tony Kubek, the
regular announcing team, would be joined in the booth
each week by a different personality from show business.
Dinah Shore one week. Pearl Bailey another. Maybe
Woodly Allen a third. Maybe even a sports announcer
from another network. Maybe even Howard Cosell.

Because, you see, Carl called me and asked me if I
would guest on one or two of the games. I told him
I'd be delighted—if Roone Arledge would clear it.
Lindemann had first told me of the idea several weeks
earlier. The only trouble was, he hadn't told Curt Gowdy.
I said to Carl at the time, "I understand your problem
with the baseball package. I'm sympathetic. But you're
going to make yourself look like a fool. The press will
be all over you because of your prior statements about
ABC and 'Monday Night Football.' "

"I know that," he said. "But I've got to do something
to liven up the package."

"You're going about it the wrong way," I answered.
"When you guys knocked us, you were off base. And
you knew it. Jackson's a professional. Gifford's a professional. I'm a professional. And Meredith was grounded

in sports, not singing and dancing [although he can do that, too]. You're going way out, and Curt's going to have a fit."

Gowdy did have a fit. The minute Carl broke the news to him, Curt, who is my closest friend in broadcasting, came to see me. We spent several hours together, talking. He even mentioned quitting. He viewed the whole idea as a slur upon his own abilities. Gowdy, of course, is as fine and as versatile a play-by-play announcer as any I have known in my lifetime. Possibly, considering the number of different sports he does, the very best.

I told Curt that I thought Carl's plan was wrong, but that I understood his problem. I said, "Curt, this whole thing has nothing to do with you. It has to do with the problems of baseball and the problems of economics. Times have changed. And baseball needs a whole new look, but the baseball leadership does nothing about it. The only new thing you have to talk about is the designated-hitter rule, and that's only in one league."

Curt, who has an undying allegiance to baseball—he was spawned on it—admitted ruefully, "I'm afraid you're right. But I still thing it demeans me."

I answered, "I think it probably does. But the point is, it's not *directed* at you. Your job is to stand tall and do your own thing."

I knew exactly how Curt felt because I had refused to do the theater telecast of the Frazier-Foreman fight when I was told that Pearl Bailey would be doing the color with me. Consequently, I did the fight only for "Wide World of Sports," and the promoters had to bring in Don Dunphy to do the blow-by-blow for theater TV.

When Curt left me that evening I thought all over again about the pressure of this traumatic business that is sports broadcasting, and how emotionally vulnerable the great announcers have been, and how quickly they can pass from sight despite their fame. Here was Curt Gowdy, a consummate professional, a veteran at his job, one of the highest-paid men in the industry for a long number of years, a man who owns three successful radio stations, all but undone over a gimmick to be used

in a major-league-baseball telecast that would vanish
from memory moments after it ended. I never knew a
man more insecure than Mel Allen, even when he was
at the top of his form. And both he and Red Barber
departed precipitously, amid a residue of bitterness. Except Allen went quietly, and Barber noisily.

In perspective, however, the NBC action illuminated
forevermore the success of the "Monday Night Football"
concept. The series was a bigger rating success the
second year than it had been the first. Of course, Bob
Wood, president of CBS Television Network, attributed
it to our great schedule. Was it such an irresistible lineup?
In the second game that year we had two teams that had
lost their openers—the Jets without Joe Namath and the
Cardinals with very little going for them, with or without
their quarterback. Take Pittsburgh versus Kansas City:
The Chiefs scored 28 points in the second quarter to
end a game that was a mismatch to begin with. Saint
Louis at San Diego: Each team went into the game at
three up and five down. Now that's a lively prospect.
And when Miami beat Chicago, 34–3, the game was
over in the first quarter. But our ratings held up on all
those games, and according to Arledge the test is how
we do when we broadcast lackluster games.

The new trio really began to mesh, I think, in the
fourth game of that season—the Giants at Dallas—with
me sitting between the two jocks, each rooting for his
old team. The game was raggedly played. There was,
to recapture a phrase I had used the first year, "a veritable plethora of fumbles." Indeed, the record for
fumbles in one game was being threatened. "Gentlemen,"
I said, "neither of your respective teams is showing me
very much this evening."

"Well, Ha'hrd," Dandy shot back, resorting to what
had now become an in joke among us, "at least we do
have respective teams."

I debated explaining to Meredith that I had been All-
Eastern Parkway for seven straight years, and that we had
never lost to the Catholic kids from Saint Theresa's.
But I decided the moment was inappropriate.

At this point I got help from an unexpected source. Forte whispered into my headset: "Howard, guess who holds the individual record for the most fumbles in an NFL game?"

I whispered back, "Dandy?" It was just one of those educated guesses that the trained observer learns to make.

Forte laughed. "Yeah. I'm going to turn the camera on him while you give the word to the viewers." I could almost see Chet chortling over his record book.

Whereupon I observed with a dry relish. "Yes, indeed, the very man at whom you were looking held the all-time NFL record for individual futility. It hardly comes as news to any of you . . . that Don Meredith fumbled more times in one game than any other man in the history of the National Football League."

Sheepishly Meredith grinned. "I did do that, didn't I, Ha'hrd?"

The second year went by so fast it was like watching a Charlie Chaplin movie on an old nickelodeon. The highlight may have been reached in Baltimore, when the Colts were to play the Rams. It was our eighth telecast, a crucial game for both teams. An hour before the game I elected to go into the Baltimore dressing room, which I'm really not supposed to do. As I walked in I stumbled over Tom Matte's foot. I immediately broke the silence in the dressing room by announcing in my most blustery way, "There he is, Tom Matte, Number Forty-one. Does nothing well, but somehow everything well enough to win. And thus typifies this curiously unspectacular but nonetheless championship Colt team."

The players laughed out loud. Even John Unitas, who was sitting next to me, smiled. Unitas cracked himself up even more by saying wittily, "You're talking through your asshole, Howard."

In a corner of the dressing room I saw Carroll Rosenbloom, the owner of the team, chatting with Vice-President Agnew, a rabid Colts' rooter. Rosenbloom noticed me and, with an obvious measure of resignation, said: "Mr. Vice-President, do you know this man?"

The vice-president replied, "Why, yes, Carroll. Howard and I have worked the banquet circuit together."

"Absolutely true, Mr. Vice-President," I said, "but presently irrelevant. Tell me, sir, what is your position on Jewish ownership?" I said it loudly enough for all the players to hear. I thought Don Klosterman was going to hide in the shower. Rosenbloom shook his head and began muttering, "I might have known what to expect from Cosell."

Mr. Agnew laughed. "There is no statute that bars them, Howard."

I then suggested that it would be a nice gesture to go from cubicle to cublicle and wish the players luck. So we went around the locker room together and immediately came to a corner occupied by four black players—John Mackey, an old friend of mine, Willie Richardson, Ray May and Roy Hilton. Just as we got within earshot I said, "Then your conclusion, Mr. Vice-President, is that this team is saddled with too many blacks?"

The black players knew me, of course, and started giggling. Agnew recovered instantly. "I didn't put it *that* way, Howard," he answered, almost peevishly. "What I said was that an intelligent reexamination of the quota is in order."

He really has a hell of a sense of humor and is a great sport. He agreed to do an interview with me to open the telecast. On the way upstairs, in the elevator, he kidded some more. He turned to Emmy and said, "You know, Howard doesn't need me. He's just giving me a break."

And I said, "Mr. Vice-President, you're telling it like it is."

A few moments later the vice-president's Secret Service men brought him to the booth. I instantly introduced him to Dandy. Dandy was wearing a cowboy hat, cowboy boots and he was in fine western fettle. "Dandy," I said, "this is the vice-president of the United States."

Mr. Agnew said, "Nice to meet you, Dandy," and he held out his hand.

Dandy, always the one to observe the formalities, said, "Great to meet you, Mr. Vice-Prez. Love ya. Didn't vote for you, but love ya. Great to meetcha." And he shook hands heartily.

Agnew couldn't stop grinning. But over in the corner of the booth, Gifford stood watching, and muttering. "How did I get into all of this? What's happened to me? I'm with a couple of lunatics. Nobody in the world would believe this scene."

Whereupon, I said, "Giff, come meet the vice-president."

Gifford came over, shook hands and said, "Nice to have you as part of the team, Mr. Vice-President. If you can escape here with your sanity, you'll be the first one. This is what I'm surrounded by every week."

Then the vice-president and I opened the show. When I finished the interview I turned the microphone over to Dandy, and as the vice-president and I watched, he tossed off one of his best lines ever: "I hope you all noticed," he said, "that the vice-president is wearing a Howard Cosell wristwatch."

There was a rustle in the booth. Some thought Gifford had fallen out.

Months later, after I had related the above story in an interview in PLAYBOY magazine, the vice-president dropped me a note. He had read the interview and he appreciated the kind reference, he said, especially in view of the fact that he knew we differed philosophically.

We wound up the second year on a high note, with a football game that had dramatic overtones. George Allen, the coach of the Rams a year earlier—and a very popular one—was now with the Washington Redskins and was coming back to Los Angeles. And if the Redskins won the game, they had made the play-offs. Roman Gabriel, his former quarterback, was making all kinds of cracks about Allen. A year later he would be begging to play for Allen again. That's football.

With this scene set we had an exciting, even thrilling game. And the Redskins won it. A sweet moment for George Allen, who had left Los Angeles under unhappy circumstances, after two ugly quarrels with the ownership.

I took cognizance of this as I was closing out the show and the season. While I was extolling Allen, there was Dandy in the background, singing "Hail to the Redskins."

For me, personally, the second year was a relatively calm sea—in contrast with the first year. A key difference was that Emmy made every trip with me.

Giff and I began the third season with an Olympics hangover. By the second game I was on the cover of *Newsweek,* with a slash line that read, "This is Howard Cosell." I wouldn't have been human if I hadn't been immensely gratified by this. The story began with an oft-quoted quip by comedian Buddy Hackett: "There have always been mixed emotions about Howard Cosell. Some people hate him like poison—and some people just hate him regular."

I could look at that line in *Newsweek* then and enjoy it. But there were times during that first year of "Monday Night Football" when the "hate" image haunted me. I made up my mind that I had to find out for myself how much truth there was in it. I spent two years of my life after the first season canvassing the country. You name it, I have been there. Middle America: Oklahoma City; Wichita; Omaha; Columbus and Lima. The Southwest: Dallas; Houston. The West Coast: Modesto; Sacramento; Seattle; San Francisco; Los Angeles; San Diego. The Rocky Mountain area: Denver; Laramie; Cheyenne. The Deep South: New Orleans; Memphis; Chattanooga; Atlanta; Miami; Winterpark; Roanoke; Pinehurst; Richmond; Alexandria. I felt like a map plotter for Rand McNally.

In all of these cities I would either be addressing civic clubs, industrial groups or college kids on campus. I have spoken before the Harvard Law School Forum, the Yale Political Union; I have been to Brown, to Columbia, to Fordham, to NYU, to Rollins, to El Centro, to SMU and TCU, to Ohio State, to the University of the Pacific, to Wilmington College, to Ohio Northern Law School. I lecture annually at the Pulitzer Graduate School of Journalism at Columbia. I have come face-to-face with America. I drove myself to the point of physical exhaustion. I learned a lot about people on that tour. And once again I learned something about myself. I learned that people would turn out in huge numbers to hear me. I found out that they wanted to know if I was the villain I had been painted. From the receptions I received after I had spoken—everywhere I went—I drew peace within myself. The "hate" image would bother me no more. It was a carefully perpetrated mirage. This doesn't carry with it the implication that I'm lovable. What it does say is that I am opinionated and there are people who differ with me. But they sure as hell respect me. And they sure do tune in.

For two years I rarely refused an invitation to speak. It's a hard habit to break. "Every Monday," Dandy observed, wrily, "Howard has to make a speech. If there wasn't a club meeting somewhere, he'd find some people in the lobby and make one."

In the summer of '72 Emmy and I were in Paris. I was off the lecture circuit, momentarily, to cover the Monzon-Bouttier fight. I picked up a copy of the *Paris Tribune* and to my amusement read a column by Rusell Baker in which he pointed out that it was honorary-degree time. He suggested that instead of going to the usual political and industrial figures they should go to the controversial people who are willing to take stands, and he mentioned, among others, Frank Sinatra and Howard Cosell.

I dropped Russell a polite note to thank him, though he was too late. I had already received two honorary degrees that spring, after having made the commencement-day speeches at Wilmington College in Ohio and the George School of Law, University of the Pacific.

The third season of "Monday Night Football" was the one our competitors were waiting for. We had a dreadful schedule. After a good opener, Washington at Minnesota, we had games like Kansas City at New Orleans, and Oakland at Houston.

The game between the Oilers and the Raiders may live in memory as the classic football telecast. Never has a worse game been played. Oakland won it, 34–0, and Oakland didn't even play well. But the Houston performance was a catastrophe. By the time the third quarter had arrived, Dandy and I threw the game to the winds. Giff joined us within the following ten minutes. At one point, after a series of pitiful turnovers, I said, "I think we better get the game films this Wednesday, Giff, and take them around to the local high schools to encourage the youngsters. There's no way they can be this futile."

Dandy jumped in with a disclaimer. "That was Ha'hrd Cosell said that, folks, not Dandy."

By the fourth quarter Chet Forte was desperate in the truck. Since we were telling the truth about the game, Chet decided to show that the people in the stands felt the same way. He panned around, catching the backs of people leaving. Then he zoomed in on a gentleman who apparently was asleep. But this particular spectator sensed the camera upon him and woke up. He looked directly into the lens and made what is known in polite circles as an obscene hand gesture. When he did this, I stopped in the middle of a sentence, aghast. But not Dandy. He jumped right in and said, "Ha'hrd, he means we're Number One."

Giff and I slumped back relievedly. Dandy had made us immortal.

In three short years "Monday Night Football" had become an American tradition. It is like a ticker-tape parade up Broadway. One moment they're showering confetti upon you, the next they might be throwing something else.

In effect that's what happened when we arrived in San Francisco where we would wind up our third season. Our next-to-the-last game was Los Angeles at San Francisco. The final telecast would be the Jets at Oakland.

We picked up a San Francisco newspaper and turning

It should be pointed out that the Oilers, Cosby's choice to improve our schedule, finished the season with a one-and-thirteen record. The only trouble with Bill's suggestion was, it wouldn't have helped him. Incredibly, our ratings held up throughout that Houston-Oakland game. They held up all year, despite the weak schedule, and to the utter dismay of CBS and NBC. Sadly, the "Bill Cosby Show" was canceled.

Dandy was right. "Monday Night Football" is a trip.

Chapter XIII

GOING BANANAS
WITH WOODY

*"When you have dinner with him,
he broadcasts the meal."*

The first time I ever saw Allan Konigsberg of Midwood High School in Brooklyn, was in the spring of 1965. I was in Fort Lauderdale, Florida, shooting a television special called "Johnny Keane: The Yankee From Texas." One day Emmy said, "Let's go down to the Diplomat Hotel tonight. Woody Allen is there. He's the comedian who got good reviews at the Bitter End in Greenwich Village." The truth was, I had never heard of Woody Allen, who, of course, had been Allan Konigsberg in Brooklyn.

Just to show you how big Woody was at the time, he was getting second billing to a singer named Kay Starr. When Woody walked out on the stage I stared at him in disbelief—a pint-sized guy with glasses as big as his face, the way-out air, the careful, subtle shyness, the low-key self-deprecation. It was all there, and I didn't like any of it. Emmy did. She thought he was great.

I never expected to see Woody Allen again. But I did, and under the most unusual circumstances. When Emmy and I were in London in May 1966 for the Ali–Henry Cooper fight, I bumped into an old friend, Telly Savalas. Telly had been the first director I ever had on

356

radio. He was a great help to me, and was one of the first to tell me I had the talent to make it big. Telly was a wild, erratic fellow, often getting to work late, sometimes not even getting to work at all, and he was a man who loved to gamble. Cards, dice, anything. So it was altogether fitting and proper that I bumped into Telly at a gambling joint called the Colony Club, at Berkeley Square. This was the place fronted by George Raft, the old movie star—gambling clubs were the big thing in London at the time—and Telly was shooting craps and had nothing but chips in front of him. "Hey," he said, "I always told you you had a big future. You're doing great."

"I'm doing great," I said, "what about you? I never imagined when you were trying that Off-Broadway stuff in Stamford, Connecticut, you'd wind up a movie star." Indeed, Telly had become a star and was, and still is, one of the finest character actors in motion pictures. It developed he was in London shooting *The Dirty Dozen*, along with Lee Marvin, Charles Bronson, John Cassavetes, Jim Brown and many others. In fact, it was then and there that I met Lee Marvin, who was giving the tables a workout himself.

We had a lot of fun that night. I lost some money, but arranged tickets for the fight for Telly, Lee and some of the others in the cast. And then we agreed to meet at a different gambling club after the fight, a place called Pair of Shoes, run by a man named Eric Steiner. There was to be a big poker game, and Telly invited me to join in.

Emmy and I drove back from the fight with Chris Schenkel, and we stopped at Pair of Shoes. It was mobbed with people, including, surprisingly, Ingemar Johansson, the onetime heavyweight champion, who had ballooned up to what appeared to be 250 pounds. It was easy to spot Jimmy Brown, who stands out in any kind of crowd, and so I went over to Jimmy and asked him to lead me to the poker game. He led us to a back room, just about big enough to hold a big table with chairs all around it, where the game was already in progress. I said hello to

Savalas and Marvin, and Telly said, "Let's make a place for Howard."

Whereupon a little figure at the far end of the table, dimly visible through the haze of smoke, said, "No. No one else in the game."

I recognized him from the Diplomat Hotel. It was Woody Allen, who was also in London to do a movie. Savalas explained that he had invited me into the game, but Allen stuck to his guns.

I was irritated, said "Forget it," and Emmy and I left. "I told you the guy was no good when we saw him in Florida," I said to Emmy. There was a matchless irrelevancy in my comment, since his performing abilities had nothing to do with his unwillingness to let me join the game.

After that I didn't see Woody again for more than two years. In 1968 I was in San Francisco to do the Quarry-Ellis fight, and one night I went to a famous Dixieland-music place called Earthquake McGoon's. There's a guy there named Turk Murphy who plays the horn and produces the best Dixieland music I've ever heard, and that includes what you get on Bourbon Street in New Orleans. So I was at McGoon's, and Turk was wailing, "I Wish That I Could Shimmy Like My Sister Kate" in a way that made you think Bunny Berrigan was alive again, when into the joint walked this little man with the glasses. "Isn't that Woody Allen?" a friend whispered to me.

"Yeh," I said. "Bad guy."

When Allen came in, he didn't even look around. He sort of tiptoed up to the stage, picked up a clarinet, joined Turk Murphy's group and started to play. I hated to admit it, but this guy could play. He did a whole set with Turk, then sat down at the table next to mine and ordered a soft drink. I recognized the guy with him as Charles Joffe, his manager.

I got up with my friends to leave and went past Woody, who said—and it surprised me—"Hello, Howard."

My first words were "Woody, you kept me out of that poker game."

He said, "You don't understand, you never—"

I interrupted. "Woody, you kept me out of the poker game."

He said, "What are you doing here?"

"I'm here to do the Quarry-Ellis fight. What are you doing here?"

"I'm making a movie for Ed Scherick—*Take the Money and Run.*" He added, "You know, I'm a fight fan. I was a fighter on Newkirk Avenue in Brooklyn."

I said, "You were, huh. [I don't know if Woody ever did fight, really, but he's still a big man at Midwood High—a member of the Midwood Hall of Fame.] Now, I'm not gonna forgive you for what you did to me in London, but how would you like to sit with me at ringside at the fight? Johnny Forsythe is coming up from L.A. to go to the fight with me, and Herman Franks, the Giants manager, is coming. You're welcome to come with us."

"Gee, that would be great. I'd give anything if . . ."

We made the date. I don't hold grudges, and let's face it, the guy was a hell of a clarinetist. I like people who entertain. I like to be around the people in show business, and I admit it.

After the fight we all went back to the Fairmont to drink. (Woody doesn't drink, by the way.) We had a great time. Finally it was time for Herman to drive me to the airport. I was taking the red-eye to New York, and Johnny Forsythe had to take the shuttle to Los Angeles.

I never thought I'd see Woody Allen again. Wrong. He opened up a whole new avenue in my life. But I had to wait two more years. In the spring of 1970 I got a call from an agent who asked me if I would do a bit in a forthcoming Woody Allen movie entitled *Bananas.* I told him I liked the idea. Send me the script. I should have known better. With Woody there's no script, only the barest outline. Anyway, I was to play myself, and open the movie by describing the assassination of a

president and the take-over by a dictator of a little
Latin American country. The scene was to be shot in San
Juan, Puerto Rico, in late May 1970.

I almost never got there because I suddenly got assigned to go to Umag, Yugoslavia. I had never heard
of Umag before, and I hope I never hear of it again,
but this was the place where Nino Benvenuti, the middleweight champion of the world, was to defend his title
against someone named Tom "the Bomb" Bethea. Bethea
was a bomb, and Nino disposed of him easily in a fight
deserving of permanent anonymity. One redeeming feature of Umag was its proximity to the interesting city
of Trieste, Italy, where there were good restaurants. The
other memorable aspect was the exquisite beauty of the
Yugoslav farmlands and the Italian cypress trees. But to
get to New York from Umag was an adventure, and I
barely made it back in time to pick up Emmy and move
on to Puerto Rico.

The humidity in San Juan was suffocating. My scene
was to be shot on the steps of the State Capitol. When
Emmy and I got there, Woody was lost in a crowd of
hundreds of Puerto Rican extras playing the roles of
rebels. Woody himself was in green chinos, the uniform
of the day. I was in my "Wide World of Sports" blazer.
I felt ridiculous and scared. But to cover my insecurity
I charged up to Woody and announced, "Well, I see
they knew I was coming. They're all here to greet me."
Woody broke up and so did the crew.

Because of the humidity I don't suppose any job I've
ever done has so enervated me. I had to set the scene
for the impending assassination of the president, then
run through the crowd (fight my way through is a
better way to put it), interview the dying president on
the steps, then thread my way back through the crowd
to interview the dictator. I really poured it on. I likened
the atmosphere to the ugliness of the scene when Ali
fought Liston for the first time, and I played it straight
right through the scene in a parody of myself and
"Wide World," and wound up throwing it back to Jim
McKay, the host of "Wide World." Woody and the tech-

nicians loved it. A perfect take, from start to finish. "Atta way to go, Howie baby," some of the technicians yelled. "Sock it to 'em."

But that was only the beginning. Although Woody used most of that first take in the movie, I had to do the scene again and again and again, and I had to do cutaway after cutaway, and all in all, excluding a break for lunch, I had to work for five hours. In that climate I was lucky that I didn't conk out.

But I have learned that you don't conk out with Woody Allen. The man is a complete professional. He knows exactly what he wants, and when he picks you for a part, he picks you because he knows what you can do and he believes in you. All he ever told me, in that quiet, whimsical way of his, was, "Do your thing." I really began to understand him at lunch that day. Woody, his manager, Emmy and I went to a picturesque place in Old San Juan called El Convento because it had, of course, been a convent. Lunch was served in a beautiful patio, and for the first time Woody explained to me why he had wanted me in the movie. "You're not just another sports announcer," he said. "You go far beyond that. You're a major personality in the industry, with the mind and talent to do far more than sports. That's why I wanted you. I also happen to think that as a sports announcer you're the dream of all the kids in the country. It's the way you put things, the urgency in your voice, your willingness to take stands, fight the establishment."

It was great to hear that from Woody, but a few months later, after "Monday Night Football" had begun and the adverse mail was streaming in, I thought to myself, "How could Woody have been so wrong?"

It's funny how little coincidences occur. While we were lunching, a slight, elderly, gray-haired man came up to say hello. At first I couldn't place him. And then he reminded me. He was Professor Paul Weiss, who had been Sterling Professor of Philosophy at Yale University when I was in residence there as a Hoyt Fellow. He had written a book in 1969 called *Sport: A Philosophic In-*

quiry, and the students had projected the professor and me into a spontaneous debate one evening. Never again. He was tough, a brilliant man. Now he was retired at Yale, but lecturing at Johns Hopkins.

When Woody finally released me that afternoon, it was too late to get a plane back to New York. So we went out to dinner with Woody. Only Woody didn't eat. It turned out that he is finicky about food, a health nut, and also a hypochondriac. He carries more bottles with more pills with him than any person I have ever known. The way he munches those pills—almost with a relish—I began to want to try them myself. He carefully explained to Emmy about food, and why he wouldn't eat. A few months later he came to our apartment for dinner, and Emmy went crazy trying to figure out what to serve. Her fears were groundless. Woody ate everything. "It's different when I go to someone's house," he told Emmy. "I wouldn't offend my hostess. Not that I didn't enjoy everything," he quickly assured her. Then, as he got into the elevator, we heard him say, "Why in the world would they serve lamb?"

Emmy and I got out on the first plane the next morning, and in our rush to escape the humidity I left my "Wide World" blazer behind. A few days later I got this letter from Woody:

Dear Howard,
Enclosed is your jacket and handsome ABC felt medallion which enables you to free admission at sporting events and one hot meal per month. Let me tell you again what a pleasure it was to work with you and now that you have gone the entire film company walks around talking in your voice.
I am glad your wife enjoyed herself and she confirms my racial theories that Gentiles have better protoplasms.
Hope to see both of you in the city.
Best,
Woody

And then, three weeks after that, I got a letter from Charles Joffe, Woody's manager, which included this paragraph:

Now I know you're going to think that I'm trying to con you, but I swear on my New York Jet tickets, that positively and without question the most talked about and appreciated piece of business in the film is your scene.

Charles' words sure came at the right time. "Monday Night Football" had just begun, and I needed all the encouragement I could get. In fact, I wondered if Charles, who is a sports fan, had just written me to be nice, since he had to be aware of some of the raps I was getting.

It turned out he was sincere. A few weeks later I got a call from him and he told me that the picture looked great but they were unhappy with the ending. Would I do a new ending for them? I asked him what the concept of the ending was, and he said he'd send me the outline. When I got the outline I thought, "Hell no, I can't do this." Woody wanted me to describe the consummation of his marriage to Louise Lasser, his costar in the picture (she was also his former wife), and then climb into bed and interview the two of them. It seemed grotesque, absurd, tasteless. I discussed it with Emmy and my younger daughter, Hilary. "Knock it off, dad," Hilary said. "With Woody it will be fun. Good satire."

So I did it. I went over to the Hotel Manhattan at one o'clock in the afternoon and it was the same routine. No rehearsing. Do your thing. And Woody loved it. He went on tour to promote the picture, and everywhere he went he built me up. Since this was when I was getting all the flak about the "Monday Night" telecasts, I couldn't have been more grateful.

Then the picture opened in New York. Emmy and I went, and I was as nervous as I've ever been. I didn't even want to look at myself. But as the opening credits came on, I could not believe my eyes. Woody had given me feature billing. And then, as the picture started, there I was, doing my thing.

The audience went wild. They really loved it. The picture got exceptional reviews, I was well treated by the critics, and I felt like ten years had been removed from my life. You better believe I like Woody Allen. He gave me a chance to show that I'm a whole human being, something more than a long-term denizen of the dugout. And he did it at the very time I most needed it.

Thus did Woody and I become friends. We had something else in common. He is a rabid sports fan, as I have indicated earlier, and he likes the New York Knicks. He couldn't get season tickets for the games, so I called Irving Mitchell Felt, the chairman of Madison Square Garden, and Irving came through. Woody was in heaven. He had his season tickets, and his only worry was the state of Willis Reed's health. Well, maybe not his only worry. When you go out socially with Woody you can go crazy with anticipation. Who'll be with him? At this time Woody was alternating between two girls—Louise Lasser, his ex-wife, and Diane Keaton, his costar in his Broadway play *Play It Again, Sam*. Emmy and I liked them both very much, but we were always afraid to talk about one in front of the other. Not Woody. We'd meet him for dinner at one of his favorite places, a Chinese restaurant named Pearl's, and he would airily say, "It's a Louise night tonight." Apparently he kept no secrets from either of them.

Woody, in his low-key way, can be a tough guy to translate. He can be remote, and you wonder what he's thinking. He moves in a very narrow circle of friends, of whom Dick Cavett is one of the most important. He has a million hang-ups of his own. Right now, for instance, he will not appear on television. He feels, for whatever reason, that it hurts rather than helps his movies. Sometimes he will startle you, in that diffident manner, with his questions.

I consider Woody a genuine nut with a cheerful hang-up about sex. One night he drove us to New Haven where he was playing a gig. As I dozed in the back seat on the way home, the last words I heard were Woody asking Emmy, "Do you think your younger daughter is a virgin? . . . And what are your feelings on that subject?"

Dixieland music is one of the important things in Woody's life. He has a pickup group that he plays with on Monday nights. The only trouble is, he says, "They keep firing me wherever I play." That's Woody. He's a star and they're firing him out of places where they desperately need his name. "It's true," insists Woody. "We're too loud for some places, and then I'm away too much." So he has been at Barney Google's on East Eighty-sixth Street in New York and gotten bounced; at Jimmy Weston's on East Fifty-fourth Street and gotten bounced; and at Michael's Pub on East Fifty-fifth Street and gotten bounced. He's consistent.

I've come to believe that he's a comic genius. Not everybody's bag, of course, because he's so special, but a rare mind with a gift for satirization of the contemporary society shared by no one else. In the years to come I suspect that Woody Allen film festivals will be an "in" thing, like Chaplin, the Marx Brothers or W. C. Fields.

At one point Woody told me he wanted to form his own company, use the same people in most of his movies. I was to be a part of it. It sounded good to me, but a problem came up. Woody bought the rights to Dr. Reuben's book, *Everything You Always Wanted to Know About Sex But Were Afraid to Ask*. He had a role for me in it. Based upon the title I was dubious. In fact, I said I would abstain. But Woody was insistent. He visited Emmy and me at the Beverly Hills Hotel when we were out there, and told us that my role would be right, that I wouldn't be embarrassed. I said fine, and we arranged a date for me to come back to Hollywood and shoot my scenes. I still didn't know what my role would be. But I found out. We were met at the airport on the day I was to do the scene by a chauffeur who had an outline of my role. I was to play a sex pervert. I never went to location. Emmy and I went to the Beverly Hills Hotel, I called Woody's producer, Jack

Grossberg, and told him to count me out. "Woody will really be hurt," Jack said. "He's been so looking forward to this. Everyone's waiting at the studio."

"Woody will be hurt," I answered. "I'll be destroyed. I have no desire to peremptorily terminate my career." And that was that.

Until I saw Woody on a Monday night at Michael's Pub. I went up to him and said, "I'm sorry, Woody. I owe you a lot. But I could not play that scene."

Woody gave me that little smile and said, "Don't worry about it. You'll be in my next movie." I shuddered to think what he had in mind.

It wasn't long before I found out. Jack Grossberg called me from Hollywood and told me that Woody's new movie was to be called *Sleeper*. Right away I was nervous. But it seems that Woody wakes up 200 years from now, opens a time capsule, out comes Nixon with one of those speeches telling us that there is no problem, we only imagine it, and out comes Cosell with a commentary, preferably on Muhammad Ali. "Glad to do it, Jack." I said. "Tell Woody I'm back."

And so I am. After all, Woody's got me pegged. When someone asked what I'm really like, he said, "Oh, just the way he is on television. When you have dinner with him, he broadcasts the meal." It takes a kid from Newkirk Avenue, Brooklyn, to come up with a line like that. Or, for that matter, to keep me out of a poker game in a gambling joint in London.

If Woody Allen helped open some new avenues for me, "Monday Night Football" cemented those avenues and provided whole new thruways. Because of the continuing Monday prime-time exposure, I became one of the most recognized personalities on television, especially in light of the controversy that surrounded me that first year. Thus the talk shows wanted me, and, to my enormous surprise, so did the likes of Flip Wilson, Dean Martin, Danny Thomas, Bob Hope and Dinah Shore.

I was delighted with the opportunity to travel new roads, emotionally and intellectually. Life in sport, and only in sport, can become life in a thimble. You are always with people whose beings are absorbed with such significant matters as the "designated pinch-hitter," the "zone defense." I have to know what these things are about, but I don't have to equate them with Vietnam, racism or drug abuse. Many in the sports world, wittingly or unwittingly, do exactly that.

So I welcomed the Johnny Carsons and Dick Cavetts of the world, and I had the opportunity to host the Dick Cavett, David Frost and Mike Douglas shows. I enjoyed those assignments more than anything I have ever done in broadcast, simply because the horizons far transcended sports. For instance, I discussed the My Lai tragedy with Richard Hammer, author of the very great book *One Morning in the War*. The case of Lieutenant Colonel Anthony Herbert was my subject with James Wooten, author of *Soldier,* and I talked motion pictures with Stanley Kramer. After years of nothing but the sports arena, it was a marvelous escape.

I learned a lot about a lot of people in television as a result of my many appearances—David Frost, for instance—and also a lot about television critics. Some of the key critics loved him. Called him a great interviewer. I suspect they loved the British accent. And maybe he was a performer of depth in Britain. I do remember one show he did, as a member of the cast of "That Was the Week That Was," that I still consider the best I have ever seen on television—anywhere. It was a moving and unique treatment of John Fitzgerald Kennedy, as seen by the British people, immediately after his assassination. But based upon my experiences as his guest, he was one of the most superficial interviewers I have ever encountered. He would sit with his silly clipboard, which contained questions written out for him by his researchers, and would read a question for you to answer. Rarely, if ever, did he show a capacity for pursuit, or, for that matter, honest interest in what purported to be the conversation. I always felt Frost was totally absorbed with himself and had a synthetic personality with a fixed smile carefully adapted to the slick phoniness of ad-agency types, show-business types and broadcast-executive types.

I have mixed feelings about Dick Cavett, another performer whom the critics have hailed. I like Dick socially, and I love to needle him, and he really doesn't know how to needle back. Once I bumped into him in the lobby of the Beverly Hills Hotel, and he was dressed in equestrian attire on his way out to ride horseback. Small and slight as he is, he makes anything but an athletic figure, so I boomed out, "There he is, the diminutive Richard Cavett, clearly one of the world's great horsemen, on his way to a gold medal in the equestrian competition at the Twenty-first Olympiad." This kind of thing undoes Cavett, who is a shy man. So does calling him Richard. I always call him Richard.

I think the critics like Cavett because of his background and apparent intellect. They know he's a Yalie, the vocabulary is good, the humor is low-key and dry and often subtle. On the surface, next to some of the others, they think, "At long last, we're getting a man with a mind." Cavett does have a good mind, I think. But I don't believe that he remotely uses it. He, too, has the prepared questions provided by "researchers." And his own interests are much too narrow. If he invites a sports figure on his show, he damn well has an obligation to take an interest in the person, and in what the person does for a living. Otherwise don't ask them on. Instead you will hear him say, "Well, I don't really care much about sports. . . ." This is not confined to sports but applies also to many other topics. I have been on with Cavett when, during commercial breaks, he would ask me to help him keep the pace of the show going. None of this comes as news to two of his ablest assistants, Sue Solomon and Jean Doumanian.

Cavett has another hang-up. He wants always to come off as a wit. Thus he will invariably take someone's answer to a question and gently deride the answer or the person with what he regards as a delicious bon mot. The net effect is to demean the interview itself and the interviewee.

Shy as Dick is, I also think he takes himself too seriously, is much too self-absorbed. His manager, Jack Rollins, once called me and told me that the New York Academy of Television Arts was honoring Dick with a dinner. Bill Cosby had been scheduled to emcee it, but had been called out of town. He asked me to fill in. I did so, but that night, when Cavett arrived with his wife, he never introduced his wife to Emmy and me, nor to Jim Duffy, the television network president, and his wife, nor to any of the other ABC brass. I just couldn't understand the omission of this common courtesy.

A few weeks later I called Jack Rollins and told him that the Bedside Network (an organization dedicated to teaching and helping hospitalized veterans to form their own broadcasting groups) was honoring me with a dinner. I asked him if Dick would emcee. Cavett was unavailable.

Withal, Cavett has also been very good to me, and I will always be available if he wants me on his show. When I first came back from the Munich Olympics, Dick had me on and allowed me the opportunity to explain some of the controversy over there, including criticism of the Stan Wright interview. And he has made his respect for me very clear on many occasions. In a nutshell, I do believe that Richard could be everything some critics have depicted him as, if he would work harder in his preparation and be less concerned with being an intellectual smart-ass.

Johnny Carson is—well, he's Johnny Carson, and that's enough for me. I like him. He is what he is, an entertainer, and a very great one. There is no intellectual pretension about him, nor need there be. Go on with Johnny and take your chances. He can cut you to ribbons with great good humor, and if you're good enough to get back at him, Johnny loves it. If you're not quick enough, you knew what you were in for in the first place. I feel much the same about Don Rickles. Don is so quick it's frightening. He also got out of Umag, Yugoslavia, just before I got in. Believe it or not, that's where he and Telly Savalas made a film called *Kelly's Heroes.*

I also like Mike Douglas very much. A lot of people have called Mike shallow, a poor interviewer, a matinee mentality. All I can say is that when I first went on with him, he asked me key questions, questions that I had not been previously asked, like "Why did you refuse to give sports news the morning after Bobby Kennedy was shot?" I respect a question like that, because you can get to the heart of the way a man thinks and feels with such a query.

In dealing with show-business people the biggest surprise I've ever had was Burt Reynolds. He's a lot, lot more than a nude figure in the centerfold of *Cosmopolitan*. He's a first-rate performer in every respect, that's what he is. A good actor. A fast man with a line. And an amazingly good interviewer. In fact, the best interview I've ever been subjected to was done by Burt when he was substituting for Johnny Carson. I had only met him once before, and that was when he sat next to me on a television show where we were roasting Joe Namath. Indeed, I couldn't understand why he had asked for me to be his guest. Once on the air with him I understood. I recognized this immediately, and the chemistry between us was perfect. That night he threw names at me, one after another, and I characterized each person in capsule form, and the audience loved it. Then he hit me with good, probative questions like, "How do you feel about parodying yourself?" This is a question I had been giving a lot of thought to, and I had just about decided to stop the parody business.

I discovered that Burt and I had a lot in common. He is a close friend of Dandy Don, and he loves "Monday Night Football." He had been a football star at Florida State, the Colts had drafted him, but he never did play pro football. So I left the studio that night a fan of Burt Reynolds.

Later Burt came to New York to make a movie called *Shamus*. He was on a brutal schedule, but despite this, when I called him he agreed to make an appearance at the Bedside Network dinner in my honor. As usual he stole the show, and that was when he introduced the line, "In the next issue of *Cosmopolitan,* Howard Cosell will be the centerfold with his vital organ covered—his mouth."

Burt and I have become friends. He and Dinah Shore, along with David Steinberg and his wife, were our guests at the Miami-Washington Super Bowl game, and if Don Meredith says life with me is a trip, then try life with Burt Reynolds. David Steinberg, by the way, is another young performer whom I greatly admire. I had a lot of fun with him when he substituted for Johnny Carson, and once again I found a man who was prepared.

A curious thing about the Carson show. I received word when I was in Munich that Johnny wanted me to guest on his show as soon as I got back to the States. I sent word back that I'd be glad to. When I came back I was told by Johnny's producer that something had happened that had never happened before. NBC refused to clear me as a guest. "They said you're getting too much publicity and they don't want to add to it since 'Monday Night Football' is about to begin. Johnny is upset as hell." I told him to forget about it, and that's when I called the Cavett show and Dick was kind enough to let me come on, because I had a lot I wanted to say about the Olympics.

A couple of months later I got a call from Jimmy Walsh, Joe Namath's lawyer, and he told me that Joe was going to host the Carson show and wanted me to guest. Would I do it? I told him I'd be glad to, and then I got another call from Jimmy, and he said, "You won't believe it, NBC won't clear you."

I said, "Jimmy, I'm not surprised. It happened once before. Forget it."

Then I got another call from Walsh, and he said, "Joe told them he wouldn't do the show unless you were on, so they agreed. Now will you do it?"

I told him, "Of course I will."

Subsequently neither of us did the show. Namath dropped out because he was to do it on a Friday night, and with a game coming up on Sunday (the Jets had lost the previous Sunday) he didn't want any needless criticism.

Finally, on Super Bowl day, as we were waiting for the game to start, David Steinberg told me that he wanted me back when he was to take over for Carson for a week, and once again NBC had refused to clear me. If I'm that much of a threat to them, then clearly we're not the "third network."

One of the best times I've had on the show-business side was doing "The Odd Couple" with Tony Randall and Jack Klugman. Get in with a couple of pros like them and you're in trouble. They could have killed me if they wanted to, but instead they were great to me. The way you do "The Odd Couple," you rehearse all week, then perform the show live before an audience on Friday night. It's like doing a Broadway play. During the week Randall carries on like a madman, changing this, changing that in the script. At some points you want to walk out of the studio. But when show time comes, this man is some performer. As for Klugman, working with him is a breeze.

And so is working with Dean Martin and Bob Hope. There's nobody bigger than Hope, and yet the way he has treated me, you'd think I batted in his league. I went out to do a cameo in one of his TV specials and the next thing I knew I got a letter from him that would have made one think I did *him* a favor, instead of him doing me one by even asking me to appear on his show.

Jack Benny is another great person. I was about to do the telecast of the Ali-Quarry fight in Las Vegas when he leaned over me at ringside. "I'm Jack Benny," he said, as if I didn't know. "I just wanted to tell you I think you're the best thing to happen in the business in ten years. Don't change a thing." What a way to begin a telecast. I was on cloud nine. When Emmy and I got back home, I tracked down Benny's home phone number, called him and told him how much his words had meant to Emmy and me.

And then there is Flip Wilson, the most dedicated, hardest-working performer I've ever seen. Begin the first day of the week with rehearsal. And then work every day until Friday. Over and over again. Finally, on Friday, do the whole show twice, in front of different audiences, use the best from each show, and you've got the perfection Flip wants. He's not funny while he's working. He's remote, far away, thinking about his scenes. He's only funny when he's on the air. He is also a perfect gentleman who will never embarrass a guest. When one of his writers suggested that Sandy Duncan call me "Horrible Howard" in a scene Sandy and I were to do, Flip caught my eye. I said nothing. As we went out to do the sketch, Flip quietly told Sandy, "Make that *Humble* Howard."

Mimicry of Howard Cosell has become a commonplace these days, but probably no one does me better than David Frye. I first watched David imitate me when he appeared on "The Dick Cavett Show." I thought at the time that he somehow wasn't getting me right. Later I learned that David's father is a fan of mine and felt the same way. He was critical of David's impression of me. Here's how I found out.

It was late on a Saturday afternoon in the autumn of 1971. I was standing on Third Avenue in New York City in front of a beauty salon waiting for Emmy who was about to come out. Two men were walking by when one suddenly stopped and asked, "Aren't you Howard Cosell?" I nodded and he extended his hand and introduced himself: "I'm David Frye. This is some coincidence."

And then he pulled a script out from under his arm, started to flip the pages, and added, "We've just left a rehearsal of 'The Kopy Kats,' and I'm imitating you interviewing Truman Capote." I was flabbergasted. The man with Frye, by the way, turned out to be Will Jordan, another fine impressionist well known for his bit on Ed Sullivan.

In a matter of minutes, Frye, Jordan, Emmy and I were in our apartment having a cocktail. This was when David starting telling me about his father who lives in Brooklyn. "Dad listens to you every day," he said, "and he doesn't think I quite catch you." Then Frye came up with a whimsical idea. "You know what I'd like to do? I'd like to call Dad right now, tell him I'm doing you interviewing Truman Capote and then put you on the phone doing your thing so that he'll think it's me."

I sparked to the idea. "Let's do it."

David called his father. He asked him how he was and then told him about the rehearsal he had just had for "The Kopy Kats" wherein he was doing me and Truman Capote. Then David added, "Dad, I really think I have got Howard Cosell now, right to a T," and I could hear his father saying that, no, there was something missing, that he had seen him do me on a recent show and he just wasn't getting me. David said, "Well you just listen and then let me know." Quickly, he handed me the phone and I said, "Hello, again everyone. This is Howard Cosell Speaking of Sports . . ." and I did a quick rundown of some fictional college football scores. Then I jammed the phone back into David's hand and I could hear his father say, excitedly, "Son, that's it! You've finally got it. That's Howard Cosell."

Only then did David Frye tell his father than he was in my apartment and that it really had been me talking, but then, his father didn't believe him and started telling him that it wasn't possible that he was with me. So I got on the phone and talked to the senior Mr. Frye and he realized that his son had been kidding him and he said, "I should have known. He just doesn't get you right." Then he said something that I'll always remember because it made me think of my own father. "You know," he said, "I never really wanted David to be in show business."

I don't really know if there's no business like show business, but certainly I have found no other people like show-biz people.

Chapter XIV

MYTH OF THE FAN

---

*"Those fools, they don't even know
what they're booing."*

Like millions of others, Emmy and I were in front of
the television set when Bobby Kennedy was shot. Like
millions of others, we recoiled in horror. Like millions
of others, we stayed up most of the night, waiting for
word on whether or not Bobby Kennedy would live. We
thought about the Kennedy family, about the unbelievable
tragedies in their lives, about all the Kennedy children.
And then, I think quite understandably, we thought
about and talked about our own two daughters, Jill and
Hilary, about the kind of society they were growing up in,
a society where assassination had become commonplace.

We have a liberal home. John Kennedy had meant
much to us. So had Martin Luther King. So had Robert
Kennedy. But if we had had opposite political views it
would not have mattered. It seemed to us the American
society had gone berserk, that we were in danger of utter
chaos. Three times in a decade. When I studied American
history and read of the assassination of Lincoln, and of
Garfield, and of McKinley, it seemed somehow remote,
abstract, part of history, but the kind of thing that could
not happen in the contemporary society. Now I knew
better. Oh, how I knew better.

I suspect that when future generations read the history
of the 1960s they'll regard it in an abstract way, too.

The whole mess of the era. The apparently endless war in Vietnam. The ecology. The racial anguish. The drug abuse. But it existed then, and most of it exists now, including the crisis of the great cities, and somehow all of it meshed and related to the disorder of many minds, the kind of disorder that could produce assassination.

In any event, at seven o'clock in the morning after Bobby Kennedy was shot I had to do my regular morning network radio show, "Speaking of Sports." I simply could not speak of sports that morning. I felt that I had to reevaluate that which I do in life, come to grips with myself and make it clear that the microcosm of sports is of small consequence in the full sweep of the society. I couldn't have faced my daughters otherwise. They were stricken with grief, with disbelief and with doubts and fears about the whole civilization around them.

So I went on the air that morning and said, "This is Howard Cosell, but this morning I cannot speak of sports." I then explained that there would be no ball scores, no routine sports items. Instead I talked of Robert Kennedy, of the three assassinations in a decade and why I had to think about what I do and why I do it, and I suggested that it might be the time for everyone to do just that because clearly there was a terrible sickness in the society.

I never dreamed what the response would be. Hundreds of letters, many of them vicious, denouncing me for not giving the sports news. "Don't tell me how to live," one said, "just give us the scores. That's what you're paid for." That was the theme of most, with profanities running through many of the letters.

I was stunned. My instant reaction: What hope is there for the country if this is the thinking? And then the attempt at rationalization. After all, there are over 200 million people in the United States, and these letter can't be the majority. But then, as the thought processes continued, the realization that it didn't matter whether or not they were a majority. What mattered was that there was, obviously, a very large number of people in the United States who didn't want their normal routines interrupted on any count, for any reason, to whom hearing a baseball score was more important than some introspective thought about the state of the nation, about the kind of society in which their children were growing up, about how three assassinations could take place in the United States within five years, and about what was wrong and what one could do about it.

I began to wonder if that "fan" kind of thinking is one of the things that makes us so prone to assassination (and assassination attempts, e.g., George Wallace) in this country. Maybe there is such an absence of intellect and sensitivity in the United States today that only violence is understandable and acceptable. The matter is deeply psychological and complex, and hardly susceptible of resolution, especially in a book about the life of a sports commentator. But one thing emerged as certain: If one has any kind of mind, one has to wonder about the people—the "fans"—who wrote those letters. I even got scurrilous phone calls: "Don't preach to us." Only their language wasn't that clean. What made it even worse, they felt they were right and within their rights. After all, they were "fans," and through all the years that I have been in sports, the "fan," generally speaking, has been sanctified by most sportswriters and sports broadcasters. I think it's time for that nonsense to stop.

The popular notion has been that since the fan pays his money, he is entitled to say or do almost anything he wants. Absurd. The payment of an admission price to a stadium does not carry with it a license to engage in disorderly conduct, unseemly behavior and the utterance of profanities that are offensive to others. This all results from the disproportionate emphasis placed upon sports in America in which people get so bound up with an event, with winning or losing, that their whole sense of values is discarded in the transitory escape from real life that the event provides. Life hardly begins or ends when Miami beats Washington in the Super Bowl, yet many act as if it does.

Sometimes it doesn't even take an event as important as the Super Bowl to arouse the "fans." As I have explained elsewhere in this book, we have had a television miracle with "Monday Night Football." But within that basic miracle a second miracle emerged—the half-time highlights. Roone Arledge felt that the public was tired of watching local high-school bands perform at half time—indeed, research had established the audience declined at half time—and he felt that it would be an audience disaster in prime time to employ such programming. So he dreamed up the notion of playing the highlights of key, or exciting, NFL games of the previous Sunday afternoon. It is a tough thing to do, logistically, because the films of the Sunday games have to be sent to Philadelphia, where NFL Films is located, and then the film must be developed and edited to time, and then transmitted to the stadium where "Monday Night Football" is taking place. This is usually done a couple of hours before the game, barring technical problems, and as the film is fed in I ad-lib over it.

The half-time highlights quickly became a "thing." Audiences stay glued to the television set, and, of course, in every city the fans hope to see their team in action. The hope cannot be fulfilled. We have five to six minutes available for the highlights, and twelve games are played every Sunday. So, as practical fact, the most we can deal with are four or five games. The games have been picked by our coproducers, Chet Forte and Dennis Lewin, with very simple criteria employed in the selection. They go for games that have the most meaning in the standings, but also the games that have the most exciting plays visually. They also have to be concerned about the number of viewers. In other words, if the two New York teams are blacked out in New York on a Sunday, and Los Angeles is similarly blacked out, it becomes important to show those teams because so many millions of viewers are involved, far more than if Denver or Miami were blacked out. All of this has been made perfectly clear to the fans during the three years of "Monday Night Football."

The fan couldn't care less. Thus, in our second year of "Monday Night Football," there came a day when

Washington crushed Saint Louis. It was a lousy football game, no excitement, but Washington was unbeaten at the time. Forte and Lewin elected not to use highlights from this game. The reaction was extraordinary. I began to get calls from Washington announcers and sportswriters demanding statements from me as to the cause of my prejudice against the Redskins. Then the mail! Hundreds upon hundreds of letters. "Get Cosell off the air. He hates Washington." We were amused and, in a sense, delighted. It showed the impact of the half-time show. Then I got word that the "fans" were hanging me in effigy in the nation's capital. As I laughingly explained to the members of the media who called, I had nothing to do with the selection of the highlights, only the performance of them. I pointed out that every week as I lead into the highlights I say on the air, "Now, yesterday's highlights as selected by the producers of 'Monday Night Football.'" The fans in Washington, every time I go there, still want to know why I hate the Redskins.

Why should they be different? Let me tell you about Miami. In 1972 the Dolphins came of age. They proved they were a truly great football team, winning 17 straight games. Their fans went wild. But they were not on the half-time highlights every week. Suddenly, out of nowhere, I began getting vile mail. The letters this time mounted into the thousands. What did I have against Miami? ABC should take action against me. The same drivel that had occurred with Washington was taking place—only a new twist was added; the mail took on a threatening tone. Several threatened my life, and one said, "Better not come to Miami, Howie, you'll not make it home again." I discussed the matter with Everett Erlick, our company's general counsel, and with Roone Arledge, and they advised me to see our ABC security man and turn the letters over to him for forwarding to the FBI. I did, in the case of the letter I quoted above. The writer turned out to be a young lady who was simply a rabid fan. I was told she apologized and invited me to visit her when I came down for the Miami–Saint Louis game. Fat chance.

While all this was going on I was advising media people in Miami of what I told the people in Washington—that I had nothing to do with selection of half-time highlights. I gave them Chet Forte's name. Now Forte started to get the mail, and I started to enjoy his discomfiture. "It's not funny," he said, "these people are nuts. Read some of this stuff." I told him I didn't have to. I was quite familiar with it.

When we got to Miami for our "Monday Night" game there, the papers were full of the "war between the fans and the ABC broadcast team." Dandy Don said, "What the hell do they mean, broadcast team? I'm no part of this. Cosell's the guy." I always said Dandy had a great sense of humor.

To our astonishment, Forte and I learned that the one man who had been stirring up the population against us most was a sports announcer on our own Miami affiliate station. We were incredulous. He had been telling the people to write me, write Roone Arledge, write Chet Forte, get the Dolphins on every half time. We bumped into this guy at a dinner, Forte did an interview with him explaining how the half-time highlights were picked, and then Chet asked me to talk to him. I did, reluctantly, and there was acid in my voice. Later Chet and I watched the interviews on television and we could not believe it when the man wound up his show saying, "Cosell and Forte are staying at the Sonesta Beach Hotel." This was one of the most professionally scurrilous acts I've ever witnessed. Within seconds after he said it Forte and I started to receive ugly, profane, threatening calls. We had our phones turned off.

By now my wife was both disturbed and disgusted with the whole series of events. I wasn't happy. And Meredith was saying, "Damn, you're unbelievable, Howard. You don't have anything to do with picking the damned highlights, and the silly business is becoming a national story." Indeed, papers around the country were writing about my life being threatened, special security was to be provided for me at the game, and all the rest.

The night of the game could not have been more uneventful. Miami won easily, as expected. There was only one thing worthy of note. The gridiron was encircled by a cordon of police, each policeman holding a vicious-looking German shepherd by the leash. The dogs were deterrents, or supposedly so, to the "fans," who had a propensity for rushing onto the field during the course of play. The fans were not deterred. Some went onto the field anyway, and one even picked up the football before the ball was snapped by the center. Fortunately none of the dogs got loose or there could have been a serious aftermath. Forte did not put his camera on the scene for fear it would lead to similar exhibitionism around the country, but Dandy and I described the situation, and Dandy said, "You know there are really some nutty people down here." Yes indeed. But some nice ones, too. Lots of them. After we left Miami I got stacks of mail from people in the Miami area apologizing for those who had been plaguing Forte and me.

And then there is Pittsburgh. One day I got a call from KQV Radio in the Steel City, one of our owned radio stations, and I was advised that the Pennsylvania State Legislature had passed a resolution which, in effect, censured me for keeping Pittsburgh off the "Monday Night" schedule and for not showing enough of the Steelers at half time. I was asked to comment. I said, "I hope that the good legislators apply the same fervor and enthusiasm to their attacks upon the problems in Appalachia as they have shown in this case." The funny thing was, I had just received a lovely letter from Art Rooney, owner of the Steelers, thanking me for characterizing Pittsburgh as the new powerhouse in the NFL. After the Pittsburgh call I telephoned Pete Rozelle to tell him I had usurped his role as league commissioner. I described the KQV call to Pete and advised him, "Since it's now clear that I arrange the 'Monday Night' schedule instead of you, Pete, I think a reexamination of your position in the pro-football structure is necessary. It has become altogether clear that I am the new commissioner as well as an announcer."

Rozelle laughed and then said, "Who would have believed the half-time show would become this big, and that people would take it so seriously?"

The "fan," that's who.

You look back on stories like these with high humor, but at some point you have to wonder again about the distortion of emphasis on sports in the United States, and wonder how grown people can take so seriously something so unimportant as 45 seconds of action footage at half time.

Then you think about some of the great athletes you've known, and you remember their involvement with the "fans."

Early Wynn, for instance, was one of the greatest pitchers I have ever seen and he's recently been elected to the Baseball Hall of Fame. I remember sitting with this very characterful and interesting man near the end of his career whn he was struggling to win his 300th career game—he could no longer win with the consistency he had once enjoyed—and he started talking about what was happening to him inside. He said, "It now becomes very hard for me to go out on the field. . . . They boo me. They boo me the minute I appear." He continued, "I think I'm a tough man. I think my whole career has proved that. I know I have no physical fear, but something happens to me. Those fools, they don't even know what they're booing. They're booing a man who's done his very best, who's never done anything less than his very best through all of the years—and I think my record will get me into the Hall of Fame—but right now I just want that three-hundredth victory and they won't let me alone. I'm beginning to think I'm never going to get it, because I can't stand what they're doing to me." It was all pouring out of him, spewing out of him, and it seemed so unnatural because Early Wynn was so tough, with that burly body and the willingness to throw at another man's head, and the willingness to storm off the mound toward the batter, or the umpire, and get into a fistfight if necessary. There was nothing weak about Early except for this: He was human, and had done his best. The fans don't recognize that in many, many cases.

I saw the hair fall out of Roger Maris's head. I was extremely close to Roger Maris during the year 1961. I saw his hands begin to shake and I knew what was going on inside him, and still the fans booed him. Why? Because Mantle was their hero, not Maris, and it began to get to him. I believe that was part of the reason the hair was falling out. It was the whole undoing of his base-ball life in New York. Sure, the 61 home runs haunted him, but what haunted him even more was when he would sit and say to me unendingly, "Do you hear them? I don't even want to go out there anymore." He would trot out to right field, and all along the right-field foul line they would boo him and they would hurl profanities, and then when they had big houses they would sit behind him and he'd wonder when they were going to start to throw things at him. What was he doing? He was hitting 61 home runs; he was going to break another man's rec-ord. But somehow, in some way, he didn't reach those people, because they had two other heroes whom they didn't want to see beaten—Mantle and Ruth. What kind of sickness is that? Instead of rewarding excellence they had debased him. They destroyed Roger Maris in New York, and he couldn't wait to get away. And now he sits, a fat man in Jacksonville, with his beer distributorship, and when he thinks back to baseball what does he think about? He thinks not about the 61 home runs, but mainly about the fans in New York, and you can't even really get him to talk about baseball anymore.

This very day, as Henry Aaron, one of the finest men and players in the game, approaches Babe Ruth's sacred home-run record, he is getting the most vicious kind of mail, with the "nigger" element thrown in. There can be only one Babe Ruth, say the letter writers, and no "black bastard" has any right to challenge his record.

These are fans?

My broadcast buddy, Don Meredith, knows something about the "fan"—that sacred person who must always be catered to. After three years of "Monday Night Foot-

ball" with Dandy Don I've gotten to know him intimately.
I know much about his personal life, I know much about
the kind of man he is and I know much about the
scars that are inside of him. As I said earlier, Don
Meredith didn't like his coach, Tom Landry, and everybody who knows football knows that. Indeed, as he sees
his relationship with Landry, Landry did many things to
him that have created deep wounds inside of him that
somehow keep cropping up and seem to live with him
forever. But I think perhaps the deepest wounds ever
inflicted upon Don Meredith, who was a first-rate quarterback, were the wounds inflicted by the "fans" of Dallas.
When the Saint Louis Cardinals crushed the Dallas Cowboys 38–0 in the first year of "Monday Night Football,"
it was almost a mockery to hear those people start to
chant, "We want Meredith, we want Meredith." It
seemed to me that this was one of the things that set
Dandy off that night, that caused him to say so many
things that he otherwise might not have said on the telecast. I remarked at the time—and the TV critic, Cleveland Amory, later took note of it in a review of "Monday
Night Football"—"Listen to them. Now they want Meredith when they booed him out of the Cotton Bowl all
those years." I think that more than Landry, more than
anything, the fans' treatment of Don Meredith caused
him to leave football prematurely. He had another good
five or six years left in him and could have won the
Super Bowl, the one thing he wanted more than anything else out of football. But their treatment of him was
just cruel, almost savage. I've indicated already that other
athletes are aware of this. He would take the field and
the "fans" would boo him. They would laugh at his
skinny legs. Here's a man who played hurt and the
"fans" never even knew. I remember once talking with
Lance Rentzel, and Rentzel told me that the greatest
demonstration of leadership and courage he had ever
known as a player occurred when he was playing in
a game and Meredith was his quarterback, his leader.
Meredith went down under a pass rush and suffered a

number of broken ribs that stifled his breathing. There were two minutes left, in the game, and Dallas was trailing. There was no way Meredith should have continued in the game, but somehow he forced himself. He could hardly call the signals in the huddle, but he drove his team down the field to victory. Later, when they discovered the broken ribs, they couldn't believe what he had done. Such was the danger of that situation that those ribs could have punctured the lungs and might, indeed, have cost Meredith his life. Rentzell tells the story very vividly and very emotionally. It's the kind of thing Meredith did as a player.

Now take that kind of courage, and take that kind of dedication, and then pit against that somebody who pays his money to get into the ball park and says that gives him the right to heap insulting verbal abuse that amounts to public slander upon a man. Decide for yourself.

One could go on and on with stories like these. Once I saw Mickey Mantle in actual physical jeopardy as he was literally mobbed by "fans," young and old, for his autograph. When Mickey finally broke free of them they shouted, almost in unison, "Where would you be without us, you bum? Who pays your salary anyway?"

I remember the Washington Touchdown Club annual dinner in January 1973. I had hosted the dinner the year before, at the behest of Andy Okershausen who is the operating head of WMAL-TV and WMAL Radio in Washington, both of which are affiliates of ABC. Andy happens to be one of the closest friends I have in broadcast, and I'm glad to be of service to him whenever he calls upon me. So I went to Washington in '72, and then I was asked back in 1973, and in both cases I went down there because of Andy, without fee, which is unusual because I'm at a stage of life when I can command a substantial fee for every appearance I make. Well, I was introduced that night as "the man who picked both Dallas and Miami to beat the Redskins," all in good fun, and this produced 2500 boos, all in good fun. During the course of the evening one had to be ready to give and take, it's that kind of affair. But when the evening ended (once again I was on a tight schedule, and the hour was late) I started to get mobbed for autographs at the dais table. And when finally I was really beginning to feel almost faint, from people over me and just throwing down the paper to be signed, I asked politely if they couldn't give me just a minute so that I could get myself together and then resume signing. Whereupon one guy said to another guy, "The dirty son of a bitch, we hate him anyway. Who wants his goddamn autograph?" I simply quietly got up and started to walk away. Behind me I heard mumblings about what a terrible person I was. One person did have the decency to run after me and try to apologize. At a moment like that you want to turn around and really let loose!

One night Emmy and I were leaving Foxboro Stadium with F. Lee Bailey, the Boston attorney, and his wife. We were rushing to get into a helicopter of Lee's to take us back to Boston. Lee couldn't get over the way the fans accosted me for autographs. If you stop and sign one you're dead. You will be mobbed, and you have to hope, as Mantle so often did, for your physical well-being. So you wave good-naturedly, say you'd love to sign but you can't, you're on a time schedule, and they move along with you and start to surround you anyway, and some of them start to abuse you. Lee was observing closely what I was going through and he was trying to help, and when we finally got to the adjacent field where the helicopter was, he looked at me and said, in his quiet, incisive way, "It's such a temptation to be rude, to let it all hang out." How right he is, and how many times I've had the temptation.

All of the above will undoubtedly be taken by some to mean that I am complaining about being in the public eye, and that athletes complain about the same thing, or that all fans are wild and unruly. Not at all. I think any person who performs in the public arena, as I do, as athletes do, has to expect some manifestation of public fervor during the course of his life. The question is to what degree, and in what ways? Does my wife have to sit at a table at Emily Shaw's Inn in Pound Ridge, New

York, and have a man come up to her to say, "I hate your husband's guts. He's a no good son of a bitch"? I think not. On the other side of the coin, I now enjoy a degree of recognition in the country that is almost ridiculous, and for every person who will invade your privacy or turn on you at the slightest opportunity, there is the person who'll make you feel good. When you walk down a street in Wichita or San Diego and a stranger recognizes you and calls out, "Hey, Howie baby, keep it up, you're doing a good job," it's only human to feel a sense of elation. That's one of the great rewards of performing.

But the point remains that the "fan" can be thoughtless, ignorant and cruel, and should not be sanctified. Yet almost unfailingly he continues to be. In February 1973 the baseball owners threatened the players with a lockout. As it began to appear that spring training might not open on schedule, a number of writers across the country wrote about their concern for the "fan." "The fan doesn't care about the squabble between the players and owners," they wrote. "They just want baseball and they're entitled to get it. Where would the players and owners be without them? So let's get started." In a broad sense this is, I suspect, carrying the mythology of the "fan" to the extreme, because it implicitly embraces the notion that, in a country founded upon individual rights, individuals should give up those rights for the "fan," even though the "fan" doesn't give up his individual rights in the conduct of his life. Specifically, this is what I mean: The "fan" is a telephone worker, a transit worker, a power-company worker, a steelworker, a teacher, whatever. He has never given up the right to strike and often does. When he does the public is inconvenienced and sometimes the public health and safety is threatened. When a ballplayer strikes, the effect upon the public health and safety is nil. Nor is public convenience disturbed for that matter. Yet the ballplayer and the owner are called upon to each give up his individual bargaining rights because the "fan" wants baseball and "is entitled to get it." You can't blame the fan for originating this type of thinking, though. Blame it on a group of baseball writers whose mental horizons are the dugout, and for whom all of life is the luxury of warm weather and spring training.

Finally, when I think about the "fan," I inevitably must think about three and a half years of my life and the life of Muhammad Ali; about the tens of thousands of letters directed to me, beginning with the general refrain, "You nigger-loving Jew bastard . . ."; and about the phone calls, some of which would . begin, "We're gonna get you. We know where you're at, and we're gonna get you." Once again it's easy to laugh all this off with the rationalization that such "fans" are in the minority, but there are too many of them and they are part of the general group termed "fans" whose interests so many seem dedicated to protecting.

To be identified with Ali was to catch the full sweep of the fans' mentality. Once, in early 1971, after I had repeatedly defended Ali's right to earn a living, I was confronted by a group of hard-hats. They were doing construction work on Fifty-second Street, across from Mike Manuche's where I often have lunch.

As I approached, one of them said, "Here he is, the Jew who loves Clay." They quickly encircled me. He continued, "We know you, Cosell. What is with you and that traitor, that black son of a bitch? The guy should never be allowed to fight again."

His name, I soon found out, was Johnny. He seemed to be the leader. He was a big, rough, potbellied guy. I looked at him and collected my thoughts. As it happened Ali was in New York that very afternoon and staying at the Hilton Hotel. "Now wait a minute," I said, as they crowded closer. "I know how we can settle this. Clay is just around the corner at the Hilton. We can go over there right now, and you—" I jabbed a finger at Johnny "—can lay that son of a bitch low."

He looked at me with suspicion. "Are you serious?" he demanded.

"Of course," I shot back. "Look at your body. You can handle him. I'm with you all the way. He's around the corner in Room nineteen ten. He's up there right now. We'll go over—you bring the others guys along—and you can have a piece of him. You can whip his ass."

So then the other hard-hats picked up the chant. "Yeah, that's right, Johnny. You can take care of him. You can whip him. Come on. Let's go."

He raised his hands to quiet them down. "What the hell is the matter with you guys?" he asked. "You crazy? The guy is a professional fighter. Gimme a hammer and I'll go over there, maybe."

I said, "Hell, you don't need a hammer to take care of a yellow traitor who wouldn't fight for his country. Just go over there and beat his ass."

The others were telling him to put up or shut up. Johnny looked at me for a long while and finally he said, "Aw, let's go back to work. You know, Howie ain't all that bad. He loved Lombardi."

I quickly ducked inside Manuche's, and my heart was palpitating. Although I had enjoyed agitating Johnny, the experience had been a distasteful one. I felt that it could just as easily have gone another way and become physically unpleasant. By great verbal dexterity I had managed to extricate myself and win them over.

But I wasn't through with Johnny the Hard-Hat. Over the next few days he grew friendlier each time I passed. One afternoon I stopped and said, "Johnny, tell you what. They're going to announce the signing of the Ali-Frazier fight next week at Toots Shor's. After the signing I'll bring him over to meet you. You might like him."

"Aw, don't you start that," he said.

I smiled. "No problem," I said.

The next week, after the signing, I persuaded Ali to take a walk with me. I led him to Fifty-second Street and found Hard-Hat Johnny at work with his friends.

"Hey, Johnny."

"Oh, hey, Howie, how are ya?"

"I want you to meet Muhammad Ali," I announced, "you know, the black son-of-a-bitch traitor." I had prepared Ali on the whole story. He was looking ferocious.

"Now, wait a minute, Champ," stammered Johnny.

"Wait a minute, Champ. You got to understand Howie, ya know?"

"Did you call me a black son-of-a-bitch traitor?" Ali stepped toward him.

"Champ, you don't understand, Champ. Kidding. You know, kidding."

In the middle of this Ali started to laugh. Within moments, he was regaling them with stories, telling them what he was going to do to Frazier, dancing and shadowboxing. The hard-hats were laughing, and hanging on every word. Johnny slapped me on the shoulder. "Hey," he shouted in my ear, *"This is some guy! They done him wrong. This guy is awright."* And as we walked down the street the hard-hats were still standing there, grinning, waving, wishing Ali luck.

Of course, the fickleness of the fans is a subject on which Joe Willie Namath could write another book. On January 12, 1969, Namath engineered the greatest upset in the history of pro football. It was a victory that changed the very face of the sport. He was truly the toast of Broadway, the overlord of Manhattan Island. For not quite 12 months.

In December, when the Jets lost the American Football Conference title to Kansas City, the Shea Stadium fans booed him off the field. *Sic transit gloria mundi.*

In my view, the "fan" does deserve certain things. With the reminder that he voluntarily pays admission to an event—no one puts a gun to his head—I think he is entitled to a clean, comfortable and safe ball park. I think he is entitled to the assurance that the ownership is doing everything it can legitimately do to produce a product of excellence—in the case of sports, a winning team. I think he is entitled to the assurance that, if the product is good (not great) and if the fan supports it so that the owner shows a reasonable profit, the owner will not desert him by moving the franchise to another city. I think he is entitled to the assurance that the athletes he pays to see will give of themselves to the utmost in their performance within the arena, and I think the athletes have a concomitant obligation to be in peak physical condition so that they can render that kind of performance. I think a reporter, like myself, with large-scale public recognition, has the same obligation to the fan that he has to his employer—namely, to do the best reporting job possible, to relay the most information, provide total accuracy, deliver the most responsible journalism, and yet deliver it in the most attention-getting manner possible. Also to deliver commentary that is probative and responsible.

If the fan gets all these things, he is getting what he is entitled to. He is also entitled to courtesy from each and every one of us, owners, athletes, reporters. But he is not entitled to impinge upon our privacy, endanger our safety, demean our dignity. Personally I feel I have lived by my responsibility to the public.

I know of no better evidence than the way I have sought to expose the carpetbaggers in baseball, nor do I know of a better way to protect the interests of the fan. I am not at all sure that many of the fans even understand, or want to be protected. This is their right, but it is just another reason why they should not be celebrated as a sacrosanct body always to be served.

There is a final reason why the fan should not be unduly celebrated—the most compelling reason of all— and that is the basic obligation to be a journalist. It is an easy thing to appeal to the fan in order to achieve his quick approval. It would have been an easy thing to have called Muhammad Ali "Cassius Clay," and to have extolled the fact that he had been barred from professional boxing. That would have been the popular thing to do. But not the right thing. To repeat what I have said elsewhere, what is popular is not always right, and what is right is not always popular. Oddly, that maxim has to be learned by Americans in every generation. I think I have practiced it throughout my career. It is a course guaranteed to cause one countless frustrations, but in the face of them you sometimes gather strength from unlikely sources.

There was a night when I felt abused by an unruly audience at the annual dinner of the Long Island Athletic Club. I had emceed this affair for five years as a personal favor to Gene Ward, a sports columnist for the *New York Daily News*.

You have to understand the climate of your typical sports banquet. It is the celebration of a season just beginning, or ending; a joining of people—usually men— with a common loyalty; a chance to hear coaches and athletes and people who inhabit the very world that so excites them. In short, it is a dream night for the fan. The fellowship is strong. So is the booze. There is often about it the roughhouse aura of a stag party.

This night the crowd, always roisterous, grew disorderly and discourteous to the point of being obnoxious. In other years this crowd had booed Allie Sherman mercilessly. It had behaved rudely during a speech by Vince Lombardi. Tonight I listened to their jeers and watched their misbehavior until I had my fill of it. I told them their conduct was inexcusable. They'd had me for the last time. At the end of the evening I refused a gift the sponsors had provided for me, and I left, to drive an hour and a half through a midwinter snow to my home.

Later that night I described my disgust and disappointment to Emmy. And the next day I was handed a letter, neatly typed, by my daughter, then 17. It was dated February 5, 1970, and I read it hungrily.

Dear Daddy,

This afternoon Mom told me about what happened at the dinner in Garden City. I wanted to let you know how sorry I am. We are all very proud of you and what you do; your courage in always speaking the truth, and your willingness to stand up for these truths. We are also admittedly proud of the adjective "controversial" which is always coupled with your name. At the same time we tend to forget that the burden of being controversial is not a light one, and that you ultimately are the one who must shoulder it. Never forget though that we are ready to help if we can.

You and I frequently talk about what a strange

*and sick time we live in. While sometimes we dis-
agree about the cause and the remedy, both of us
are firm in our stand that the remedy must be found
and the disease cured. The only way that this will
ever happen is by people telling the truth, no matter
how ugly and unpalatable it may be. Your truths,
though not so immediately significant as those of
a Martin Luther King or a John Kennedy, are important. It doesn't really matter if the particular
truth concerns poverty, Muhammad Ali or Joe Willie's knees. What I believe is important now is the
realization that at this particular period in our country the truth, while rarely easily to swallow, is now
impossible to choke down. Nearly every American
knows that there is something terribly wrong with
our society. Though they may differ in their opinion
of the cause of the problem, they are alike in their
desire to hear their anxieties explained away by pat
phrases, worn-out rhetoric, and half-truths. You
well know, and I am slowly learning, that there is no
place in such a world for those few who will not
lie or compromise with soothing half-truths. You
are one of those few.*

*I'm glad that you stayed at the dinner and showed
them that it takes more than behavior like theirs
to stop those who tell the truth.*

*When I heard of this ugly occurrence I remem-
bered a tape I saw of Robert Kennedy speaking at
Kansas University during the campaign. Those students wanted to hear pleasant lies about themselves
and their country. But Bobby told them the ugly
facts about poverty, war and racism. And they booed
him and jeered him. They wouldn't let him finish
a sentence. He stood up to them and told them that
they had better listen and change their attitudes
because there was a very real possibility that they
might be the last generation to have the chance to
change things before it was too late.*

*It must have been humiliating for him then, as it
was for you last night. But he had every right to*

be proud of himself. And I'm sure that his family
was proud of him too. No matter how that audience,
or any audience, treated him he knew he spoke the
truth. No one, not even Sirhan Sirhan, could rob
Robert Kennedy or his family of that knowledge and
the strength it gives. And while I in all honesty
cannot, despite the greatness you possess, attribute to
you all the greatness of the Senator, I can compare you. There is much that is comparable. And
coming from me, you know that that is the highest
praise I can give.

> Peace,
>> Much love,
>>> Hilary Jennifer

Raising a daughter capable of such feelings gives meaning to a man's life. Hilary's letter is with me always.
She is one fan I want forever.

Chapter XV

OUT OF THE CROWD

---

*"Hey, Roone, come help me listen
to Howard."*

As I look back upon my career in broadcasting—the places I have been, the events I have seen—I have an admixture of feelings. I shall probably always wish that the career had been in the area of news. But even this feeling is tempered by the realization that sports does have a major place in society; that it provides entertainment the country needs; it offers escape. It is tempered even more by what I really take out of sports: people. People like Jackie Robinson, Vince Lombardi, Bill Toomey and Muhammad Ali.

I have learned that age-old lesson—people are what matter—and without question, in my mind, there are many great people in sports. The events are transitory; they come and go. And fame is indeed fleeting. The athletes, even the great ones, learn that early. But people are infinite in the mind, and in the memory.

The procession has been long and full, and many of the names prominent in my own career have been covered elsewhere. There were some for whom I really didn't care, and some who didn't care for me. But all of them have left impressions upon me that are indelible.

Fred Hutchinson was one. From the very first broadcast I ever did, Fred Hutchinson was there to help me. When I started the "Little League Clubhouse" show on radio, Fred was managing the Detroit Tigers and he brought his two great rookies, Al Kaline and Harvey Kuenn, to the studio to guest for me. I was with him in a New York hotel when he spoke to Detroit and learned that his days were numbered as the manager of the Tigers. Not a word of complaint. No whimpering.

He was a big man. Six-four, 235 pounds, with a face that could have been chiseled out of the granite of Mount Rushmore. Everything about him betokened strength. And he had a violent temper. Once when he was pitching for the Tigers—and he had been a fine pitcher—he was removed from the game. He broke 36 light bulbs on his way to the clubhouse. When he became manager he learned to control that temper. Sometimes.

In the next years Hutch managed the Cardinals and then the Cincinnati Reds. Always he would come to our apartment in New York when his team was in town. And then, suddenly, it happened. Fred Hutchinson had cancer. I watched his body shrivel. Not once did he ever indicate the pain. Once we were having a drink at Toots Shor's when he couldn't withstand the wracking ache of his body. Quietly he said, "You must excuse me." And he left.

The last time I saw Fred Hutchinson alive was in the winner's clubhouse at Shea Stadium in 1964. He was a coach on the National League All-Star team, which had just beaten the American League. He came out of the shower. It seemed as though everybody's eyes were averted. This man, with that once strapping body, seemed now inches shorter and untold pounds lighter. He was a shrunken shell of what he had been. Fred Hutchinson died not too many months later. But he went out the way he wanted to. He had done his thing—baseball was his life—and having done it he departed with a dignity that I have not ever seen before or since. Never one word of self-pity. Never one visible evidence of self-martyrization. No single sign of morbidity. This was a man.

*　　*　　*

Tony Lema was another—and, ironically, another tragic story; ironically because Tony Lema was one of the brightest and most bubbling guys in the whole human race. His nickname, Champagne Tony, referred as much to his personality as to his taste in beverages. He was a great golfer, great enough to have won the British Open and the Thunderbird, among others.

He flew back from the British Open one year and came straight to my home in Pound Ridge. We were to shoot a special the next day at the Westchester Country Club, a profile of Tony to be called, "Champagne on the Green." We did that show against four different backdrops at the club. Tony was his usual self. Buoyant, charming, outspoken. He had had enough, he said, of all the publicity that Palmer and Nicklaus and Player were getting. What about guys like him, and Doug Sanders? We wound up the show on the veranda of the club, a bottle of champagne nestled between us. "How about a glass of the bubbly?" he asked me.

"Fine, if you'll open," I answered.

He popped the cork—he was as good at that as he was at golf—and he poured. I then lifted the glass and, in the final scene of the show, said, "Tony, when it's all over, how would you like to be remembered? As Tony Lema, great golfer, or Tony Lema, great guy?" (He was, at the time, only in his thirties.)

"As Tony Lema, great guy," he said. And then he raised his glass, touched it to mine and said, "Cheers."

That ended the show. I put him in a limousine for the airport. He had to go to Ohio to play in a tournament. This was on a Monday. The following Monday Emmy got a letter from Tony Lema, thanking her for a pleasant stay at Pound Ridge. When Emmy got the letter and saw his name on the envelope she cried. She didn't want to open it. Tony Lema was already dead.

He had died the night before, with his wife, in the crash of a private airplane they had chartered after the golf tournament ended. Tony was to play in a golf charity the day Emmy got the letter.

*　　　*　　　*

There is a simple, basic decency about Ralph Branca that is given to few men. This tall, slow-spoken, slow-walking, cracked-voice former Dodger pitcher from Mount Vernon, New York, has been a good friend and a consequential figure in my life.

In 1962 and 1963, the first two years of the Mets, we carried their games on local radio in New York and Ralph teamed up with me on the pre- and postgame shows. I would introduce him as "Big Ralph Number Thirteen Branca," and we steadfastly refused to take the Mets seriously. Every day for two solid seasons we would try to satirize their futility. We would do it in many ways. Once, after a particularly inept performance—one got to a point where grades were given for degrees of ineptitude—we parodied the Lerner-Lowe classic "I've Grown Accustomed to Her Face" with lines like, "We've grown accustomed to your pace. . . ." Indeed, at that time the Mets did make our "day begin." Some of their night games would linger until one in the morning and sometimes even later.

We would broadcast the shows from my home at Pound Ridge when the night games took place. Ralph would arrive for dinner, then we would do the pregame show and settle back to watch the game on television. We rarely succeeded. Almost invariably we would fall asleep, and Emmy would wake us up in time for the postgame show. At that time the Mets were the perfect antidote for insomnia.

The shows were a tremendous success, and over the past three years, working with Don Meredith, I have often thought about Ralph. Like Don, Ralph was a perfect opposite to me and provided an ideal personality chemistry. How odd that my two broadcast buddies should both be from Mount Vernon, one in New York and the other in Texas.

Every time I see Ralph now he reminds me of the old days. "Ali says he made you and so does Meredith," Ralph will say. "Why don't you tell the truth? I made you."

I have never known a man more loyal or honest than

Ralph Branca. Both qualities are ingrained in his up-bringing and are reflected in his home. His wife, Ann Mulvey, is the daughter of the late "Deary" Mulvey, one of the long-term owners of the Dodgers, and she is a charming, attractive lady. They have two lovely daughters, and all will always be part and parcel of the Dodgers. To this day Ralph is sensitive about the fact that he threw the home-run ball to Bobby Thomson on October 3, 1951, a blow that has been immortalized. But as the years have passed, Ralph has developed a quiet resignation about that moment of ill fortune. He has a sense of where it's at. Two of his best friends, Gil Hodges and Jackie Robinson, are gone. A home run and a pennant pale next to that fact.

Willie Mays came to New York in 1951, and through Monte Irvin I became his lawyer for a time. He was not then and is not now a man of intellect. But he is a man of sensitivity. Through the years he has grown enormously; he is no longer the kid who played stickball in the streets of Harlem, when he wasn't patrolling center field at the Polo Grounds. But even in the early years he had instinct. He called me one day and wanted me to go with him to Englewood Cliffs, New Jersey, to look at a house that was for sale.

We looked at it. It was lovely. But as Willie drove away he said, "One of my people just moved into the neighborhood. That's why they want to sell to me." Willie learned more about that in San Francisco.

Don Drysdale was a 19-year-old gangling kid when I met him. He had just pitched and won his first major-league game, 9–2, over the Phillies. I took him uptown to do my "Little League" show and then over to our apartment for dinner. I never dreamed then that he would become one of the finest pitchers of his time and wind up as a Hollywood sophisticate and an announcer with the California Angels. But that's what he did.

As a pitcher he was not only outstanding but also mean and tough. The naïveté and the boyishness went out of him early. If you were a right-handed batter you took your life in your hands when Drysdale side-wheeled one at you. On his good days he was a replica of Ewell Blackwell.

Sandy Koufax, a Jewish kid from Lafayette High School who went on to the University of Cincinnati, joined the Brooklyn Dodgers when they were at their peak, in the mid-Fifties. He would sit alone and unnoticed in a corner of the dugout, looking on almost in awe at Robinson, Reese, Hodges, Furillo, Campanella, Newcombe, Erskine, Rowe and the rest of the great troupe. One could not possibly envision that Koufax would become the greatest left-hander of his time and a Hall of Famer. But he did.

As the years passed, these three—Mays, Drysdale and Koufax—became and stayed good friends of mine. But the climax was reached on Labor Day, in 1965, when they banded together in an incident I will never forget. That was when ABC had the baseball "Game of the Week" package, and I was doing the pre- and postgame show. The Dodgers and Giants were locked in a wild battle for the pennant. The series opening on this day could not have been more critical, nor could the atmosphere have been more tense.

The last time the teams met, Giant pitcher Juan Marichal, standing in the batter's box, had turned and hit catcher John Roseboro with his bat as Roseboro was crouching behind the plate. Roseboro's head was cut open by the blow and he was hospitalized.

Now on this Labor Day everyone wondered what might happen, especially with Drysdale scheduled to pitch for the Dodgers and always ready to throw at the Giants' bodies rather than at the plate.

So I did my pregame show with Koufax representing the Dodgers, Mays representing the Giants and, finally, Drysdale, who was to pitch for Los Angeles. The questions were pointed: no holds barred. I asked Drysdale if he was going to throw at the Giants. I asked Koufax and Mays about their individual feelings and about their respective teams' feelings.

It was a helluva show to set up the game itself for Chris Schenkel and Leo Durocher, who were doing the broadcast, and I felt exultant when I had completed it. Drysdale went back to get ready for his warm-up. Mays and Koufax went back to their clubhouses. And then I heard from Chuck Howard in the ABC truck. "The tape didn't take," he told me. "You better plan to ad-lib."

I exploded. One profanity followed another as I denounced the "amateurs" in the truck. Then I looked at the clock. There were 25 minutes left to game time. I said, "Get everything ready. I'll be back."

I raced into the Giants' clubhouse. Herman Franks, the Giants' manager, was with his team captain, Mays, behind closed doors. They were going over the Dodgers' lineup. I banged on the door. Franks shouted, "Who is it?" I said, "Herman, I've got a crisis. I've got to have Willie." (Talk about *chutzpah*.)

He opened the door. "Are you crazy?" he asked me. "We've never had a bigger game. And you want my captain?"

I said, "Herman, you don't understand. I've got a crisis and I need Willie." I explained to him how the tape had been fouled up.

Franks turned to Willie and said, "Go ahead." I went out with Willie, put him in camera position and said, "Give me two minutes." I then shot into the Dodgers' clubhouse, where Koufax was undressing, getting ready for a shower and a change of uniform.

I said, "Sandy, you've got to put your shirt back on and do the interview again."

He said, "You've got to be kidding."

I said, "Sandy, the damned tape didn't take. Willie's out there now and we've got to do it again."

He said, "You're the only guy in the country who'd even have the nerve to try this. There's no way."

I said, "Sandy, you were just a damned snit from Brooklyn sitting in the corner of the dugout surrounded by the great ones when I first met you. You owe me this."

He said, "I don't owe you one goddamn thing, but I'll do it." He put his shirt and cap on and out he came.

We did the show again. And Chuck Howard couldn't believe it. And then, to make the whole insane story complete, Drysdale did another interview with me. It took me an hour and a half to recover from the emotional stress I had gone through. But I'll carry that memory with me forever. Mays, Drysdale and Koufax. They're the kind of men you take out of sport.

Leo Durocher, too. As a member of our broadcast team that year, Leo was—well, Leo was Leo, and there is no one else quite like him in sports. One day you hate him, the next you love him. You never trust him. He is the brassy figure he has always been pictured as, sartorially impeccable, with a quick turn of the tongue that can either level you or charm you, as his momentary disposition dictates. During that whole season he would unfailingly arrive for the telecast the same way. With those short, mincing steps of his, he would come tripping down the grandstand steps and make his entrance on the playing field during batting practice.

No sooner would he step onto the field than he would shoot those gorgeous cuffs of his handmade shirt and give you a quick glimpse of the ornate cuff links, and then flash the watch with the gold band that encased his wrist. It was as if he hadn't done it last week and the week before. "The Man gave me this," he would say. "The Man," of course, was Frank Sinatra, who had given Leo the watch.

For the first time on a baseball telecast we put cameras in the center-field stands so the viewer could see the catcher give the signal and also get a better view of the pitch. Most of the staid managements fought this, and Durocher berated them. "Dammit," he said, "let's give the public what they want, what they're entitled to." When Leo was on the outside, looking in, he was anti-establishment.

As the season wound down we got to our next-to-the last game, Milwaukee at Pittsburgh. This was shortly after I had done my one-hour special with Mantle that attracted wide attention. After we left the ball park for the airport that day, Leo talked to me about it. "That was some show that you did with Mantle," he said. "I'd like to do one like that with you. I'll tell *everything*. Lower the boom on these guys, once and for all. How much can I get for it?"

"Leo," I said, "with the career you've had, the stories you've got, your personality, we'll pay you five thousand for a half-hour interview and we'll do it right in our Los Angeles studios after the season ends. You won't have to make a move."

"Great," he told me. "It's a deal. Just call me."

The season ended, and I called Leo some days later. "It's all set," I told him. "We'll do it at the ABC Studios on Prospect Street next Wednesday at two."

"What's that?" Leo said. He had just been named the manager of the Chicago Cubs. "Kid," he said, "I can't do it. I'm back in. Do you understand, kid? I'm back."

Every time I see Leo, I chuckle.

I never liked Casey Stengel. And he never liked me. That's putting it mildly. Now in his late eighties, I'll give him this: He has the most enduring and remarkable physical vitality I have ever seen in a man. But I found him rude, crude and uncultured. And I always believed he did not like young people. I found him downright cruel to his young players. He would make cracks about them, in their presence, to what he called "my writers." That was another thing I didn't like about him. He viewed the media as a personal arm, for personal publicity, and he got away with it. He would wink, and he would double-talk, and he would drink with them, and he would be great copy for them, and he *owned* them, as no other sports figure in my time has owned the writers.

I view him as part of a distant past, victimized by obsolescence. The young people of America today couldn't possibly buy his act. He remains a figure of romantic nostalgia for those with 19th Century dugout vision.

One other thing I always resented about Stengel. He was deliberately and cannily used by the Mets when they first began, as a publicity gimmick, to make futility entertaining. Coming as it did, at a time when Lombardi was glamorizing the quest for excellence, I was appalled. I deeply resented the hypocrisy that underlay the whole approach of the Mets at that time.

Bobby Bragan was never a good ballplayer, and he was fired time and again as a manager. As a player he never had the necessary ability. As a manager he was overqualified. His problem was that he was bright and creative. Where do you find a place in baseball for a man like that?

He also had color, the way Leo Durocher did, and a mind and a capacity for growth. Southern-born, I have earlier described how he wanted to quit the Brooklyn Dodgers when Jackie Robinson joined the club. Of course, he wound up a friend of Robinson's and managed more black players in his time than any other manager in the big leagues. He would try new things. Like having his best hitter lead off, rather than bat third or fourth in the lineup. What better way to induce quick disfavor in baseball than to violate tradition?

He managed Maury Wills at Spokane. Maury was going nowhere. Bobby made him a switch-hitter, got him to bat from the left side of the plate, and that made Maury's major-league career possible. To this day Maury will tell you that.

Bragan needs a challenge, a stimulus. Sameness destroys him. And there is something defiant about him. Thus it was that I arrived one Saturday at Milwaukee County Stadium, in 1965. Bobby was managing the Braves, and they were to play the Giants in our "Game of the Week."

The night before, Bob Shaw of the Giants had allegedly been throwing one spitball after another, and there was a major rhubarb during the game as Bragan protested again and again. I read about it in the *Milwaukee Sentinel* as I rode from the airport to the stadium. The minute I got to the ball park I went to Bragan and I said, "I see where Shaw threw the wet one at you guys all night long."

Bobby answered, "The umpires stink. They've got no guts."

I said, "Bobby, you can expose the whole damned thing. Let's you and I do the pregame show on the spitter."

"Great," he said. "How do you want to do it?"

I said, "Who throws it best for you guys?"

Without batting an eyelash he said, "Danny Osinski. I tell you what we'll do," Bobby added. "Let's open with a shot of the slippery elm on Osinski's index finger, and then pan up to his mouth while he puts it on his tongue. Then you guys can shoot him from the back while he delivers the pitch, and the fans can see the reaction of the spitball."

The idea was intriguing. Bragan had become a producer. The slippery elm, by the way, is a tablet that increases the saliva flow in the mouth. We did the show with Bobby doing the voice-over. It was probably one of the most honest shows ever done on baseball. When we finished I said, "Bobbin', you can get fired for this."

He said, "It's a helluva way to go. It's about time people knew that we throw it."

To this day Bragan and I are close friends. We always will be. If NBC wants to liven up their baseball package, this is the guy to do it with. In my opinion he's another Meredith, only he has a better voice. Bobby sings with barbershop quartets wherever he goes. And when he does the score of *The Music Man* he makes Robert Preston pale by comparison.

Bobby is now the president of the Texas League and has become baseball's resident expert on the spitter. In July 1973 Bobby and I did a film piece on Cleveland pitcher Gaylord Perry in which Bobby declared that Perry was doctoring the ball with a foreign substance that he had planted under his left armpit.

*   *   *

Take a guy who is new to sportscasting, send him to spring training in 1956, have him visit Sarasota, Florida, where the Boston Red Sox are training, put him in with the greatest hitter of his time, an erratic, tempestuous man named Ted Williams. John Podres, the young pitcher who won the seventh game of the World Series for the Dodgers in 1955, has, at that time, just been drafted by the military. Give that young sportscaster a microphone and let him fearfully go up to Williams, who was called up to the service for the second time in the early Fifties to do battle in Korea. Let the sportscaster dare to ask Williams for his reaction to the induction of Podres, and this is what you'll get:

"I think they're discriminating against the athletes and I don't give a damn who knows it. And I know from my own case, for that matter." Right there you've got the beginning of Howard Cosell and Ted Williams. And it stayed that way always, at every crisis in his then remaining baseball career. When he spat at the fans of Boston in Fenway Park he went on with me to explain why he had done it. When he hit his final home run as a player he went on and said, "I'll not manage ever. It's a lousy job, a thankless job." Through his whole career Ted Williams was a dead-honest guy. He would meet any issue head on. I respect him and I admire him.

Ted later changed his mind about managing, but managing didn't work for him. He had a lousy team. The only thing I ever regretted about Ted Williams was the way he went out. He should have quit when the Washington team moved to Arlington, Texas. To put Ted Williams in Arlington, Texas, is like having Helen Hayes play Victoria Regina in Mason City, Iowa.

When Ted was managing Washington, and the Senators were at the stadium, I stopped by to do an interview with him. He said, "Before we do it, let me get you something." He disappeared into the clubhouse, came out a moment later with a copy of his book, *My Turn at Bat*. He handed it to me. "Take this," he said, "I want you to have it."

The inscription read, "To Howard, Who was always on my side."

I don't really remember exactly when I first became friendly with Joe DiMaggio. Or, put it another way, I don't really remember when I felt that Joe and I were communicating. As a young lawyer I would see him eating at a favorite table in Toots Shor's and I would look at him with a kind of awe. The man reeked with class. He is one of those unusual cases: a man who grows increasingly more handsome, more dignified, with the passing years.

But I suspect we really felt a kinship at the Yankee training camp in Fort Lauderdale, Florida, when Joe would come in to help out with the early training. I don't know how it's possible, really, not to like and even admire Joe DiMaggio. He handles himself the way he played. Remember how he used to run, with the effortless grace of an antelope? His manners have that same style.

It was at Fort Lauderdale that we first began to talk about his career, about what he was doing and about whether or not he wanted to return to baseball on a full-time basis. Joe is a very private man. You don't pry with him. What he wants you to know he will tell you. We've run across each other often, and he has taken my success with as much pride as if it were his. If Mike Burke had stayed with the Yankees, Joe would have been back with them in some capacity. With the new ownership I don't know. But I know Joe wants to go back.

I also know this: When I go to Yankee Stadium, as much as the place is Ruth and Gehrig, it's Joe DiMaggio. He's the classiest ballplayer I've ever known.

The 1973 baseball season opened as usual. The scribes were writing about Aaron's race for Ruth—could he catch the 714 career homers the Babe had achieved? They were writing about whether or not Mays should still be playing. Could Oakland do it again? These were typical topics. My own mind drifted to another man, a center fielder who wasn't even playing but who probably could have started for any one of the 24 teams. If he were in his prime, that is.

His name is Curt Flood. He had sacrificed his career to fight the reserve clause. He had lost his battle in the Supreme Court of the United States. He had given up a salary of $100,000 a year. I learned he was tending bar at the Rustic Inn on the island of Majorca off the coast of Spain. I did a show with Curt Flood that week. He walked the streets of Majorca, and unwound. He talked about what his life had become, as against what it had been. Then, on the terrace of his flat, with the harbor in the background, he lowered his head and said, "Look, this is me." He pointed to his body. "Nobody can own me. Nobody can buy me. Nobody can sell me. Nobody can trade me. This belongs to me. I don't know of any other business in the world—outside of slavery—like baseball, where they own you, where they can sell you or trade you. That's what they did in slavery. They sent you from one plantation to another. The hundred thousand a year doesn't matter. A slave is still a slave." He ended the Majorca interview with this observation: "I've got my wife. I've got my son. And I've got my dog. That's all a man needs."

Curt had quit baseball and challenged the reserve clause when Saint Louis traded him to Philadelphia. He lost his case but left an imprint on the game he left behind. Everyone in America now knows what the reserve clause is. It's the clause that binds one man to one team forever. And in the new agreement with the owners, the players gained substantial advantages, such as compulsory arbitration of salary disputes. In fact, under the new agreement, based upon the tenure of service that he had enjoyed as a member of the Saint Louis Cardinals, Flood could not have been traded to Philadelphia. Among the players this is known as the "Curt Flood Amendment." Curt Flood, like Muhammad Ali and

Jackie Robinson, has thus become something more than a name for the sports tomes.

Arnold Palmer has been one of the most celebrated figures in contemporary sports. He was even named the athlete of the decade for the 1960s. He was a very great golfer, though never so good as Nicklaus, but he captured the public through what I can only call a physical charisma. He has a kind of rugged good looks, a quick, winning, flashing smile and the kind of game to match his appeal—the late charge on the course, the ability to come from behind dramatically and seize the victory. Put this together with certain familiar mannerisms— the casual discharge of the cigarette, the lock of hair strewn loosely across the brow, the approach to the ball itself, the tortured but powerful swing, and then the appreciative relief in the face as the crowd oohed and aahed—and it all adds up to the phrase "physical charisma."

Palmer's appeal as a personality is at its best from a distance. In a room—except for the fact that he's Arnold Palmer, golfer—you wouldn't know him. The plain truth is that he's dull. He does not articulate well, often speaks ungrammatically, and his conversation is neither witty nor thoughtful nor penetrating. Joe Namath doesn't have the biggest mind in the world, but when he's in a room he fills it. The physical appeal is there, but so is the personality. That's the difference.

Lee Trevino is a golfer with personality, whether from near or afar. He gives golf what little middle-class appeal it has. A Chicano, with a lusty sense of humor, who doesn't always observe the niceties of deportment on the course, he's down-to-earth, refreshing and honest. Well, not so honest. The son of a gun still has a great pair of German sunglasses that he appropriated from me four years ago. He keeps writing me that they're the best he ever had.

When they played the U.S. Open in 1969 Trevino came to the eighteenth one day, putted out, looked up and saw me and waved. "There he is," I announced loudly, "the young Mexican-American who was a total unknown until I elected to make him famous."

Trevino grinned, showed all the teeth, and then answered back, "Don't believe a word of it, ladies and gentlemen. He never did a damned thing for me. But he *made* Muhammad Ali."

"That's what I keep telling Ali," I said, "but he doesn't believe it either."

The man Trevino admires most is Jack Nicklaus. Indeed, it was Jack who talked Lee into going back into the Masters tournament after he had refrained from playing in it for one year. Only Jack could have done this.

I think Jack Nicklaus is one of the genuine articles in American sport. In all the things that matter—home, family, friendship, loyalty, character and kindness—Jack Nicklaus is a winner. He's also, in my opinion, the greatest golfer who has yet lived.

Gary Player, the diminutive gentleman from South Africa, is another genuine article. He has been unfairly maligned because of the apartheid policies of his native land. He didn't ask to be born and brought up there, and it was unjust in the first instance to expect him to constantly divest himself of every vestige of training that he had during his formative years.

Player is not a racist, nor is he anything like it. Back in 1961 Gary told me that he would like to meet Jackie Robinson and talk about the racial problems. He wanted to talk about America and about South Africa. He wanted to make it clear that, while he was reared in an apartheid country, he did not cling to the practice of it. I put the two of them together at a pro-am held at what was then the Vernon Hills Country Club, in Mount Vernon, New York. In the year when Gary Player had to play a couple of major tournaments accompanied by security guards, I couldn't help thinking, "These pressure groups, these people who are all over Gary Player because he is from South Africa, they don't even know him. They don't even know how he thinks. They don't care. They would ask of him what they never ask of themselves. They would ask him to forsake his home, his property, his duly acquired possessions, even his relatives and old friends. It seems to me that's asking a lot of a man."

What they might better have thought about Gary Player was, "This man has made every effort to show his concern." They could have asked Lee Elder about that. Nor did he limit his concern to the black. When he won the U.S. Open at the Bellerive Country Club in Saint Louis, he turned over the prize money to charity. Name the American golfers who have done that.

I'm for Gary Player.

I'm also for Bill Russell. Bill Russell was the *authentic* athlete of the Sixties. He dominated his sport—basketball—as no other athlete has dominated a sport in my lifetime. But that's not why I'm for Bill Russell. I'm for Russell because he's the proudest man I know, as proud as he is tall. He will not give in, he will never knuckle under to those who would want him to bend to expediency in the daily course of human life. He shows this in many ways. A fan asks for an autograph. Russell will look at him coolly and say, "I'm sorry, I don't sign." And he will tell you why. "It is not a personal thing that they want. To sign my name on the back of a matchbox or on some little loose slip of paper is not a personal thing, and I will not submit myself to that. I would rather they ask me to shake hands and look me in the eye as they do it."

It seemed to me that at Jackie Robinson's funeral, of all the athletes there, Bill Russell most understood what Jackie was. Bill is a thinker. He has an exceptional mind. You realize this when you spend time with him. You don't wind up talking about basketball. You wind up talking about government, about racism, and Bill will look at you searchingly and say, "What do you think you really accomplish if you get the big leagues to name a black manager? That's not the problem. The problem is to create a society where there will be black managers, black owners, black general managers, black sportscasters. What we need is a society where the black normally, routinely has a place in every stratum."

He's right. But you have to begin somewhere.

Bill is a definite on-the-air talent. A natural. Not just a sportscaster but a personality. I know from the many shows I have done with him. He began his own syndicated television talk show, and I thought it was excellent. I did the pilot for the show with Muhammad Ali. I also did a show for Bill with Joe Namath. Russell handles himself beautifully. He has a great sense of humor and he displays it every night on local radio in Los Angeles for two solid hours, as he parries phone calls from listeners. But he must give up that show for his new job as coach and general manager of the Seattle Sonics.

Of course, when he gives out with that gusty cackle you just find yourself laughing along with him.

In Munich, at the Olympics, Bill did color on the basketball competition for ABC. But the thing I most remember about Russell, the thing most typical, is that when Bill wasn't working a game he would put on that little cap of his, stroke his beard and go off to hear the glockenspiel.

If my wife had her pick of all the handsome, interesting young athletes who have paraded through our home, and through my career, over the last 17 years, her choice for a second son-in-law would be Bill Bradley of Princeton. And Emmy would admit it readily.

Bradley matters to me because he is the direct antithesis of the jock stereotype. There is a terrible contradiction in seeing this man run around a wooden floor in underwear, trying to put an inflated ball through a hoop. He just seems above it. This is a man of rare brilliance. He has a mind that cuts through the most complex problems. A former Rhodes scholar, he can discuss every nuance of international affairs, is conversant with every current book (he's an omnivorous reader), has strong social convictions and definitely will undertake a political future.

With all of this, he almost had a fistfight with Don Nelson in the 1973 play-offs against Boston. How can you resist a man like this? But even for Emmy, Bradley presents a problem. He eats like a horse. He had dinner at our place one night and he consumed the whole damned roast. Hilary could never cook for him. Emmy's dream died.

If I were in trouble and needed help, the two men in the world I would turn to immediately would be my two neighbors in nearby Stamford, Connecticut—Andy Robustelli and Walter Kennedy. These men are staunch friends and have been for years. Robustelli never went to Princeton, never won a Rhodes Scholarship. He went to little Arnold College—which doesn't even exist anymore—but he made himself a Hall of Fame defensive end. He did it the way he does everything else in life, with hard work and resolution. To this day I regret that he never became a head coach in the National Football League. He would have been a great one. There is a lot of Lombardi in him. And to this day, though he won't admit it, it is Andy's great regret, too.

But Andy is doing well in a thousand and one ventures, and besides, if he's ever in trouble his kids can support him. They make their money baby-sitting for my grandchildren.

Emmy and I have traveled the world with Walter and Marion Kennedy. I have known him since he broadcast college games with Ted Husing and have watched the development of his career from the time he was the publicist for the Harlem Globetrotters, to when he became mayor of Stamford, and to his present high estate as commissioner of the National Basketball Association. He is a man without a mean bone in his body. He loves to kid and he knows how to take a kidding. During all the years he was mayor of Stamford I would address the Stamford Old-Timers' banquet and denounce Walter for his annual breakdown in snow removal.

As a commissioner Walter had done his damnedest and, overall, has done well. But in perfect honesty—and this has hurt him deep inside—some of the owners have betrayed him and undercut him. As a group the NBA owners simply don't have much class or brains.

Pancho Gonzales has a special place in my heart. Next to Jackie Robinson, he was the most competitive athlete I have ever known. I remember once, when he was long past his prime, watching him in a tournament at the White Plains County Center, where he consecutively defeated Ken Rosewall, Lew Hoad and a young, strong, tireless Rod Laver to win the tournament. Gonzales did it on memory and on will. It struck me as one of the extraordinary achievements in my lifetime in sports.

In his whole career Gonzales had feared only one player—Lew Hoad, the brilliant Australian who later was undermined by an ailing back. But Hoad was in his prime when he turned pro, and Pancho and I were in a taxi going to a party when he talked about Lew. Even then, Pancho was no longer youthful. He said, "This fellow will be the toughest I have ever played against. He has everything—power, movement, guile, everything." But Pancho beat him.

Hoadie himself is quite a guy. I often feel he should have been a boxer. His wrists were so enormously powerful, and his hands so quick. I used to talk to him about it, because Hoadie was a boxing fan. But then, he was a fan of all sports. And he's a kook. Once, at three in the morning, the phone rang. I was petrified. A call at that hour could only mean a family disaster. But, no. It was Lew Hoad, calling from Melbourne, Australia. Two Catholic nuns, good friends of his, wanted to see the Mets game the next day. Would I leave tickets. Only Lew Hoad could do that.

*　　*　　*

There are few vestiges left of the sports generation with which I grew up. Williams and DiMaggio are two. But the overriding one is Joe Louis. Because of my association with boxing, Joe has been a continuing part of my life. He is a man for whom I have an uncommon affection and whom I will always respect. I will always respect him because he has about him an inherent dignity and he carries with him, for all of us who remember, the strength of his greatness as a fighter. More than that, he will ever be a symbol—he was the first one to dispel the myth of German supremacy.

Now, today, it is impossible for me to be with Joe and not feel sadness. He is not a well man. He has become a recurrent showpiece for major boxing events. You find him hanging around the tables at Caesar's Palace in Las Vegas, and you are offended—remembering his greatness—by the loose, casual, hey-champ-sign-this treatment he gets from the fly-by-night bettors hovering nearby. I resent the fact that they have made Joe Louis the white man's black man.

I'll remember Joe Louis my own way. I'll remember him coming down from the house at Pompton Lakes, New Jersey, head swathed in a towel, swami-fashion, getting ready for a workout in preparation for a bout with Billy Conn. I'll remember Joe Louis answering those around him who were talking about Conn's swiftness and how Billy would hit and run against Joe; I'll remember Joe saying, "He can run but he can't hide."

I learned early on that sports is a part of life, that it is human life in microcosm, and that the virtues and flaws of the society exist in sports even as they exist everywhere else. I have viewed it as part of my function to reveal this in the course of my pursuit of every avenue of the sports beat. I can not be reverential about the Masters Golf Tournament. For me such an event is an attempt to return to the age of Rhett and Scarlett, the two of them on a veranda in the misty distance as one walks the eighteenth fairway. Nor can I equate the Super Bowl, the World Series or the Rose Bowl with the very real and often overwhelming problems of the society.

Many sports announcers and sportswriters do. Perhaps this is why I have been a shock treatment to many people, especially older ones who have grown up subject to the carefully created notion that the world of sports is, in fact, Shangri-La, the Lost Horizon. Perhaps. Part of it has to be my own personality, the way I am, often abrasive, impatient, even intolerant with people. Emmy talks to me about this often. And she is always right.

But I do feel I have been right about one thing. The attempt to bring some decent journalism into sports broadcast. The most disturbing facet of my career has been the general absence of journalism in sports coverage, both in broadcast and print.

In some ways the failure of sports print journalism has been the more distressing. I am not interested in petty feuds with some writers. Let them do their thing, and some have done it to me pretty well. Those are passing things. What is sad is that, as I mentioned earlier, so many sportswriters who travel with teams become a part of those teams, become in effect, a house publicity organ. To this day there are teams who still pay travel and living expenses for writers who cover their activities. Blame the newspapers themselves for allowing this, but sadly the independence of the writer is severely inhibited. Then there are still the writers who will cover a team and get paid to write the annual promotion film of the team. A clear conflict of interest.

What sports print journalism does have that sports broadcast does not have is a whole host of sports columnists throughout the nation who can and do speak out. Not enough, in my judgment, on the great issues in sports today, but enough to at least provide some measure of journalism that does not exist in the form of regular sports commentary in broadcast.

Personally I have no quarrel with the press treatment I have received. It has been good, and it has been bad, and that is part of life. When the bad notices almost got to me, I not only survived but prospered. And as a matter of fact I have made it clear that I have brought writers to the television industry, and that they were the hard core of every documentary I have produced. So I bear no grudges.

I just want them to get better, a lot better, since they have a freedom, a latitude, that the average sportscaster simply does not enjoy. They can do things that we broadcasters cannot do. They have the luxury of space. We do not have the luxury of time. So their space might be better used in creative writing, providing insights into the people and the issues of sport, than in envying the salaries of the broadcasters and refusing to accept the fact that television is here to stay and that it is the single most important medium of communication in the contemporary civilization.

As a final comment on sports print journalism, I shall never get over the fact that the nation's most circulated newspaper, the *New York Daily News,* did not send one correspondent to the Munich Olympics, where the biggest story in the world broke. Their sportswriters were covering the pennant races.

Sad, isn't it?

In broadcast I feel the blame for the absence of journalism lies with the industry more than it does with the announcers. At the local broadcast level—when it comes to the transmission of events—in most cases the announcers are hired by the teams. I believe this defeats journalism at the inception. How can a man tell truths about a team, or a game, if such truths are deleterious to the interests of his employer? And how can local stations, publicly licensed and transmitting over publicly owned airwaves, forfeit their own programming obligations to a sports franchise? The FCC has finally become interested in this very question and has started an investigation into sports announcing that will hopefully lead to an uplifting of sports broadcasting standards.

On the network level the problem is more complex. The competing networks are ever in quest of the great events as part of their programming structures. If one network has an announcer who speaks out, that announcer might alienate the commissioner of the sport, the league's owners and the sponsors. And all three will find another network ready and willing to move in and carry the events. More than that, they are, on the average, ready and willing to allow the parties the privilege of choosing announcers. Under these circumstances announcers are handcuffed. They become salesmen. This is honest work; there is no pretense about it. But it is not journalism.

Personally I have been fortunate in this regard. Whatever my problems in my climb up the corporate wall, I have had support from ABC. I do not think I would have gotten it elsewhere. I do not know if I will always get it.

I do know that only once in my entire career in broadcasting has anybody tried to tell me what to say or what not to say and nobody at ABC was involved in that.

The incident occurred at Madison Square Garden. Joe Frazier was fighting Jerry Quarry and I was taping the opening of the telecast. The fight took place at the time when Muhammad Ali was inactive. Jimmy Ellis was recognized as the heavyweight champion of the World Boxing Association and Joe Frazier was recognized as the heavyweight champion by New York and one other state. In taping the opening I identified Frazier as the recognized champion in two states. Harry Markson, then the director of boxing at the Garden, grabbed me and said, "You're in the Garden now, you're in New York. You've got to say that Frazier is the heavyweight champion of the world. How can you do that to us?"

I was enraged. I advised Markson to go out to our truck and tell Chet Forte, our producer, what he wanted me to say. I told Markson that if Forte ordered me to identify Frazier in the manner Markson wanted I would instantly leave the premises. Forte, of course, gave me no such order. Subsequently Markson wrote ABC Sports a letter of apology. But I will never forget the incident and I have nothing but contempt for the Madison Square Garden boxing department. That is one of several reasons why I would have nothing to do with ABL's summer Saturday afternoon "club" boxing from the Felt Forum in the Garden.

I have bullied and blustered my way into situations—and out of them—that some writers and broadcasters would never even have attempted. Yes, there is a good deal of put-on in my personality, and I respond best to those who understand this. But at the same time, and especially in the case of Muhammad Ali, that put-on has enabled me to get answers to searching questions that few would ask.

And let's face it. You must have humor, particularly in sport, where, without humor and perspective, one tends to live in a closet. I am at a stage where, naturally, I need new stimuli, new challenges, new outlets, whether in the field of television entertainment—or in politics. I do not mean that I intend to leave sports. What I do mean is this: The one thing that would take me out of broadcast would be the opportunity to serve in the Senate of the United States.

But realistically it seems much too late for that. In fact, that is my one regret to this day about leaving the law. So I will continue to get my kicks out of people who play in the romper room of sports. The ones who count in my life are drawn to it, inevitably, just as I have been.

One of the questions I'm frequently asked is whether I am the same off-camera as I am on. Is my public image—the often flowery language, the often overbearing manner—a calculated pose? The biblical truth is that I am *always* on. I am the same in private, among friends, as I am on the air, at the podium of a banquet hall or in a crowd of absolute strangers. I know of no other way to be. I needle my friends as mercilessly as my enemies. Sometimes more so. In the words of Sammy Davis, "I gotta be me."

My good friends understand this, and I am partial to the ones who can zing back. Such as Don Klosterman. There was a day during the U.S. Open in Houston when Klosterman and I sat in the clubhouse at Champions. I was sounding off on one of my favorite subjects, the universe, when Roone Arledge happened to walk past. Klosterman looked up. "Hey, Roone," he pleaded, "come help me listen to Howard."

And then there was the time Klosterman was to enter a Baltimore hospital for nose surgery, to have a deviated septum corrected. Jim Mahoney was staying with Emmy and me at our New York apartment. It was 2:00 A.M., and we were listening to Sinatra records. Suddenly Jim said, "You know, we owe it to the Duke to call him and wish him luck." I agreed. We called Klosterman in Baltimore and, sleepily, he picked up the phone.

"Duke," I said.

"Huh," he mumbled.

"Duke, I'm with Mahoney. We thought we owed it to you to call before the operation. Jim and I have done all the necessary research. Only three people have died from the operation that you'll undergo tomorrow. So we called to reassure you. You're in good shape." And I handed the phone to Mahoney, who took it from there.

An hour later, at three, Sinatra was singing "My Way," and Mahoney had an inspiration. He picked up the phone and called Klosterman again. "Duke," he told him excitedly, "our research was wrong. Only *two* have died. Your odds are even better."

Klosterman banged the phone.

A half hour later Mahoney dialed Klosterman again. This time Jim never said a word. He just listened. Then he put down the phone and couldn't stop laughing.

I said, "What did he say?"

Mahoney answered, "It was Klosterman. He said, 'This is a recording. Mr. Klosterman can be reached after one P.M. tomorrow at Room four-oh-nine, Union Memorial Hospital.' And then he hung up."

Don had had the last word. Not only that, he survived the surgery.

Erich Segal came late to the sassy repartee of sport. In his gentle way, and of all the people who have tried, Erich may have inadvertently best characterized me.

Erich ran in his eighteenth Boston Marathon last April. I was doing a show on the Marathon. It was a blistering, unseasonably hot day. Nonetheless I persuaded Erich to run the 26 miles, 385 yards with a power pack weighing between five and seven pounds strapped to his back so that he could record his reactions during the race.

You have to understand what the additional weight means to a runner covering that distance. In this event the participants seek every tiny edge, every advantage they can steal. Their track togs are of tissue weight. Some shave their heads. Others station friends along the route to spray them with water as they pass. No one, NO ONE, intentionally takes on a handicap.

Erich finished the race. One hour behind the leaders. But he finished. He was a source of constant puzzlement to the observers who saw his frail back bent slightly under the accumulating burden of our gear. I say "accumulating" because it got heavier as the race wore on.

At the finish a Boston TV reporter grabbed him for an interview. What in the world, the reporter wondered, was Erich doing with that contraption? How could he carry that unwanted and unwarranted load for more than 26 torturous miles?

With his last gasps of breath, Erich panted, "Have you—have you ever—have you ever tried—to say no to Howard Cosell?"

For the Sunday cyclist... for the cross-country tourist... whether you ride for better health, for sport, or for the sheer fun of it,

GET

THE COMPLETE BOOK OF BICYCLING

The First Comprehensive Guide
To All Aspects of Bicycles and Bicycling

JUST A FEW OF THE HUNDREDS OF EXCITING TIPS YOU'LL FIND:

- A simple way to increase your cycling efficiency by 30 to 40%—breeze over hilltops while others are struggling behind.
- 13 special safety tips for youngsters.
- How to read a bicycle's specifications to know if you're getting a superior one or a dud.
- How to know whether to buy a 3-speed to start with, or a 10-speed.
- How to select the right kind of equipment for touring or camping.
- How to minimize danger when cycling in the city.

▼ **AT YOUR BOOKSTORE OR MAIL THIS COUPON NOW FOR FREE 30-DAY TRIAL** ▼